D1484041

MULTIETHNIC
JAPAN

MULTIETHNIC JAPAN

John Lie

HARVARD UNIVERSITY PRESS

Cambridge, Massachusetts

London, England · 2001

Library of Congress Cataloging-in-Publication Data

Lie, John.
Multiethnic Japan / John Lie.
p.   cm.
Includes bibliographical references and index.
ISBN 0-674-00299-7
1. Aliens—Japan. 2. Japan—Ethnic relations.
3. Japan—Civilization—1868– I. Title.
DS832.7A1 L53 2000
952'.004—dc21   00-057503

for Charis

Contents

Preface

Wielding my rusty Korean or rudimentary Thai, or interspersing a few Tagalog or Farsi phrases with English, I began this project by interviewing foreign workers in Japan in order to delineate their working and living conditions. Although there wasn't an obvious moment of epiphany, my project eventually underwent what was tantamount to a Copernican Revolution. Perhaps the matter-of-fact narratives about the foreign workers' trajectories to Japan bored me. The reams of documents and statistics I collected didn't seem to lead anywhere, leaving me with answers in search of questions. Here the efflorescence of whiteness studies in the United States was inspiring. Rather than taking the majority population—whether white Americans or mainstream Japanese—for granted, the challenge was to explicate why and how the majority became the norm that escaped scrutiny, free from historical reflection or contemporary critique. Intellectually stimulating too was the seemingly endless flow of books on the social construction, invention, and making of various nationalities and ethnicities.

The course of research never does run smoothly, but in retrospect I seemed to have merely elaborated on some of my initial insights, articulated in my first published essay. In any case, the cleansed picture of social research encapsulated in textbooks—formulate a coherent hypothesis, use certified methods to collect data, and analyze rigorously and systematically—hardly does justice to the life course of many projects. My experience is, rather, closer to the view of Dencombe in Henry James's masterly story, "The Middle Years": "We work in the dark—we do what we can—we give what we have. Our doubt is our passion and our passion is our task. The rest is the madness of art." Surely, social research would be better off with a dash of madness and art, rather than the hygienic view that would only sanction sanity and scientificity.

I used multiple methods and sources. I conducted over one hundred unstructured and lengthy interviews with Japanese people of varying backgrounds. Structured and mechanical interviews, however they may offer a sense of objectivity, neutrality, and even certainty, almost inevitably generate pat responses. It is often in the asides and the afterthoughts that I found insights into how people think about others and themselves. This is all the more true for sensitive questions about which most Japanese would prefer to proffer the correct answers. I made special efforts to interview people of different social and educational backgrounds. Although nearly all of them lived in the Tokyo metropolitan area, I also conducted interviews in Nagoya, Kyoto, Osaka, and Fukuoka. Tokyo is, of course, not Japan *tout court*, and the hold of monoethnic ideology is weaker outside of Tokyo. The significant presence of Burakumin and Koreans in Osaka, for example, renders the idea of monoethnic Japan less convincing to Osaka residents.

In addition, I spent a great deal of time observing and engaging in informal conversations with both Japanese and non-Japanese (i.e., nonethnic) Japanese in the Tokyo metropolitan area. As sightings of the new foreign workers became common, there were numerous occasions to overhear Japanese people's spontaneous reactions to one another, as well as to observe instances of interethnic contact.

I have also drawn extensively on comparative studies, particularly of Britain, France, Germany, and the United States, on race, ethnicity, nation, diaspora, and identity. Reading numerous studies replete with acute theoretical insights and suggestive empirical findings provided useful benchmarks to think about the case of Japan.

Most visible in the text are the documentary sources I collected, ranging from government publications to popular and scholarly publications. Because Japan is a highly literate society with an active publishing culture, the sheer volume of printed materials is staggering. Given that not just professional scribes but ordinary people publish their thoughts in pamphlets, newspapers, magazines, and books, they offer an indispensable and rich repository of information.

My reliance on documentary sources forces me, willy-nilly, to use extensive citations and quotations. I wish that authority flowed naturally from authorship. One yearns to transcend the cumbersome scholarly apparatus, to *aufgehoben* our predecessors. Worse, my aesthetic preference for simplicity is severely challenged by a plethora of parentheses. T. S. Eliot once quipped: "immature poets imitate; mature poets steal." However, scholars, whether mature or immature, cannot, alas, steal for that is plagiarism. The least one can hope for is that whereas bad scholars deface what they take, good scholars transfigure it into something better. In any case, acknowledging the authorities may very well be the best way to relieve the burden of the past and the anxiety of influence.

Unforgettably, C. Wright Mills called for sociologists "to grasp history and biography and the relations between the two within society." Perhaps I have read him too literally, but I have spent the past decade attempting to illuminate my life against my Korean and Korean diasporic background. *Blue Dreams* (Abelmann and Lie 1995) explored the Korean diaspora in the United States, and *Han Unbound* (Lie 1998) analyzed South Korea, the place of my birth. This book completes my sociological imagination trilogy, although it should have been written much earlier. Because I had spent my formative years in Tokyo, I experienced a year spent in Tokyo in 1985 as something of a homecoming. Participating in the periphery of the anti-fingerprinting movement—the struggle waged by foreigners living in Japan for civic respect—I came to realize, rather belatedly, some of the unsavory aspects of Japanese society. Intoxicated by high theory, however, I could not bring myself to focus on the issues that the struggle had raised. In the past decade I have sought to rectify my erstwhile intellectual hubris, and to begin, if unconsciously at first, to make sense of the worlds that have shaped me. The belated result is this book.

Solitary as I am in my work habits, I received a lot of help in writing this book. The University of Illinois at Urbana-Champaign, Keio University, and the Japan Foundation provided financial and institutional support. Watanabe Hideki generously sponsored my affiliation with Keio University. Aya Ezawa, Eri Fujieda, Hiroshi Ishida, Machimura Takashi, Miho Matsugu, Mineshige Miyuki, Mitani Hiromi, Nakayama Keiko, Ann Saphir, Akwi Seo, Sugiura Ako, Takenoshita Hirohisa, Uemura Hideaki, David Wank, and Alan Wolfe made my time in Japan productive and pleasurable. In the course of writing, I benefited immeasurably from the friendship of Megan Greene, as well as the support of Emin Adas, Aya Ezawa, Serife Genis, Tom Hove, Miwako Kuno, Will Leggett, Monica Shoemaker, and Charis Thompson.

Michael Aronson at Harvard University Press once again proved to be a kind and supportive editor. I am also grateful to Richard Audet for his sensitive and scrupulous copyediting. Two reviewers for the Press gave me useful comments and criticisms. I would like to thank Andrea Dodge, who facilitated the production process, and Aya Ezawa, who fashioned the index.

I completed the manuscript in September 1998. Therefore, I was unable to incorporate the ever expanding literature on multiethnic Japan published after fall 1998 in this book. Nec scire fas est omnia.

A Note on Terminology

By modern Japan, I mean Japan after the Meiji Restoration (1868). Postwar *(sengo)* refers to the post–World War II era, from the end of World War II in 1945 to the death of Emperor Shōwa (Hirohito) in 1989.

I have used pseudonyms to identify people whom I interviewed. Asian names are listed surnames first, save for two exceptions: those who write principally in a Western language and those listed in the reference section. In transliterating Japanese names and words, I have followed the guideline in Masuda (1974:xiii). Names and words familiar to Anglophone readers are in their Anglicized form: thus Tokyo, not Tōkyō. All translations are mine, unless otherwise noted.

O, happy is he who can still hope
To escape from this sea of error!
What we don't know, we truly need
And what we do know, we cannot use.
—JOHANN WOLFGANG VON GOETHE, Faust

Introduction

If the dominant view of modern Japanese society were correct, then *Multiethnic Japan* would be either an oxymoron or an occasion for a very short essay. The received wisdom is that Japan is monoethnic. Edwin O. Reischauer (1988:33), the leading Japanologist of his generation, wrote: "the Japanese today are the most thoroughly unified and culturally homogeneous large bloc of people in the world," with "the possible exception of the North Chinese" (see, however, Eberhard 1982; Honig 1992). Moreover: "Race looms large in the self-image of the Japanese, who pride themselves on the 'purity' of their blood" (Reischauer 1988:396). In *Japan Today*, Roger Buckley (1990:82) declaims: "No other major industrial society has anything approaching the racial homogeneity of Japan." The opinion of Western Japanologists is shared by Japanese scholars. Bitō Masahide (1993:17), an eminent Japanese historian, remarks: "we are in reality of a singular ethnicity." A Japanese sociologist asserts: "Japan is more racially and ethnically homogeneous than almost any other modern nation" (Kumagai 1996:9). In 1986 Prime Minister Nakasone Yasuhiro declared that "Japan has one ethnicity *(minzoku)*, one state *(kokka)*, and one language *(gengo)*," and drew a favorable contrast to the multiethnic United States (Terazawa 1990:64–65).

Many Japanese believe that they live in a monoethnic society, which they also regard as one of their most distinctive—and, some would add, positive—characteristics. The assumption that Japan is a monoethnic society is widely shared not just by scholars of Japan and the Japanese themselves but also by virtually everyone else. A study of Japanese Americans, for example, notes that Japanese "are among the most homogeneous people in the world, on both physical and cultural dimensions" (O'Brien and Fugita

1

1991:3). The philosopher Allan Bloom (1990:21–22) asserts: "Japanese society . . . is intransigently homogeneous." In a book devoted to the subject of polyethnicity, the historian William H. McNeill (1986:18) remarks: "More than any other civilized land . . . the Japanese islands maintained ethnic and cultural homogeneity throughout their history."

Given that no one would deny that there are non-Japanese people living in Japan, whether Japan is monoethnic or multiethnic is a matter of degrees and definitions. Indeed, the very term ethnicity—as well as its cognates, race, nation, and people—is contentious. The philosopher W. B. Gallie (1964:158) is right to observe that most social terms are "essentially contested concepts . . . which inevitably involve endless disputes about [their] proper uses." Suffice it to say that I stress the historically and socially contingent character of social classification and categorization. That putatively deep differences between people justify hatred, war, and even genocide does not deny their ultimate ephemerality and superficiality—however natural and necessary they may seem at any particular place and time.

Contemporary categories of peoplehood are fraught with confusion and contention, but there are only three terms that are widely used: race, ethnicity, and nation. Slaves and castes—people with legal or customary proscription on intergenerational social mobility and intermarriage—are rapidly disappearing. The categories of race, ethnicity, and nation all grope toward a social grouping larger than kinship (whether family or lineage) but smaller than humanity. They seek, so to speak, to divide people horizontally. They are categories salient in the modern era, in contradistinction to the preponderance of vertical, hierarchical categories, such as caste and status, in premodern civilizations. To be sure, a proto-national or proto-ethnic sentiment—a sense of peoplehood—can be found in all social situations. Nonetheless, whether articulated as a transition from status to contract (Maine) or aristocratic to democratic (Tocqueville), the transition to modernity signals a shift away from explicit vertical hierarchy. Notwithstanding the salience of class stratification, the horizontal categories supersede the vertical ones in the transition from the premodern civilization, empire, or state to the modern nation-state.

I eschew the term race because of the biological unity of the human race (Marks 1995). National or ethnic distinctions, in any case, often incorporate socially salient physiological features. Some distinguish between race and ethnicity in order to emphasize the ferocity of racism (such as the legacy of slavery in categorizing African Americans as a distinct race). Although I am sympathetic to the political impulse, I am skeptical about its analytical—and, ultimately, political—benefit. Should we consider Jews in Nazi Germany to be a race because of the Holocaust, but regard Jews in the contemporary United States as an ethnic group? Most disturbingly, the language of race almost inevitably accentuates the role of biology in what is fundamentally a matter of social analysis.

There is no getting around the essentially ambiguous definition of nation or ethnicity. I follow E. J. Hobsbawm (1990:8) in considering "any sufficiently large body of people whose members regard themselves as members of a 'nation'" as a national or ethnic group. In addition to ethnic or national consciousness, discrimination and differentiation by outsiders sustain national and ethnic distinctions. In this regard, there is really no simple criterion or a set of criteria to differentiate nation and ethnicity. Formally, it is possible to posit a distinction by noting whether there is a sovereign state attached to a group. However, in practice, the distinction is conflated. Although there is no Palestinian state in the late 1990s, some would like to see its formation, whereas others have denied its existence altogether, whether in the name of monoethnic Israel or pan-Arabism (Said 1979:5–8; Khalidi 1997:180–182). Whether to call Palestinians in Israel a national or ethnic minority seems ultimately moot.

The principal ethnic groups in contemporary Japan include Ainu, Okinawans, Burakumin, Koreans, Chinese, and, of course, Japanese (mainstream Japanese, Yamato people, or Japanese Japanese). Most Japanese regard Ainu people as racially distinct from mainstream Japanese, or Yamato, people. Because both Korea and China are nation-states, with their own languages and cultures, no one would question their distinctiveness. The matter is more controversial for Okinawans because many Japanese regard Okinawa as a region and its language as a dialect. However, Okinawa was an independent kingdom until the late nineteenth century, and Okinawan ethnic or national consciousness remains palpable in the 1990s. Finally, Burakumin pose the most contentious case. Burakumin are—to use the simplest designation—descendants of Tokugawa-era outcastes. Although they have been regarded as racially distinct in the past, most contemporary Japanese consider them to be physically indistinguishable from mainstream Japanese. Some scholars designate them as a caste, but Burakumin face no formal barriers to intergenerational mobility or intermarriage. However, there is considerable identification as members of a distinct group, and many Japanese continue to recognize and then discriminate against them in marriage and employment. Identification and discrimination offer, therefore, good grounds to consider them as an ethnic group.

Because neither the Japanese government census nor sociologists' surveys recognize ethnic diversity in Japan, we can only estimate the population of non-Japanese Japanese. Statistics—as neutral and objective as they may seem—are steeped in political and social assumptions. For example, because we have no systematic data on how many Korean Japanese have become naturalized Japanese, we have no way of ascertaining how many Korean Japanese there are. The problem is compounded by the persistence of discrimination against non-Japanese Japanese. Fearing obstacles in employment and marriage, many people attempt to pass as "ordinary" Japanese and hide their ethnic background. Hence, people of Ainu ancestry may identify themselves as ethnic Japanese. Although the official Ainu population was about 25,000 in the early 1990s, some estimates run as high as 300,000 (Sjöberg 1993:152), and others suggest even higher figures. If the fluctuation seems dubious, then consider the case of American Indians. The United States census counted roughly 350,000 American Indians between 1930 and 1950, but there were nearly 1.9 million by 1990 (Nagel 1996:85). The sociologist Joane Nagel (1996:140–141) argues that the massive increase is due principally to the renewal of American Indian ethnic pride. A similar ethnic renewal among the Ainu would presumably increase their population figure as well.

The estimated total of non-Japanese Japanese living in Japan in the 1990s is 4–6 million in a country of 125 million people: Ainu (25,000–300,000), Burakumin (2–3 million), Okinawans (1.6 million), Koreans (700,000–1 million), Chinese (200,000), children of mixed ancestry (10,000–25,000), and foreigners (150,00–700,000)) (for various estimates, see, inter alia, Ōhashi 1971:7; Sugimoto 1997:171; Taira 1997:142). Although the proportion of ethnic minorities is lower than that of the United States, it is far from negligible and comparable to the 1992 figure in the United Kingdom (Mason 1995:35). My case for multiethnic Japan, however, relies not so much on the demographic estimate but on its constitutive role in modern Japanese history and society.

Let me briefly sketch the path that I will traverse in this book. I begin by recounting the debate on foreign workers, which revealed and reified the presumption of Japanese monoethnicity. I delve deeper by identifying the animating assumptions of the contemporary discourse of Japaneseness, or

Japanese identity, which insist on the class, cultural, and ethnic homogeneity of Japan. In contrast, I demonstrate the centrality of multiethnicity in modern Japan. Postwar popular culture, which provided a sense of national identity, cannot be understand apart from ethnic heterogeneity and cultural hybridity. Indeed, the fundamental forces that shaped modern Japan—state-making, colonialism, and capitalism—made it into a multiethnic society. Given the centrality of multiethnicity in modern Japanese history, perhaps it is not surprising that the ideology of monoethnicity become dominant only after the 1960s, when it became a principal predicate of Japaneseness. Finally, I analyze the conceptual foundations of the discourse of Japaneseness. Thus, as much as I seek to show modern Japan to be a multiethnic society, I devote considerable energy to explaining the contemporary belief in Japanese monoethnicity.

This book is but one effort that depicts contemporary Japanese society as multiethnic (for others, see, inter alia, Ōnuma 1986; Field 1991; Fukuoka 1993; Nakano and Imazu 1993; Maher and Macdonald 1995; Oguma 1995, 1998; Smith 1995; Denoon et al. 1996; Howell 1996; Ryang 1997; Weiner 1997; and Morris-Suzuki 1998a). It has become more difficult to deny the existence of ethnic others in Japan, but many people continue to insist that Japan is a monoethnic society. The repeated appeal to rectify ethnic discrimination—indeed, to recognize the very existence of ethnic diversity—encounters the shibboleth about Japanese monoethnicity. The ethnic minorities in Japan suffer twice; although teased mercilessly in schools and barred from many jobs, their existence is not recognized by the government (except as foreigners), most Japanese people, or, for that matter, by many Western Japanologists and Japanese social scientists. Nonetheless, the voices of the previously silent and silenced members of non-Japanese Japanese make the claim of monoethnicity increasingly implausible in the 1990s. If the owl of Minerva does fly at dusk, then the dawn of a new Japan may mercifully be not so far off.

CHAPTER

1

The Second Opening
of Japan

In the late 1980s the influx of foreign workers became the most widely discussed social issue in Japan. Hardly a day passed without a newspaper headline, a major magazine article, or a television documentary on the problem of foreign workers. Scores of books appeared; students eagerly wrote theses on the topic. The truly historical proportion of the phenomenon was underscored by the terms of the debate, which was analogous to the mid-nineteenth century discussion whether Japan should end seclusion *(sakoku)* or open the country to the West *(kaikoku)*. The brouhaha led even the sober-minded, such as the economist Shimada Haruo (1994:vii), to declare: "Japan has a serious foreign worker problem which is likely to play a major role in shaping the nation's future."

The spotlight on the foreign workers problem faded rapidly. By 1993, when I conducted my interviews in Japan, several people told me that the topic was passé; some were kind enough to suggest other, more au courant, projects to the hapless researcher. As Japan entered a prolonged economic slump, and the authorities intensified surveillance, the new Asian migrant workers became less conspicuous. At the same time, Japanese people became inured to them, and the mass media moved to newer and more copyworthy topics. However, the waning interest belied the steady, even slightly increasing, number of foreigners in Japan.

What is puzzling about the debate is that there was no obvious cause for concern. In spite of their growing presence, foreigners constituted about 1 percent of the total Japanese population by the early 1990s (*Asahi Shinbun,* Aug. 22, 1993). Most of them were long-term Korean and Chinese residents and their descendants. Furthermore, the new foreign workers, who in the late 1980s hailed principally from Asian countries, performed tasks that most Japanese shunned. Why then were there intense and intermina-ble—indeed, inescapable—discussions of the problem of foreign workers between the late 1980s and the early 1990s? Beyond dissenting opinions on whether to allow more migrant workers into Japan, the new foreign work-ers challenged, as well as reproduced, the prevailing preconception of Ja-pan as an ethnically homogeneous society.

International Labor Migration and Contemporary Japan

International labor migration is hardly unique to contemporary Japan. After all, industrialization and international labor migration cannot be considered apart. The nineteenth-century industrialist Frederick Engels (1975:389) observed that the "rapid expansion of English industry could not have taken place if England had not possessed in the numerous and impoverished population of Ireland a reserve at command." More recently, the postwar economic growth of western Europe depended on low-wage immigrant labor (Freeman 1979:3–5). The transnational flow of labor, along with the globalization of finance and production, has come to char-acterize the late twentieth century (Sassen 1988:186–188).

What accounts for the pervasiveness of international labor migration? In the post–World War II era, enforced labor migration virtually vanished (Potts 1990:199–207). Unlike the seventeenth-century migration of Afri-cans to Europe and the Americas, the late twentieth-century transnational labor migration is largely voluntary. In this context the foremost source of international migration is the inequality between nations. As the historian William McNeill (1990:69) notes, "Globally, there remain billions of peas-ants and ex-peasants who are ready and eager to move into places vacated by wealthier, urbanized populations." For example, per capita Japanese GNP was 30 times that of the Philippines and 125 times that of Bangla-desh in the late 1980s (Keizai Kikakuchō Sōgō Keikakukyoku 1989:44). A Bangladeshi worker could earn in a day in Japan what would take months to earn back home. As a Bangladeshi man explained, "Do you realize how much this [money] is? I am going to live like a king when I get back to Dacca."

International inequality in and of itself, however, is insufficient to gener-ate a large scale cross-border migration. Migrant workers neither embody nor exemplify microeconomic motivations or macroeconomic forces. Al-though they may move from one country to another more or less voluntarily, individual initiatives are often inadequate. Because state sovereignty is bound up with territorial surveillance, border patrol, as part of national security, regulates the influx of migrant workers. Barriers to a free market in labor are formidable, and most individuals by themselves are incapable of scaling them. Furthermore, states provide privileged access to domestic employment opportunities and distribute the bulk of welfare benefits to their citizens. Hence, large-scale international labor migration does not occur spontaneously as a free play of the international labor market; rather, it results from specific efforts by governments, employers, and migrants to initiate and sustain a transnational labor flow.

The pressing need for low-wage labor, usually in times of economic expansion and corresponding labor shortage, is frequently a necessary precondition for states to relax immigration restrictions. A notable example is western Europe during the rapid economic recovery of the 1950s and 1960s. Almost immediately after the end of World War II, the French government aggressively promoted international labor migration because of perceived labor shortages (Freeman 1979:68–72). By the mid-1950s, well over 100,000 migrant workers entered France annually, and the state "lost control in the face of intense industrial demand for immigrant workers" (Ireland 1994:40). In West Germany the influx of foreign workers began later than in France (Tezuka 1989:152–158). The West German government was concerned less about labor shortages and more about the deleterious effects, such as inflation, of rapid growth at full employment (Hollifield 1992:58). In spite of the late start, the number of immigrant workers in West Germany had reached 280,000 by 1960 (Bade 1992:395). Any adequate explanation of postwar French and West German economic growth must consider the impact of immigrant labor (Hollifield 1992:chaps. 3–5).

From a Labor-Surplus to a Full-Employment Economy

Unlike western Europe, Japan's rapid economic growth in the 1960s and 1970s did not depend on foreign workers (Morita 1987:21). Given that the prewar Japanese economy depended on Korean and other migrant workers, and that almost all growth economies rely on immigrant labor, why didn't postwar Japan employ foreign workers? Quite simply, Japan remained a labor-surplus economy until the 1960s. After Japan's defeat in World War II, 6.6 million Japanese were repatriated to the main islands from the far-flung empire (Mori 1997:34; cf. Umemura 1964:63–67). The constant labor surplus led the Japan Emigration Agency to "stimulate emigration through various measures such as posters and propaganda films, [and take] extensive measures to help emigrants with technical and financial assistance to support successful settlement abroad" (Mori 1997:35; cf. Suzuki J. 1992:257–261). The last ship to carry Japanese emigrants to Brazil departed Japan in 1973 (Fujisaki 1991:54).

Rather than immigrant workers, internal migration from rural areas and women's entrance into paid work satisfied the growing Japanese labor demand from the 1950s to the 1970s. The postwar Japanese labor market proved to be remarkably flexible (Umemura 1964:80–89). Postwar Japan experienced perhaps the most rapid rural exodus in world history; four million farmers became urban workers annually in the late 1960s (Mori 1997:55–57). In addition to the structural shift from a rural agrarian into an urban industrial society, predominantly male farmers labored in the off-farm season in construction and manufacturing (Watanabe and Haneda 1977; Kumito 1990). Indeed, the economist Ōkōchi Kazuo (1980:173–176) famously defined the uniqueness of the Japanese labor market by singling out the significance of *dekasegi* (seasonal migrant) labor. Many *dekasegi* workers, incidentally, were Burakumin, Okinawans, and other minorities. By the mid-1960s, the depopulated countryside was dominated by the *sanchan* (three-chan) agriculture of *obāchan* (grandmother), *ojīchan* (grandfather), and *okāchan* (mother) (Ueno 1995:159). For many rural areas, postwar history is one of rapid rural exodus and seasonal labor migration (Kamata 1984:128; Niigata Nippō Hōdōbu 1985:3).

Women's labor force participation was equally remarkable. From the early phases of industrialization, Japanese women worked in a variety of jobs, and their presence in the labor force was higher than that of their European counterparts until the 1970s (Koike 1981:248–249). Between 1960 and 1980, the number of women in paid work nearly doubled. Not only did women enter the labor force in larger numbers, but many of them worked as part-timers to fulfill the fluctuating demands for low-wage labor (Hirota 1979:138–141; Shioda 1985:187–192). Part-time labor is defined not so much by the length of working hours but rather by its status as dispensable low-paid labor (Ōsawa 1993:79–85). The proportion of part-timers, who were mainly married and older, among all women workers increased from 9 percent in 1970 to 23 percent in 1981 (Matsubara 1983:102–104). In general, women worked in light manufacturing and in the peripheral sectors, which were vulnerable to labor market fluctuations

(Ōmori 1990:17–18). Although women performed more than half the labor, they received between a fourth and fifth of all earnings (Ōsawa 1993:46).

As the Japanese economy continued its rapid growth in the 1960s, it transformed from a labor-surplus economy to a full-employment economy. In addition to rural migrants, seasonal workers, and women, part-time students and older workers joined the labor force (Koike 1981:189–192), but by 1970 the economy was facing serious labor shortages (Kobayashi 1977:118–129). In response to rising wages and labor demands, there were some efforts in the late 1960s to recruit workers from South Korea and elsewhere (Ochiai 1974:chap. 6). However, the 1973 oil crisis and the ensuing economic slump dampened labor demand (Mori 1997:55–57).

By the 1980s, however, Japanese economic growth had once again dried up the domestic sources of low-wage labor. Rural exodus was nearing its limits, and the number of *dekasegi* workers had reached its peak around 1970 (Kobayashi 1977:90). The number of *dekasegi* halved between 1972 and 1982 (Haneda 1987:2). In a similar fashion the number of part-time female workers diminished by the 1980s (Tsutsui and Yamaoka 1991:100–101).

The demand for low-wage manual and service labor became pressing by the late 1980s (Shimada 1994:33). The labor shortage was palpable in industrial towns around the Tokyo metropolitan area. Small manufacturing firms or town factories had been relying on older employees. One elderly owner said, "Young people just don't want to work in a place like this. My youngest employee is in his 40s." Hence, young Asian migrant workers were snapped up quickly, resulting in a situation of older Japanese employees working side by side with young foreign workers. One survey of small manufacturing employers showed that the overwhelming majority (77 percent) cited the inability to hire Japanese as the reason for employing foreigners (Inagami et al. 1992:73).

In particular, 3K (*kitsui, kitanai,* and *kiken*) jobs—which may be rendered as 3D in English (difficult, dirty, and dangerous)—faced severe shortages. Whether because of its low wages or low prestige, most Japanese were not willing to tolerate the conditions of 3K work, such as sexual work and construction. "I hate sweating," several young Japanese told me. A similar story can be told about Japan's vast sex industry. Although fancy-bar hostesses and expensive call girls remained the preserves of Japanese and white women, many of the lower-paying sex work jobs were filled by recent immigrants, who were willing to work for less than their Japanese counterparts (Ishiyama 1989:18–25). Many urban red-light districts transformed into global villages. In this regard, it may be tempting to conclude that the much-vaunted Japanese work ethic has become corrupted, but it is important to note the steadily improving labor market prospects for almost all Japanese during the postwar period. In any case, the very assumption of a Japanese work ethic as a cultural trait is questionable (Cole 1979:240), as are other traits of Japanese employment relations (Gordon 1998).

There were also specific conditions conducive to labor flow from underdeveloped Asian countries to Japan. In addition to improvements in transportation and communication exemplified by Boeing 747s and fax machines, many Asian governments encouraged their citizens to work abroad in order to enhance foreign exchange accumulation (Komai 1993:chap. 4). The Philippines, for example, established the Overseas Employment Administration to promote migrant labor (Kikuchi 1992). The Japanese economic expansion in Asia also projected the image of Japan as a rich and desirable country. As the Filipino migrant worker Rey Ventura (1992:165–166) wrote, "There is no Japanese Dream, and yet Japan, for the Filipino, has become a second America. . . . The Japanese are now the largest investors and aid donors to the Philippines. They are our wealthiest tourists." Certainly, Japanese cultural influences were pervasive in Southeast Asia (Asahi Shinbun Shakaibu 1989:65–67). In the mid-1980s, moreover, Asian workers living in the Middle East suffered from a downturn in the economy there and were seeking a new place to work (Abella 1995:420). Thus, Japan became an attractive destination for aspiring Asian migrant workers.

The initial influx of immigrant labor to Japan in the 1980s did not result from an explicit government policy, as in postwar France or West Germany, but rather from the nexus of employers' demands and workers' desires. Given the enormous legal and linguistic barriers posed by working in Japan, most migrant workers had to rely initially on labor brokers and other organized networks (Sellek and Weiner 1992:220–222). Labor brokers located potential workers and arranged for their transportation (Komai 1993:43–54). Because the principal occupations of immigrant workers—construction and sex work—were closely associated with *yakuza* (Japanese mafia), *yakuza* and *bōryokudan* (gangs) were initially the most important labor brokers (Asahi Shinbun Shakaibu 1989:117–141). Many Burakumin and Korean Japanese are, incidentally, members of *yakuza* and *bōryokudan* (Ino 1993:266–260), and Japanese mafia and gangs in turn had been aggressively expanding their networks beyond the Japanese national borders (Yamanaka 1989:38–44). Once in Japan, the expanding social networks of foreign workers conveyed employment and other information to their fellow nationals. Thereby relatives and friends, as well as various media outlets and organizations, supported the transnational movement of migrant workers to Japan.

Structural Vacancy and Ethnic Transitions

The acute labor shortages in several low-paying and low-prestige occupations contributed to the belated influx of foreign migrant workers into Japan. The migrant workers from Asia filled the niches in the secondary labor market previously held by rural migrants, *dekasegi* workers, and women. In other words, the structure of the labor market remained robust; different groups of people assumed its lowest reaches.

Consider the construction industry. The prewar construction industry relied heavily on Burakumin, Okinawans, and Koreans (Hippō 1992:131–151). In the postwar period, it continued to draw on Burakumin—many of whom were *dekasegi* workers—and other minorities in the informal labor market, or *yoseba*, where employers hire casual day laborers (*dokata* or *ninpu*) (Nishizawa 1995:chaps.2–3). Famous *yoseba*, such as San'ya in Tokyo and Kotobuki in Yokohama, are synonyms in Japanese for a slum or skid row *(doyagai)*, with nefarious connotations of addiction, crime, and madness. The gradual decline of *dekasegi* workers and day laborers underlay the labor market shortage in the postwar construction industry (Hippō 1992:456–463). Beginning in the 1980s, Filipino, Thai, Iranian, and other foreign workers thronged to Kotobuki, which was a veritable melting pot of all the major Japanese ethnic minority groups (Fowler 1996:15). The informal labor market in the early 1990s expressed an ethnic hierarchy with Japanese workers at the top, older Korean and Burakumin workers in the middle, and the new migrant workers at the bottom (Aoki 1989:97–98, 1992:325–326), thereby reconstructing the ethnic hierarchy of the Greater East Asia Co-Prosperity Sphere.

The structural transition can also be gleaned from other examples. Some Asian migrant workers lived in the low-cost housing units previously occupied by *dekasegi* workers (Okuda and Tajima 1991:23–26). Also, not far from where I was staying in Yokohama was a well-known prostitution area, which began in the immediate postwar years for American GIs. As one pimp told me, "Yes, years ago we had some Koreans but most prostitutes were country girls *(inaka no nēchan)*. Now, it's the United Nations; you can have a Taiwanese girl or a Filipina."

The Diversity of Foreign Workers

The situation of the Asian migrant workers in Japan was no different from that of their counterparts elsewhere (cf. Piore 1979:50–51). In the late 1980s and early 1990s Asian migrants worked predominantly in the worst jobs that Japanese society offered, characterized by poor pay, dismal working conditions, low status, job insecurity, and no chance of promotion. In 1992 Asian male migrants worked mostly in construction (51 percent) and factory work (28 percent), while women worked as hostesses (34 percent), factory workers (17 percent), and prostitutes (11 percent) (Shimada 1994:30–31). Many Japanese enterprises and industries became heavily dependent on these migrants by the early 1990s. When the job market was especially tight, there was considerable competition for foreign workers (Shinano Mainichi Shinbunsha 1992:19–21). Some employers even claimed to prefer the non-Japanese labor force. A small factory owner— half of whose employees were foreigners—told me that he preferred non-Japanese workers because they worked harder than their Japanese counterparts. In fact, he had no choice but to hire them. In the Tsukiji Fish Market—the principal market for sea food in Tokyo—several wholesalers noted that the place would not function without foreigners. One-fourth of Tokyo newspaper delivery people were said to be non-Japanese.

The new foreign workers did not form a homogeneous group. Ethnic diversity characteristic of immigrant labor populations in most societies was true for Japan as well (Castles and Kosack 1985:3–6). In 1990 the highest numbers were from the Philippines, South Korea, Thailand, China, Pakistan, Malaysia, and Bangladesh. By 1992 Thai, Malaysians, Filipinos, and Iranians were the largest nationalities. As the government cracked down on illegal foreign workers, labor brokers and employers recruited ethnic Japanese from South America (Yamanaka 1993) as well as those who were easier able to pass as Japanese, such as South Koreans and Chinese. In 1987 Brazilian citizens in Japan amounted to little over 2,000; by 1993 their total skyrocketed to over 150,000 (Watanabe M. 1995:23).

The profiles of the newly arriving migrant workers were far from uniform. Their visa status, national origin, and gender were among the variables that led to significant inequality in income (Inagami et al. 1992:17–27). Some national groups were strongly represented in particular industries, such as Bangladeshis in the printing industry and Chinese in the restaurant business (Aoki 1992:348). Inequality could exist in the same industry. For example, an estimated 30,000 Korean bar hostesses worked in well-appointed and expensive establishments (Mainichi Shinbun Gaishinbu 1990:30); the same cannot be said for many Filipina prostitutes, who worked at the bottom tier of the sex industry.

The worst fate awaited illegal workers. Because the Japanese government does not issue work visas for most manual and service jobs, defined as simple *(tanjun)* labor, many migrants work illegally, compounding their vulnerable status in Japan. Employed in industries that are illegal (e.g., sex work) or loosely regulated (e.g., smaller construction firms), the structure of exploitation often depends on the legal vulnerability of the new foreign workers and their informal dependence (e.g., debt) vis-à-vis their brokers or employers (Ishiyama 1989:89–96). In the informal day-labor market *(yoseba)*, employers would sometimes not pay workers or assign them to dangerous tasks (Kobayashi 1992:74–79). Many foreign workers found only limited access to medical facilities (Takayama 1992), welfare benefits (Satō Susumu 1992), and other supporting institutions.

By the early 1990s the new Asian migrant workers—Filipina dancers, South Korean hostesses, Thai masseuses, Iranian telephone-card sellers, and Bangladeshi construction workers—became recognizable character types in the Tokyo metropolitan area, so much so that they began to appear in popular television shows and comic books. Beyond newspaper headlines and television documentaries, the new foreign workers were to be found not only in Tokyo but across the Japanese archipelago. They increasingly became part of everyday life.

Like immigrant workers elsewhere, most of the new foreign workers in Japan intended to return to their homelands. There were, however, by the early 1990s some harbingers of their settlement in Japan (Okuda and Tajima 1993:54–60). The emergence of ethnic media, stores, and even neighborhoods became palpable (Machimura 1993). In addition, older ethnic communities, especially of Koreans and Chinese, provided havens for their compatriots (Ko 1995:234). Here again, western European and North American examples suggest the near inevitability of short-term migrants turning into long-run settlers or constituting transnational communities (Piore 1979:84–85).

The Problem of Foreign Workers in Japan

Immigration has generated a major political debate in the rich countries. In Britain "immigration [became] one of the most hotly debated public issues" in the 1980s (Castles and Kosack 1985:1). Britain is, of course, hardly unique in this matter; whether one considers the anti-immigration movement in France or the immigration debate in the United States, the politics of the industrial countries is inextricably intertwined with immigration. Even the newly industrialized countries, such as South Korea and Taiwan, experienced national debates on immigrant labor by the 1990s (Kim 1994).

In spite of some significant similarities, each national debate has its particularities. And, in the case of Japan, the problem of foreign workers was often articulated as a reprise of the question Japan faced in the mid-nineteenth century. According to the dominant Japanese historiography, Japan had been sequestered from foreign contact until the coming of Commodore Perry in 1853, when Japanese leaders were forced to decide whether to open the country (kaikoku) or to keep it closed (sakoku). In the late twentieth century, Japan was said to face a problem of comparable magnitude to this turning point in modern Japanese history (Tezuka 1989:9–21).

The sakoku faction argued that foreign workers would undermine Japanese uniqueness. Yano Tōru (1988:46–49), for example, wrote that the emperor system and the Japanese worldview are unique and should be protected from foreigners. In a similar vein, Nishio Kanji (1988) warned that the non-Japanese population would cause the social disorganization that he observed in other countries. The subtitle of one of his books reads "foreign workers will destroy Japan" (Nishio 1989a). Immigrants and their children would threaten well-functioning schools and other institutions and thereby undermine social cohesion and order. As Nishio (1989b:330) summarized: "This is not necessarily an economic problem. Frankly speaking, it is a problem of 'cultural defense.'"

The kaikoku side advocated allowing entry to foreigners from poor countries. One common reason was to let them earn money in Japan, thereby fulfilling Japan's obligation as a wealthy country (Miyajima 1989:11–12; cf. Nishio 1989a:144–150). Ōnuma Yasuaki (1988b) argued that accepting immigrants would not only make Japan a better member of the international community, but it would also open the closed spirit of Japan. In a similar vein, Keizai Dōyūkai (1989:3) wrote that "we believe that living with foreigners is important for the future of Japanese society."

In summary, the *sakoku* side stressed social costs, whereas the *kaikoku* argument accentuated human rights and Japan's international responsibility. The debate did not, however, follow obvious ideological cleavages. Major employers' associations and the largest labor unions generally advocated the *sakoku* side in the early stages of the debate, although there were significant exceptions among organizations of both capital and labor (Nimura 1992:256). Various national ministries were far from uniform in their outlook, and some local governments actively advocated open immigration (Kantō Bengoshikai Rengōkai 1990:124–142). Over time the response to the Asian migrant workers became more positive (Hachiya 1992:42–48).

Opinion surveys were inconclusive. In the 1988 *Sōrifu* (Prime Minister's Office) survey of 10,000 adult Japanese, 8 percent argued that Japan should not admit foreign workers, 26 percent advocated some restrictions, and 35 percent favored open immigration (Sōrifu 1988:5; Nyūkan Tōkei Kenkyūkai 1990:183). The 1992 figures were, respectively, 14, 57, and 15 percent (Sōrifu 1992:74; cf. Sōrifu 1990:3–6). A Mainichi newspaper survey of December 1988 reported 45 percent "for" as opposed to 48 percent "against" the influx of foreign workers. By January 1990 "for" had increased to 51 percent while "against" had declined to 44 percent (Mainichi Shinbun Tokyo Honsha Shakaibu 1990:275). The main reason for opposing immigration was fear of crime (Sōrifu 1992:76). The primary rationale for opening the country was the need for migrant workers who would undertake tasks that most Japanese shunned (Yorimitsu 1993:14–26).

The problem of foreign workers engendered many points of discussion beyond the simplified terms of the *kaikoku-sakoku* debate. A business executive in his fifties argued that because Japan is a small country, it would be "physically impossible" for too many more people to live in Japan. Another man, a proprietor of a small eatery, expressed his sympathy for foreigners but wondered how easily they would assimilate into Japan. Something of a dominant life philosophy in urban Japan is to respect individuality as long as one doesn't bother others *(meiwaku o kakenai)* (Shūkan Daiyamondo Bessatsu 1993:52). Several interviewees actively affirmed that the Asian workers were welcome as long as they didn't bother people. A middle-aged housewife expressed her hope that the foreign workers would learn Japanese quickly. The critic Kure Tomofusa (1993b:68), in his usual outlandish fashion, argued that they should be made "slaves of democracy." Many people, it should be noted, were indifferent.

There were, in addition, many scholarly studies. Some invoked econometric models and comparative examples to illuminate the Japanese situation (Gotō 1990; Tezuka, Komai, Ono, and Ogata 1992). Many people discussed seriously the potential impact of immigration and its unintended consequences for Japanese society. The desire to forestall the formation of an underclass, such as those existing in contemporary Europe, is not necessarily a covert expression of racism. Very few would, after all, advocate the end of all border control. Many people sharply indicted Japanese society for the horrible working conditions and human rights abuses that some foreign workers suffered.

By 1993 the dominant mood was to accept the inevitable. As some scholars argued in the late 1980s, the influx of migrant workers was ineluctable (Furuta 1989:32–34). The economist Kuwahara Yasuo (1991:277) suggested that the *kaikoku-sakoku* debate was meaningless because it did not reflect reality—the very presence of foreign workers refuted the *sakoku* argument. By the early 1990s most people acknowledged that Japan had become considerably less ethnically homogeneous than it had been.

Nonetheless, the dominant media articulation was in terms of the *kaikoku-sakoku* binary. What was the point of this debate? Why should a small group of non-Japanese manual and service workers have generated such intense media coverage? The number of the new foreign workers in Japan was minuscule compared to that of most other wealthy nation-states. International labor migration in contemporary Japan differs from its western European counterparts in the belated beginning of the influx and the small size of the migrant worker population. "By 1975 foreign workers had come to constitute 10 percent of the labor force in Western Europe as a whole" (Piore 1979:1). The ratio of foreign workers to the total employed German and French population in the 1970s was twenty times that of Japan in the early 1990s. In addition, elite, well-paying jobs in the government bureaucracy and large corporations remained restricted to Japanese college graduates, whereas there was an acute labor shortage in 3K jobs. The small number of the new foreign workers and the absence of economic competition suggest that the debate was not primarily economic in nature. Day laborers, who were perhaps most directly in competition with the new migrant workers, did not express strong resistance to foreigners.

Furthermore, the 1989 Revised Immigration Act did not restrict the inflow of all foreign workers. As articulated in the government's 1992 *Basic*

Plan for Immigration Control, the distinction was made between skilled workers, who would benefit Japan, and unskilled workers. The term simple labor *(tanjun rōdō)* is itself a neologism that came to be associated with the foreign worker debate (Inagami et al. 1992:41). The Plan noted that "the admittance of 'unskilled' foreign workers is not a mere introduction of labor force into Japan but acceptance of human beings having their own cultures and ways of living, and there are many problems resulting therefrom that cannot be judged only by economic principles" (Japan Immigration Association 1992:41). The uneasy mixture of economic utilitarianism and cultural conservatism is not out of line with the immigration law of many countries. Interestingly, the original postwar Japanese immigration law had been patterned after that of the United States (Hirowatari 1992:70).

Given that some employers were eager to hire foreign workers, who were in turn willing to work at low wages, and that there was no strong opposition movement, the media attention must be located in the perceived novelty and the symbolic significance of the Asian migrant workers. The new foreign workers unleashed a national discussion because their presence—especially the media focus on the ostensible novelty of ethnic heterogeneity—challenged the idea of Japan as an ethnically homogeneous society. In the late 1980s these workers were racialized and transmogrified into a problem.

The Racialization of the New Foreign Workers

The new foreign workers constituted a problem insofar as they posed a potential, and largely symbolic, threat to Japanese society because of their racialization and social visibility. By racialization I mean the process by which a group comes to be marked by its physical and cultural distinctiveness. More often than not, of course, shorthand characterizations misrepresent the population that they seek to signify. In spite of the fact that two-thirds of the immigrants were white in Britain in the mid-1980s, Castles and Kosack (1985:1) noted that the "term 'immigrant' has come to mean 'black man' in popular speech, and social scientists and politicians have, on the whole, adopted this usage" (cf. Gilroy 1991:46). Similarly, "To many French, 'immigrants' means 'Algerians,' but the Portuguese are actually more numerous" (Ireland 1994:15). The French anti-immigrant movement targeted Beurs (second-generation North Africans) (Silverman 1992:70–78; Hargreaves 1995:157–160), and the immigrant problem there is inevitably about Beurs, not Italian or Portuguese immigrants (Grillo

1985:30–35). In a similar fashion, the new foreign workers—principally from poor Asian countries—came to stand for all foreign workers in Japan.

In spite of their visibility and the discussions that they generated, the new Asian migrant workers constituted a small proportion not only of the total Japanese labor force but also of the total foreign population in Japan. In 1992 an estimated 1.3 million registered foreigners lived in Japan, or about 1 percent of the total Japanese population (for these figures, see Kunitomo 1992; Nyūkan Kyōkai 1993). The largest nationalities were 688,000 Koreans and 195,000 Chinese, who accounted for about 70 percent of all the registered foreigners, and whose number has not fluctuated significantly in the postwar period. Neither did 85,000 foreigners with work visas constitute a significant population. The largest group was 22,000 people on entertainment visas. Fewer people, mostly North Americans and Europeans, were on commercial, professorial, religious, and other professional visas.

Discussions of the new foreign workers referred neither to the Koreans and Chinese nor to Europeans and North Americans, but rather to the manual and service workers from poor Asian countries and, in particular, to illegal workers from underdeveloped countries who performed simple labor (Umetani 1993:77–80). In 1992 there were nearly 68,000 deportees and 300,000 visa overstays. In addition, those on student visas (113,000) and trainee visas (19,000) may have worked illegally. In 1990 the Ministry of Labour (1992:164–165) estimated that there were 280,000 "illegal disguised foreign employees" and 500,000 foreign workers overall. Even accepting the largest estimate, 5 percent of the total foreign population of Japan came to stand for all foreigners.

The Japanese discourse on the new Asian migrants shifted rapidly over time. Racialization does not imply stasis; like social science theories, evidence has an impact on its formulation and reformulation. The prevailing term for foreigners until the 1980s was *gaijin* (outsiders), and most Japanese associated the term with white Americans and Europeans. For example, when I made an appointment to see Japanese people, many of them were surprised to find that I looked very much like them. My name (John) and nationality (American) led them to expect a white man, as in John Kennedy or John Reed. Frequently a prospective rendezvous almost failed because the other person persisted in looking for a *gaijin* or *hakujin* (white person).

In the 1980s the Japanese mass media used the term *Japayukisan* to denote the new migrant workers. The term derives from *Karayukisan,* who were Japanese prostitutes overseas in the late nineteenth century (Suzuki 1993:224–236). *Japayukisan* thus implies sexual workers, who are engaged in what Japanese call the water trade *(mizushōbai)* (Itō 1992). Until 1988 the vast majority (80–90 percent) of deported workers were women working in the water trade as bar hostesses and prostitutes. The decline of sex tours to South Korea and Taiwan and the high cost of Japanese sex workers contributed to the inflow of sex workers from the Philippines, Thailand, and other countries into Japan (Hinago 1986:143–144). Because of the shifting gender composition of the new foreign workers, as well as a movement by Japanese progressives to extirpate the use of the term, *Japayukisan* became less frequently used by the early 1990s.

If *Japayukisan* connoted the sexualization of female foreign workers, the eventual dominance of the term *gaijin rōdōsha* and, later, *gaikokujin rōdōsha* (foreign workers) signified the incorporation of class identity in the racialization process. The shift from *gaijin* to *gaikokujin* denoted not only that the new foreign workers were not white but was also an effort to rectify discriminatory language. Whereas *gaijin* was deemed discriminatory, *gaikokujin* was considered proper. I was admonished several times not to use the term *gaijin rōdōsha* because *gaijin* expressed the exclusionary, or xenophobic, spirit of Japanese people. However, the very need to qualify the word for foreigners with that for workers—which has a connotation of manual or industrial work—distinguished the predominantly middle- and upper-class Euro-Americans from their proletarian counterparts. Hence, *gaikokujin rōdōsha* almost inevitably referred to the new Asian migrant workers engaged in manual labor, and not to Euro-Americans or even an Asian American academic such as myself. Whenever I asked Japanese people whether I should count myself as a *gaikokujin rōdōsha,* all of them denied it, and often vehemently so. The new foreign workers were, as I elaborate in the following chapter, not only racial but also class others.

The new foreign workers were, above all else, visible in urban Japanese life. Racialization highlights appearance—usually somatic features—as the basis of social classification. Although Southeast Asians are darker-skinned than most urban Japanese, they are readily identifiable by most Japanese people even without this somatic marker. Differences in clothing, gesticulation, and the general presentation of the self render them as obviously non-Japanese. For example, non-Japanese do not generally bow when they encounter other people.

The popular perception of the massive growth of the foreign worker population in the late 1980s was due to the racialized Asians. Consider this confident report on the incredible growth of the foreign worker population: "In the past, I saw perhaps one or two foreigners every few months. But now, I see them every day" (Kunitomo 1992:8; cf. Okuda and Tajima 1991:14). Never mind that this person would have seen hundreds of Korean Japanese without recognizing them as foreigners all his life. Korean Japanese, of course, look and gesticulate like Japanese and hence are indistinguishable from other Japanese by mere appearance or even extended social interaction. In a similar fashion, Hatada Kunio (1990:130) wrote sensationally that two-thirds of the people on Ōkubo-dōri, a major street in Tokyo, were foreign workers. He neglected to note that many Korean Japanese and Burakumin, among others, had been walking on the same road for decades.

It is not simply from the media coverage but from individual experience—the undeniable phenomenology of visual perception—that many Japanese viscerally understood the growth of the foreign worker population and that provided the crucial underpinning of the foreign worker debate. As a salesclerk in her forties summed up: "Well, it is now almost impossible to avoid [foreign workers]. Go outside and you will see that Tokyo has become a crucible of the human race [jinrui no rutsubo]. Everyone knows that there is a foreign worker problem in Japan." Experience, as indubitable as it may seem, is mediated by assumptions: in this case, the belief that Japan has been an ethnically homogeneous country until the recent influx of the Asian migrant workers. The spotlight on the new foreign workers obscured the old foreign workers and other ethnic minorities.

The visibility of the new foreign workers, however, dimmed rather rapidly. In a bustling cosmopolitan city like Tokyo, civil indifference is the hegemonic mode of social interaction. In repeated observations in public places, I rarely spotted anyone showing interest in the Asian workers. Several times, my hope was raised only to be dashed by the realization that the interest was being expressed by South Korean or Taiwanese tourists. Once, when I was talking to a Filipino worker, I noticed two middle-aged women stubbornly staring at us. When I talked to them, I learned quickly that they were not interested in the Filipino worker—it was a natural occurrence (atarimae no koto), they said later—but rather in my apparent fluency in English. They wondered whether I could offer private lessons to their school-aged children.

Was Japan Ever Closed or Ethnically Homogeneous?

Not only were the new Asian migrant workers racialized, but their presence challenged the vision of the social integrity and solidarity of the Japanese body politic, which is widely believed to be ethnically homogeneous. Thus, the Japanese discussion reflected ethnocultural issues that also dominated the debates on immigrant labor in West European and North American countries. For example: "In France in the 1980s the problem of immigration has come to be defined in terms of citizenship and identity, rather than demography or economics" (Hollifield 1992:188; see also Silverman 1992:140–147; Hargreaves 1995:165–168). As we have seen, the demand of the receiving country usually initiated the transnational flow of labor. Because the labor performed by foreign workers cannot be separated from the foreign workers themselves, ethnocultural issues supersede economic ones.

The problem posed by the new foreign workers encompassed ethnic Japanese as well, including the return of orphaned Japanese children in China and of the descendants of Japanese emigrants to South America (*Nikkeijin*). Some Japanese commentators argued that *Nikkeijin* were incapable of living and working in homogeneous Japan (Ishi 1995). In a similar vein, Japanese students returning from a spell abroad (*kikoku shijo*) generated serious discussions (Goodman 1990:1–2). Some believed that extended exposure to a foreign culture and educational system rendered the internationalized students ill-suited for their home country. The sociologist Merry White (1988:122) observed that "the returnees must remain a stigmatized deviant," who exist "in a cultural no-man's-land." The anthropologist Roger Goodman (1990:174) has called them a new minority group. More generally, any Japanese with extended exposure to life outside of Japan was suspect; the older epithet, *bata kusai* (butter smelly), viscerally expressed the suspicion of those tainted by the West.

What is curious is that the public attention to the new foreign workers occurred in a period of great Japanese political and economic expansion. The *kaikoku-sakoku* debate reached its apogee precisely when nearly everyone agreed on the need for Japan to be international. Nihon Keizai Shinbunsha (1982:18)—the publisher of the leading Japanese business paper—had advocated in the early 1980s: "It is time to open all of Japan to the world." Others, whether business-oriented conservatives or liberal internationalists, wrote of the need to break open the closed nature of Japanese society (Nagai 1988:220; Ōmae 1989:178). In a mid-1980s survey, only 8 percent of the respondents felt negatively about internationalization (Keizai Kikakuchō Kokumin Seikatsukyoku 1987:15). Prime Minister Nakasone's call for the internationalization of Japan was perhaps the dominant political slogan of the mid-1980s (Ogata 1992:63). Many books on the topic appeared, ranging from a discussion of how international Japan was in the fifth century (Asahi Shinbunsha 1990) to a non-Eurocentric vision of international society (Ōnuma 1988a), but I cannot recall a single title that was against internationalization. The most negative accounts were those that lamented the insufficient internationalization of Japanese society.

In this regard, the foreign worker debate bypassed the obvious obverse of the influx of foreign workers: the significant economic expansion of Japanese corporations and the outflow of Japanese people to the rest of the world. From 1970 to 1988 there was a threefold increase in the number of foreigners entering Japan, while the population of Japanese going abroad rose thirteenfold (Mainichi Shinbun Tokyo Honsha Shakaibu 1990:app. 7). An estimated tenth of Japanese people have traveled abroad (Katō 1992:24). Well over a million Japanese left Japan for business purposes annually (Skeldon 1992:42–43). The profound impact of Japanese corporations on the rest of Asia, ranging from worker exploitation to environmental degradation, has been amply documented (Shiozawa 1986; Steven 1990). While Japanese were debating the threat of foreign workers, the major discussion about Japan abroad was the Japanese threat to the rest of the world (Shimada 1991:171–176).

Historically, Japanese have emigrated to other countries seeking better economic opportunities. As I noted, Japanese emigration to Brazil continued until the 1970s (Valente 1978:22–31). The Japanese diaspora spanned Asia and the Americas; the total number of Japanese living abroad exceeded 1.4 million by 1940, and was over 1.6 million fifty years later (Taeuber 1958:201; Tanaka H. 1991:193; Suzuki J. 1992:4). By the early 1990s there were over 200,000 Japanese citizens residing in the United States alone, in addition to over 700,000 Japanese Americans (Tanaka H. 1991:185–186). Japanese business people, tourists, and immigrants are everywhere (Iwauchi et al. 1992). A neglected aspect of the Japanese diaspora, incidentally, is its ethnic heterogeneity, especially the overrepresentation of Burakumin and Okinawans among Meiji-era emigrants and Korean Japanese and mixed-race people more recently.

If internationalization was such a widely shared goal—as well as an indisputable social fact—for Japan, why was there such a heated debate on foreign workers? As the economist Tezuka Kazuaki (1989:23) had pointed out early in the *kaikoku-sakoku* debate, the internationalization of Japan inevitably pointed to the influx of foreign workers. What made them and returning Japanese students problematic was the assumption that Japan has been closed to foreigners and that it has been an ethnically homogeneous society.

Japan has in fact never been closed to foreign contact, whether of ideas, goods, or people. During the Tokugawa period (1603–1867), Japan was not closed to all foreign contact (Toby 1984; Jansen 1992:2–4). The Tokugawa state monopolized all foreign trade, but state monopoly did not preclude foreign, even Western, ideas from entering the three major islands (Tsuruta 1992). During the Tokugawa period there was a well-developed discourse on Asia, and over 200 books on foreign countries were translated (Torii 1993:221; Arano 1994:228–229). As I elaborate in Chapter 4, Japan became a modern nation-state by incorporating diverse ethnic groups. Meiji state-making included the colonization of Hokkaidō and Okinawa, and Japanese imperialist expansion led many Koreans and Chinese to enter Japan.

The origins of the Korean and Chinese populations in Japan point to a more obvious way in which the belief in ethnic homogeneity is untenable. The debate on the new foreign workers frequently neglected the long-term Korean and Chinese residents in Japan. The last great Japanese attempt at internationalization—before and during World War II—resulted in the immigration of Korean and Chinese workers into the Japanese archipelago. The Korean migration into Japan alone totaled 2.3 million people in 1945. However, the colonial period was effaced during the debate. It is not surprising that the *kaikoku-sakoku* debate harked back to the nineteenth century, when Japan was putatively closed from foreign contact. The twentieth century—when Japan had embarked on colonial expansion and forcefully brought over foreign workers—was conveniently bypassed.

The problem of the new foreign workers arose precisely at a time when the idea of monoethnic Japan faced challenges from the previously silenced legacy of Japanese colonialism. The 1980s witnessed the rise of vibrant social movements that revived the repressed colonial past. In the mid-1980s, the effort to end fingerprinting *(shimon ōnatsu)* of resident foreigners became a celebrated cause. Led by Korean Japanese, the movement mobilized not only a large number of people, but it also became a major foreign policy issue between Japan and South Korea (Lie 1987). By the late 1980s another legacy of the colonial period, "comfort women," became a major media sensation. The international effort to redress the enforced prostitution of Korean and other women was transformed into a serious diplomatic issue (Takasaki 1993:128–138). Postwar immigration is, of course, often associated with the colonial past. "British people confronted with immigrants from what used to be the Empire, cannot but be expected to react to them in terms of the role which the immigrants used to fill" (Rex and Tomlinson 1979:91). "Any account of the contemporary response to migration and migrants in France must, therefore, acknowledge the impact of a colonial past in defining and shaping interethnic relations" (Grillo 1985:289).

The spotlight on the new foreign workers obscured the various diasporic communities in Japan. The amnesia of Japanese colonialism effaced the past atrocities and elided the problems raised by the earlier foreign workers. Hence, the Japanese debate in the late 1980s both crystallized the presumption of an ethnically homogeneous Japan and defined the new foreign workers as a major problem. They contradicted and reinforced the ideology of Japanese ethnic homogeneity. As countless publications and television documentaries depicted the problems of foreign workers and ethnic minorities in other countries, they accentuated the assumption of Japanese monoethnicity. As a self-proclaimed critic of Japanese xenophobia commented while we viewed a documentary on Europe, "It is horrible that German and French governments treat the minorities so badly. At least Japan doesn't have this problem." The unquestionably multiethnic face of other societies made Japan seem monoethnic and veiled its ethnic heterogeneity.

In Japan the inevitable dialectic of internationalization and ethnic heterogeneity has been repeatedly denied. Every major effort to internationalize Japan begins from the assumption that Japan had been closed, thereby neglecting both the past and present reality of multiethnicity. Whether one focuses on the 1890s debate to allow Chinese to live in Japan or the 1920s discussion to permit Korean workers in Japan or the 1960s effort to introduce Korean immigrant workers, each occasion obfuscated the prior existence of foreigners on Japanese soil (Yamawaki 1994). Each new call for internationalization generated alarming prospects of foreigners within, which reaffirmed and strengthened the assumption of Japanese ethnic homogeneity by occluding the multiethnic past.

The problem of the new foreign workers—the second opening of Japan—refracted a powerful belief in Japanese monoethnicity in contemporary Japanese society. The dominant terms of the debate obfuscated the actually existing ethnic minorities and the colonial legacy. The transnational realities of the Japanese economy, past and present, made it impossible for Japan to be a major global economic player and simultaneously close off its national borders. The contradiction between the dynamic of the expansionary political economy and the ideology of a pure and homogeneous nation manifested itself starkly in the foreign workers debate. The reality of multiethnicity once again threatened *and* affirmed the belief in monoethnicity. Precisely when multiethnicity became incontrovertible, people asserted that Japan has been, always and already, monoethnic.

2

The Contemporary Discourse
of Japaneseness

One Sunday in 1993 I took a train to Ishikawa Station, perhaps half an hour away from where I was living in Yokohama. Walking westward from the station, I entered Chinatown and ate at a restaurant remarkable as much for its sordid interior as for its savory noodles. Walking eastward amidst Chinese-language signs and speakers, I explored Kotobuki, one of the most notorious *doyagai* (slums) in Japan. Beyond shabby buildings and sleeping drunks—the inescapable sight and stench of poverty—I passed by people talking animatedly in various Asian tongues, including Tagalog and Thai. Passing a Korean restaurant, I was overwhelmed by the aroma of Korean food as well as by loud conversations in Korean.

Later in the afternoon, I went to Roppongi, one of the most fashionable areas in Tokyo. Navigating a crowd of well-dressed people, I felt as underdressed as I had felt overdressed in Kotobuki. I passed Israelis hawking cheap jewelry and Iranians peddling telephone cards. At a fancy French café I ordered the most expensive cup of coffee of my life from a Bangladeshi waiter. Conversing with a Japanese friend, I recounted my day and my inescapable impression of Japanese multiethnicity. But she begged to differ and insisted that I had gotten Japan all wrong. She remained unconvinced as I talked about Ikaino, the Korean area of Osaka (Kim 1985), and other notably multiethnic areas of Japan, such as the Chikuhō region in Kyūshū (Shindō T. 1985:37–66). When I pointed to the foreign workers I met in Kotobuki, she said that Yokohama had always been an exception. She went on to say that Yokohama, Nagasaki, Kōbe, and Tokyo were all port cities and therefore were atypical. Neither Kotobuki nor Roppongi, nor Ikaino nor Chikuhō, was really Japan.

What is the real Japan? In Chapter 1, I argued that the debate over the new foreign workers revealed and reified the widespread assumption of Japanese monoethnicity. Why is it that so many Japanese people insist that Japan has been and remains an ethnically homogeneous society? Many Japanese share a particular vision of Japan, or a discourse of Japaneseness, which highlights homogeneity. In reconstructing the discursive domain within which this belief is articulated against the influx of the new foreign workers, I highlight its three critical assumptions about class, culture, and ethnicity. The new foreign workers are relationally constructed as the antipodes of Japanese people; they are the class, cultural, and ethnic others.

Japan as a Middle-Strata Society

In the contemporary discourse of Japaneseness, Japan is often characterized as a middle-class society. Surveys show that 90 percent of adult Japanese place themselves in the middle strata *(chū kaisō)* (Murakami 1984:167–172; Mamada 1990:24), leading many to characterize Japan as a classless society (Ueno 1985:99–101; Umesao 1986:61–62). Alternative characterizations of Japan, such as those describing it as a mass society *(taishū shakai)*, envision Japan as an egalitarian society (cf. Ueno 1989:59–53). Matsuyama Yukio (1985:143–144) explained that he was happy to be Japanese because Japan "does not have class and is an egalitarian society." The belief in an egalitarian Japan is confirmed by the common reaction to the new foreign workers, who are almost always viewed as less educated and of lower status than the Japanese. A middle-aged white-collar worker argued that the influx of the new migrant workers would destroy Japan's "classless society."

The reality of past and present inequality in Japan contradicts the assumption of a universal middle-class society. In the Tokugawa period the rigid status hierarchy, encapsulated in the shorthand *shi-nō-kō-shō* (samurai, farmer, craftsperson, merchant), precluded status mobility and interstatus marriage (Minegishi 1989:chap. 2). Although the Meiji Restoration introduced features of formally egalitarian citizenship, prewar Japan clearly distinguished the hereditary elite—the imperial household *(kōzoku)*, nobility *(kazoku)*, and former samurai *(shizoku)*—and commoners *(heimin)* (Lebra 1993:57–60), as well as Burakumin *(shin heimin)*. There was a conspicuous elite in prewar Japan, exemplified on the one hand by its hereditary members and on the other hand by a meritocratic elite forged through the nexus of imperial universities and the government bureaucracy (Silberman 1964:108). In fact, the two factions were interdependent; although *shizoku* accounted for only 6 percent of the total population, they constituted over half of imperial university students in the early twentieth century (Amano 1983:260–262). If formal barriers to marriage and employment ended, informal restrictions remained robust. Furthermore, blights of urban poverty (Yokoyama 1949) and, even worse, rural poverty (Inomata 1982) dotted the archipelago.

Formal status inequality ended with the postwar eradication of the hereditary elite, but substantive inequality persists in postwar Japan. Perhaps the best-known textbook on postwar Japanese society—Nakane Chie's *Japanese Society* (1970:87)—delineates Japan as a "vertical society" *(tate shakai)*, characterized by "vertical stratification by institution or group of institutions." As one wag put it, her book may be a very astute ethnography of the University of Tokyo, which is steeped in rank consciousness. Be that as it may, hierarchy remains a constant in characterizations of Japanese society. An American scholar, for example, matter-of-factly notes: "The Japanese view of the world . . . is essentially hierarchical" (Greenbie 1988:12).

Beyond the issue of vertical hierarchy as a component of Japanese culture or consciousness, inequality is an undeniable fact of contemporary Japanese society. For a long time the Japanese Dream was to gain entrance to a prestigious university. No one seriously questions the university hierarchy, with the University of Tokyo (Tōdai) and Kyoto University at its apex (Ehara 1984:265–266). In the late 1970s Tōdai graduates dominated the two most powerful state bureaucracies, representing 89 percent of the employees of the Ministry of Finance and 76 percent of the Ministry of Foreign Affairs (Rohlen 1983:91; cf. Passin 1982:135–136). Moreover, the quality of primary and secondary schools differs widely, the access to better schools depending on preexisting social position (Smith 1995:chaps.2–3). As Hiroshi Ishida (1998:307) concludes: "the unequal distribution of occupational outcomes is related not only to different levels of educational credentials . . . but also to the difference by type and quality within the same level of educational credentials." Especially in poorer areas, high schools—contrary to the dominant image of the Japanese educational miracle in the United States—are wracked by absenteeism, violence, prostitution, and drug use (Rohlen 1983:294–301; Sōmuchō Seishōnen Taisakuhonbu 1996:174–188).

Indeed, some scholars characterize Japan as a class-stratified society (Shōji 1982:23–26; Steven 1983:319; Gotō 1985:147–159). Although 90 percent of Japanese may identify themselves as middle strata, nearly 40 percent in a 1982 survey experienced some economic difficulties *(kurushii)* in everyday life, and the majority reported that they had no leisure time (Gotō 1985:143). Poverty persists, including an estimated 100,000 homeless people in the early 1990s (Iwata 1995:27). If we explore different dimensions of social life, whether health care or cultural life, we find significant stratification (Mouer and Sugimoto 1989:187–192). Occupational and corporate hierarchy remains formidable (Takeuchi Y. 1995:181–187). Japan is no more egalitarian or open to intergenerational mobility than Britain or the United States (Ishida 1993:253–257).

Most Japanese are in fact acutely aware of educational and occupational hierarchy. When the language of class is used, Japanese sort themselves differently than they do when employing the language of status. In a 1975 survey 90 percent of respondents placed themselves in the middle strata *(kaisō)* but only 4 percent in the middle class *(kaikyū);* 71 percent said that they were working class (Naoi 1979:365). In factories, industrial workers readily distinguish themselves from the educated management (Nakamura 1982:220–226). In spite of the ideology of managerial paternalism, workplace hierarchy is obvious (Hamashima 1985:122–127). Although Japanese people are not necessarily class-conscious, we should be wary of the claim that Japan is a statusless or classless society (cf. Misumi 1990).

Given the reality and consciousness of inequality, why do people claim that Japan is an egalitarian society? To put it simply, Japan became significantly more egalitarian after 1945. The postwar era began with a spate of progressive reforms. Legal distinctions based on status ended; constitutional monarchy gave way to democracy. The postwar universalist ideologies, whether Marxism or progressive liberalism, buttressed the egalitarian ethos. The memory of status hierarchy faded rapidly in the postwar period. The novelist Yasuoka Shōtarō (1983:23), born in 1920, wrote in the early 1980s, "In our heart of hearts, the idea of status distinction *(shi-nō-kō-shō)* peculiarly but persistently remains." When in the early 1990s I mentioned this passage to people in their twenties, they were surprised—and some were even dismayed—by the survival of the feudal past as recently as a decade before.

Claims of status equality were confirmed by lessening economic inequality and rapid economic growth. Massive land reform purged large landlords from the countryside, and the dissolution of family-owned business groups *(zaibatsu)* eroded the dominance of large capitalists (Iwamoto

1985:84–90). Postwar Japanese society become significantly more egalitarian in terms of income and experienced nearly uninterrupted growth until the 1973 oil crisis. In the course of one generation, the images of poverty and desperation captured in the 1950s films of Kurosawa Akira were superseded by the visions of plenty and playfulness in the 1980s films of Itami Jūzō. Luxury goods, such as the three Cs—car, color television, and cooler (air conditioner)—were transformed from desire into necessity in a matter of a decade. As Takeuchi Shizuko (1982:166) put it: "Workers had nothing to lose but their chains, but they now have washing machines and television sets." My home-ism *(mai hōmushugi)* and consumer society became key catchphrases to describe Japanese society (Kaneko 1985:72–76). The transformation was rapid and compressed. While 1966 was dubbed the beginning of private car ownership *(mai kā gannen)* (Plath 1992:230), by 1974 the economist Uzawa Hirofumi (1974:67–76) was already complaining about its social costs.

The postwar economic transformation generated the new ideal of the middle strata in the guise of the *sararīman* (salary man, or white-collar worker). Returning in 1969 to a Tokyo suburb he had studied a decade earlier, Ezra Vogel (1971:271) observed: "By now all . . . aspirations for security, material possessions, and regular hours have been realized not only by the salary man, but by most of the population of Japan. The model and the vision that were provided by the salary man a decade ago have been essentially achieved already." In other words, the salary man, or middle-strata, status became normative in postwar Japan (Vogel 1971:267). The ideal penetrated the countryside as well: "In some rural communities, farmers now turn over their income to the co-operative, draw it out in the form of 'sarari' (salary) and proudly claim that they are just like salary men" (Vogel 1971:267–268). Factory workers similarly struggled to become ordinary Japanese *(hyōjunteki na kokumin)* (Kumazawa 1981:71). The postwar labor struggles narrowed the social distance between blue-collar and white-collar workers (Kumazawa 1983:37–38), closing not only the wage gap but status distinction. After the mid-1950s visible status or class markers, such as clothes that until then had distinguished occupational groups, disappeared (Kumazawa 1981:73). Factory workers donned the uniform of the bourgeoisie: a suit and a tie.

In this regard, the competitive examination system underscored meritocracy—a career as *sararīman*—that superseded the hereditary and entrenched elite. There is a continuity from the prewar period in the Japanese ideology of self-reliance and success *(risshin shusse)*, in which school was the principal institutional route of upward mobility (Kinmonth 1981:331–339). The putatively objective nature of entrance examinations underscored the meritocratic educational and employment system.

By 1990, buoyed by the bubble economy, the dominant Japanese self-image projected a society of affluence. The vocabulary of class had declined along with the support for socialists and other leftist parties (Kosaka 1994:96–97). However, labor market conditions in themselves did not discourage people from assuming less prestigious jobs; in this context, the new foreign workers—employed predominantly in undesirable jobs—enhanced the widespread sense of Japan as a society of middle-strata, and even middle-class, people. In other words, Japanese are middle class, and foreign workers are lower class.

Some foreign workers, such as refugees, are, of course, poor and in desperate straits (Nakano 1993:77–79). However, some come to study electrical engineering and security laws, and others wish to work for a Japanese company or to marry a Japanese person (Okuda and Tajima 1991:44–45). I was struck time and again by the fluent English, suggesting high educational attainment, of the Filipinos and Iranians I met in Kotobuki and elsewhere (Kikuchi 1992:182). If we were to identify the modal Asian migrant workers in Japan in the early 1990s, they would be far from impoverished and ill-educated (Okuda and Tajima 1993:49–54).

Nonetheless, the Asian migrant workers' significant diversity of educational attainment or class background escapes the dominant Japanese view. Never mind that a Bangladeshi construction worker may be a college graduate, a Filipina bar maid a professionally certified nurse, or an Iranian telephone-card seller a son of a medical doctor: upper class and lower class, college educated and illiterate are all lumped into the category of foreign workers, who assume manual and menial jobs. Hence, the middle-class (and affluent) Japanese are opposed to the lower-class (and impoverished) foreign workers.

Ironically, politically progressive people most clearly articulated the class contrast. A self-appointed supporter of the foreign workers' struggle argued that they should be allowed to work in Japan because they are pitiful and poor. Progressive Japanese analyses of the foreign workers stressed structural factors, such as their poverty, rather than their individual desires and initiatives (Tou 1992:29–33). Media coverage, ever in search of interesting copy, highlighted sensational stories of suffering. It is, of course, problematic to emphasize only the exploitation and the pathos of the new foreign workers. After all, most of them enter Japan voluntarily and consciously endure the demanding working conditions.

The unwanted sympathy and the thinly veiled presumption of superiority led many foreign workers to resent Japanese haughtiness. After the October 1987 death of a starving Bangladeshi student, Japanese activists launched a movement to feed foreign students, but many foreign students found the effort offensive (Tanaka H. 1991:178–179). A Thai worker surprised the concerned Japanese Okabe Kazuaki (1991:i) by saying that he "felt sorry for Japanese people because there was no foreign country where they can make ten or twenty times the going wage in Japan." Very few Japanese discerned the disjuncture between some foreign workers' upper- or middle-class background back home and their lower-class employment in Japan. Most Japanese were shocked to realize that some workers belong to the upper crust of their home countries by virtue of their college education (Kokusai Kyōryoku Jitsugyōdan 1994:123). Their multifaceted reality cannot be captured by an unrelenting narrative of suffering and exploitation.

Underlying the contrast between the middle-class Japanese and the lower-class foreign workers is the widely diffused belief in Japanese affluence and Third World poverty. To be sure, the proposition of Japanese prosperity and Third World poverty is unassailable in and of itself. However, just as not all Japanese are rich, not all Third World people are poor. Class and nation are, however, fused in the regnant Japanese view. By neglecting inequality in their own country, many Japanese have little sense of inequality elsewhere. The nationalist and essentialist framework leads many Japanese to ignore intranational variations in favor of international comparisons. Motoyama Yoshihiko (1991), one of the leading Japanese economists, begins his survey of developing countries with a chapter entitled "the desperate poverty of developing countries," but does not mention the significant inequality within a developing country or among developing countries. Reflecting a widespread view, the Third World is, simply, "desperately poor." Although many foreign workers may be relatively well-educated, the recognition that they hail from countries poorer than Japan—and, more obviously, that they seek employment in affluent Japan—confirm many Japanese in their equation of impoverished Third World countries with low-class foreign workers.

If Japanese are middle class and the new foreign workers are lower class, then who are the upper class? In short, white foreigners (*gaijin* or *hakujin*). *Gaijin* (outsiders) in postwar Japan almost inevitably referred to white North Americans and Europeans. Although Europeans and Americans may have low educational attainment and occupational status back home, they are likely to be regarded as of higher class than the Japanese. Commercials that evoke elegance inevitably employ white models. The archetypal Japanese depiction of upper-class life is a Swiss chateau or a British country house. Hence, Japanese who wish to differentiate themselves often assume aspects of European culture. Imada Minako's fashionable school in Harajuku teaches classical French cuisine, including "Diane de Poitiers' cheesecake, Ludwig II's *choux* swans and Catherine de Medici's sabayon" (Petkanas 1993:7). Shino Rinji owns three French restaurants and built a museum in his native Wakayama Prefecture that resembled the Louvre. For his country club "French lampposts line the driveway to the chateau-like clubhouse. . . . And those who lose their way among the French rose bushes can refer to a French-Japanese guidebook" (Thornton 1995:70). Whether haute cuisine or home design, the West denotes class (Rosenberger 1992:106).

These examples of Europhilia and penchants for Western aristocratic culture reflect a country where the superiority of Europe and the United States was taken for granted. As a man in his forties paradigmatically stated, "But, of course, *gaijin* are rich. Don't they live in a large mansion, relax in a swimming pool, and eat fat, juicy beefsteaks for breakfast?" When Katō Hidetoshi (1980:3) visited Harvard in 1954, he was impressed most deeply by fat steaks and plentiful coffee. Yamamoto Akira (1986:110–112), a scholar of popular culture, recalls that the first thing he did when he arrived in the United States in the 1960s was to make himself a Dagwood sandwich. The popularity of the cartoon *Blondie,* one of whose comic staples was the sumptuous sandwiches that the male protagonist Dagwood concocted, projected an indelible image of American wealth (Dore 1958:84).

White Europeans and North Americans personify the upper class in part because the Japanese domestic upper class is invisible. The remnants of the hereditary elite lead lives of quiet opulence. Beyond their small numbers, they are not only residentially segregated but attend special schools, shop in designated stores, and eat at exclusive restaurants (Lebra 1993:148–155). The breakup of large family firms and the postwar land reform reduced the fortunes and the size of the prewar upper class. The postwar corporate elites are paid professionals, and in status, if not in income, *sararīman*. The meritocratic elite do not constitute an aristocracy.

Cultural Superiority

An implicit corollary of the contrast—Japanese as middle class, foreign workers as working or lower class—is that Japanese are more advanced in terms of culture and civilization than foreign workers. The superstructure of cultural superiority overlies the infrastructure of class advantage. To put it crudely, Japanese believe themselves to be more cultured and civilized than foreign workers.

In the discourse of Japaneseness, status homogeneity accompanies cultural essentialism. Most Japanese assume the equivalence of the nation-state and national culture, and comfortably talk about *the* Japanese culture as if it were a static and homogeneous thing. Japanese tend to adopt an ethnonationalist frame when they delve beyond the simple dichotomy between Japanese and non-Japanese. Because Japan is believed to be homogeneous, almost all other countries are believed to be so as well. That Filipinos may group themselves according to their place of origin (Ventura 1992:49–50) or that Indonesia comprises a myriad of cultures (Anderson 1990:119–123) bypasses the consciousness of most Japanese. The assumption of homogeneity is, of course, paradoxical, given that one of the ostensibly unique attributes of Japanese society is its homogeneity. However, the nationalist habit of thought is apparently infectious. Hence, Japan is a haven for national character studies, in which national cultures are personalities writ large.

National cultures are, moreover, unequal. The idea of ranking civilizations or cultures along a unilineal scale of progress is deeply entrenched in Japan. Influenced by Thomas Buckle and François Guizot, Fukuzawa Yukichi, perhaps the greatest social thinker of modern Japan, delineated a hierarchy of civilizations in his widely disseminated books. In his view European countries and the United States are civilized *(bunmeikoku)*, Turkey, China, Japan, and some other countries are semi-civilized *(hankai no kuni)*, and Australia and Africa are savage *(yaban no kuni)* (Fukuzawa 1981a:20). The tradition of grand history—the rise and fall of civilizations and the attendant assumption of a moral hierarchy of nations—remains a popular genre in Japan, exemplified in the postwar period by the popularity of Arnold Toynbee. To be sure, postwar intellectuals and the reading public found Toynbee's cosmopolitan spirit attractive, but they also found reasonable his view of cultural hierarchy (Toynbee 1976:21; cf. McNeill 1989:268–270).

That Japan ranked below the West was an accepted, albeit occasionally contested, fact since the Meiji Restoration. Catching up with the West was perhaps the most important prewar national mandate. The slogan *wakon yōsai* (Japanese spirit, Western technology) underestimates the extent to which Japanese political, military, business, and educational leaders acknowledged Western superiority and sought to emulate the West. The very word for culture or civilization *(bunmei)* had extremely positive connotations and was associated above all with the West. As the Foreign Minister Inoue Kaoru said in 1887: "Let us change our empire into a European-style empire. Let us change our people into a European-style people. Let us create a new European-style empire on the Eastern sea" (Jansen 1980:69). The scholar-bureaucrat Nitobe Inazō (1984:129) observed that just as "our ancestors sought knowledge from Korea and China," the Japanese of his time "should emulate [their ancestors] and must absorb knowledge from the West."

To desire to catch up is to acknowledge backwardness. Cultural inferiority is an abiding theme of modern Japanese history (Irokawa 1970:70–78). To again quote Nitobe (1972a:232), writing in the early twentieth century: "We are still far behind America and Europe. Instead of being self-satisfied, our duty still is, and will be for some years to come, to be conscious of our inferiority." This sentiment survives in the late twentieth century. "Japan has been until 1975 or 1976 a backward country *(kōshinkoku).* It is an extremely special country in never having been an advanced country" (Tanizawa 1991:84). Many Japanese intellectuals have been ashamed of Japanese culture and glorified Western culture (Tsurumi 1989:67). Sekikawa Natsuo (1996:271) writes: "I believed in modernization and Westernization. That is, I had some reservations—some shame—about being Japanese."

In literature European influences frequently eclipsed native traditions. As Katō Shūichi (1971:143) noted, "the special characteristic of Japanese literature is the overwhelming influence of foreign literature." All the leading novelists of modern Japan—from Natsume Sōseki and Mori Ōgai to Tanizaki Jun'ichirō, Nagai Kafū, and Mishima Yukio—were deeply engaged with the West and wrote in large part in reaction to their Western experience or their reading of Western literature (Nakamura 1983:140–

157; cf. Nakamura 1987). At times, things Japanese were so devalued that Japan was said to be missing from modern Japanese literature (Shimada 1970:54). The leading thinkers of modern Japan—Nishida Kitarō and Watsuji Tetsurō, or Kuki Shūzō and Miki Kiyoshi—cut their philosophical teeth on Western classics, whether Nietzsche or Kierkegaard, Bergson or Heidegger (Sakabe 1990:8–9). Reverently reading the spines of foreign books in a bookstore, the celebrated writer Akutagawa Ryūnosuke's (1978:311) memorable line—"Life is not worth a line of Baudelaire"—is but an exaggerated expression of this mindset.

The glorification of Western civilization manifested itself in valorizing the ideal of *kyōyō* (cultural literacy, or *Bildung*) (cf. Conze and Kocka 1985). Fukuzawa Yukichi's (1980) *Gakumon no susume* (The Encouragement of Learning) set the tone by selling 220,000 copies, or one for every 160 Japanese at the time (Koizumi 1966:28). Fukuzawa himself read and reread Sugita Genpaku's (1959) paean to Dutch learning, originally published in 1815; Sugita's chronicle of learning painfully acquired became a role model in modern Japan. As Sugita and Fukuzawa exemplified, *kyōyō* was quintessentially about acquiring and displaying Western culture (Tsutsui 1995:32–36).

The unquestioned prestige of Western learning (Maruyama 1961:8–15) explains the heightened role of critics and translators in modern Japanese intellectual life. Japan was a "translators' heaven" (Kamei 1994:8) or a "culture of translation" (Isoda 1983a:33). Purveyors of *kyōyō*, or *chishikijin* (intellectuals), translated and introduced Western writings (Nakamura 1960:288–292). Some writers went so far as to buy up all the copies of a particular Western-language title to conceal their dependence on it for one or another essay (Ōoka and Haniya 1984:271). Maruzen—the main importer of Western books in prewar Tokyo—became a veritable intellectual shrine (Terada 1947:119–124). Ambitious pupils sought to read through the collected works of great writers. *Bunko* (small paperbacks) that are ubiquitous in contemporary Japan began when the leading publisher Iwanami Shoten adopted the ideal of the German Reklam editions *(Universal Bibliothek)*. Even in the 1980s the publisher's bookshop held the complete collection of Reklam titles. Iwanami, in turn, signified intellectual seriousness and prestige. As the novelist Haniya Yutaka remarked: "We are all of the Iwanami *bunko* generation" (Ōoka and Haniya 1984:98).

The indisputable dominance of Western intellectual culture can be gleaned from Japanese memoirs. Yasuda Takeshi's (1985) memoir of reading begins with Alexandre Dumas's *The Count of Monte Christo* and ends with Erich Maria Remarque's *All Quiet on the Western Front.* In his memoir Katō Shūichi (1968:i, 190) emphasizes the pleasure and influence of Pascal, Gide, Racine, and Proust. The Kyoto University professor Ashizu Takeo recalls that his college friends argued vociferously about whether Wilhelm Furtwängler's or Arturo Toscanini's rendition of Beethoven symphonies was superior (Waki and Ashizu 1984:105–106). As postwar Japan's most celebrated intellectual Maruyama Masao recorded in his diary in 1954, "No event gave me a greater shock recently than Furtwängler's sudden death. The desire to listen in person to Beethoven's Ninth conducted by him and performed by the Berlin Philharmonic—this is 90 percent of my reason to want to go to Europe—has now finally become forever an unrealizable dream" (Waki and Ashizu 1984:115). Maruyama goes on to note, after an excursus on Maria Callas, that many Japanese are known to be Furtwängler maniacs (Waki and Ashizu 1984:122). Regardless of the accuracy of Maruyama's observation, the lure of the West and its place as a cultural center are undeniable.

Postwar intellectual life continued to valorize European and American intellectual imports. The manga (comics) artist Tsuge Yoshiharu (1983:55), for example, includes Edgar Allan Poe and Feodor Dostoevsky among his influences. The popular novelist Murakami Haruki describes his youth as a time when he read *The Brothers Karamazov, Jean Christophe, War and Peace,* and *Quiet Flows the Don* three times each, noting: "I thought that *Crime and Punishment* was too short" (Murakami and Anzai 1986:144). Although few might share his lament, Murakami's zeal is suggestive of the Japanese desire for *Bildung.*

What is more striking is that the immersion in Western classics is not the sole preserve of the educated elite. Gail Bernstein (1983:123) was surprised to discover Fumiko, "the genteel farm woman," in a peripheral farming community in Ehime, who "read in translation a surprising number of American classics, including Louisa May Alcott's *Little Women* and some of Hemingway's novels, as well as books on race problems in America." Edward Fowler (1996:61) encountered in the famous *doyagai* San'ya a day laborer who told him, "You're from the United States and teach Japanese literature! I should tell you that I'm not entirely ignorant of your field. I know the name of Donald Keene."

The Japanese defeat in World War II devastatingly reinforced the sense of cultural inferiority (Takeyama 1985:276). Shiga Naoya (1955:127)—

dubbed the god of the novel—proposed in 1946 that Japan should institute French as the national language: "France is a culturally advanced
country . . . there are some commonalities with Japanese." His reasoning
harked back to an earlier idea to institute English as the national language: "During this war, I frequently recalled that some 60 years ago, Mori
Arinori attempted to adopt English as the national language (kokugo). If
that had been realized, I thought of what might have been. Japanese culture would have become far more advanced than it is now. And, most
likely, this war would not have happened" (Shiga 1955:126). Needless to
say, Shiga's proposal was ignored, but the belief in the cultural bankruptcy
of Japan was widely shared.

The impact of Europe, particularly Germany, was pervasive in the prewar period, both in scholarly endeavors and in cultural pursuits (Rimer
1992:268–273). The tyranny of Europe over Japanese high culture waned,
only to be superseded by the reign of the United States after 1945 (Ishida
1984:28–29). In social theory the prewar period was characterized by obsession with German sociology and especially with the close reading of
Marx and Weber, which gave way to the attentive perusal of Talcott Parsons
and Robert K. Merton in the postwar period (Hashizume 1989:81, 161). In
all spheres of cultural life, whether sport or music, American influence became ascendant. Even when the ideal of kyōyō and chishikijin declined
(Karatani 1995:203–212), the sense of the superiority of the West persisted.
Consider the hold of English on contemporary Japanese life. For many
Japanese, to be international means to learn English (Manabe 1990:6). To
use Japanese names for musical instruments has been considered déclassé
(yabo kusai) (Suzuki T. 1990:226–227). Whatever is cool (kakkoii) is in-
scribed in English. In the 1990s the names of almost all the popular rock
groups not only were English-sounding but were transliterated in rōmaji
(Roman alphabets)—thirty-seven of the fifty best-selling records in 1992
had rōmaji titles (Minoshima 1993:45).

The dominance of the West generated ambivalence and assertions of
Japaneseness. The first explicit articulation of modern nationalism—
Nihonshugi (Japanism) in the 1880s—arose in conscious reaction to the
onslaught of Western culture (Banno 1993:164–174). The very idea of nationalism, after all, was au fond a Western ideal. Preeminent prewar theorists of Japaneseness, such as Kuki Shūzō or Watsuji Tetsurō, were steeped
in European philosophy. The search for a Japanese essence was in large
part a reaction to the Westernization of Japan. Given the dialectic of

Westernization and Japanese reaction, Natsume Sōseki (1986:26, 34) castigated the superficial character of modern Japanese civilization.

The converse of Western superiority was Asian inferiority. *Datsua nyūō*
(escape Asia, enter Europe) became a shorthand slogan for this modern
Japanese attitude, which became palpable as early as the mid-nineteenth-
century Iwakura Mission that toured the Western powers (Tanaka
1984:214–215; cf. Fukuzawa 1981b:224). There are two sources of this
mindset: Japan succeeded in industrializing and averting colonialism, and
Japan itself became a colonial power. Might makes right, or at least smug-
ness. This belief was later legitimated by the Western idea of progress,
whether in the form of social Darwinism or Marxism (Kotani 1992:63–
66).

Imperial Japan engaged in its own *mission civilisatrice*, disseminating
everything from the emperor ideology to the Japanese language in East
and Southeast Asia (Kawamura 1994a). While Shiga advocated adopting
French as the national language after World War II, and English is the de
facto second language in contemporary Japanese life, there was a concerted
government effort to make Japanese into an international language from
the late 1930s (Tanaka 1989:13–14). Colonial rule accentuated the belief
in Japanese advancement over the uncivilized colonized. Albeit "an in-
ternationalist, Christian, and liberal" (Hunter 1984:150), Nitobe Inazō's
(1972a:327) description of Korea in the early twentieth century was far
from positive: "The very physiognomy and living of this people are so
bland, unsophisticated and primitive. . . . They belong to a prehistoric age."
Japanese colonialism was to impart progress to this benighted land (Nitobe 1972b:228–230). Acknowledging Western superiority, Nitobe remained even more convinced of Asian inferiority. Historical writings compared Japanese progress with Chinese and Korean stagnation (Tanaka
1993:267–276).

Japan is, in this line of thinking, not an Asian or an Eastern country—a
point made by Fukuzawa Yukichi himself (Matsuzawa 1993:352). The prevailing cultural distinction, whether in clothes, cuisine, or music, is between Japanese and Western, not between Eastern and Western (Dore
1964:237). The equation of modernity and the West (and backwardness
and the East) implied that modern Japan was, if not Western, at least not
Eastern. In fact, the critic Noguchi Takehiko (1993b:3–4) suggests that Japan has been part of the West at least since 1990. Umesao Tadao (1986:39)
writes: "One key to understanding Japan is to think of Japan as another

Europe." In ordinary usage continental Asia is distinguished from Japan. "Asia" was written in *kanji* (Chinese characters) in the prewar period; it is now written in *katakana*, a script used to denote foreign names and words. When I lived in Tokyo in the mid-1980s, several of my politically progressive friends recommended that I read *Ajia wa naze mazushiika?* (Why Is Asia Poor?) by Tsurumi Yoshiyuki (1982). Asia for Tsurumi and my progressive friends did not include Japan. In fact, postwar Japanese intellectual and political life has largely ignored Asia (Sonoda 1993:22–25). Only recently has scholarly interest in Asia begun to revive (Ishida 1995:78–82).

Nonetheless, there is also a strong strand of Asian identification and respect for Asian cultures in modern Japanese history. In early modern Japan there was a well-developed discourse on Asia (Torii 1993; Hiraishi 1994). Furthermore, not all modern reactions to the West separated Japan from Asia (Ishida 1983:45–51). Okakura Kakuzō (1928:6) asserted Asia as "the true source of our inspirations." Although some used the same idea to justify Japanese imperialism (Matsuzawa 1979:26), Okakura and others highlighted historical relations with and respect for continental Asian cultures, especially Chinese civilization.

The respect for classical Chinese culture survived Japanese nationalism and imperialism (Naitō 1976:i, 16–24). Consider the following two government proclamations: the 1879 Imperial Rescript on Education—"For morality, the study of Confucius is the best guide" (Passin 1982:227)—and the 1943 Ministry of Education Policy on Instruction—"Through classical Chinese, the students shall study the thought and culture of the Empire and of East Asia . . . so that they may contribute to the cultivation of our national spirit" (Passin 1982:269). The aesthete Yanagi Muneyoshi (1984), among others, wrote appreciatively about Korean culture (Tsurumi 1984:163–185). Most important, the fact of colonialism, encapsulated in the ideology of the Greater East Asia Co-Prosperity Sphere, positioned Japan at the center of Asia as a "Pacific state" and the corresponding ideology of Asiaism *(Ajiashugi)* (Shinobu 1992:40–42). Hence, the contemporary right-wing nationalist writer Watanabe Shōichi (1995:355–356) defends the Japanese role in World War II as an "emancipatory war from white domination" and argues that Japan should "teach" Southeast Asian countries. In other words, pan-Asian sentiments and the belief in Japanese superiority often go hand in hand.

The postwar Japanese economic miracle has once again distinguished Japan from its poor Asian counterparts (McCormack 1996:171–174). Just as Westerners represent the upper class and signify cultural superiority, Asians come to stand for the lower class and denote cultural inferiority. Domestic class relations can be easily transposed onto the world system of national hierarchies, where Japan stands near the top. It is only another step to affirm Japanese cultural superiority. In various college cafeterias, I often overheard students discussing their impressions of poverty in other East and Southeast Asian countries where they had spent their vacations. Although some lamented the poverty, others enthusiastically exchanged tales of horror, which at times degenerated into comparative scatology. When a day laborer can go on a sex tour to Thailand (Fowler 1996:72–73), the belief in Japanese superiority seems irresistible, even if it derives largely from prosperity.

Most people were, however, reluctant to state that Japan is, as it were, number one. Intellectuals, in particular, remain predominantly critical of contemporary Japanese society. The economist Sawa Takamitsu (1992:76) contrasts the idea of Japan as an economic power *(keizai taikoku)* against the idea that it is a cultural wimp *(bunka shōkoku)*. No one I interviewed pontificated on Japanese greatness. The Japanese defeat in World War II was catastrophic for such boasting, and even in the 1990s few are outright chauvinists. Only right-wing nationalists, conservative politicians, and some very old and very young people expressed unqualified pride in Japaneseness. Even then, the statements are not so much about Japanese greatness as about American decline. The critic Yasuhara Ken (1993:3) is exceedingly critical of the United States, but he is even more critical of a Japan that continues to admire it. Whether because of political correctness or plain politeness, Japanese people rarely express an encomium about their own country. In addition, many Japanese are sympathetic to the problems of underdeveloped nations and are aware of the peril of prejudice. The earnestness of progressive writers, such as Motoyama (1991) or Tsurumi Yoshiyuki (1982), is simultaneously a conscious effort to affirm global solidarity.

Expressions of Japanese superiority occur indirectly, which effectively masks ethnocentric and even chauvinistic views. A common response to the new foreign workers concerned their personal hygiene. A young man who had just returned from a trip to China said that toilets in China were abominably dirty, and concluded that many Chinese are dirty. Such a statement reveals the visceral way in which social distinction is often articulated. As George Orwell (1958:127) noted in *The Road to Wigan Pier:*

Here you come to the real secret of class distinctions in the West—the real reason why a European of bourgeois upbringing, even when he calls himself a Communist, cannot without a hard effort think of a working man as his equal. It is summed up in four frightful words which people nowadays are chary of uttering, but which were bandied about quite freely in my childhood. The words were: *The lower classes smell.*

The new foreign workers smelled and seemed dirty to many Japanese urbanites. A self-identified progressive, who had been working on behalf of foreign workers, said that they smell for an objective reason; according to him, they cannot afford to take a bath every day as Japanese people can. Consider in this regard that many Western tourists complain about the poor state of Japanese toilets. An American academic told me ad nauseam about the disgust she felt riding a commuter train, sandwiched between a *sararīman* with halitosis and another with psoriasis.

In a similar vein, fashion distinguished Japanese from the migrant workers. Japanese often regard white Westerners as smart or cool *(kakkoii)* because of their physique (e.g., tall) or appearance (e.g., well-dressed). In contrast, the migrant workers are said to be short and shabbily dressed. A young female office worker said that white people are fashionable *(sensu ga aru)*, but Iranians and Filipinos are unfashionable *(dasai)*. She went on to list the flaws of Iranian and Filipino men, including their ugly mustaches, stonewashed jeans, and so on.

When I asked Japanese people about their opposition, or at least emotional resistance, to the weekly gatherings of Iranians, one of the most common responses was that Japanese people don't like people who gather in groups. As one young man exclaimed: "I just don't understand why they have to stick together like a herd of animals. Why can't they act as individuals?" Another college-age woman said, "Iranians gather *(tamurou)* like an ant colony." Images of the Iranian Revolution frightened some people, who feared that Iranians might engage in collective action. An unpublished survey by some Japanese sociologists cited the propensity of Iranians to gather in a crowd as the chief reason why Japanese held Iranians in low esteem. The underlying contrast was between the individualistic Japanese and the group-oriented Iranians. The irony is that the reigning stereotype of Japanese in the United States and elsewhere is that they only act in groups, as for example in a tour group (Katō 1992:25–27). The anthropologist Nakane Chie (1978:40–42) has emphasized the Japanese propensity toward group action as their distinguishing feature (cf. Katō 1981:20–21). The journalist Honda Katsuichi (1993b:129) decried Japanese society as a tadpole society: "The Japanese behavioral principle is like that of tadpoles. Neither theory nor logic nor ethics underlies or informs Japanese behavior. Quite simply, a Japanese looks around and does what others are doing."

Another displaced expression of cultural superiority, often articulated by women, was gender relations. One office worker discoursed at length about Arabs, although she clearly meant Iranians. According to her, they come from a culture that oppresses women. Based on a television documentary she had recently watched, she recounted in horror that Arab women had to wear a veil in public and to submit to their husbands. In contrast, she noted, Japanese women are free and independent, and she could wear a miniskirt whenever she liked and could go out at any time of the night. It is ironic that, at least in comparison to advanced industrial societies, Japanese women lag behind their counterparts in most measures, such as gender wage inequality (Brinton 1993:222–224; Ōsawa 1993:110–116). In the 1970s Joyce Lebra (1978:297) articulated an opinion still common among Western visitors to Japan in the late 1990s: "The majority of women in Japan, whether married or single, cling to the traditional definition of women as 'good wife and wise mother.' There has been no fundamental questioning of this traditional ideal." Furthermore, American feminists have noted that Japanese women are subservient and that their clothing caters to male tastes. The woman I interviewed, however, had no inkling that Western feminists might regard Japan in the same way that she regarded Arab societies.

In general, many cross-cultural comparisons use gender relations as a gauge of cultural hierarchy. There was, in fact, a merry-go-round of cultural comparisons. Just as Americans derided the patriarchal Japanese, Japanese castigated the patriarchal Iranians. An Iranian man, who claimed to shuttle back and forth between Paris, Los Angeles, and Tokyo, told me about the infernal situation of American women. When I asked why the situation of women in the United States was worse than that in Iran, he cited the endemic violence against women in the United States. "Our women are well cared for," he said. He found young Japanese women to be sex-starved, which was a view shared by some Japanese men as well. A Japanese stockbroker said, "Women who hang around foreigners are like *pan pan* (prostitutes) during the U.S. occupation period."

Given the many approaches that one may use to compare female advancement, it is easy for one group to claim superiority over others based on its choice of measurement. Certainly, many Japanese would agree with Sumiko Iwao's observation (1993:265) that "[w]e must question the often-heard line that Japanese women 'lag behind' women in the United States and Europe. . . . Japanese women have made equality based on mutual dependence acceptable and workable." That another group may not share the same criteria is taken to be merely another indicator of Japanese superiority—their capacity for sound judgment.

In cultural expressions and practices, then, we find indirect articulations of Japanese pride. They are intimately intertwined with Japanese economic might and its consequences. Although outright expressions of chauvinism occur from time to time, what is more striking is the ways in which cultural confidence is often expressed indirectly and unintentionally. The prewar legacy should not be overemphasized. Although older Japanese feel inferior to the West and superior to Asia, the same mix of sentiments does not exist across generations. The sources of cultural superiority, along with modes of expression, are diverse, although they are united in affirming Japanese superiority over the new foreign workers.

Ethnic Homogeneity

A cardinal axiom about Japanese society is its ethnic homogeneity. The debate in the late 1980s on foreign workers presumed that Japan was pristine before the onslaught of the new foreign workers on the archipelago. In spite of concerted efforts by some scholars and activists to challenge the belief in Japanese ethnic homogeneity, many Japanese people persist in believing that they live in a monoethnic society.

The belief in a classless society and cultural essentialism is part and parcel of the widespread assumption that Japan is homogeneous, whether in language (see Appendix), cuisine, popular culture, or ethnicity. Being Japanese is a natural and ineffable quality. The equation between the state, nation, and ethnicity (as well as class and culture) means that Japan is a distinctively homogeneous country. Geography and history provide compelling reasons for Japanese homogeneity; the Tokugawa state's policy of seclusion (sakoku) accentuated the "natural" isolation of the Japanese archipelago. The received wisdom is well expressed by Satō Seizaburō (1992:10): "Japan continued to be extremely homogeneous racially and culturally. . . . Throughout the Tokugawa period when peace continued for over two centuries, Japanese society became extremely integrated and homogeneous." In this view, to speak of modern Japan, is to recognize a constant elision between all manners of homogeneity. The immutability of its history, geography, and culture further marks this homogeneity as something of an ethnonational essence.

The implicit assumption became an explicitly articulated view when I asked Japanese people about the existing minorities. Many people produced puzzled looks. Confronted with evidence of ethnic diversity, most either ignored or denied it. Like my friend in the opening vignette of this chapter, people asserted and reasserted the certitude that Japan has been and remains a monoethnic society.

There was a persistent fissure between the articulated assumption of monoethnicity and the tacit awareness of multiethnicity. Paradoxically, many people acknowledged the existence of one or another exception to the monoethnic rule, all the while insisting on it. As a bank employee in his fifties concluded after we discussed the Ainu, Burakumin, and Korean Japanese for half an hour, "But, of course, Japan is an ethnically homogeneous society." Quite a few people, moreover, noted the hybrid ethnic origins of Japanese people and readily admitted that Japanese blood is, so to speak, mixed. Many people were aware of *toraijin* (immigrants from the Korean peninsula) a millennium ago. Furthermore, people from the peripheries, such as Hokkaidō and Okinawa, were acutely aware of the Ainu and Okinawans as distinct groups, as were people in Osaka, who were more conscious of Koreans and Burakumin.

Most people in the Tokyo metropolitan area, however, were only vaguely aware of ethnic diversity. The most common acknowledgment of existing Japanese minorities indicated awareness of the Ainu. Many people sensed that they were somehow different from ordinary [*futsū*] Japanese, although the specification of these differences remained vague. As one middle-aged man said, "They are Japanese but they are not really Japanese." Responses about the Ainu ranged from superficial remarks, such as their hirsute character, to some outright racist remarks about their uncivilized *(mikai)* culture. The Japanese government having had refused to acknowledge the Ainu as an indigenous people, the repercussion in the public at large has been widespread ignorance and vaguely held prejudices (Uemura 1992a:85–99). Interestingly, when asked how many Ainu there were in Japan, no one mentioned a figure higher than 1,000, although some estimates, as I noted in the Introduction, run as high as 300,000. The low figures underscored the widespread view of the Ainu as a virtually vanished and vanquished people.

Okinawans, in contrast, were often regarded as much closer to, indeed a part of, mainstream Japanese people and culture. Several people mentioned a recent popular television drama in which Okinawa was portrayed as a feudal domain during the Tokugawa period. In this view Okinawa acquires a regional identity. A self-described "citizen of the world" *(chikyūjin)* and "ordinary *sararīman*" said that Okinawans are "really Japanese," but he quickly added that he did not mind if they felt differently. Others considered them to be an ethnic minority group, including an Okinawan youth who advocated national independence and a Japanese youth who had studied Okinawan history in school. One man who had spent his junior high school years in Okinawa regarded Okinawans as inferior to the mainland Japanese. A Japanese Brazilian of Okinawan descent also asserted the ethnic distinctiveness of Okinawans. This was due to her experience of discrimination in Brazil by other Japanese Brazilians. She noted, however, that they did not discriminate against her as an Okinawan but rather as a *Nikkeijin* (person of Japanese descent) (cf. Ike 1995:202). A young office worker went to Okinawa on a vacation and was shocked to discover that she couldn't understand Okinawan speech. Although she thought that they were Japanese before, she now had serious doubts. A civil servant in his forties suggested that Korean Japanese may be more Japanese than Okinawans, all the while insisting that this was a very subtle point.

Almost everyone was reluctant to classify the Burakumin as an ethnic group. In the Tokyo metropolitan area, education regarding the Burakumin *(dōwa kyōiku)* is uncommon. No one mentioned them as an ethnic group, and young people were even ignorant of the prejudice they face. When I said that they should be regarded as an ethnic group, most people disagreed strongly. One man in his thirties exclaimed "eh!" and remained silent for a while. At last he suggested that the language of class should be used, not that of ethnicity. A housewife in her forties told me, "I can't believe that you would classify people like that." She suggested that the Burakumin are really a vestige of the feudal past, and that they should be regarded just like any other Japanese. For many people, Burakumin status is a historical relic that holds no contemporary relevance. Even when differences were acknowledged, ethnic status was denied because ethnicity is racialized in Japan. Although the Burakumin face discrimination in employment and marriage, they are not considered to be an ethnic minority because they belong to the same ethnoracial stock as other Japanese.

Burakumin identity becomes more explicit when they are classified as a "minority" (*mainaritī*, the Japanese pronunciation of the English word) or as people who are discriminated against. Several people grouped Burakumin with the physically disabled as instances of minority populations in Japan. A part-time factory worker in her forties claimed that racial discrimination is not any different from Burakumin discrimination. Japanese progressives have a tendency to lump all sorts of people into the category of the oppressed (*yokuatsu*) or of people who are discriminated against (*sabetsu*). In an "encyclopedia" of prejudice and discrimination, there are entries on Korean Japanese, Ainu, Burakumin, and Okinawans, but also women, the elderly, religious minorities, people with low educational attainment, the physically disabled, *hibakusha* (victims of atomic bombs), pollution victims, and so on (Shinsensha Henshūbu 1981). A more recent volume on discrimination includes entries on Burakumin, religious minorities, women, and pupils who are bullied (Kurihara 1996).

Most Japanese were aware of the existence of Korean and Chinese residents in Japan. However, their knowledge tended to be shallow and sparse. One indication is the wonder bordering on astonishment expressed by several people when I told them that many famous athletes and entertainers were in fact Korean Japanese, although they used Japanese names in public. Younger Japanese especially insisted that Korean Japanese were basically Japanese. An employee of a large publishing house said that Korean Japanese live amidst other Japanese, whereas Ainu people live apart. Hence, Korean Japanese are Japanese, but Ainu people are not. The salient point here, however, is that few would brook the idea of a hybrid identity for Korean Japanese; almost everyone insisted that one has to be either Japanese or Korean.

That many Japanese are more or less aware of various nonethnic Japanese living in Japan does not challenge the assumption of Japanese ethnic homogeneity. The strategy of normalization is to insist on the binary and distinct categories of Japanese and foreigners; everyone is either one or the other. On several occasions in the course of daily interaction, Japanese were shocked and even became angry when I revealed that I am not a Japanese national. A woman who cut my hair said "Why didn't you tell me?" as if it were my obligation to identify my citizenship status before every encounter with Japanese people.

Given the dominant belief in Japan as an ethnically homogeneous country, the new foreign workers represent the potential of heterogeneity. Against the pristine simplicity of homogeneous Japan, they pose, in effect, the heterogeneous complexity of the world outside of Japan. Against the stability of Japanese national identity lies the potential of uncertain change. A small shop owner in his fifties expressed his worries about the migrant workers because he was uncertain whether they came from the mountain or the sea *(yama no mono ka umi no mono ka wakaranai)*. In effect, he expressed an essentially conservative vision that any change may upset his world of peace and stability.

Indeed, there was a relationship between the idea of homogeneity and that of stability. Rapid economic growth and an egalitarian ethos had brought reasonable satisfaction to the majority of Japanese people by the 1970s. In this context, many supported the conservative Liberal Democratic Party not so much as a principled ideological position but rather to preserve the stability of everyday life (Ueno 1985:101–104; Sawa 1991:102–104). As a 1980s poster for the Liberal Democratic Party put it: "security *(anshin)*, safety *(anzen)*, stability *(antei)*" (Sasaki 1986:71–72). Given that homogeneity was widely believed to be a, if not *the*, major feature of Japanese society, virtually all aspects of homogeneity became something that should be valued and preserved.

To be sure, others hoped to change the homogeneous character of Japan. A college student was in favor of opening the country because he found Japan boring. His friend thought that Japan should admit more foreigners in order to make the country more international and therefore more interesting. The journalist Yaneyama Tarō wrote in the late 1980s that Japanese monoethnicity is "the greatest weakness [of Japan] in the internationalized world" (Ōtake 1994:246). The salient point is, however, that these views presumed Japan to be ethnically homogeneous. As I have emphasized, the explicit discussion about the new foreign workers almost always brought the presumption of Japanese monoethnicity to the forefront. Having expressed his gratitude for being born in Japan after a period of travel abroad, a Japanese writer noted, "It is rare to find a country so unperturbed by ethnic or racial problems" (Matsuyama 1985:143–144). The urgency of the foreign worker debate stemmed in part from the perceived absence of any ethnic problem—in fact, any ethnic minority—in Japan.

The Discourse of Japaneseness

The discourse of Japaneseness articulates Japan as a homogeneous society. Unencumbered by significant inequalities, cultural cleavages, and ethnic diversity, the class, cultural, and ethnic divides that characterize most advanced industrial countries are missing in this view of Japan. Furthermore, Japan is an affluent, middle-class, and culturally advanced society, unlike the impoverished, lower-class, and less civilized societies from whence the new foreign workers come. What makes this contrast all the more striking is the image of a pure Japan encroached on by polluted outsiders, who are, by virtue of their lower class and cultural status, ultimately inimical to the Japanese body politic.

Recall Émile Durkheim's (1984:chaps. 2–3) classic distinction between mechanical solidarity and organic solidarity. He argued that preindustrial social solidarity (mechanical solidarity) was based on homology, or likeness, among individuals. The solidarity of complex societies (organic solidarity) is, in contrast, based on interdependence. Needless to say, contemporary Japanese society is a complex entity with a great deal of role differentiation, not to mention income inequalities, gender differences, regional disparities, and distinct lifestyles and life goals. Nonetheless, the discourse of Japaneseness casts 125 million Japanese citizens into an essentialized receptacle of homologous individuals whose primary identity is Japanese. The crucible of the state provides the mold for the enduring form of Japaneseness. By equating class, nation, and ethnicity, Japan emerges a society of mechanical solidarity. This discourse effaces salient social divisions as well as the past, which is the chronicle of differences and dissension. In delineating a clear boundary between Japanese and non-Japanese, the discourse of Japaneseness opposes insiders against outsiders.

Thus, the discourse of Japaneseness equates nation and ethnicity with the state, effacing class and other divisions as well as eliding the past. It pits Japanese against foreign workers as antipodal groups and provides a powerful basis for regarding Japan as a monoethnic society. It is a deductive and dogmatic assumption that seeks to reject the empirical reality of ethnic diversity. Although Europeans and North Americans have served as cultural superiors whom Japanese emulated, Koreans and Chinese, like other existing minorities in Japan, have been suppressed—either assimilating to the wider Japanese culture or eking out an existence as foreigners on Japanese soil. The specter of multiethnicity haunts, and reinforces, the assumption of monoethnicity. Thus, my friend whom I described in the opening vignette can endlessly accept exceptions to the hegemonic vision of Japan as an ethnically homogeneous society, and yet ultimately insist on Japanese monoethnicity.

The particular social vision of Japan, as articulated in the discourse of

Japaneseness, is ironically shared by progressive critics as well as by the new foreign workers themselves. The assumption of Japanese monoethnicity affects even those who attempt to articulate an oppositional discourse and criticize the xenophobic elements in Japanese society. Although progressives wish more humane treatment of foreign workers and criticize the repressive practices of the government, their assumptions and utterances often are the same as those of their opponents. They regard the new foreign workers as poor persons, with undesirable cultural practices and beliefs, who are entering an ethnically homogeneous country. Many foreign workers share the same vision of Japan: as an affluent, culturally advanced, and ethnically homogeneous nation. Whether treated well or poorly, their images of Japan, as ill-informed as many of them may be, mirror those advanced by the Japanese themselves. The workers' judgments, like those of the progressive Japanese, may be quite negative; I heard charges of xenophobia, racism, close-mindedness, and other hard-hitting indictments of Japanese society. Nonetheless, they all share the terrain grounded in the discourse of Japaneseness.

How do Japanese people discuss differences, then? As Kären Wigen (1995:216) argues, the Meiji state had tolerated regional differences, and "geography emerged as the permissible language of difference in Meiji Japan." Regional differences, including dialectal differences and variations in interpersonal relations and cultural norms, persist to this day (Yoneyama 1989:27–30). Many Japanese discourse at length on regional or prefectural differences. There are books on prefectural characters *(kenminsei)* (Sofue 1993:9–26). A Japanese scholar of European politics who grew up in Tokyo said that he feels more foreign when he is in Osaka than when he is in Rome. A Japanese boss told the journalist Lesley Downer (1989:18) about Tōhoku, "You don't want to go there. . . . They're all yokels. You won't understand their dialect." In addition, there are other ostensibly random ways to divide Japanese people. The phenomenal popularity of blood type as a means of differentiating Japanese people is one example. These articulations of internal heterogeneity, however, do not fundamentally challenge the belief in essential Japanese homogeneity.

It is not only against the new foreign workers that Japanese have articulated their views of themselves and others. After all, the contemporary discourse of Japaneseness did not spontaneously generate itself during the debate on the new foreign workers. It drew on a very robust discourse of

Japaneseness—*Nihonjinron*, or theories of Japanese people and culture—that identifies essential elements about Japanese people in contradistinction to others. Consider the extensive Japanese writings on Koreans. In addition to the veritable library produced during the colonial period, postwar Japanese society was awash with books and articles that sought to nourish the narcissism of minor differences. We learn in one book that Japanese are modest whereas Koreans are aggressive, and Japanese are indifferent to history whereas Koreans are obsessed with history (Toyota 1985:174, 194). In another book the author confidently distinguishes Koreans, who are easy to unify, egalitarian, and populist (bottom-up history), from Japanese, who are difficult to unify, hierarchical, and leader-oriented (top-down history) (Kim 1983:271). Never mind that a stereotype has Koreans being conflictual and hierarchical, and Japanese as consensual and egalitarian.

According to David Goodman and Masanori Miyazawa (1995:11–12), "the Japanese have produced enough writing on the Jews to fill a small library." The fact of the matter is that they have produced scores of small libraries. Though the substantive propositions may be different, a similar discursive pattern that accentuates differences exists. Beyond the obvious empirical failings of grand generalizations lies a particular way of classifying and understanding the world, which I elaborate in Chapter 6. Before I proceed, however, let me discuss in the following two chapters the constitutive character of multiethnicity in modern Japan.

3

Pop Multiethnicity

Izoku (Different Tribes) is the last, sprawling, and unfinished work of Nakagami Kenji (1993). Symptomatic of his style, the novel features moments of lyric beauty amid prolix prose of extreme digressiveness. Although he admired and emulated William Faulkner (Sengoku 1993:60), Nakagami was in fact more of a Thomas Wolfe without Maxwell Perkins. What interests me about *Izoku*, however, is not just its polyphonic and multilingual narrative but the ethnic heterogeneity of its protagonists.

The three central characters, who share a blue birthmark and an interest in karate, are the right-wing youth Tatsuya, the Korean Japanese Simu, and the Ainu Utari. They encounter not only disparate worlds within contemporary Japan—right-wing nationalists, motorcycle gangs *(bōsōzoku)*, teenage nymphs, and so on—but also a series of individuals of different ethnic backgrounds with the same blue birthmark. Cultural universals, such as sex and violence, are experienced by people of different ethnic backgrounds and in various places across Asia. We also find the unity of Asia in the existence of outcastes (cf. Noma and Okiura 1983; Tsukada 1992). One of the novel's central threads is the right-wing figure Makinohara's plot to resuscitate the prewar Japanese empire in Manchuria; Makinohara himself, it turns out, is of Chinese descent. In *Izoku*, then, we encounter multiethnic Japan in all its diversity and expansiveness.

Nakagami's (1978, 1980, 1983) trilogy on Roji—his Yoknapatawpa County—not only rehearses the universalistic themes of sex, violence, and family romance but also the particular ethnography of a Burakumin village in Kishū Kumano in Wakayama Prefecture, where Nakagami was born in 1946 as a Burakumin. Nakagami's trilogy captures the web of human relationships in Roji—centering on *dokata* (construction workers) and *ninpu* (day laborers) and their family members—and delineates in detail a world far away from the romantic views of Japan, the glitz of Tokyo or the serenity of Kyoto.

Nakagami is by no means the only writer of significance to be of Burakumin descent or to feature Burakumin and other non-Japanese Japanese in his writings (Watanabe 1994:17–32). One of the masterpieces of the modern Japanese novel, and the paradigmatic work of Japanese naturalism, is *Hakai* (Broken Commandment) by Shimazaki Tōson (1957), originally published in 1906. Natsume Sōseki, surely the emblematic modern Japanese writer, called it the only genuine novel of the Meiji era (Keene 1984:255). Shimazaki's naturalism is a literary ancestor of Nakagami, especially of his Roji trilogy. The continuity is not merely a matter of literary genre but of subject matter as well. *Hakai* traces the trajectory of a popular teacher, Segawa Ushimatsu, as he struggles toward confessing his Burakumin ancestry. The novel ends with the protagonist's departure for a Japanese American community (Nihon *mura*) in Texas. Noma Hiroshi's (1966–1971) roman-fleuve, *Seinen no wa* (The Cycle of Youth), features Burakumin characters and, more important, takes Burakumin discrimination as one of its main concerns. Takeda Taijun's (1972) *Mori to mizuumi no matsuri* (The Festival of the Forest and the Lake) depicts the entanglement of a Japanese Ainu scholar, an Ainu activist, and a Japanese woman painter. The novel poses the question of Ainu survival and Japanese colonialism against the landscape of Hokkaidō. If these novels are not as well known in the West as those by Tanizaki Jun'ichirō or Mishima Yukio, they are nonetheless central to the history of modern Japanese literature. Indeed, modern Japanese literature cannot be considered apart from Japanese imperialism; colonial relationships engendered numerous writings on ethnic encounters both within the main Japanese islands as well as in the colonies (Ozaki 1971).

Fiction, needless to say, does not simply reflect reality. If social conditions do not directly determine the world of literature, imaginative works still tell us something about the social situations from which they arise. Manifold representations of ethnic others in modern Japanese literature point toward ethnic heterogeneity in modern Japanese history.

Popular Culture in the Era of High-Speed Growth

When I was growing up in Tokyo, not far from the Olympic Stadium, in the 1960s, every child was said to love "Kyojin, Taihō, Tamagoyaki" (Kobayashi 1997:75). Kyojin is the nickname of the Yomiuri Giants, a professional baseball team that won nine successive championships. Taihō was a *yokozuna,* the highest rank for a professional sumō wrestler, who was widely regarded as the premier wrestler of his generation, perhaps of the century (Kitade 1991:151–152). Tamagoyaki is a pan-fried mixture of beaten eggs, sugar, and soy sauce. The troika of every child's desire—or should it be every boy's?—exemplified a national popular culture that was disseminated by television, which by then had infiltrated practically every household. "Kyojin, Taihō, Tamagoyaki" represented potent symbols of Japaneseness in the 1960s—sufficiently so as to be parodied mercilessly by the 1980s (Yoshida 1990:85). But they were also irremediably multiethnic and multicultural. Beneath the patina of a monoethnic, national culture in the 1960s, ethnic others were frequently the representative figures of—and the exogenous forces that shaped—putatively national activities. Multiethnicity emerges not as marginal but as quite central to what it meant to be Japanese in the 1960s.

Why the 1960s? Why popular culture? If a case for monoethnic Japan can be made, then the 1960s present the most promising period. The 1960s were the era of high-speed growth *(kōdo seichōki)* when the devastation of World War II receded rapidly from popular memory and the Japanese economic recovery reached its symbolic apogee in the 1964 Tokyo Olympics (Isoda 1983b; Sekikawa 1993). As I elaborate in the following chapter, pre–World War II Japan was replete with non-Japanese people; as we saw in Chapter 1, the influx of Asian migrant workers challenged the idea of monoethnic Japan by the late 1980s. Between these two periods of incontrovertible multiethnicity, Japan seemed relatively monoethnic.

Periodization is, of course, a matter of convenience, and the 1960s of this chapter are the long 1960s—the '30s and '40s of the Shōwa era (1955–1974)—or the high tide of the postwar period. In these two decades the contemporary meaning of Japan and Japaneseness was forged. By the 1960s it became possible to talk of a genuine national culture and national homogeneity that superseded the rural-urban divide and regional diversity (Yamamoto 1986:21–23). While 41 percent of the employed population was engaged in the primary sector in 1955, this figure dropped to 14 percent by 1975 (Tsurumi 1984:58). Farmers became a minority; urban workers became the indisputable majority. Television and manga (comics)—for many Japanese the defining features of popular culture—became commonplace beginning in the late 1950s (Kure 1986:135). Everyone seemed to read the same magazines and watch the same television shows (Katō

1964:236). By the 1980s, however, the time had passed when popular culture meant nationally shared reading, singing, and watching (Miyadai, Ishihara, and Ōtsuka 1993:4).

By popular culture, I refer to widely dispersed and shared activities and artifacts (cf. Hebdige 1988:47; Frow 1995:82–83). In the postwar era, and especially in the 1960s, Japanese popular culture was truly national. National culture is often equated with high culture as in Matthew Arnold's definition (1993:190): "the best which has been thought and said in the world." The Arnoldian sense of Japanese culture evokes kabuki and tea ceremony, in which very few Japanese people in fact take part. If, as Raymond Williams (1963:306) wrote, "[c]ulture is the product of the old leisured classes who seek now to defend it against new and destructive forces," then popular culture, which is what most people engage in, encompasses these "new and destructive forces" (Willis 1978:170).

Popular culture is a crucial sphere in which modern identities are forged. In many premodern societies, rituals of solidarity form a common identity, defining one group of people apart from others. In the late twentieth century, rituals of solidarity and identity occur not so much in the tangible realm of rites and festivals but in the intangible realm of media-dominated communication and culture. The nationwide distribution of newspapers and magazines, popular songs and games, and movies and television programs bridges a geographically far-flung population (Thompson 1990:225–238). Victor Turner (1967:30) once observed that "[r]itual . . . is precisely a mechanism that periodically converts the obligatory into the desirable." Rituals of popular culture—sitting in front of a television, for example—presume the primacy of desire but come tantalizingly close to duty; in the name of leisure and pleasure, the dull compulsions of popular culture become well-nigh inescapable.

Experiences of popular culture are, to be sure, differentiated, whether because of region or religion, gender or generation. An individual may change over time, and frequently exhibits ambivalence. Culture cleaves; it unites people and it differentiates them. There are well-recognized subcultures, so much so that it may be more accurate to accentuate culture's plurality (Hebdige 1979). Indeed, distinction and discrimination, denoting a dynamic stratification of taste and status, lie at the heart of culture in action (Bourdieu 1984).

Yet these facts do not gainsay that certain events and experiences constitute a crucial part of national identity. Popular culture defines in profound ways cultural citizenship and popular nationality. Even in the heterogeneous United States, there are certain songs or shows that capture the national imagination. To have been away even for a year makes one a partial exile from one's own country. The paradoxical mixture of ubiquity and ephemerality renders markers and makers of national identity all the more difficult to emulate for outsiders: one has to be there. Consider a simple thought experiment: imagine a native-born and -reared American who is unfamiliar with contemporary U.S. popular culture—that is, ignorant of Michael Jordan or Michael Jackson, *The Simpsons* or *Seinfeld*. How long can one spend time with him before finding him utterly unworldly? The converse phenomenon is that this book will seem dated precisely by the irrevocable shift in ephemeral markers. Although Elvis may continue to live, virtually every other popular cultural figure or activity is doomed to die a symbolic as well as a physiological death. No wonder that serious authors who hanker for literary immortality often seek classical, Arnoldian references.

Popular cultural literacy—born of immersion in a particular space and time—is a crucial constituent of the contemporary structure of feelings and of national identity (cf. Williams 1977:133–134). Historically transient though it may be, its singularity and ephemerality charge it with meaning. Indeed, when I asked Japanese people what makes a person Japanese, the answers often involved elements of popular culture. A middle-aged housewife said, "You can tell Japanese [from non-Japanese] by what they eat and what they watch on television." Some Japanese claimed a taste for sushi and *sashimi* (raw fish) to be key ingredients of Japaneseness. Others, aware of the immense popularity of sushi among some Americans, pointed to *nattō* (fermented beans), conveniently ignoring that many Japanese find the dish unpalatable. An office worker in her twenties declared me an honorary Japanese after I discoursed on the popular comic-turned-television-show *Tokyo rabu sutōrī* (*Tokyo Love Story*) (Saimon 1990–1991). For many people, to speak of the soul of Japan, or Japaneseness, means to highlight elements of popular culture. In the United States, for example, "American as apple pie" is but one way in which food comes to stand for national identity, as fish and chips may for British people. Similarly, the Dallas Cowboys or Manchester United may plausibly claim to be a quintessential element of national popular culture and, hence, of national identity.

National popular culture is, however, hardly nationalist. Popular culture does not express, as German Romantics believed, the spirit of the people.

Precisely at the moment when radio, film, and television enabled the far-flung dispersal of popular cultural artifacts, extranational influences became dominant. The media, in other words, made possible a nationwide diffusion but simultaneously imported international messages. It would be misleading to write a history of Japanese popular music in the 1960s without mentioning the Beatles (cf. Nakano 1995:276–288). Since then, the globalization of the media has further eroded the salience of national borders. Japanese popular culture—from manga to music—pervades Southeast Asia and elsewhere (Ching 1996). In Japan in the 1960s, however, the basic boundaries of popular culture remained national, and I wish to focus on the resolutely Japanese elements.

Sport

Sport is undoubtedly universal across cultures and history, and modern sport has been central to popular culture (cf. Guttmann 1978:54–55). Sport is also a potent marker of personal identification, gender differentiation, and social distinction. An enthusiasm for squash or lacrosse marks a particular educational and class trajectory in contradistinction, for example, to bowling or bingo. Furthermore, in any given country there are significant gender or geographical differences in allegiance to one sport or another. Very few sports, moreover, are purely national, but there are certain sports that become emblematic of a given nation.

Let me consider three of the most popular Japanese sports in the 1960s: baseball, professional wrestling, and sumō. To be sure, many girls, affected by the superb performance of female athletes in the Tokyo Olympics, preferred volleyball. In addition, some Japanese were fanatical about tennis, which denoted aristocratic tastes, and others avidly followed boxing, with its plebeian connotation. But the three sports I consider were immensely popular in Japan during the 1960s.

Baseball

In the 1960s even central Tokyo was full of empty lots. In one of these small fields, my schoolmates and I would often gather after school to play baseball. Because of differing fortunes, not every child owned a glove, but we often had enough among us to equip the defending team. All of us idolized the stars of the Yomiuri Giants, better known as the Kyojin. One of our favorite manga was *Kyojin no hoshi* (The Star of the Giants) (Kajiwara

and Kawasaki 1966–1971), which depicted Hoshi Hyūma's struggle to become an ace for the Kyojin. A middle-aged employee of a publishing company whom I interviewed thought that Hoshi's struggle was an allegory of
Burakumin liberation; as a child I regarded it as a gripping tale of heroism
(cf. Yoshihiro 1993:38). In particular, it exemplified *konjō* (the spirit of persistence), personified at the time by the victorious volleyball team at the
Tokyo Olympics (Kure 1993c:84; Kobayashi 1997:112).

My brother and I would eagerly run to the local bookstore to buy the
latest issue of the weekly *Shōnen magajin* in which *Kyojin no hoshi* was seri-
alized; we dropped everything for the Saturday evening broadcast of its
televised animation. When my family emigrated to the United States, my
chief regret was that I would not be able to read and watch *Kyojin no hoshi*.
My enthusiasm was far from deviant. In the 1960s *Shōnen magajin* sold 1.5
million copies a week; the animated series was seen in 30 percent of all
television-owning households; and nearly 60 percent of youths in one survey regarded *Kyojin no hoshi* as their favorite manga (Saitō 1995:37–40). By
the mid-1980s when I did get around to reading its conclusion, *Kyojin no
hoshi* had become an object of both nostalgia and parody (Kubo 1987:21;
Ueno 1996:164–165).

Baseball was indisputably the most popular Japanese sport in the 1960s
(Whiting 1977:5, 1989:5; Iyer 1988:318), if not of the twentieth century
(Nitobe 1972b:107). Baseball has, of course, an unquestionably American
origin. "Whoever wants to know the hearts and minds of America had
better learn baseball" (Barzun 1954:159); it is a "national pastime, idyllic
imprint of youth, mirror of American character, creator of heroes, enduring communal event" (Bruck 1997:84). In a similar spirit, many aficio-
nados and commentators have noted the national character of Japanese
baseball (*bēsubōru* or *yakyū* as it is called in Japan) (Ikei 1991:8). Indeed,
Western writers on Japanese baseball inevitably mention *bushidō* (the way
of the samurai), Confucianism, or Zen to characterize the Japaneseness of
Japanese baseball. Cultural adaptations and variations are themselves universal; whether baseball or badminton, there is more than one way to play
a seemingly singular game.

But these observations rarely amount to more than platitudes. Robert
Whiting (1989:49) wrote: "Baseball's grip on Japan's collective psyche is
due, ultimately, to the fact that it suits the national character." However
sensible such a generalization may seem, each proposition, taken one by
one, does not withstand serious scrutiny. For example, Whiting prognosti-
cated that it is "extremely unlikely that any [Japanese player] will ever play

on an American team. Leaving one's team to play in America would be regarded as an act of national disloyalty" (Whiting 1977:113). Nomo Hideo and Irabu Hideki—two Japanese pitching sensations in the U.S. major leagues in the mid-1990s—were feted, not scorned, by Japanese fans.

In the 1960s the Kyojin were widely regarded as Japan's Team. A fan told Robert Whiting (1977:211), "I'm a Japanese! That's why I like the Giants." As any dissenter to the Cowboys' claim to be America's Team will readily understand, the Kyojin, as popular as the team was, had many detractors as well. The Tokyo-centric myopia of the Tokyo-based media systematically overlooks the differentiation in Japanese tastes, even in baseball.

The nationalist credential of the Kyojin is, however, indisputable. The national icon was nationalist as well; its name, Kyojin (giant), was a product of wartime militarism, when the team was renamed Kyojin-gun (giant battalion). The Kyojin were owned by the family of the Yomiuri newspaper mogul Shōriki Matsutarō, who was a Class A war criminal notorious for his pro-Nazi and militarist views in the 1930s and 1940s (Ushijima 1995:138–140). More significantly, Kawakami Tetsuharu, the manager who led the Kyojin to nine straight championships, claimed that he would "build a team of pure-blooded and pure-hearted Japanese" when he took over the team in 1960 (Whiting 1977:145). Kawakami—dubbed the god of batting *(dageki no kamisama)* during his illustrious career as a first baseman for the Kyojin—made *kanri yakyū* (administrative baseball) his managerial philosophy. It is no wonder that the Giants were so popular among government bureaucrats and business executives.

In spite of his nationalist impulse, Kawakami fell far short of realizing the goal of managing a monoethnic team. An indisputable giant among the Giants was Oh Sadaharu. Oh hit 868 home runs during his career and won the Triple Crown back to back in 1973 and 1974 (Oh and Falkner 1984:5). In tribute to his outstanding career, he was the first person ever to receive the government's highest honor *(kokumin eiyoshō)* (Yamamoto 1979:209). As his surname attests, Oh is a second-generation Taiwanese Japanese. It is true that he was regarded as an honorary Japanese by many people. As a fan who boasted that the Kyojin "won nine straight Japanese Championships without any foreign players" remarked, "Oh has a Japanese heart. He was born and raised in Japan. He went to school here. He has a Japanese mother and a Japanese wife. He looks like a Japanese. He talks like a Japanese. He *is* a Japanese" (Whiting 1977:211). Because of his Taiwanese citizenship, however, Oh was ineligible to participate in the National Amateur Athletic Competition *(Kokutai)* as a high school student.

The rejection was devastating: "How could this happen to *me, who was a Japanese!* My father was Chinese, and I was his son, that was true, but I had grown up as a Japanese, treated fully as such by neighborhood friends and schoolmates alike. It never entered my mind that I was 'different.' I had never felt 'different'" (Oh and Falkner 1984:54–55).

Oh was not the only non-Japanese Japanese member of the Kyojin in the 1960s and 1970s. The mandate of victory torpedoed Kawakami's nationalist aspirations. The person Oh regarded as "Japan's best pitcher—ever" (Oh and Falkner 1984:84), Kaneda Masaichi, was of Korean descent. Another ace, Niura Kazuo, was also Korean Japanese. Like Oh, he was not able to participate in the *Kokutai* in 1968, but he was able to join the Kyojin despite his ethnicity (Chŏng 1989:34). In the 1970s Harimoto Isao (Chang Hun), one of the greatest hitters in Japanese baseball history, joined the Kyojin. Incidentally, these three Korean Japanese stars of the Giants were far from uniform in their ethnic sentiments. A man of immense ethnic pride, Harimoto contributed to the formation of professional baseball in South Korea (Yamamoto 1995:271–272). However, though Niura later pitched in the South Korean professional league, he claimed not even to eat *kimch'i*, perhaps the most distinctive Korean staple (Chŏng 1989:22; cf. Sekikawa 1988:20–29).

Before Kawakami's declaration of ethnic purity, the Kyojin featured many non-Japanese stars. Victor Starfin, a Russian ethnic from Hokkaidō without citizenship, won over 300 games between 1936 and 1955 (Whiting 1977:109). Wally Yonamine, a Japanese American from Hawaii, was a successful hitter. Kawakami, a lifelong rival of Yonamine, purged him after taking over the team (Whiting 1977:143). Yonamine was, incidentally, not the first Japanese American player in Japanese baseball (Nagata 1994:13). Beyond the Kyojin, many prominent baseball players—aside from foreigners from the United States and elsewhere—belied the veneer of monoethnic Japan. For example, Kinugasa Sachio, who superseded Lou Gehrig's record of most consecutive games played (until he was in turn overtaken by Cal Ripken), had an African American GI father (Whiting 1989:61–65), as did Irabu Hideki, who joined the New York Yankees in 1997 to great fanfare.

Professional Wrestling

Oh Sadaharu's childhood hero was Rikidōzan (Oh and Falkner 1984:17), who, for some people, was "the greatest postwar hero" (Hwang 1992:51).

Beginning as a sumō wrestler, he pioneered professional wrestling (*puro resu*) in Japan. In the immediate postwar era, when many Japanese were still smarting from the material and symbolic wounds inflicted by the United States, Rikidōzan performed a redemptive ritual in the ring. Fighting an oversized white (American to most Japanese viewers) wrestler who would fight in the most treacherous way imaginable, Rikidōzan would pent up his righteous anger until he could no longer suppress it and then unleash his karate chops to beat resoundingly and mercilessly the hapless opponent. It was a powerful display of national pride and masculinity and an occasion to restore wounded Japanese pride (Saitō 1995:131–136). Rikidōzan was a national hero until his death in 1963 at the age of 39, and was to cast a long shadow as a paragon for a generation of Japanese men. Konaka Yōtarō (1993:219) called him "a reflection of Japanese spirituality" *(shinsei);* Rikidōzan's name remained lionized and *puro resu* was wildly popular during the 1960s.

Rikidōzan, the symbol of Japanese masculinity and national pride, was born in colonial Korea to Korean parents. He became a successful sumō wrestler but quit in 1950 at the height of his career. Although he claimed financial motivation, discrimination against Koreans (preventing his promotion to *yokozuna*) may have contributed to his decision to leave sumō (Ushijima 1995:61–63). A chance meeting with the Japanese American wrestler Harold Sakata, a.k.a. Toshi Tōgō, alerted him to the prospect of professional wrestling, and Rikidōzan went to Hawaii in 1952. Cultivating his "Japanese" karate chops, he became a wrestler in the United States (Ushijima 1995:74–75).

Returning to Japan, Rikidōzan pioneered professional wrestling in 1953. Riding on the growth of television, he in turn contributed to its popularity (Shiga 1990:196–198). The famous broadcast of Rikidōzan, teaming with the judo champion Kimura Masahiko, to defeat the Sharp Brothers spawned a national obsession with the sport. In 1957, for example, one match was viewed by over 20,000 spectators from a single television set placed outside Shinbashi Station in Tokyo. Another match was seen by 87 percent of television-owning households (Ushijima 1995:126–129). Interestingly, the person perhaps most responsible for television broadcast of wrestling was Shōriki Matsutarō, the owner of the Kyojin (Ushijima 1995:143–144). Rikidōzan's tie with right-wing figures, such as Kodama Yoshio, and *yakuza* exemplified an unholy alliance between ethnic Koreans and right-wing Japanese nationalists (Ino 1993:283–284).

As a nationalist hero of Japan, Rikidōzan veiled his Korean heritage. Harimoto Isao once visited him and the wrestler played a record of Korean folk songs. When Harimoto turned the volume up, Rikidōzan became angry, fearing that neighbors would hear the music. In response to Harimoto's challenge to be open about his Korean ethnicity, Rikidōzan replied, "I can't say [that I am Korean]. I became a star because people think that I am Japanese. If they know I am Korean . . . my popularity would end" (Yamamoto 1995:268). This exchange occurred in the early 1960s, when Rikidōzan was said to be "the most famous person after the emperor" in Japan (Ushijima 1995:266).

Sumō

Yakyū and *puro resu* were popular but few would deny their non-Japanese origins. Sumō, however, exemplified traditional Japanese athletics. The Hawaii-born Jesse Kuhaulua (1973:24), better known as Takamiyama, observed, "Sumo is as old as Japan and the gods who created her. For more than fifteen hundred years sumo has, in one form or another, played an important part in the fabric of Japanese life. . . . It has always endured as a vital expression of the Japanese spirit." Shrouded in tradition and strewn with Shintō symbols, sumō struck many of my friends as a relic of the feudal past. The archaic costumes of the referees, their ancient-sounding calls, the difficult Chinese characters of wrestlers' names, the staid broadcast by the establishment television station NHK, and, most unmistakably, the overweight wrestlers rendered the sport a paragon of uncoolness *(kakko warui)*. There is no question that sumō, both in its ideology and organization, is tradition-bound (Oinuma 1994:17–19) and has been identified as a national sport *(kokugi)* since the late Meiji period (Nitta 1994:283).

In the 1980s the Hawaii-born Konishiki's imminent promotion to the rank of *yokozuna* generated a heated debate (Matsubara 1994:3). Nationalists and traditionalists argued against the possibility of a non-Japanese *yokozuna* in this most Japanese of all sports. Although another Hawaiian wrestler, Akebono, achieved the exalted status in 1993, another non-Japanese, or at least not "pure" Japanese, wrestler had in fact become the youngest *yokozuna* in history in 1961, and remained the dominant figure throughout the 1960s. His name was Taihō, as in "Kyojin, Taihō, Tamagoyaki."

Taihō was a phenomenon. He once won forty-five straight matches, and he achieved the elusive grand slam twice (*Shōwa no ōzumō 60-nen* 1986:107). A grand slam in professional sumō entails winning all six tournaments held in a calendar year. Taihō was not, however, "pure-blooded Japanese"; his father was an ethnic Russian who had fled his homeland after the Bolshevik Revolution (Cuyler 1985:124). In fact, other popular wrestlers in the postwar period were not Japanese, including the Korean Japanese Rikidōzan and the Hawaii-born Takamiyama. To be sure, Takamiyama's mentor thought that "no one [was] more . . . Japanese" (Kuhaulua 1973:173; cf. Whiting 1986:128–130). The same honor is often accorded to Akebono (Morita 1993:57). Indeed, some wrestlers begin to look Japanese. Ogiwara Mitsuo said that the Hawaii-born Musashimaru, who became a *yokozuna* in 1999, looked like the Meiji-era hero Saigō Takamori (Strom 1999:A9). In any case, at least two other non-Japanese Japanese wrestlers—Tamanoshima and Mienoumi—have been *yokozuna* (Matsubara 1994:10–11).

In spite of its close entanglement with state Shintō and the emperor system, sumō is hardly the pure national sport that some of its enthusiasts believe it to be. Originating in Mongolia, the current form of Japanese sumō took shape in the mid-eighteenth century, and it shows close affinities with its Okinawan and Korean variants (Miyamoto 1985:12–16, 30; Hasegawa 1993:233–234). Sumō is neither unique to Japan nor does its heritage reveal a pure nationalist descent.

There were nonethnic Japanese figures of renown in other postwar Japanese sports, from boxing (Yamamoto 1993) to golf (Chi 1997:32). Even in the seemingly Japanese sport, karate, the person most responsible for its popularity in the West was the Korean Japanese Ōyama Masutatsu (Saitō 1995:258). Professional soccer, which became a national obsession in the early 1990s, features not only Korean Japanese stars but also many other nonethnic Japanese players (Yoshizawa 1993; Nomura 1996:chap. 11).

Varieties of Entertainment

The enrichment of Japan became perceptible by the late 1950s. Freed from the struggle to satisfy their basic needs, people sought solace in leisure (Plath 1964:96; Minami et al. 1983:384–386). Puritans everywhere decry leisurely pursuits, but we should be mindful of Friedrich Schiller's (1965:79) argument: "But why call it a *mere* game, when we consider that in every condition of humanity it is precisely play, and play alone, that makes man complete." Not only is play a condition sine qua non of fully realized humanity, but it is also a fundamental marker of cultural identity (Caillois 1979:66–67). In postwar Japan movies and television became mass obsessions, and people passed their time playing games. Fashion *(ryūkō)* ruled urban life (Ueda 1987:59) to the extent that the sociologist Mita Munesuke (1978:8–11) regarded its existence as expressing something quintessentially Japanese. To a significant extent, people listened to the same songs, read the same magazines and books, and played the same games.

Popular Music: *Enka*

In the immediate postwar period all genres of Western music filled the air, from classical to jazz and blues. In the 1960s the Beatles, Edith Piaf, and Maria Callas had loyal followings. However, a particular favorite of middle-aged *sararīman* (white-collar workers) and housewives was *enka*. The Japanese "soul music" sung of love and loyalty as well as tears and farewells (Zakō 1983:68). Although many Japanese regard *enka* as Japanese music, not only did it have transnational origins but its representative singers were Korean Japanese.

In the mid-1960s, Miyako Harumi emerged as a powerful exemplar of *enka* singing. Debuting in 1964, the year Oh hit fifty-five home runs and the year of the Tokyo Olympics, she became by the following year the youngest female singer to participate in the Kōhaku Utagassen (Red-White Song Festival), held annually on New Year's Eve (Arita 1994:14). Her series of million-sellers, such as "Namida no renrakusen" (The Ferry of Tears) and "Kita no yado kara" (From a Northern Inn), have become part of the standard karaoke repertoire. Almost always clad in a traditional kimono, Miyako remains one of the most popular *enka* singers in contemporary Japan. Her life story, including her impoverished childhood in Kyoto and her mother's devotion to her, is well known (Nakagami 1987) but her ethnicity is not: her father was Korean.

Miyako's inspiration was Misora Hibari (Arita 1994:11–26). Some regard Misora and Miyako as the two leading singers of the postwar period (Kata 1985:250–252). The critic Mori Akihide (1981:140) argues that *enka* reached its peak of popularity in 1960, with Misora Hibari's "Aishū hatoba" (The Wharf of Sorrow). Although derided by some intellectuals, others sang her praise: for the journalist Honda Yasuharu (1987:17, 394), Misora exemplified the postwar period (Shindō 1977:242). Her funeral was described in a language "normally reserved for imperial funerals, [which] had been used only five months earlier for Hirohito's last rites" (Fujitani 1996:241). A teen sensation who excelled not only in singing but also in acting, she became the prototype of all idols (aidoru) in postwar Japanese popular culture (Hiraoka 1993:38). It would not be an exaggeration to say that Misora personified "what was 'authentically' Japanese" (Tansman 1996:108). But she, too, was of Korean descent, as was her husband, the singer-actor Kobayashi Akira (Hwang 1992:52).

Postwar Japanese popular music is replete with non-Japanese Japanese, and especially Korean Japanese, singers. Miyako and Misora are perhaps the best known, but many teenage idols are Korean Japanese. One of them boasted that the "Kōhaku Utagassen on New Year's Eve couldn't take place without [Korean Japanese]" (Nomura 1996:15). Rather than engaging in a who's who of Japanese popular music, however, I want to discuss enka itself because of its status as the quintessential national music.

Enka generates strong likes and dislikes among Japanese people. It signifies mass (taishū) taste, as opposed to the high or refined preference for classical music. In other words, enka epitomizes the popular, traditional, and native as opposed to the refined, modern, and Western. It also marks an age differentiation: whereas techno pop, hip hop, and heavy metal are popular among youth, enka appeals to older people. Furthermore, as the musicologist Koizumi Fumio (1984:153) observes, enka "preserves the fundamental rhythm of Japanese language." Both the musical structure and the lyrics speak, in this line of thinking, to the Japanese soul.

Nonetheless, enka is far from purely Japanese in origin or development. Since the mid-1970s, speculations about the Korean origins of enka have been rife, fueled by the successes of South Korean enka-style singers, such as Yi Sŏng-ae and Cho Yŏng-p'il (e.g., Mori 1981:19–22). Ironically, in South Korea enka-style music is considered Japanese. The singer Yi Mi-ja was named as one of the 100 most influential South Koreans by the newspaper Han'guk Ilbo in 1985, but several of her songs were banned by the government because of their putative Japanese influences (Okano 1988:86–93).

The debate about national origins is moot; enka was formed in the crucible of transnational influences, including not only Japanese and Korean music but Western music as well. The musical structure and lyrics of enka may seem traditionally Japanese, but Western influences were crucial in its development as a musical genre (Okano 1988:177–183). It consolidated by distinguishing itself from, while being influenced by, a variety of Western music, especially choral music, that entered Japan in the late nineteenth and early twentieth centuries (Tansman 1996:111–112). The composers most responsible for the popularity of *enka*—Koga Masao and Miyagi Michio—spent their childhood in colonial Korea. They claimed Korean influence not only from Korean folk music but also from Korean instruments, such as *kayagŭm,* and Korean sounds, such as that of *kinuta* (fulling blocks against which clothes were beaten) (Mori 1981:22–26; Okano 1988:23–28, 106). For many people, however, Koga's music expressed a common Japanese sensibility (Shindō K. 1985:136–140).

Beyond *enka,* Japanese musical tastes are eclectic and transnational (Uchida 1993:307–317). European music has, however, dominated modern Japan, particularly in music education (Tsurumi 1984:139–142). Perhaps the most popular song in Japan is "Hotaru no hikari"—the Japanese adaptation of the Scottish folk song "Auld Lang Syne"—which is sung at the end of Kōhaku Utagassen on New Year's Eve and at any event that marks an end (Tsurumi 1984:163–164). Probably more Japanese know its lyric than that of the national anthem, "Kimigayo." The principal composer of "Kimigayo," incidentally, was the nineteenth-century German Franz Eckert (Kagotani 1994:176–177). More generally, various musical traditions, such as those of Tibet and Yunnan, influenced traditional Japanese music (Koizumi 1977:14–15; Kojima 1982:29–30). National purity cannot be found in music; sound does not respect national borders.

Television

No activity came closer to defining entertainment in the decade after 1945 than movies, and particularly Hollywood movies (Minami et al. 1983:398). But by the 1960s the most popular leisure activity was watching television (Kawauchi 1979:135–142). Its ubiquity in the 1960s is all the more remarkable because television broadcasts only began in 1953 (Tsurumi 1984:108). Because just a few networks dominated the airwaves, watching television amounted to a common national activity (cf. Williams 1975:30–31). Not only did television take a central place in many living rooms across the country, but it dominated discussions, within and without the household, as well (Fujitake 1985:141–145). It would be trite indeed to mention the

Western origins of movies and television. The most popular television genres—dramas, variety shows, and sports—emulated those of the United States (Stronach 1989:138–140; cf. Williams 1975:39–43). By the 1960s, however, television emerged as a central cultural institution in Japan, and television was as Japanese as anything else (Kitamura 1983).

As in popular music, many prominent actresses and actors were non-Japanese Japanese. Matsuzaka Keiko was one of the most glamorous Japanese actresses. Her mother hoped that she would become another Ingrid Bergman (Matsuzaka and Matsuzaka 1993:170), and sent her to a variety of lessons, including music lessons with the composer Koga Masao (Matsuzaka and Matsuzaka 1993:199). Perhaps predictably, she is of Korean descent. In the early 1990s several surveys named the actress Yasuda Narumi as the woman male college students would most like to marry. When I told one student that she was Korean Japanese, he was incredulous and indignant. After verifying this fact, he vowed that he would enter a graduate program in sociology to study ethnic relations in Japan. Rather than drawing up a long list of non-Japanese Japanese movie and television personalities, I will focus on a television series that exemplified one aspect of 1960s popular culture.

Urutoraman (Ultraman), a series that continues to be rebroadcast in the 1990s, was a forerunner of other superheroes, including the Power Rangers. The initial director of *Urutoraman,* Tsuburaya Eiji, is best known around the world for *Gojira* (or *Godzilla*). After its forerunner, *Urutora Q,* commanded viewer ratings of over 30 percent in 1965, *Urutoraman,* which premiered in 1967, was viewed by over 40 percent of all television-owning households (Yamada 1992:120, 146). Its offshoots, such as *Urutora Sebun* (Ultra 7) and *Kaettekita Urutoraman* (The Return of Ultraman), have also captivated generations of children. To be sure, I was not particularly fond of the program, but I can still vividly recall the monsters from the series that materialized in my nightmares and terrorized me during my sleeping hours. The Nobel laureate Ōe Kenzaburō (1981) castigated *Urutoraman,* and worried about its impact on children. Urutoraman dolls dominated the toy sections of department stores even in the 1990s. Japanese cultural studies scholarship has generated a long list of titles on nearly every aspect of the *Urutoraman* series, from its physics to its cultural valence. In its popularity and influence, *Urutoraman* defined a generation.

For the uninitiated viewer, a *Urutoraman* episode usually features a plot of infantile simplicity; Urutoraman—an alien from another galaxy—and his ilk fight monsters to save humanity. Beneath the exoteric reading, however, lies a myriad of esoteric readings, one of which is about multiethnic Japan. The creator and the most important scriptwriter of the original series was Kinjō Tetsuo, an Okinawan Japanese who attended high school and college in Tokyo. One of his goals was to "become a bridge between Okinawa and Japan" (Kiridōshi 1993:34). Not only did he use Okinawan to name monsters, but he also wrote *Urutoraman* as an allegory of the U.S. military occupation of Okinawa (Yamada 1992:168, 160). One episode from *Urutora Sebun,* "Nonmaruto no shisha" (The Messenger from Nonmaruto), defied the simple equations of Japan and humanity, and of Okinawans and monsters. The show depicts the original inhabitants of the earth—Nonmaruto, from non-Martians (Mars being the "god of war")—who had descended under the seabed because they were defeated by the current inhabitants—namely, us. The episode can be easily read as a transposition of Okinawan history and of Japanese colonialism (Kiridōshi 1993:62–66).

In anticipation of the 1972 return of Okinawa to Japan, Kinjō went to Okinawa in 1969 and became active in Okinawan theater and television (Yamada 1992:186–191). As proud of his Okinawan heritage as he was, he faced difficulties once in Okinawa. He was unable to master Okinawan speech, and other Okinawans regarded him as insufficiently anti-Japanese (Tsushima 1992:18; Yamada 1992:233–234; cf. Satō K. 1992:150–152). In 1976, having become a heavy drinker, he died accidentally at the age of 37 (Yamada 1992:205–208). Few in Okinawa even knew that he was the originator of *Urutoraman* (Yamada 1992:220).

The story does not end with Kinjō's death, however. Another principal writer of the *Urutoraman* series was Uehara Shōzō, another Okinawan Japanese. Other writers also continued to explore the issues originally raised by Kinjō. In one episode from *Kaettekita Urutoraman* (1971), an old man named Kaneyama, who is an alien, is killed by his neighbors in Kawasaki. Kaneyama is a common Japanized name for Korean Japanese with the surname Kim, and Kawasaki is a city known for the large number of Koreans, Okinawans, and other ethnic minorities. In response to Kaneyama's death, the monster Muruchi wreaks havoc on the city. Urutoraman does not, however, aid the denizens of Kawasaki. When one man pleads "Please! Get rid of the monster quickly!" Urutoraman thinks to himself, "Don't be selfish. You people brought on the monster. Oh, it's as if the anger of Kaneyama took over [the monster]" (Kiridōshi 1993:190). The part of

Urutoraman in this show was, incidentally, played by the *hāfu* (mixed descent) actor Dan Jirō (Kiridōshi 1993:194). In 1993 Ichikawa Shin'ichi wrote a television drama, "Watashi ga aishita Urutora Sebun" (Urutora 7 That I Loved), based on the life of Kinjō and Urutoraman. In one scene Ichikawa traces the origin of "Nonmaruto no shisha." Kinjō recognizes the equation between Urutora Sebun and the U.S. Seventh Fleet, between the police force that Urutora Sebun is helping and the Japanese Self-Defense Force, and between the monsters and Okinawans. He then writes the Nonmaruto episode to indict the Japanese colonization of Okinawa and leaves Japan (Kiridōshi 1993:296–297).

Popular Literature and Theater

Q. D. Leavis's (1979:31) snobbish characterization of Britain in the 1930s can easily be applied to postwar Japan: "novel-reading is now largely a drug habit." A lively culture of reading existed, even if what people read most often were manga and pornography.

In literature we see the inescapable fact of multiethnic Japan. One intriguing case is Tachihara Masaaki. He was twice nominated for the Akutagawa Prize; he eventually won the Naoki Prize but declined it because of his identity as a writer of serious fiction (Suzuki 1991:236–237). In Japan, the distinction between pure literature *(jun bungaku)* and mass literature *(taishū bungaku)* is institutionalized in the form of these two major awards: the Akutagawa Prize for the serious and the Naoki Prize for the frivolous. Considered the most Japanese of writers, Tachihara's Korean ancestry was revealed after his death. His biographer, however, affirms his Japaneseness by asserting "[o]riginally, the ancestry of eight or nine out of ten Japanese are Korean, so it was not so unnatural for Mr. Tachihara to have lived as Japanese" (Suzuki 1991:235).

Tachihara is hardly alone. In the realm of literary fiction, as we have seen, the fact of Japanese multiethnicity has been irrefutable. The Okinawan Japanese Ōshiro Tatsuhiro won the Akutagawa Prize in 1967 for his story "Kakuteru—pātī" (Cocktail Party), which focused on the rape of a Japanese woman by an American soldier. The list of prominent Korean Japanese writers is long and distinguished, generating a substantial critical literature in its own right (Takeda 1983). The achievements of the 1960s pale in comparison to the efflorescence of non-Japanese Japanese writings in the 1980s and 1990s. Two Korean Japanese writers—Yi Yang-ji and Yu

Mi-ri—have recently received the Akutagawa Prize. The Naoki Prize recipient Ijūin Shizuka (1989:46) is also of Korean descent. Finally, theater is a realm in which Korean Japanese have been especially active. Perhaps the dominant playwright of the 1970s was Tsuka Kōhei (Senda 1995:160–166), who has written on his Korean ethnic background (Tsuka 1990).

Manga

Contemporary manga have disparate roots, including native pictorial traditions and foreign influences such as American cartoons (Tsurumi 1984:54–57). One proximate precursor was the *kami shibai,* or picture shows (Kata 1979). Many men who entertained children with *kami shibai* were Burakumin (Allen 1994:100). One survey revealed that manga were the foremost concern for high school students in the early 1990s (Kure 1993a:9). Similarly, manga were not merely an entertainment but a way of life for many of my friends in the 1960s. *Kyojin no hoshi* and other *supokon manga* (sports *konjō manga*) instilled a life philosophy (Kure 1993b). One man recalls that he "realized that he could do whatever he wanted" by reading *supokon manga* (Inui 1971:281).

In the late 1960s manga became something of a hegemonic print genre (Ishiko 1975:5). The progressive cast of 1960s and 1970s manga is undeniable. Tsuge Yoshiharu, a manga artist with a cult following, was said to exemplify postwar democratic ideology (Kayatori 1980:142–144; cf. Schodt 1996:200–203). The common saying in the late 1960s was "te ni wa Jānaru, kokoro wa Magajin" (*Asahi jānaru* [a progressive weekly] in my hand, *Shōnen magajin* in my heart) (Ishiko 1975:130–131). *Shōnen magajin* is the serial that ran *Kyojin no hoshi.* It was widely said that student radicals read Shirato Sanpei's *Ninja bugeichō* (1976) after they went home after demonstrations. As the novelist Mishima Yukio (1996:110) wrote in 1970, "It has already become a myth that the youth of *Zengakuren* [a progressive national student organization] developed a revolutionary movement from the manga [*gekiga*] of Shirato Sanpei." Although Mishima claimed to dislike Shirato's epic, many intellectuals felt otherwise. At a small conference of Marxist historians, I was amused to hear a famous scholar mention with great gusto Shirato's epic. What was even more striking was the smile of recognition on everyone's face. Shirato's impact on the 1960s generation was profound: "I learned about the lives of the downtrodden," "I learned historical materialism," and "I learned about revolution" are typical assessments (Bungei Shunjūsha 1992:108). A nightwatchman in his forties told me that I can learn all I need to know about Burakumin by reading *Kamuiden* (Shirato 1979), where Shirato delineated the dialectics of status and class struggles in early modern Japan. *Kamuiden*—from *kamuy*, the Ainu word for god—was intended as a story of the Ainu people's struggle (Nagai 1996:52–53). Manga are thus inextricable from the theme of multiethnicity.

One of the appeals of manga is not only that they provide something to suit everyone's taste, but that they have been one of the most liberating means of expression in postwar Japanese society. Over two-thirds of 4 to 12-year-olds watched the weekly television broadcast *Kureyon Shinchan* in the early 1990s (Saiki 1994:A13); the show featured a young boy who punctured the pretensions and euphemisms of adult society. To use the Japanese cliché, he told *honne* (real feeling), not *tatemae* (pretended feeling). Similarly, another popular manga of the early 1990s was *Gōmanizumu sengen* (Arrogantism Manifesto), in which the author Kobayashi Yoshinori cut wide swaths through conventional wisdom. He depicted and denounced the deplorable discrimination against Burakumin (Kobayashi 1993:38–39, 46–51). As a right-wing nationalist (McGregor 1996:244), however, he also insisted on the superiority of the Japanese penis and urged the exclusion of foreigners from sumō (Kobayashi 1993:22–23, 32–33). If some manga have been accused of racist depictions (Russell 1991:86–101; Takeuchi O. 1995:175–181), one reason is that manga have been one of the few popular genres in which ethnic minorities in Japanese life are openly presented (Kure 1986:264). A very popular manga in the early 1990s, *Master Keaton*, featured Taichi Hiraga-Keaton, alias Master Keaton, who is an archaeologist-detective—a cross between Indiana Jones and Colombo—and of mixed descent of a Japanese father and a British mother. One episode features a nefarious plot by neo-Nazis and conveys an antiracist and antixenophobic message (Hokusei and Urasawa 1993:chaps. 7–8).

Games

When we consider what many Japanese people actually do in their leisure time, pachinko—Japanese-style pinball—may very well have occupied more time than any other leisure activity beside television. In 1994 the total revenue generated by pachinko was over 30 trillion yen, or about

250,000 yen per Japanese (Nomura 1996:94). There are 18,000 pachinko parlors in Japan, more than the number of bookstores (Nomura 1996:93). In the mid-1980s, an estimated 2.7 million Japanese were serious fans of pachinko, and perhaps 30 million played with some frequency (Ishige 1989:174).

A visitor to pachinko parlors usually finds not only people who are jammed closely together under wafts of cigarette smoke but also a noise level of deafening proportions—jarring metal balls, employees greeting customers, and speakers blasting military music and *enka*. The atmosphere seems, well, Japanese: "pachinko was a representative leisure activity of postwar Japanese" (Tada 1974:44) or "the greatest entertainment *(asobi)* that postwar Japan developed" (Ueno 1995:69). Given that "pachinko is a game machine invented in Japan" (Ishige 1989:178), few would deny its Japaneseness, and no serious study of postwar popular culture can ignore it (Takarajima 1992:132–133).

Nonetheless, pachinko reveals the multiethnic contours of Japanese society. The game was a variant of an American game and became popular among children in the 1920s and 1930s. Known as *gachanko* in Kantō and *pachipachi* in Kansai in the 1930s, pachinko became a game for adults after 1945 (Ishige 1989:181). And Korean Japanese spearheaded the industry. In the immediate postwar years most Korean Japanese could find employment only as day laborers or through self-employment in recycling, *yakiniku* (grilled meat) restaurants, or pachinko parlors. The popular culture scholar Katō Hidetoshi, "despite his sympathies for popular culture, had misgivings about patronizing" pachinko parlors because "most of these new enterprises [were] owned by Chinese and Koreans" (Riesman and Riesman 1976:109). In the 1990s an estimated 60 to 70 percent of pachinko parlor owners were Korean Japanese (Nomura 1996:93). The most successful chain is owned by the first-generation Korean Japanese Han Ch'ang-u. Han, a graduate of the elite Hōsei University and an eager reader of Marx and Engels, could not find suitable employment and therefore devoted his life to the pachinko business (Nomura 1996:96–98).

No matter where one looks, we find ethnic diversity and cultural hybridity in Japanese entertainment and the arts before and after the 1960s. Even in the seemingly most Japanese of art forms, kabuki, at least one famous modern actor, Ichimura Hazaemon the fifteenth, had a French father (Tsurumi 1984:147). The fact of multiethnicity should not be surprising in a genre that featured many outcastes in the Tokugawa period (Hattori 1993:109–113). Kabuki itself originated from Kawata, or premodern Burakumin, culture (Noma and Okiura 1983:268–269). Indeed, urban entertainment *(dōgei)* in general was the domain of Burakumin culture and occupations (Rei 1969:23–31; Ishizuka 1993:174; Morita 1995:32–34). The weakening taboo against non-Japanese ethnicity has made it increasingly possible to assess the irreducibly multiethnic character of Japanese popular culture. Perhaps the leading entertainer in Japan since the 1980s has been Kitano Takeshi, better known in Japan as Bīto, or Beat, Takeshi, and better known abroad as the director of *Sonatine* and other films (Kumazaka 1985:109). Kitano is, in fact, part Korean (Nomura 1996:8–9). We cannot write a history of postwar Japanese entertainment without mentioning non-Japanese Japanese.

Food

"We are what we eat"—the memorable adage by Ludwig Feuerbach intuitively captures the centrality of food in our lives. Beyond being a cultural universal, however, food and cuisine are vivid and visceral markers of social distinction (Mennell 1985:17). What is distasteful and disgusting to one group may very well be desirable and delicious to another. That taste may be the most conservative of the five senses only heightens the role of food as a cultural marker (Inoue 1989:138–139). Common national epithets—"Froggy" or "Kraut"—suggest the significance of food in the work of making national distinctions.

Certainly, many Japanese people are wont to associate Japanese food with Japaneseness. The essence of culture, in this view, is understood through the stomach. The popular *enka* singer Yashiro Aki—who herself is Korean Japanese (Chi 1997:32)—answered the question, what is *enka?*, by saying, "*Nattō* [fermented beans] and seaweed and tamagoyaki and breakfast with miso soup. That is, what every Japanese person likes" (Zakō 1983:40). Foreign travel for some Japanese unleashes a longing for miso soup (miso *shiru*), which reveals food to be a powerful marker of home. The manga *Oishinbō* (Gourmet) chronicles the inextricable link between food and culture. In one episode a Greek singer is hopelessly homesick and is unable to perform. The protagonist finds an octopus and olive oil and feeds her. Sated by her "soul food," she delivers a magnificent performance (Kariya and Hanasaki 1985:173–174). The Japanese character who finds octopus and olive oil odoriferous states in the concluding scene that miso soup is "our soul food" (Kariya and Hanasaki 1985:177).

The very idea of Japanese national cuisine arose in reaction against the spread of Western food—whence the contemporary distinction between *washoku* (Japanese food) and *yōshoku* (Western food) (Harada 1993:20–23). To be sure, many elements of contemporary Japanese cuisine can be found in the distant past (Hanley 1997:85), and urban Tokugawa-era cuisine would be recognizable today (Watanabe 1988:162–169). However, although it seems obvious that Japanese people eat Japanese food, such an assumption presumes the unity and continuity of Japanese culture and history. Before the centralizing thrust of the Meiji state, Japanese people's food consumption was differentiated across regions and status groups (Hanley 1997:85; cf. Bloch 1954). Outside of coastal areas, *sashimi* (raw fish) or Edo-style sushi (what contemporary Japanese simply call sushi) was rare (Yanagita 1976:i, 70–74). What samurai ate differed considerably from what peasants ate (Watanabe 1964:240–246). Contemporary Japanese cuisine is a cultural hybrid of manifold foreign influences (Tada 1972:22–24, 51–52).

Rice

Rice is a potent symbol of Japaneseness. The folklorist Yanagita Kunio (1978:50–55) regarded rice cultivation as the basis of a distinct Japanese culture, and many scholars link rice with the emperor system *(tennōsei)* (Amino 1996:244). A corner of my elementary school playground, which was completely paved, was a small rice paddy in a concrete frame. The association of Japan with rice is such that some Japanese mistakenly believe that Westerners don't eat rice, despite the prevalence of *raisu* (rice) in Japanese-style Western cuisine. Most Japanese realize that other Asians eat rice, but they often insist that Japanese rice is different. The obvious point that rice originated elsewhere, proximately from the Korean peninsula, is ignored (Okazaki 1993:271–272).

The centrality of rice cultivation cannot be observed in Hokkaidō or Okinawa before the Meiji Restoration (Harada 1993:219–23). In fact, rice has been the chief staple in Japan only since the nineteenth century (Ohnuki-Tierney 1993:39–40). Medieval peasants in Honshū principally ate millet and wild grass (Nagahara 1990:325–326). The extensiveness of taro cultivation even suggests the existence of a distinct culture—what

Tsuboi Hirofumi (1979:274–285) calls Azuma. In any case, the proto-typical Japanese rice of today is distinct from what most people in the Japanese archipelago ate in the past (Ohnuki-Tierney 1993:15).

Karē Raisu and Other National Food

The food historian Morieda Takashi (1989:196–198) regards *karē raisu* (curry rice) and *rāmen* (instant noodles) as Japan's two national dishes *(kokumin shoku)* (Minami et al. 1983:97). *Karē raisu* often ranks as the favorite food of Japanese people (Morieda 1989:16; cf. NHK Hōsō Yoron Chōsabu 1983:82, 103). *Rāmen* is, as far as I can surmise, the most consumed item in Japan. Itami Jūzō's film *Tampopo* gives a glimpse of the Japanese obsession with *rāmen*. Both dishes became popular during the instant food boom of the 1960s and are not Japanese in origin (Yamaguchi 1983:13; Suigyū Kurabu 1990:67–78). *Rāmen* was introduced initially as *shina soba* (Chinese noodles) (Morieda 1989:197–198). *Karē raisu* is an intriguing case.

Karē is ubiquitous in contemporary Japan. There is a wide variety of curry-flavored products; innumerable restaurants serve *karē*, ranging from the most inexpensive of greasy spoons to the very expensive "authentic" Indian restaurants. This most ordinary of Japanese food became popular in the 1910s (Morieda 1989:194–196). It arrived via Britain in the form of curry powder in the 1880s, and hence it was introduced as Western, not Indian (Asian), food (Morieda 1989:78–80, 209–210). The three common vegetables in *karē*—potato, onion, and carrot—are all Western imports that became common in Japan after the Meiji Restoration (Morieda 1989:127–131). The most popular brand in Japan, Hausu Bāmonto Karē, evokes the American state of Vermont and its reputation for health and longevity. The leading endorser of the brand in the 1970s was Saijō Hideki, a Korean Japanese singer (Takarajima 1992:162–163).

Karē raisu is far from the only post-Meiji import that has enthralled the Japanese palate. Whenever I spoke to Japanese children in the early 1990s, they often mentioned even more recent imports as their favorites: hamburger, pizza, and spaghetti. In the 1960s the responses would have included *korokke* (croquette), *omuretsu* (omelette), and *tonkatsu* (pork cutlet), which are all early twentieth-century Japanese adaptations of French cuisine (Watanabe 1988:210–216). By the 1970s salad was the favorite food of women under 30, and *yakiniku* (grilled meat) had become the favorite food of men under 30 (Yamaguchi 1983:225). Given menus with *kimch'i* and other Korean dishes, many Japanese categorize *yakiniku* as Korean cuisine. Although it is true that *p'ulgogi* and *k'albi*—two Korean meat dishes—resemble *yakiniku,* there are in fact significant differences. This is not surprising given that *yakiniku* originated as *horumonyaki* (*horumon* in the Kansai dialect is "thrown-away things") in the black market by Korean Japanese in the immediate postwar years (Morieda 1988:182–183). *Horumonyaki* first became popular among Korean Japanese in the Osaka area and then among poor and working people nationwide. In the early 1990s, 70 to 80 percent of *yakiniku* establishments were said to be owned by Korean Japanese (Hoyano 1993:38). In this respect, a Korean Japanese producer of Korean food predicted, "Not too long from now, we [Koreans] will conquer Japanese through their stomach."

Purin and Other Childhood Favorites from the 1960s

Let me return to tamagoyaki, as in "Kyojin, Taihō, Tamagoyaki." Its antecedent appears to be Western omelettes, which were served in Japan in the early Meiji period (Watanabe 1964:282). I wondered as a child about this third member of the trio. Kyojin and Taihō certainly seemed popular, but tamagoyaki? My friends and I liked other dishes, such as *karē raisu, supagetti* (spaghetti), and sushi. My favorite dish was *guratan* (gratin; actually, macaroni and cheese). In my elementary school, however, we inevitably had two slices of bread, milk, and soup for lunch. U.S. food aid, especially of wheat, and the associated idea about proper nutrition, dictated the proliferation of bread and milk as the chief staples of school lunches (Watanabe 1964:312–314). Milk itself was foreign to most Japanese until the Meiji period (Kumakura 1988:16–18). School lunch, in any case, provided a common denominator for the postwar generations of Japanese children and profoundly shaped their taste buds.

If the truth is to be told about popular food, however, we cannot bypass candies and desserts. Who can forswear the childhood delight in sweets? Virtually all the childhood favorites in the 1960s were non-Japanese in origin. My friends and I devoured *purin* (flan) and *kasutera* (pound cake), Coca Cola and *karupisu* (fermented milk drink), and chewing gums and chocolate. *Karupisu* and *kasutera* certainly dominated the 1960s (Nakagawa 1995:128).

The non-Japanese origins of all the childhood favorites from the 1960s are obvious and would be acknowledged even by ardent nationalists. *Purin* was initially marketed in 1963 (Katō 1977:187–188). *Kasutera* has a longer history, manufactured and marketed by the food giant Bunmeidō in 1900 (Katō 1977:109–110). *Bunmei* (civilization) was a code word for Western in the Meiji period, and as the illustration on the box readily suggests, *kasutera*'s model is the Portuguese *castella*. Coca Cola became popular during the U.S. occupation; as a favorite drink of the GIs, it proliferated on the black market. The unrestricted import of Coca Cola began in 1961, and it soon became standard Japanese fare (Katō 1977:184). *Karupisu* has a longer history in Japan. A cross between American yogurt and a Mongolian fermented drink, it was first sold in 1919 (Katō 1977:142–143). Chewing gums, like Coca Cola, became popular during the U.S. occupation when GIs dispensed them freely to Japanese children. Although chocolate was introduced in 1874 (Katō 1977:67–68), it became a mass consumption commodity only after 1945.

In contemporary Japan the name Lotte is inescapable when one looks for chewing gums, chocolate, and other candies. Lotte has controlled about 70 percent of the chewing gum market since the 1960s (Ch'oe 1987:70). Named after the heroine in Johann Wolfgang von Goethe's *Die Leiden des jungen Werthers* (The Sorrows of Young Werther), the company was founded and operated by the Korean Japanese entrepreneur Sin Kyŏk-ho. Initially hiding his Korean identity, Sin began by delivering newspapers and milk (Ch'oe 1987:73–77). Characterized by inspired and insistent advertisement campaigns, Lotte emerged as the principal purveyor of chewing gums in postwar Japan (Takarajima 1992:160–161).

Most of my interviews, incidentally, took place in cafés or bars. As I conversed over *kōhī* (coffee) and *kēki* (cake), or *bīru* (beer) and *shishamo* (Ainu word for small fish), the multiethnic and multicultural dimensions of Japanese life became all the more visceral. Cafés and bars are sites of conspicuous consumption (Veblen 1953:61–65) that dominated the *sakariba,* or the shopping-entertainment districts, by the 1960s (Yoshimi 1987:22–25).

Contemporary Japanese cuisine is a thorough hybrid. Most traditional dishes and ingredients hail from outside of the archipelago. Even the most Japanese of offerings, such as sake and sushi, have Korean roots (Chŏng 1992:49–54). Beyond foreign traditions of cookery, many of the very ingredients and items that Japanese consume are non-native in their origins. Tea and tofu come from China and Korea (Kumakura 1988:18–20; Tanaka 1988:170–172). Carnivorous as contemporary Japanese are, the revival of meat eating by non-Burakumin Japanese stems from the Western impact (Tada 1972:239–246).

The non-Japanese origins of food items are also true in a literal sense. Already by the 1970s, 60 percent of Japanese food consumption was accomplished through imports (Katō 1977:48). Even rice depended heavily on colonial production before 1945 (Ōmameuda 1993:310–317). Tofu and miso—two crucial items in any authentic Japanese cuisine—are made from soy beans, which were cultivated heavily in Manchuria in the early twentieth century (Katō 1977:167), and in the 1990s the Japanese relied heavily on North American soy beans. It is ironic that many Japanese are suspicious of foreign-grown food (*Asahi Shinbun*, Mar. 17, 1993), when so much of what they consume hails from outside the Japanese archipelago. The Japanese appetite in fact enmeshes the whole world. The demand for shrimp has transformed the economy and ecology of Southeast Asia and elsewhere (Murai 1988).

Finally, ethnic differentiation has been and remains coterminous with ethnic heterogeneity. The Ainu distinguish themselves from the Japanese, the Gilyak (Nivkhi), and others by their stress on thorough cooking (Ohnuki-Tierney 1993:3). Burakumin, along with people in Ezochi and Ryūkyū, were marked from mainstream Japanese by their carnivorous cuisine. People from Korea and China had their distinct culinary traditions. Multiethnic Japan is multialimentary as well.

Hybridity and Heterogeneity

No national culture is immune from transnational influences; hybridity, not purity, is the norm. In spite of the nationalist stress on cultural homogeneity and endogenous development, any contemporary culture inevitably reveals its heterogeneous and exogenous roots and influences. Whether one considers Britain or Japan—two cultures often noted for their literal and metaphorical insularity—purity and homogeneity are at best wishful projections.

Consider Britain. Rastafarianism and reggae seem far from representing the received understanding of British culture, but few would deny their place and popularity in contemporary Britain. For that matter, no serious scholar would deny that Kazuo Ishiguro and Salman Rushdie are two of the leading contemporary British novelists. Even fish and chips, the seemingly timeless national food, not only has a history but a history inflected by multiethnic Britain. Fish and chips "expressed ethnic diversity as well as simplistic national solidarity, from the strong East End Jewish element in the early days of fish frying in London, through the strong Italian presence in the trade from the turn of the century, in urban Scotland and Ireland especially, to the growing importance of the Chinese and Greek Cypriots in the post–Second World War decades" (Walton 1992:2). The reality of multiethnic Britain is denied by the nationalist discourse that privileges tradition and organic community. Paul Gilroy (1991:69) argues that "the language of British nationalism . . . is stained with the memory of imperial greatness. . . . [T]hese apparently unique customs and practices are understood as expressions of a pure and homogeneous nationality."

The idea of Britain and British culture is, of course, a modern phenomenon (Colley 1992). The vision of a homogeneous and organic nation, however, effaces not only the contemporary heterogeneity of British society but also the hybridization process that constituted its past. According to the historian Conrad Russell (1993:3), "It was during the years from 1968 to 1979 that English history courses began to pay lip-service to the notion of British history." Until then, England and Britain were usually conflated (Bogdanor 1997:4). Although they are constitutive elements of modern Britain, the effaced groups still hanker for recognition in both history books and contemporary debates.

The Politics of the Ethnic Closet

One reason for the invisibility of non-Japanese Japanese in 1960s popular culture is the irrevocable fact of discrimination. The ideology of monoethnicity shrouded popular cultural multiethnicity. Ethnic discrimination, however, contributed to the overrepresentation of ethnic minorities in sports and entertainment. It was commonly said among Korean Japanese parents in the 1960s, "If it's a boy, make him a baseball player; if a girl, then a singer." The Korean ethnics in Japan play the functional role of African Americans—as sports stars and singers—whereas Koreans in the United States are feted as a model minority (Abelmann and Lie 1995:165–170).

The paradox of ethnic overrepresentation and ethnic invisibility is by no means unique to Japan. Although few would deny the multiethnic constitution of the United States in the late twentieth century or the Jewish influence on American cultural life, Jewish Americans attempted not so long ago to pass as ordinary white Americans. The pressures toward Anglo-conformity led Betty Joan Perske and Samille Diane Friesen to become Lauren Bacall and Dyan Cannon, and Bernard Schwartz and Issur Daniel-ovitch to rename themselves Tony Curtis and Kirk Douglas (Kaplan and Bernays 1997:62–63). "The paradox is that the American film industry . . . called 'the quintessence of what we mean by "America,"' was founded and for more than thirty years operated by East European Jews who themselves seemed to be anything *but* the quintessence of America" (Gabler 1988:1).

Consider in this regard lesbians, gays, and other sexual minorities in the Unites States. Where homophobia is prevalent, people with homosexual orientations frequently hide their sexual preference. The closet becomes a repository of secret knowledge, at once a realm of respite and of prevarication (Halperin 1995:29). Just as outing in the context of an extremely homophobic culture means the demise of one's career, the disclosure of ethnic status, such as Korean descent, threatens the loss of popularity in Japan. The actress Matsuzaka Keiko, for example, suffered from a controversy over her Korean heritage (Matsuzaka and Matsuzaka 1993:220–223). Divulging Korean Japanese singers' Korean descent was considered tantamount to ending their career in the 1970s (Mori 1981:10–21). Rikidōzan sought to hide his Korean descent, as did numerous other figures, famous and nonfamous.

Discrimination does not disappear by confining people to the closet. In fact, the acts of passing may reinforce discrimination. But outing is a morally complicated deed. Matsuzaka's father risked lynching from his fellow coal miners if they had become aware of his Korean identity (Matsuzaka and Matsuzaka 1993:87, 93). Although no one is likely to suffer lynching in contemporary Japan, many non-Japanese Japanese fear that they could lose their popularity, friends, lovers, jobs, and so on if their ethnic backgrounds are revealed. Hence, I have consciously passed over people who have not self-identified themselves as non-Japanese Japanese, except for the deceased, such as Rikidōzan and Misora Hibari.

That the facts of multiethnic Japan still remain occluded, then, is in part because of monoethnic ideology. In spite of the proliferation of books on ostensibly every topic in publisher-happy Japan, there is, for example, still no serious history of pachinko. Korean Japanese owners of pachinko parlors are wary of researchers who may harm their business, whether because of ethnic discrimination or because of the Japanese tax bureau (Nomura

1996:94–95). I have written little on Burakumin because, until recently, many were reluctant to reveal their identity.

When I look back on my childhood in Tokyo, it is not only "Kyojin, Taihō, Tamagoyaki" that comes to mind. My classmates often beat me up after school because of my Korean name. Excluded from our usual after-school baseball game, I would walk over to the shopping district near Shibuya Station. My favorite haunt was Seibu, which remains a fashionable department store. It hardly occurred to me then that the owner of Seibu (and its corporate parent Saison Group) was of Korean descent (Downer 1994:11–12). Whether one regards individual stars or dishes, or games or genres, we inevitably encounter ethnic heterogeneity and cultural hybridity in postwar Japanese popular culture. The presumption of monoethnic Japan must be jettisoned in favor of the reality of multiethnic Japan.

4

Modern Japan, Multiethnic Japan

The contemporary discourse of Japaneseness posits that Japan has been and remains an ethnically homogeneous country. Thus, nationalist historiography delineates a pure descent of Japanese people, especially since the long period of seclusion *(sakoku)* under Tokugawa rule. In the previous chapter I focused on multiethnicity as a central feature of postwar Japanese popular culture. In this chapter I broaden my horizon to encompass the terrain of modern Japanese history. The seemingly singular light of modern Japanese history refracts and reveals a spectrum of ethnic contacts, competitions, and constructions. Indeed, the fundamental forces of modern Japanese history—state-making, colonial expansion, and capitalist industrialization—engendered ethnic heterogeneity. To speak of modern Japan is to speak of multiethnic Japan.

The Making of Multiethnicity

Why do nation-states become multiethnic? There are three major mechanisms: state-making, colonization, and migration.

First, by identifying the nation-state with a dominant group, the modern nation-state transforms all remaining groups into ethnic others. Because most modern nation-states hail from status-based societies, low-status groups often become ethnic groups: a religious minority, such as the Jews, or a migratory group, such as the Gypsies, or an occupational group, such as the outcastes. In all these instances claims about shared decent and common culture, in addition to discrimination by the larger society, sustain social differentiation.

Second, when a nation-state colonizes a contiguous or, for that matter, distant, territory, it willy-nilly incorporates people living on the land. Except in the case of irredentism, territorial expansion incorporates ethnically distinct people. Political expansion, in other words, leads to ethnic heterogeneity. To be sure, successful integration may expunge memories of difference and markers of distinction, but that process frequently takes generations. Conversely, the revival of regional identity, which often indicates successful integration, may occur and resemble ethnic renewal.

The third path toward multiethnicity occurs when people enter another nation-state, whether as traders, students, missionaries, or workers. Frequently, sojourners, by establishing residence in a new land where they may not initially have intended to stay, become immigrants, and hence ethnic minorities. Immigration has been, at least in the nineteenth and twentieth centuries, the most common route to ethnic differentiation.

In general, the more powerful and prosperous the nation-state, the more multiethnic it will be. Powerful states not only expand territorially, but they also attract outsiders because of a thriving economy or culture. All world-historical civilizations display a considerable mixture of peoples; all major metropolises are heterogeneous, whether ancient Athens or imperial Rome, or nineteenth-century Paris or twentieth-century New York.

It should not be surprising, then, that modern Japan should be multiethnic. As an increasingly powerful and wealthy nation-state, modern Japan became multiethnic via all three paths that I have briefly sketched. In the course of modern state-making, one large group, the Burakumin, became an ethnic minority. Territorial expansion of modern Japan incorporated Hokkaidō and Okinawa, as well as Taiwan, Korea, and other parts of Asia and the Pacific. Finally, capitalist industrialization encouraged immigration, especially of the colonized people, into the Japanese archipelago. The fundamental forces of modern Japan—state-making, colonialism, and capitalist industrialization—engendered ethnic heterogeneity. The history of modern Japan is simultaneously the history of its multiethnic constitution.

From Outcastes to Burakumin

The origins of the Burakumin have generated a great debate in Japan. Some believe in their racial distinctiveness because of their putative Korean origins (Fujino 1994:162–165), whereas others assert a long lineage of polluted people *(eta)* (Uesugi 1990:13–18). Ishio Yoshihisa (1986:28–29) suggests the political origins of early modern *senmin* (outcastes) by pointing out that they were Christians and other religious heretics, as well as insurgent peasants (Noma and Okiura 1986:35–36). Rather than sorting out the complicated genealogy of the Burakumin, I wish to stress their modernity as an ethnic identity. Before the Meiji Restoration, the future Burakumin comprised numerous status categories (ranging from leather and funerary workers to lepers and the handicapped to the homeless and the poor), with considerable regional variations, and cannot be generalized as a unitary group (Ninouya 1993:62, 1994:217–220). We should not retrospectively conflate the motley category of social inferiors (Kasamatsu 1984:41–46; Wakita 1985:245), although they had begun to consolidate their identity, principally against peasants *(hyakushō)*, during the Tokugawa period (Kobayashi 1979:4–5). In any case, establishing ancestry before the Meiji period is difficult (Fujiwara 1993:231–232); it is more illuminating to highlight the modernity of Burakumin identity.

The designation of the Burakumin as an ethnic group is controversial because most contemporary Japanese equate ethnicity with race. Because Burakumin and Japanese are said to belong to the same race—there are no obvious sources of phenotypical distinction—they are not regarded as distinct ethnic groups. In spite of the continuing discrimination and the impoverished status of the Burakumin, most Japanese, including the Burakumin themselves, insist on their Japaneseness (Yoshino and Murakoshi 1977:130). However, if shared descent and common culture, as well as discrimination, characterize an ethnic group, then the Burakumin are as ethnic as the Ainu or Okinawans. Although they have never had their own country, neither did the Ainu, Indian outcastes, or European Gypsies.

After the Tokugawa *bakufu* (government) collapsed, the new Meiji state faced enormous challenges. Internally, *han* (domains) threatened to become autonomous powers. From the 1868–1869 Boshin War to the 1877 Satsuma Rebellion, armed resistance contested central rule. In addition, peasant uprisings and the popular rights movement challenged state legitimacy (Unno and Watanabe 1975:225–228). Externally, European powers posed a potent threat to Japanese autonomy. In response, the Meiji state sought to consolidate central rule and to become a major industrial and military power, encapsulated in the slogan "rich nation, strong army" *(fukoku kyōhei)*. It also abolished status distinctions and sought to transform townspeople and peasants divided by regional and status differences into loyal national subjects.

The 1871 Emancipation Decree transformed the outcastes into formally free new commoners *(shin heimin)* (Kobayashi 1979:69–75). Rather than the rigid status distinctions that had proscribed occupational mobility and interstatus marriage during Tokugawa rule, the Meiji state guaranteed occupational mobility, residential freedom, the right to surnames, and other features of formally egalitarian citizenship. The Decree granted the new commoners the same rights as those held by the *heimin,* the traditional commoners.

Thus, there was a transition from caste—defined by customary or legal proscription on occupational mobility or exogamy—to ethnicity. Social discrimination and cultural stigma against the new commoners did not disappear. The very fact that the family registry system *(koseki)* distinguished *heimin* from *shin heimin* allowed a simple documentary basis for differentiation. More important, the new commoners, who lived in special villages *(tokushu buraku),* were considered a breed apart from the mainstream Japanese. After the 1871 Emancipation Decree, there were anti-Burakumin riots (Totten and Wagatsuma 1966:36–37). The conscious effort by farmers to put the Burakumin in their place enhanced their respective identities. In the early twentieth-century "popular notion," Burakumin had "one rib-bone lacking; they have one dog's bone in them; they have distorted sexual organs; they have defective excretory systems; if they walk in moonlight their neck will not cast shadows; and, they being animals, dirt does not stick to their feet when they walk barefooted" (Ooms 1996:303).

The Meiji state not only destroyed the legal basis of discrimination but simultaneously withdrew protective measures, such as a monopoly over several occupations, that had sustained the livelihood of the ancestors of the Burakumin. The Burakumin therefore lost their principal sources of livelihood and were forced to cultivate meager plots of land, engage in low-wage crafts, such as footwear and matches (Akisada 1993:60–77), or work in the secondary labor market, especially in construction and coal mines (Kobayashi 1985:306–323; Yoshimura 1986:30–32). The Meiji state was slow to expand schooling or transportation and communication to Burakumin villages. In short, the Burakumin held the worst jobs and housing of modern Japanese society. Legal discrimination was replaced by economic competition and class reproduction.

The ferment of social reformism in the 1890s contributed to the stirring of Burakumin liberation. Some younger Burakumin became educated and began to agitate. Suiheisha (Leveling Society), an organization devoted to ending discrimination against the Burakumin, was organized in 1922, and had 53,000 members by 1928. Despite wartime repression, Suiheisha remained the largest left-leaning organization in existence, with 40,000 members in 1940 (Neary 1989:50–56, 91). Its principal activity was a campaign of denunciations *(kyūdan tōsō)* (Neary 1989:85). Leftist and Communist supporters dominated the organization before and after 1945 (Totten and Wagatsuma 1966:62–63).

The Japanese government engaged in a policy of repression and integration. Liberal social thinking and the fear of popular uprising—symbolized by the 1918 Rice Riots—goaded the government to pursue welfare measures for the Burakumin—the so-called *yūwa* (assimilation and harmony) policy (Neary 1989:130–132, 166). The first state aid occurred in 1920 in the form of various improvement projects for Burakumin villages (Neary 1989:59–61). Poverty, geographical segregation, and social stigmatization characterized most Burakumin. In the 1930s Burakumin households earned income perhaps one-half of the national average, and experienced lower wages and poorer living conditions than the ethnic Japanese (Neary 1989:148–149).

Suiheisha and the *yūwa* policy consolidated the Burakumin identity. On the one hand, Suiheisha organized Burakumin qua Burakumin, thereby entrenching the Burakumin identity. On the other hand, the state, especially via its *yūwa* policy, treated the Burakumin as a distinct group.

In the postwar period, the Burakumin continued to occupy a distinct niche in Japanese society. Although no longer called *buraku* but *dōwa chiku* (assimilated areas), many postwar Burakumin neighborhoods were socially segregated, with inferior infrastructures (Fukuoka et al. 1987:18–19). Poverty continued to mark Burakumin areas, and the Burakumin themselves were characterized by low educational attainment and high welfare dependency (Wagatsuma and De Vos 1966:125–128). Not unlike the Jim Crow South in the United States, Burakumin day laborers in rural areas had separate and substandard facilities for dining and sanitation (Neary 1989:3).

In spite of legal equality, the Burakumin continued to be excluded from prestigious corporate jobs and marriages with mainstream Japanese people. Many large corporations used name books *(chimei sōkan)* to identify individuals with Burakumin ancestry and not to hire them (Upham 1987:114–116). Although some consider the cause of this ostracism to be groupism or the village mentality *(mura ishiki)* of Japanese bureaucrats and managers, it may have more to do with the association of the Burakumin with communism and political activism (cf. Uesugi 1990:173–177).

In addition to residential and economic segregation, Burakumin culture showed distinct characteristics that further indicated and inspired discrimination from the mainstream population. In the early 1960s the Burakumin diet reflected a tradition of meat eating—the consumption of internal organs—that many Japanese abhor, and Burakumin dress included the wearing of distinctive sandals (Sasaki and De Vos 1966:135). The Japanese people whom John Cornell (1967:347) interviewed in the 1960s regarded the Burakumin as "rough in speech, crude or brutal in relations with each other, having a low boiling point, quarrelsome, highly sensitive to insult, born traders, and relatively much more cohesive than any other community" (cf. Nakagawa 1983:366–367). In the classic language of otherness, the Burakumin were "darkly disreputable, mysterious, and substantially unknown" (Cornell 1967:348). The most common reason that the Japanese give for Burakumin discrimination is that the Burakumin act in unison (Tamiya 1991:20–21). National and local governments have largely denied or neglected the condition of the Burakumin, and most Japanese people have been indifferent to their plight (Yagi 1984:175).

If political and economic factors contributed to the crystallization of Burakumin identity in the early twentieth century, the same causes led to the partial dissolution of that identity in the late twentieth century. In 1946 Suiheisha and the more moderate supporters of the *yūwa* policy consolidated to form what came to be known after 1955 as the Buraku Kaihō Dōmei (Buraku Liberation League) (Wagatsuma 1966:73). In part in response to Burakumin activism, the 1965 Cabinet Dōwa Policy pointed to the persistence of discrimination against the Burakumin (Upham 1987:84–86). Consequently, beginning in 1969 the Japanese government initiated special measures to improve Burakumin residences and neighborhoods (Neary 1997:64–65), spending some 6 billion yen between 1969 and 1981 (Shimahara 1991:336). The fundamental spur that integrated many Burakumin into the mainstream labor market was, however, rapid economic growth and the tight labor market of the 1960s, underscoring W. Arthur Lewis's (1985:44) generalization that the "most effective destroyer of discrimination is fast economic growth."

Nonetheless, the conditions of the Burakumin in the last decade have yet to reach the egalitarian ideal. Welfare dependency and discrimination still mark the lives of many Burakumin. However, significant improvements in educational attainment and employment opportunities have taken place (Shimahara 1991:338–345). In particular, the Buraku Liberation League and other activist organizations have worked closely with international human rights efforts (Tsurushima 1984:84). The League's most important activity, however, remains protest and denunciation of writers, publishers, and politicians who defame the Burakumin. The political strategy of the Buraku Liberation League nonetheless does not deny the ideology of monoethnicity and thereby maintains the silence on and the invisibility of ethnic differentiation.

Territorial Expansion

Tokugawa sovereignty extended to Honshū, Shikoku, and Kyūshū. Its fluctuating claims over Hokkaidō entailed at most the southern tip. Ryūkyū, although a tributary state, was an independent kingdom. Even in the three major islands, as I elaborate in the following chapter, regional differentiation and a rigid status hierarchy prevented a well-disseminated national identity. Modern state-making strengthened popular Japanese national identity, but it also led to ethnic heterogeneity. Defining the national boundaries proceeded hand in hand with their expansion (Iriye 1989:739). The Meiji state first annexed Hokkaidō in 1873, Ryūkyū in 1879, Taiwan in 1895, Korea in 1910, and made significant conquests in Asia and the western Pacific. In so doing, Ainu and Okinawans, as well as Taiwanese, Koreans, and other Asians, became incorporated into the Japanese polity. The rise of imperial Japan was coeval with the growth of multiethnic Japan.

From Ainu Mosir to Hokkaidō

Ainu people (from *aynu*, meaning human beings in Ainu) inhabited the northern part of the Honshū, Hokkaidō, Sakhalin, and Kurile islands since the beginning of recorded history. Given geographical dispersion and cultural diversity, one cannot convincingly talk of Ainu ethnicity until the fifteenth century. Like the Inuits of North America, there was nary a sense of larger cultural unity. That outsiders may detect a family resemblance among the Ainu does not deny their own sense of significant differences. Even today there are very small but distinct groups from among the Ainu, such as the Uilta and the Gilyak (Nivkhi), living in Hokkaidō. By the fifteenth century Ainu people were principally hunter-fisher-gatherers and engaged in far-flung trade with others, ranging from Aleutian islanders to the east, Russians and Chinese to the west, and Shamo (as the Ainu call Wajin, or Japanese people) to the south (Uemura 1990:part 1). The Ainu developed a sophisticated material culture and a noteworthy literature, including *yukar* (epic poetry) (Ainu Minzoku Hakubutsukan 1993).

The Tokugawa-era appellation for Ainu Mosir (human land in Ainu) was Ezotō or Ezochi (Tamura 1992:87–88). Before the fifteenth century, Ezochi—then encompassing northern Honshū and Hokkaidō—existed as a politically autonomous area (Kaiho 1989:58–60). Neither the distinction between Shamo or Ainu nor the boundaries between Tokugawa territory and Ezochi were well delineated (Kaiho 1989:48–51). From the mid-fifteenth century the Matsumae *han* sought to control trade ports and routes in the area, which generated continual skirmishes between the 1457 Koshamain's Rebellion and the 1550 peace treaty (Uemura 1990:59–69).

The conflict was not ethnic but, rather, political, pitting Matsumae against Ezochi (Kaiho 1989:76–78). The continuing encroachment of the Matsumae domain, however, contributed to ethnic differentiation (Howell 1994:79). In spite of intermittent resistance by Ainu people (the last armed resistance occurred in 1789) and their control over much of Hokkaidō (Kikuchi 1984:193–196), the Shamo held key trading ports and sustained their military superiority. The 1669–1672 Shakushain's War ensured Matsumae's dominion over the southern tip of Hokkaidō and its monopoly over the profitable Ainu trade (Uemura 1990:92–105). However, Ainu people continued to live in northern Honshū until the early nineteenth century (Namikawa 1992:290–295). In part to ensure its monopoly in Ainu trade, Matsumae sought to maintain rigid distinctions between the two peoples—Ainu were forbidden to speak Japanese or to don Japanese clothing (Kikuchi 1991:35–46).

The exploitation of Ainu people and land intensified during the nineteenth century. The Ainu economy became dependent on Matsumae *han* (Howell 1995:44–47). In particular, the rise of contract fisheries incorporated Ainu people as low-wage workers, as many Ainu became dependent on tobacco and alcohol (Kikuchi 1989:136–137). The Shamo also used Ainu people as forced labor (Kayano 1994:26–28). Interestingly, Tokugawa-era intellectuals speculated on projects to colonize Ezochi by using Burakumin ancestors (Ooms 1996:296–298). Fearing Russian advances and striving to protect the profitable Ainu trade, the *bakufu* (Tokugawa government) claimed control over Hokkaidō in 1807 (Kikuchi 1995:234– 235). Although Matsumae *han* regained control in 1821, the *bakufu* once again placed Ezochi under its direct rule when Hakodate became a treaty port in 1854 (Howell 1995:42–43). Japanese influences penetrated Ezochi (Kikuchi 1995:240–244).

The Meiji state renamed Ezochi as Hokkaidō in 1869 and declared the territory as imperial land in 1873 (Tamura 1992:92–93). Until the mid-nineteenth century, Ezochi was a foreign territory *(iiki)* for Tokugawa Japan (Kaiho 1992:15). Thereafter, it became part of Meiji Japan. National security concerns against Russia appeared foremost in the decision to seize Ezochi (Gabe and Kawabata 1994:227). No organized resistance faced the Meiji state, which appropriated over 20 percent of the current Japanese landmass. A greater part of the land was distributed to the former samurai, who transformed themselves into pioneers *(kaitakusha)* (Tamura 1992:93– 94). Although Japanese in Hokkaidō numbered only 168,000 in 1873, the figure increased to 786,000 by 1897 (Shin'ya 1977:179). In addition to the ex-samurai, other Japanese came to exploit the natural bounty of Hokkaidō, resulting in a near depletion of deer and salmon by the 1880s (Horiuchi 1993:17–18). Deforestation proceeded at a rapid place (Honda 1993a:7–11). Most significantly, the spread of infectious diseases that accompanied Shamo immigration led to a significant decline in the Ainu population (Seki 1983:230–231).

The Meiji state pursued an aggressive policy to integrate Ainu people, whom they regarded as aborigines *(dojin)*, into the modern Japanese polity. The Japanese state forcefully relocated some Ainu people and transformed them into farmers (Kaiho 1992:100–102). Nearly all aspects of Ainu culture were banned outright or became objects of scorn (Shin'ya 1977:183–185). The Ainu were forced to adopt Japanese names (Asahi Shinbun Ainu Minzoku Shuzaihan 1993:92–98) and placed under the national registry *(koseki)* (Kaiho 1992:18). Kayano Shigeru (1994:44) describes the thoughtless manner by which a government official named Ainu people: "I see; so this village is called Pirautur [now Biratori]. Then let's name the Ainu here Hiramura [Pira village]. Next is Niputani [now Nibutani], so their name should be Nitani." Thus, the state pursued a policy of assimilation, seeking to transform the Ainu into Japanese, or civilized, people (Kaiho 1992:22–28; Takagi 1994:166–168).

The culmination of the Meiji policy toward Ainu people was the 1899

Hokkaidō Aborigine Protection Act *(Hokkaidō kyūdojin hogohō)* (Ogawa and Yamada 1998:409–412). The appellation *kyūdojin*—former aborigines—captures the dominant Japanese presupposition of Ainu backwardness. Although claiming to protect the Ainu, the legislation sought to transform and, in fact, destroy the Ainu way of life (Shin'ya 1977:188–193). Its two main pillars were to make them farmers and to assimilate them as Japanese. Henceforth, Ainu people were forbidden to fish, barred from cutting trees, and banned from speaking their native language. The end of contract fishery had simultaneously liberated Ainu workers and ended their chief means of livelihood. Prevented from pursuing their traditional way of life, they were to become either farmers or day laborers (Uemura 1990:262–265). By the turn of the century, the forced integration of Ainu people into mainstream Japanese culture was in full force. Beginning in 1877 the Meiji state had established special schools for Ainu children (Ogawa 1997:69–73). The educational opportunities for Ainu children, however, lagged behind their Shamo counterparts (Kamijō 1994:128). Assimilation intensified in the 1930s, leading to the abolition of special schools (Ogawa 1997:371–375).

Thus, Hokkaidō became a Japanese version of the American western frontier, exemplified by the injunction of Hokkaidō University President W. S. Clark to the graduates: "Boys, be ambitious" (Yamakawa 1996:53). The northern frontier became the chief conduit of Japanese expansionist energy until Japan began to colonize Asia in the late nineteenth century. The parallels with the conquest of the American West are striking: the native economy, culture, and nation were destroyed; the indigenous people suffered from diseases and exploitative pioneers and were later confined to a small landmass; and the winners got to write history. As the historian Tanaka Osamu (1986:4–5) observes, the modern Japanese history of Hokkaidō has been a history of development *(kaitaku)* (Ebina 1983), which effaced the indigenous and expropriated population. The Japanese who settled or traveled to Hokkaidō found a defeated people, whom they considered "lazy natives," suffering from alcoholism and other social ills (Uemura 1990:269–273; Horiuchi 1993:123–129).

The process of Japanese assimilation ironically contributed to an ethnically diverse Hokkaidō. Intensive mining not only had devastating ecological consequences (Kuwabara 1993:101–106), but it also led to the use of prison workers (Tanaka 1986:102–132) and Koreans. By 1944 over 60 percent of all the miners in Hokkaidō were Koreans (Kuwabara 1993:188–189), which also led to intermarriage between Korean men and Ainu women (Asahi Shinbun Ainu Minzoku Shuzaihan 1993:154).

The tale of Ainu abuse and exploitation does not end after the destruction of Ainu sovereignty in the late nineteenth century. After the end of World War II, when a major land reform was enacted, many Ainu lost land due to deceptions by Japanese farmers (Horiuchi 1993:32–36). In general, they have been poor, with low educational attainment. In one study, 61 percent of the Ainu were on welfare, whereas only 8 percent had graduated from high school (Sjöberg 1993:152). Ainu people are also targets of considerable discrimination. For example, the Japanese sentence "Ainu da" (That is an Ainu) is rendered as "Ah! Inu da" (Oh! That is a dog) in order to taunt Ainu people (Horiuchi 1993:129–130). When Ainu people engage in salmon fishing, they are arrested for breaking the Japanese law. The two conflicting claims can be gleaned from the following exchange between a Japanese prosecutor and an Ainu trespasser: "'If you aren't satisfied with Japanese law, why don't you go to China or the Soviet Union?' 'What are you saying? This is our Ainu land. Why don't you leave?'" (Asahi Shinbun Ainu Minzoku Shuzaihan 1993:176–177).

Official neglect has occluded Ainu history and culture from the mainstream Japanese view. Although the Japanese government had recognized the Ainu as a distinct culture in 1950, it ceased to do so after 1953 and until 1987 (Uemura 1987:238–240, 1992a:91, 129). The journalist Honda Katsuichi (1993a:338) recalls that the very mention of Ainu was taboo in the early 1960s. In contemporary Japan Ainu people appear principally in posters promoting tourism to Hokkaidō. When Japanese tourists visit Ainu villages, they are surprised that Ainu people eat white rice and are disappointed that they have refrigerators and television (Asahi Shinbun Ainu Minzoku Shuzaihan 1993:184). In a survey of over a dozen high school Japanese history textbooks, only one mentioned anything about the Ainu (Horiuchi 1993:28). Although most textbooks mention the first Japanese person to reach Antarctica in 1912, there is nothing about the two Ainu who accompanied him (Asahi Shinbun Ainu Minzoku Shuzaihan 1993:103). Nearly all the Japanese I talked to regarded the Ainu as nearly extinct. When I asked people to estimate their population, no one gave a figure higher than 1,000. Not surprisingly, they are frequently described as a "vanishing people" (Creighton 1995:69–70).

Japanese scholars of the Ainu have largely buttressed popular prejudices, regarding them as a dying people, and have been chiefly interested in their racial classification (Siddle 1996:97–112). Shin'ya Gyō's indictment (1977:264) from the 1970s still rings true: "I think that people called Ainu scholars are the last agent of Yamato [Japanese] people's massacre of Ainu people."

In the postwar period, the Ainu Kyōkai (Ainu Association) remained generally passive and accommodated itself to the Japanese assimilation policy. Indeed, the group renamed itself Utari Kyōkai (Utari Association; Utari means comrade in Ainu) in 1961 in part because of the pejorative connotation of the word Ainu (Siddle 1997:27). The resurgence of Ainu pride and activism dates from the late 1960s. Inspired by external events, including the rise of the student movement, Burakumin activism, and the global struggles of indigenous peoples, some Ainu began to engage in political and cultural activities (Uemura 1992b:39–61; Siddle 1996:24, 1997:28–30).

In the early 1990s the Hokkaidō Utari Association claimed about 16,000 members, while the estimated number of Ainu in the mid-1980s was 24,000 (Uemura 1990:281). Because of the gradual reassertion of Ainu pride, more identify themselves as Ainu. Hence, Uemura Hideaki (1992a:76) estimates that the number of people with Ainu ancestry may well exceed ten times the 24,000 figure (cf. Sjöberg 1993:152; DeChicchis 1995:106). There are, moreover, concerted efforts to reclaim Ainu language, culture, and land. The effort to overturn the 1889 Hokkaidō Aborigine Protection Act (Yamakawa 1989:172–182; Ainu Association of Hokkaido 1993) succeeded in 1997.

The insurgence of Ainu ethnic identity articulates anger against historical injustices and amnesia (Chikappu 1991:17–19). As Kayano Shigeru (1994:59–60)—a noted Ainu carver, lexicographer, and politician—writes in his memoir, "We are not 'former aborigines.' We were a nation who lived in Hokkaidō, on the national land called Ainu Mosir, which means 'a peaceful land for humans.' 'Japanese people' who belonged to the 'nation of Japan' invaded our national land. Beyond doubt, Ainu Mosir was a territory indigenous to the Ainu." Meanwhile, its sovereignty over Hokkaidō secure, the Japanese state engages in efforts to claim the Northern Territories—the islands that belong to the indigenous population (Wada 1990:chap. 3).

From Ryūkyū to Okinawa

Although most Japanese regard the Ainu as a distinct ethnic group, many Japanese consider Okinawans as essentially Japanese. It is easy for Japanese to accept the ethnic distinctiveness of the Ainu because of their putatively distinct physical appearances. As Anton Chekhov (1967:198) noted, "the bearded Ainu closely resemble Russian peasants." Swathed in their traditional costume and makeup, Ainu people would stand out in any Japanese town. However, so would Okinawans in their traditional attire (Horiba 1990:151–152). Yet many Japanese would insist on the ethnic homogeneity between Okinawans and Japanese. Undoubtedly, there are grounds to justify this view; many linguists, for example, regard Ryūkyūan as a Japanese dialect, whereas Ainu is indisputably a distinct language (Shibatani 1990:191–196). Manifest differences can therefore be regarded as merely regional differences.

Nonetheless, the distinctiveness of Okinawan culture—its southern climate, its history as an independent kingdom and as a virtual U.S. colony, and its idiosyncratic arts and customs—leads many people, both Japanese and Okinawans, to seek to reconcile its place in mainstream Japanese culture. Nantō (southern island) ideology asserts the ethnic homogeneity between Okinawans and Japanese *(Nichiryū dōsoron)* (Christy 1993:623–627; Murai 1995:8–9). Even Iha Fuyū (Ifa Fuyiu), the father of Okinawa studies who traced his ancestry to China (Kano 1993:1), believed in the common origins of Japanese and Okinawans (Smits 1999:151–153). The folklorist Yanagita Kunio (1978) famously regarded Okinawa as the source of Japanese culture, especially the origin of rice culture. In this vein, Okamoto Tarō (1972:185–186) called for the Japanese to return to Okinawa as a repository of an authentic Japanese culture (cf. Yanagi 1985:31). In these efforts we can detect Okinawa's ambiguous place in the ideology of Japanese monoethnicity and monoculturalism. What unites them, however, is the impulse to link Okinawa to Japan and to minimize, if not obliterate, the geographical, cultural, and historical distance between them (Watanabe 1990:55–56).

The central fact, however, is that Ryūkyū was an independent kingdom until the Meiji state annexed it in the late nineteenth century. The Ainu and the Okinawans became ethnic groups in Japan because they were colonized in the nineteenth century. Although Japanese influence on early modern Ryūkyū should not be ignored, it would be misleading to squelch the distinct trajectory of Ryūkyū and its people, and to conflate it to Japanese history (Taira 1997:145–148). The Tokugawa state regarded Ryūkyū as a foreign country *(ikoku)* (Kamiya 1990:264–265), no differently than it did Korea (Toby 1984:45–52). That Okinawa seems part of Japan in the 1990s is less obvious in Okinawa than it seems in the main Japanese islands.

Ryūkyū is itself an extended archipelago, and geographic dispersion sustained considerable linguistic divergence and cultural differences among the islands (Matsumori 1995:30–31). At the same time, whether in mythology or music, Ryūkyūan culture reveals profound affinities with Southeast Asian and western Pacific cultures (Hokama 1986:4–6). Neighboring islands, such as Iriomotejima, became integrated into the Ryūkyū sphere of cultural influence over time, just as much as Ryūkyū itself became integrated into the Japanese sphere of influence (Takara 1992b:383–384). From the fourteenth to the sixteenth centuries Ryūkyū was a node in active seaborne trade that spanned East and Southeast Asia (Takara 1993:chap. 3).

Ryūkyū became an independent and unified kingdom in 1429, albeit as a tributary state of Ming-dynasty China (Takara 1993:44–46). Under King Shōshin's long rule (1477–1526), the Ryūkyū islands became centralized with a new religion. Both Chinese and Japanese influences were palpable in the language and culture of the Ryūkyū kingdom. Ryūkyū's most significant literary achievement, *Omorosaushi*, twenty-two volumes compiling Ryūkyūan songs from the twelfth to the seventeenth centuries, dates from this period, published between 1531 and 1623 (Hokama 1986:127–128).

The Tokugawa state regarded Ryūkyū as a foreign country, but there were significant cultural and political contacts between them. Satsuma *han* invaded Ryūkyū in 1609 (Kamiya 1989:253–260). As a result, the Amami islands came under Satsuma rule. The Ryūkyū kingdom became a dependent state that maintained tributary relations to both Qing and Tokugawa rulers (Takara 1993:68–74), although Ryūkyū hid its relationship to Japan from China (Kamiya 1989:281–284; Smits 1999:44–46). Because Ming or Qing China did not pursue a policy of sinification, Japanese influence became increasingly paramount in the islands (Kamiya 1989:283–284).

Okinawa became part of Japan in the late nineteenth century. The decision to incorporate Ryūkyū was one of the first steps on the road to the

Japanese empire (Gabe 1979:48–49). The initial pretext of Japanese rule was the Formosan Incident (Taiwan *jiken*), when several Ryūkyūans were killed in Taiwan in 1871. The dispute with Qing China escalated into competing claims over Ryūkyū (Gabe 1992:105–106). After Japan invaded and conquered Ryūkyū between 1872 and 1879, the islands became a province of Japan in 1879 (Ryūkyū *shobun*) (Maehira 1994:263–264). Although it threatened to develop into a major international dispute, China was in no position to contest Japan's action, and Western powers showed little interest. Hence, incapacity and indifference left Ryūkyū in the hands of Japan (Kerr 1958:384–392).

The conquest of Okinawa was also the first step toward extensive Japanese rule over Micronesia (Nan'yō). Japan acquired the unpopulated Ogasawara, or Bonin, Islands, in 1878. Although used by British and American whalers in the nineteenth century, no Western power expressed interest in controlling the small islands near Japan (Gabe and Kawabata 1994:241). The "southward advance" *(nanshin)* argument that began in the 1880s became a reality by the 1920s (Peattie 1988:2). In the aftermath of World War I, Japan became the preponderant power over Micronesian islands that had been under Spanish or German rule. In Rota in the Marianas, for example, by 1935 there were 5,000 Japanese people, as opposed to an indigenous population of 800 (Peattie 1988:167, 1992:203–204). Japanese emigrants to Nan'yō numbered 50,000 by 1935, many of whom were in fact Okinawans (Tomiyama 1995:385). Ethnic heterogeneity ensued in many of the islands. To offer one small example: both parents of the first Palauan to earn an American doctorate are half-Japanese (Wurth 1998). Yet most Japanese are ignorant of the history of Nan'yō, save for tourists who are shocked to discover Japanese influences in the tropical Pacific islands (cf. Kawamura 1994b:5–7).

The Meiji state unilaterally abdicated the sovereignty of the Ryūkyūan royalty and aristocracy (Gabe 1992:107). Whereas the Ainu were not politically organized and therefore did not engage in collective resistance in the late nineteenth century, Ryūkyū, which was a kingdom, did. Some leaders sought alliance with Qing China (Gabe and Kawabata 1994:235–237), and others refused to heed Japanese imperatives (Gabe 1979:80–85). The Meiji state dispatched the military (Gabe 1979:99–103) and appointed central local leadership (Hokama 1986:84). Organized resistance, both by the traditional elite and peasants, failed due to internal disorganization and the superior might of Japan (Gabe 1992:113–117). However, local resistance was sufficiently serious that a dual power existed in Okinawa in the late nineteenth century (Kikuyama 1992:77–79).

The Meiji state sought to integrate Okinawa into the Japanese political economy. It undertook a land survey and promoted commercial agriculture in Okinawa (Yoshimura 1981:81–84). Okinawa became a classical colonial economy in the early twentieth century. The most developed sectors were sugar (Mukai 1992) and coal (Miki 1992), while nearly three-fourths of the households were engaged in agriculture (Aniya 1977:152). Furthermore, in spite of being the poorest province in Japan, Okinawa bore the heaviest tax burdens during this period (Smits 1999:149).

Like many colonial economies, Okinawa remained poor. Limited economic opportunities in the islands led many young Okinawans to seek their fortune in the main Japanese islands and other South Sea islands, including Taiwan. Beginning in 1905, and especially after the 1920s depression, many Okinawans emigrated to foreign countries or moved to Honshū, particularly to the Kansai region, as migrant *(dekasegi)* workers (Tomiyama 1992:175–176). Up to one-sixth of the population, or 75,000 Okinawans, had emigrated abroad by the 1940s, and 50,000 became *dekasegi* workers (Aniya 1977:145; Yoshimura 1981:140). In Wakayama *ken,* perhaps 40 percent of the textile workers were Okinawans by 1941 (Tomiyama 1992:185). Okinawans in Japan occupied the secondary labor market—not unlike the Asian migrant workers of the 1980s and 1990s— and became targets of considerable prejudice. Ironically, the demand for low-wage labor in coal mining led to the rise of migrant workers from Fujian, Korea, and Taiwan in Okinawa (Miki 1992:242–244). In Ishigakijima, for example, there continues to be a significant population of Taiwanese. Like Hokkaidō, modern Okinawa experienced considerable ethnic heterogeneity.

In spite of the effort to integrate Okinawa into Japan, there was considerable discrimination against Okinawans by Yamato people, or Yamatōnchū as Okinawans still call them. As George Kerr (1958:448) wrote of the early twentieth century, "The Japanese government was winning the campaign to have Okinawans think of themselves as Japanese subjects, but in general there was little done to overcome the widespread Japanese sense of superiority toward the Okinawans as an 'out-group,' a minority of rather second-class, country cousins." In 1903, for example, an anthropological exhibit in Osaka displayed Okinawans along with Ainu, Koreans, and Taiwanese (Tomiyama 1992:171); Okinawans were explicitly regarded as aborigines *(dojin)* (Kano 1987:9).

Ethnic discrimination solidified both Okinawan and Japanese identities. Labor market and linguistic differentiation were two major factors. In particular, the large number of Okinawan *dekasegi* workers occupied a distinct labor market niche as day laborers, often residing in Okinawa *mura* (villages) in large cities (Tomiyama 1990:131–132, 166–169). Employers regarded Okinawans as lazy and unreliable, which justified their low wages, in contradistinction to the diligent and reliable Japanese (Tomiyama 1992:186–187). The identification of an Okinawan wage delineated the identity of both Japanese and Okinawan workers. As mentioned previously, some linguists regard Okinawan as a dialect of Japanese; nonetheless, linguistic difference provided a major source of prejudice and a basis for discrimination against Okinawans (Tomiyama 1992:179–181).

In time, the Yamato instituted a policy of cultural integration in Okinawa. Standard Japanese was taught at schools, traditional clothing was discouraged, long hair that characterized Ryūkyūans was ordered to be cut, and surnames had to be provided under the registry system *(koseki)* (Kano 1993:237–239). The process of Japanization *(Yamatoka)* intensified after the late 1930s (Arakawa 1995:146–147). The effort to integrate into Yamato society and the countereffort to distinguish Okinawan culture mark the modern history of Okinawa (cf. Kano 1987:26–52).

During World War II Okinawa became the only Japanese site of armed combat. The Japanese military had regarded Okinawans as unreliable, believing them lacking in martial spirit, unable to speak Japanese, and insufficiently loyal to the emperor (Ishihara 1992:253–255). In particular, the return migrants from the United States were particularly suspect (Ishihara 1992:269–270). Not surprisingly, many Okinawans in turn considered the Japanese military as an occupying army (Yoshimi 1995:145–147). The military consciously used Okinawa as the last line of defense before the anticipated American invasion of the main Japanese islands (Ishihara 1992:263–265). The Battle of Okinawa resulted in one-fourth of all Okinawans dying (Takara 1992a:13; cf. Fujiwara 1987:11). The scar remains a potent reminder of the difference between Okinawa and Japan.

After Japan's defeat, Okinawa became the Ryukyu Islands under U.S. rule. The United States regarded Okinawans as an ethnic minority (Satō 1985:246). Okinawa's strategic significance mandated that it become an American military outpost, playing an important role during the Vietnam War (Makino 1992:319–321). In the process, Okinawa itself became highly militarized. By 1954, 12 percent of all the land, or 20 percent of the arable land, belonged to the U.S. military (Yoshimura 1981:212). Although Okinawa constituted only 6 percent of the total Japanese landmass, 75 percent of American military bases were located there in the 1980s (Fujiwara 1987:12).

The economy became U.S.-dominated as well. American aid at its height in 1953 accounted for 30 percent of the Okinawan government budget, and fluctuated between 9 and 15 percent throughout the 1960s (Matsuda 1981:334). Military revenues exceeded all others during most years of the occupation (Yoshimura 1981:223). Interestingly, the U.S.-led economy contributed to Japanese economic recovery. As late as the 1950s, the positive Japanese balance of trade with Okinawa accounted for nearly 30 percent of Japanese foreign exchange reserves (Makino 1992:355–356).

U.S. occupation had significant ethnic consequences. Intermarriages between American GIs and Okinawan women occurred. Their children, often referred to as *hāfu* ("half," signifying half-Japanese and half-American ancestry), numbered about 4,000 by the 1980s (Murphy-Shigematsu 1994:53; Honda 1982). Many of them were bereft of nationality (Ōshiro 1985:176) and stigmatized because some of their mothers were prostitutes (Ikemiyagushiku 1996:98).

U.S. occupation also generated considerable anti-American sentiments (Arasaki 1995:225–229), which contributed in turn to pro-Japanese sentiments. Inspired at first by the land appropriated for military bases (Matsuda 1981:167–171), the local resistance expanded to excoriate American soldiers' behavior as well as the war in Vietnam (Yoshiwara 1973:261–262). Many activists attempted to hasten the end of U.S. rule by strengthening Okinawan allegiance to Japan (Arasaki 1995:225–229). Concomitantly, there was a widespread denial of Okinawa's colonial subjugation by Japan or its historic ties to China (Ōshiro 1993:24). Thus, "reversion" to Japan, rather than independence, became the rallying cry of Okinawan activists.

In 1972 Okinawa once again became a Japanese territory (Havens 1987:136–141). The 1970 Nixon Doctrine had set in motion the retrenchment of the U.S. presence in Asia (Matsuda 1981:819–822). The waning military significance of Okinawa and the increasing importance of the Japanese alliance led to America's decision to turn over Okinawa to Japan. In Japan the irrendentist claim—the return of Okinawa and the Northern Territories—had become a charged symbolic issue (Iwanaga 1985:158–167). In any case, Okinawans were not consulted in the U.S.-Japanese negotiations on their fate (Ōta 1972:447–448).

Okinawans have gradually asserted Okinawan autonomy and difference. Until the 1970s assimilation and the assumption of inferiority dominated Okinawan sentiments regarding Japan (Ōta 1976:369–407). At the same time, even casual visitors notice the distinct quality of social interaction in Okinawa compared to Tokyo (Feifer 1993:23–24). In the 1990s a dual consciousness was palpable (Arakawa 1995:162). The three-time governor of Okinawa, Nishime Junji, said, "although *vis-à-vis* Americans, Okinawans insisted that they were Japanese, they felt that in Japanese society they were a different kind of people" (Taira 1997:165). Certainly, Uchinānchu (as Okinawans call themselves) and Yamatōnchū remain salient categories of distinction (Takara 1987:366–367; Ōkida 1996:32). In fact, voices for cultural and even political independence are ascendant. Some Okinawans assert Okinawan cultural difference from Japan—such as the idea of Okinesia (Miki 1988:37–39)—and critically write of "brainwashing" by the dominant Japanese culture (Kamiesu 1996:3–4). Others call for political independence (Taira 1997:164–169). Ōyama Chōjō (1997:172), the former mayor of Koza, decries Okinawa's "enslavement to Japan": "Now we Okinawans should separate from Japan, and hold hands with other southern islanders and Asians" (Ōyama 1997:200). Furthermore, he regards the Ainu as their brothers: "the deep commonality between Okinawans and Ainu is that they both lost independence to Yamato people and have been discriminated against by them" (Ōyama 1997:184).

Colonialism, Capitalism, and Migration

The traditional Japanese worldview was Sinocentric, but the Meiji leaders emulated Western imperial powers. After consolidating territorial claims over Hokkaidō and Okinawa, Japan continued on its expansionist course, which culminated in catastrophic defeat a half-century later. However, its three victories—the Sino-Japanese War, the Russo-Japanese War, and World War I—resulted in a large empire that encompassed Taiwan, Korea, Sakhalin, Nan'yō (South Sea islands), Southeast Asia, and a de facto control of Manchuria. The colonial population was as numerous as the Japanese Japanese, and the colonized area was four times the size of present-day Japan (Asada 1994:2–3).

Internal conflicts and contingencies marked the Japanese path to empire-building (Iriye 1989:734–746). Although there was no master plan, a master ideology emerged: the Greater East Asia Co-Prosperity Sphere, which promised Asian unity and liberation from Western colonial rule. The new regional order would have Japan as the oldest sibling, its older and closer colonials—the Koreans and Taiwanese—as younger siblings, and all other Asians as the youngest family members (Kurasawa 1992:147–148). Although many colonized people resisted the ideology, it had a profound impact on Japanese self-perception.

The Japanese empire was, like all empires, multiethnic. Conquest and capitalist industrialization, ever in search of low-wage labor, set into motion a massive movement of peoples, rendering virtually all areas increasingly multiethnic, as we have already seen for Hokkaidō and Okinawa. Imperial expansion was accompanied by the influx of colonized people into the Japanese archipelago. The expansion of the Japanese empire, in conjunction with capitalist industrialization, transformed even the populations of the main Japanese islands.

Taiwan, Manchukuo, and the Chinese Minority in Japan

Soon after Japan had colonized Ezochi, Japan became involved in the 1874 Formosa Expedition that resulted in Japanese claims over Ryūkyū. It was also the beginning of Japan's extended foray into China.

Taiwan became a Japanese colony after the Sino-Japanese War. The war itself had originated from the Sino-Japanese rivalry over Korea, and its proximate cause was Japanese intervention in Korea during the 1894 Kabo peasant war (Fujimura 1973:43–52). The conquest of Taiwan was a protracted process (Kiyasu 1979:chap. 2). Although the initial takeover lasted less than a year, it claimed over 17,000 Chinese lives in Taiwan (Ōe 1992b:7). Thereafter, a guerilla war raged until 1915 that claimed at least 12,000 lives (Ōe 1992b:8). Various minorities in Taiwan, who live principally in the central mountain areas, took twenty years to pacify (Kondō 1992:35–36). The aborigines (Banjin, or barbarians as the Japanese called them) had their last major uprising—the Musha Incident—in 1930 (Kondō 1992:52–54). In spite of widespread claims of harmony, anti-Japanese sentiments in Taiwan remained a powerful undercurrent during and after Japanese occupation (Wakabayashi 1983:chap. 2).

Japan transformed Taiwan into a classical colonial economy. Rice cultivation and sugar production became the two primary industries (Kazama 1994:119–123). The colonizers seized land and forced aborigenes, who had been engaged in slash-and-burn agriculture or hunting, to relocate and become rice cultivators (Kondō 1992:48–49). Yanaihara Tadao (1988:198–200), in a study originally published in 1929, famously compared colonial Taiwan to Ireland, and stressed the growth of class differentiation and nationalist sentiments. Like other areas of Japanese expansion, Taiwan became ethnically heterogeneous. Seeking opportunities in the colony, 280,000 Japanese had moved to Taiwan by 1936 (Kō 1972:5), and an estimated 30,000 Okinawans had moved to Taiwan by the end of World War II (Matayoshi 1992:4).

Manchuria, as part of the Japanese expansion in China, came under the Japanese sphere of influence after the Russo-Japanese War. The year following the 1931 Manchurian Incident, Manchukuo was formed as a Japanese puppet state, with Pu Yi of *The Last Emperor* fame as its titular leader (Yamamuro 1993:6–8). As in other Japanese colonies, Japanization efforts ensued as well as resistance to Japanese colonialism (Shi 1993:chap. 2).

The Japanese leaders envisioned Manchukuo as an ethnic melting pot. The ideology of *gozoku kyōwa* (the cooperation of five ethnic groups) projected an extended family of Han Chinese, Manchurians, Mongolians, Japanese, and Koreans living together harmoniously in Manchuria (Yamamuro 1993:130–132). Although the Chinese, estimated at 30 million, were by far the largest group, 800,000 Koreans streamed into Manchuria in large part because of dislocations caused by Japanese colonial policy (Yamamuro 1993:37).

Manchukuo was also the most important frontier for land-hungry Japanese farmers. The Japanese rural exodus had resulted in farmers emigrating not only to Hokkaidō but also to the Americas. Beginning in 1932 the Japanese state also promoted Japanese emigration to the colonies, especially to Manchuria and Korea *(Man-Chō imin shūchūron)* (Duus 1995:297). This state-sponsored migration to Northeast Asia intensified after 1936 (Asada 1993:82–88). By 1945 there were approximately 230,000 Japanese emigrants in Manchukuo (Asada 1993:77; cf. Young 1998:395). Facing a multiethnic population, emigrants from Japan solidified their identity as Japanese (Araragi 1994:290–293). Despite their role as colonial settlers (Young 1998:409–410), they are regarded in Japan as tragic victims because up to a third of them died before they could be repatriated to Japan (Gotō 1992:172–173).

The colonization of Taiwan, Manchukuo, and other parts of Asia led to the inflow of people from these areas into the Japanese archipelago. Needless to say, Chinese immigrants comprised diverse linguistic and social groups. As early as 1875 there were 2,500 Chinese mainlanders in Japan as workers and traders (Vasishth 1997:118). Hailing principally from Guangdong and Fujian, most Chinese lived in one of the major port cities, such as Nagasaki, Kōbe, and Yokohama.

Immigrants from Taiwan, Manchuria, and other Chinese cultural areas never rivaled the numbers of those from the Korean peninsula. The major reason was the 1899 Meiji state directive, which limited the number of Chinese workers in Japan. Citing among other factors the protection of Japanese workers, the directive curtailed the influx of Taiwanese, Manchurian, and Chinese into Japan (Yamawaki 1994:173–174). However, the wartime labor shortage in the early 1940s led roughly 40,000 immigrants each from China and Taiwan to emigrate to Japan (Nagano 1994:59). By the early 1940s there were about 7,000 students and 150,000 workers from Taiwan, China, and Manchukuo in Japan (Vasishth 1997:125). After 1945 the vast majority of Chinese left Japan, leaving only an estimated 30,000 by 1949 (Nagano 1994:209).

The low estimate of the ethnic Chinese population in Japan in the 1990s is 70,000, but this figure does not include many who have become naturalized Japanese citizens and their descendants. In addition, there has been a significant influx of Chinese mainlanders since the 1980s (Vasishth 1997:134), which depends on networks between Chinese and Taiwanese in Japan as well as in Taiwan and China (Sugawara 1979:99–104). Most of them live in Chinatowns, especially in Kōbe and Yokohama, and in major cities, especially Tokyo. In contrast to the prevailing negative stereotypes, these immigrants have considerable diversity in terms of educational and occupational attainment and regional origins (Nagano 1994:56–59).

Korea

Late Chosŏn-dynasty Korea faced some of the same difficulties that plagued Qing China and Tokugawa Japan: peasant unrest and the Western threat. The failure of reformist efforts doomed Korea to become a colony of one of the imperialist powers. Japan's victories in the Sino-Japanese and the Russo-Japanese Wars ensured its hegemonic position over Korea. Japan turned Korea into a protectorate in 1905 and annexed it outright five years later. Thus began thirty-five years of Japanese rule over Korea (Lie 1998:179–183).

Japan's path toward empire may not have been inevitable, but its effort to become an industrial and military power entailed emulating the West, including colonial expansion. The anxiety over Western imperialism and national security ironically fueled an aggressive "Subdue Korea" argument *(Sei-Kan ron)* (Duus 1995:38–43). Furthermore, some political and business leaders sought economic opportunities in Korea, whether as a conduit to the continent for trade and natural resources or, later, for land for farmers (Duus 1995:17–18).

Japanese rule initially relied on military domination, and sought to transform Korea into a classic colonial economy. Rice cultivation was encouraged (Kazama 1994:116–119). Over time, however, Japan promoted industrialization and used Korea as the base of expansion into China. Korea, as the most developed and nationally integrated of all Japanese colonies, proved resistant. Even before Japanese annexation, the *Wibyŏng* (righteous soldiers) contested the Japanese presence in Korea (Unno 1995:185–196). A nascent push for independence culminating in the March First Movement in 1919—inspired and led in part by expatriate Korean students in Japan (Mitchell 1967:19–22)—marked the limitations of authoritarianism and ushered in a period of cultural rule *(bunka seiji)*. A massive police and military presence, however, continued to underscore Japan's assimilationist policy (Kasuya 1992:130–132).

From the 1920s the principal Japanese strategy was to assimilate Koreans. In effect, Koreans were placed on the same path as the Ainu and Okinawans had been several decades before. The Oriental Development Company achieved in a more organized manner what the pioneers had done in Hokkaidō. Similar to the imposition of standard Japanese on the Ainu and Okinawan people, the use of the Korean language was banned. Education sought to instill the Japanese imperialist worldview. In general, the Japanese policy toward Korea sought to extirpate Korean culture and to transform Koreans into the "emperor's people" *(kōminka)*.

Especially after the mid-1930s, Japan instituted a policy of complete Japanization. The Korean school curriculum became the same as that of the Japanese in 1938, while Koreans were forced to adopt Japanese names in 1940 (Miyata 1994:161–163). Over time, Japanese leaders asserted the harmony *(Naisen yūwa)* and unity *(Naisen ittai)* of Japan and Korea (Miyata 1985:148–150; Nishinarita 1997:176–196). The policy of assimilation reached its ideological height in the idea of Japanese and Koreans sharing the same ancestry *(Nissen dōsoron)* (Fujino 1994:162–165). Koreans—as despised as they were by many Japanese—were touted as the "emperor's baby" *(tennō no sekishi)* and regarded as imperial subjects *(kōkoku shinmin)* (Miyata 1994:152–158).

Colonial rule also introduced Japanese settlers into Korea. Although there were fewer than 1,000 Japanese in Korea in 1880, the population grew rapidly: 172,000 in 1900 and 348,000 in 1920 (Duus 1995:290). Like the Japanese settlers in Manchuria, most of them were poor farmers from peripheral areas (Kimura 1989:13–14).

A more profound movement of people occurred in the other direction. Many Koreans, leaving the impoverished rural areas in search of better opportunities, as well as responding to the insistent Japanese demand for cheap labor, sought employment in Japanese mines and factories. Most of them hailed from the southern part of Korea and were farmers or laborers (Nishinarita 1997:43–46). After the abolition of entry restriction in 1922, the number of Koreans in the main Japanese islands increased rapidly (Weiner 1989:78). In spite of the limitations placed on the Korean labor influx between 1925 and 1939, their numbers rose fivefold (Totsuka 1976:96–98). For example, 60 percent of the coal miners in Hokkaidō and 10 percent of all workers in Osaka were Korean by the early 1940s (Totsuka 1977:190–191).

If a low estimate of Korean culture had been a pretext for colonizing Korea, then actual colonization confirmed it. In the prewar period, most Japanese regarded Koreans as racially inferior. In Japanese travel accounts of Korea in the early twentieth century, "laziness ranked with backwardness, poverty, and filth among the most salient characteristic of Korean life" (Duus 1995:404). The nadir of Korean Japanese history occurred in the aftermath of the 1923 Kantō earthquake. The rumor that Koreans were poisoning the water supply unleashed a massive pogrom, leading to thousands of deaths not only of Koreans but also of Okinawans and Chinese (Kang 1975:159–160).

As the Japanese war effort intensified in the 1930s, the state recruited Korean workers, at times forcefully (Mitchell 1967:84–86). From 810,000 to 940,000 Koreans were conscripted to work in mining, construction, and other manual labor in the Japanese archipelago between 1939 and 1945 (Unno 1993:122), soon dominating these fields while Japanese men were increasingly dispatched to war fronts (Weiner 1994:197). Within the Korean peninsula, some 3.2 million Koreans were relocated (Unno 1993:122). In this regard, the organization of the notorious "comfort divisions" or *teishintai (chŏngsindae* in Korean) was initially designed not to produce sexual serfs for Japanese soldiers, but rather to force Korean women workers into ammunition, textiles, and other factories (Lie 1995). By 1944 the Korean population in the Japanese archipelago reached its height of 2.4 million people. Pak Kyŏng-sik (1995:301) estimates that between 1 and 1.5 million of them were forcefully relocated.

Korean migrant workers, being predominantly poor farmers, were largely illiterate and ill-prepared for urban employment. Neither Japanese-speaking nor skilled, most of them took on demanding manual work (Weiner 1989:65–69, 1994:91), occupying along with Burakumin and Okinawans the lowest tier in the urban labor market. Because of poverty and discrimination, Koreans became concentrated in their own ethnic ghettoes (Weiner 1994:140–144), often in proximity to Burakumin and Okinawan neighborhoods (Iwamura 1972:226–229).

Korean immigrant workers were far from passive victims. They engaged in collective action to improve their working conditions, occasionally even in solidarity with ethnic Japanese workers (Smith 1995:110–115). In addition, a sizable minority were involved in independence and communist agitations in the Japanese archipelago (Mun 1995:175), which is one of the reasons that Korean immigrants were frequently targeted for intensive surveillance (Mitchell 1983:193–195). Koreans in Japan constituted "a highly vocal, emotional and cohesive group" (Wagner 1951:1–2).

The proximate origin of the Korean minority in postwar Japanese society is therefore due to the labor demands of prewar Japan. Although two-thirds of the Koreans in Japan returned to the Korean peninsula after 1945, the repatriation effort was snagged by international politics, political confusion in Korea, and the decision of Korean Japanese to eke out a living in postwar Japan (Wagner 1951:43). In the immediate postwar years many Koreans, along with Burakumin, sought survival and fortune in the black market (Nishinarita 1997:331–334). Anti-Korean hysteria in 1946 was due in part to the perceived evils of Korean black marketeers (Mitchell 1967:109–111). Most significantly, the destructive Korean War and the rapidly improving Japanese economy persuaded many Koreans to stake their immediate futures in Japan. The continuing poverty of the two Koreas in the 1960s, in contrast to the rapid growth in Japan, provided enough time for second generations, many of whom grew up without an adequate command of Korean, to settle in Japan.

Until 1965, when the Japan-South Korea Peace Treaty was concluded, the status of Koreans in Japan was ambiguous and under constant siege.

Although Koreans were considered Japanese nationals under colonial rule, they were stripped of their citizenship after the end of World War II (Yun 1994:28–31). The 1950 nationality law decreed patrilineality as the fundamental basis of Japanese citizenship; the 1952 law decreed governmental registration and surveillance of foreigners (Nishinarita 1997:347–348). By the conclusion of the 1965 peace treaty, South Korean citizenship was imposed on most ethnic Koreans in Japan (Kim 1987:143–150).

Both the Japanese government and leading Korean organizations regarded Koreans in Japan as foreigners or sojourners. The postwar Japanese government, in contrast to its prewar counterpart, assiduously sought to differentiate Japanese from Koreans. It constantly interfered in Korean ethnic education and sought to suppress Korean ethnic organizations (O 1992:54–57). The ethnic Koreans in Japan identified themselves as Koreans and regarded their residence in Japan as temporary. Their sojourner status and their conflicting allegiance to the two Koreas—represented by the North Korea-affiliated Sōren (Chongryun) and the South Korea-allied Mindan (Ryang 1997:3–5)—have stunted their identification as Korean Japanese. Although most Koreans in Japan hail from southern Korea, many of them have identified themselves ideologically with North Korea. They lean, like the Burakumin, to the left, and have participated in labor unions as well as the Communist Party (Mitchell 1967:115–118).

In the postwar period, the Korean Japanese faced all manner of discrimination. Because of their status as foreigners, many are ineligible for governmental and corporate jobs. Indeed, the vast majority have had to seek self-employment in such arenas as petty manufacturing, recycling, restaurants, and pachinko parlors, or secondary or informal sector jobs in construction, cleaning, and so on (Kang and Kim 1989:130–133). Many Japanese in turn have regarded Korean Japanese with considerable prejudice not only because of the colonial legacy but also because of their impoverished state. Surveys from the 1950s consistently showed Koreans to be the most disliked national group in Japan (Mitchell 1967:131–133). Hence, Richard Mitchell (1967:158) concluded his mid-1960s study on a pessimistic note: "The traditional Japanese dislike for Koreans remains strong, and may even have increased."

Nonetheless, there are indisputable signs of improvement, stemming in part from a series of legal and political struggles by Korean Japanese, including the 1974 Hitachi employment discrimination lawsuit and the 1980s effort to amend the foreign registration law (the anti-fingerprinting

movement). Generational shifts—from first-generation Koreans to sec-
ond- and third-generation Koreans in Japan or Korean Japanese—underlie
the politics of ethnic recognition and inclusion. By the mid-1970s over
three-fourths of Korean Japanese were Japanese-born and Japanese-edu-
cated (Kang and Kim 1989:143–154), and by 1985 an estimated 70 percent
of marriages by Korean Japanese were to ethnic Japanese (Kang and Kim
1989:156). Korean Japanese names can be found in prestigious professions:
to cite one example, the Bill Gates of Japan is a Korean Japanese, Son
Masayoshi.

Some Ethnic Consequences of Colonialism and Migration

The Japanese territorial conquest and the subsequent transnational movement of people led to ethnic heterogeneity not only in the conquered territories but also in the Japanese archipelago as well. Non-Japanese Japanese
occupied the secondary and informal labor markets and lived in segregated areas, which heightened ethnic identification and differentiation.
Japanese wages and workers became relationally defined against inferior,
non-Japanese wages and workers. Japanese ethnonational identity became
crystallized via encounters with the colonized others. Colonial expansion
in turn heightened not only Japanese national identity but forged local
identities, which were articulated as anticolonial, nationalist movements.

Simultaneously, Japanese colonialism accentuated, if not generated, the
Japanese sense of superiority over the colonized population. Following
Fukuzawa Yukichi's tripartite division of countries into civilized, semi-
civilized, and savage, the Japanese colonial worldview envisioned ethnic
Japanese as more advanced than Koreans and Chinese, who were in turn
superior to Southeast Asians and Pacific islanders. Ethnoracial hierarchy,
in other words, closely resembled colonial hierarchy (Yamada Shūji
1994:69–70).

The relatively privileged positions of Korean and Chinese colonials did
not prevent the expression of racist sentiments against them. Japanese encounters with China, both within and without Japan, enhanced not only
Japanese national identity but also Japanese people's sense of superiority
over the colonized Chinese people. Anti-Chinese sentiments became part
of the Japanese racist repertory. By the 1870s there was a well-developed
anti-Chinese discourse among Japanese (Vasishht 1997:172) that escalated
during the Sino-Japanese War. Chinese—disparagingly called *Chankoro*—

were widely considered dirty, lazy, and poor. For the Japanese government, Koreans constituted the dangerous class, often categorized with Burakumin and socialists (Yamazaki 1982:221–235). Some Japanese recalled that the worst thing about Japan's defeat in World War II was not losing to the United States but to be insulted by Korean and Chinese colonials (Yamada Shōji 1994:173–174). Certainly, Japanese military victories and the ensuing colonization process heightened racist sentiments (Yamada Shūji 1994:69–70). In particular, Koreans—being the most numerous and the most visible colonials—frequently became the target of ferocious racial discrimination (Smith and Wiswell 1982:21). However, it was not necessarily the case that Koreans were regarded as worse than the Ainu or Okinawans, or the Burakumin or Taiwanese.

In this chapter I have traced the making of multiethnic Japan. The destruction of Tokugawa status hierarchies created a distinct minority group: the former outcastes became Burakumin. The Meiji state annexed Ezochi and Ryūkyū and thereby transformed the Ainu and Okinawans into minority groups. Japan's Asian conquest resulted in the influx of Taiwanese, Koreans, and other colonized peoples, some of whom settled in Japan after the war. The making of modern Japan was simultaneously the making of multiethnic Japan.

The loss of Japan's colonial empire and the repatriation of many colonials reduced ethnic heterogeneity in the Japanese archipelago after 1945. As I discussed in Chapter 1, until the new foreign workers became a significant presence in the late 1980s, Japan was widely presumed to be monoethnic. As we saw in the previous chapter, however, it would be highly misleading to consider postwar Japan ethnically homogeneous. If I am right, then the question is not whether Japan was or is multiethnic but, rather, why anyone should believe that Japan has been and remains monoethnic.

5

Genealogies of Japanese Identity and Monoethnic Ideology

Imagine France: the tricolor flag, the republican ideal, and the French language evoke a long-unified country with a single national symbol, ideal, and tongue. The historian Crane Brinton (1948:50) expresses this image of *la France éternelle:* "France has been . . . so nearly the complete nation-state, so nearly unified in culture and habits." Consider, however, Douglas Johnson's (1993:52) description:

> Even in 1863, according to official figures, about a quarter of the country's population spoke no French, and there is every reason to believe that this is an underestimate. The persistence of languages other than French, and of many patois and dialects of the French provinces, lasted well into the twentieth century. There is ample evidence to suggest that substantial parts of the population did not feel that they belonged to a French nation, just as they were ignorant of the vital facts of French history, such as the significance of 1789 or of 1870 and just as there were many communes which did not possess a tricolour flag.

The national integration of France in the late nineteenth century resulted from the expansion of state infrastructures: mass schooling, universal male military service, and nationwide transportation and communication networks, as well as the concomitant circulation of people, commodities, and culture at the national level. As Eugen Weber (1976:218) emphasized: "There could be no national unity before there was national circulation." Local identity, however, continued to take precedence over national identity in many parts of France (e.g., Ford 1993).

Given the belated—and in many ways incomplete—national integration

111

in nineteenth-century France, the Breton-French Ernest Renan's (1990:20) hazy conceptualization of the nation in his celebrated 1882 lecture seems sensible: "Man is a slave neither of his race nor of his language, nor of his religion, nor of the course of rivers nor of the direction taken by mountain chains. A large aggregate of men, healthy in spirit and warm of heart, creates the kind of moral conscience which we call a nation." In Renan's view, a shared memory and ideal—in the realm of the mind and the imagination—bring people together as a nation, not a shared geographical or biological endowment or language or culture. In short, a nation is a political and historical construct.

Nationalism provides a powerful prism that shapes not only the present but the past as well. Nationalist historiography delineates a heroic and singular lineage of a nation from the misty past to the present. Sanctioned national history is teleological; the triumphant progress to the present is projected back into the past. Narratives of origins are hardly innocent, however. In pursuing contemporary questions and using current categories, the paucity of reliable documentation becomes a spur to fanciful speculations. These mythohistories are no different from their counterparts in oral, nonindustrial societies where the belief in a common origin underscores tribal unity. The current nation-state is projected onto the past and elides a myriad of differences, whether of languages, such as Provençal or patois, or of regional identities, such as Breton or Basque. Indeed, nationalist accounts often lament the multiethnic and multicultural present by wishfully reconstructing a nonexistent past that was pristine and pure.

In the previous two chapters I explored the multiethnic constitution of modern Japan. Here I trace the origins of Japanese national identity and monoethnic ideology. In spite of proto-national discourse in the Tokugawa period, regional differences and status hierarchies stunted the development of a popular national identity. By the time Japanese national identity became well entrenched in the larger population, however, there were ethnic and foreign populations in Japan, as we saw in the previous chapter. Modern Japan was characterized by (multiethnic) imperialism, not (monoethnic) nationalism. We can speak neither of a Japanese national identity before the making of modern Japan nor of modern Japan without ethnic diversity. The belief in Japanese ethnic homogeneity became dominant in the postwar decades.

National Integration and National Identity

According to the contemporary discourse of Japaneseness, Japan has achieved the condition of "one nation, one people." This claim is a species of nationalism. A core idea of nationalism, especially among late developing countries, is the equivalence of a political entity with one nation, ethnicity, or people (Plessner 1959). As Ernest Gellner (1983:1) writes, "nationalism is a theory of political legitimacy, which requires that ethnic boundaries should not cut across political ones, and, in particular, that ethnic boundaries within a given state . . . should not separate the power-holders from the rest." Nationalists idealize the congruence of the state with the nation and, moreover, with its people, not just the ruling class. In this sense, nationalism—and its corresponding ideal of the nation-state—is a modern idea (Hobsbawm 1990; Calhoun 1997). Nationalist ideology and identity become powerful forces in modern nation-states. Not only must the state protect its political boundaries against foreign challenges, but it must also seek internal pacification and popular legitimation. In the dual challenge of the modern nation-state, nationalism promotes social solidarity and thereby often contributes to national development.

Whether as empires or city-states, there is nary a case of a one-to-one correspondence between a people and a premodern state. Premodern states lacked the infrastructural capacity to instill a uniform identity over a large territory. As the French example suggests, popular national identity had to await nationwide systems of schooling, transportation, communication, and so on. Xenophobic sentiments may have been common, but the ideology of "one nation, one state" did not exist in the premodern era. In many premodern societies status was the guiding principle of social organization. In these societies slaves, lower castes, or peasants were considered to be distinct from their rulers; they were, literally, different races of people. The reality of vertical hierarchy shunned a formally egalitarian and inclusionary political identity.

Because the modern state and nationalism assert some form of equality among citizens, status hierarchy no longer becomes the fundamental division. Although aristocrats and peasants may have been different races earlier, they become part and parcel of a new national entity. It is only against the background of modern state-making and its assertion of an inclusive identity that ethnicity arises as a salient category. Whether because of resistance to national incorporation or migration, new boundary lines are drawn and categories of people become crystallized on either side of them. Neither nationalism nor ethnic identity is autonomous; they are mutually constituted and constructed.

By arguing for the modernity of nationalism and ethnicity, I am not denying either the antiquity of some ethnonational identities or the premodern existence of proto-national or proto-ethnic identities. For villagers to consider themselves French or Japanese requires two historic achievements, however: the development of national integration and the decline of vertical, status-based, hierarchy. Only then can we speak, in the modern sense, of being French or Japanese.

The Disunity of Premodern Japan

When did Japanese national identity emerge? Imperial historiography *(kōkoku shikan)*, which assumed an equivalence of nation, ethnicity, state, and the imperial household since the accession of Emperor Jinmu in 660 B.C., provided an influential answer, which continues to affect even progressive historians (Brown 1993:1). The Japanese Ministry of Education did not approve Ienaga Saburō's Japanese history textbook because of its negative description of prewar militarism, but his one-volume cultural history limns a "unified tradition": "the Japanese national body [*kokutai*] has preserved . . . its character from the Yayoi period [c.300 BCE–c.300]" (Ienaga 1982:5, 21). The quest for Japanese origins is presumably focused on tracing at least some family resemblance to contemporary Japanese people.

Contemporary urban Japanese, however, have more in common with their urban French or American counterparts than with their ancestors in the third century. When a Japanese scholar visited me in the U.S. Midwest, he was struck by people who sported tattoos and a colleague who walked about barefoot. Finding Americanness everywhere, he also declared at a party that "Japanese people don't eat fresh vegetables." According to the earliest extant description of proto-Japanese people in a third-century Chinese-language tract, however, they had body tattoos, walked barefoot, and ate fresh vegetables (Ishihara 1985:79–80). Ancestors of people living in the Japanese archipelago today came from all the neighboring landmasses (Hanihara 1996:199–209). If we include present-day Hokkaidō and Okinawa as part of Japan, then the mix becomes all the more heterogeneous (Pearson 1996:102–107). The influx of different peoples into the Japanese archipelago, such as present-day Koreans, Chinese, Manchus, Mongolians, and others in early Japanese history renders nonsensical any claim about the pure descent of homogeneous Japanese people. As the earliest extant Japanese texts, *Kojiki* and *Nihon shoki*, attest, there were numerous types of countries or people—Emishi, Ezo, Ebisu, Kumaso, Hayato, and so on—represented in Honshū and Kyūshū.

The earliest mention of Japan (*Nihon*, or at least the two Chinese characters that are read as such today) occurs in the seventh century (Nishijima 1994:201–203), when the *ritsuryō* (legal code) state emerged. Hence, many scholars point to the seventh century, with the rise of the first ethnic Japanese state, as the beginning of Japan (Kitō 1975:115–119; Yasumoto 1991:23). However, it was geographically circumscribed to the Kinai region and regarded people of the present-day Kantō or Tōhoku region as foreign (Amino 1991:202). Furthermore, its earliest history—the introduction of steel production and new agricultural tools, and the dissemination of new political and religious ideas—cannot be told apart from the arrival of immigrants from the Korean peninsula (*toraijin*) (Hirano 1993:307). Indeed, Sawada Yōtarō (1995:2), among others, argues that the Japanese imperial household hailed from the Korean peninsula.

It is possible to seek manifestations of proto-Japanese national identity in the distant past. Certainly, even the ruling elite of the seventh-century state were undoubtedly conscious of being different from their counterparts on the Asian continent. The aristocratic culture of the Heian or Kamakura periods offers glimpses of proto-Japan (Yoneda 1984:241–245), as does the Japan of the Muromachi period (Hayashiya 1953:1–24). Nationalist historiography has attempted to narrate a gradual and uninterrupted growth of Japan, and hence people versed in it recognize elements of the narrative in Jōmon-period pottery, the *ritsuryō* state, Heian-period literature, or the people of Kyoto during the middle ages. Only hindsight, however, allows us to recognize elements of proto-Japan and, in doing so, neglect discontinuities and differences, and systematically distort our understanding of these periods. The trivial truism that the past led to the present obscures the great gulf between the two.

Consider in this regard the disunity of the Japanese archipelago in the fifteenth century. Although warring *daimyō* (lords) used the modern term for the nation-state (*kokka*), it referred to their local domain (Katsumata 1994:28–33; cf. Kamada 1988:27–28). As I argued in the previous chapter,

Ezochi (northern Honshū and Hokkaidō) and the Ryūkyū kingdom were not under central control. The Andō clan in Tōhoku claimed political independence as Hinomoto, going so far as to send an emissary to China (Namikawa 1992:6–9). The Pan-China Sea area functioned as an autonomous area that brought traders from all over East and Southeast Asia together (Murai 1987:112–113). A distinct language and clothing characterized these people (Wajin or Wakō), who claimed autonomy both from the Muromachi government *(bakufu)* and Chosŏn-dynasty Korea (Tanaka 1997:27–33). Furthermore, cultural integration was far from complete even in Honshū. According to the historian Amino Yoshihiko (1992), the division between eastern and western Honshū was serious enough to constitute two distinct cultures.

Status distinctions, moreover, severely curtailed social solidarity. There were numerous subdivisions among the peasantry (Nagahara 1990:306–310). Status was racialized and given physical expression (Kuroda 1987:65–67). The style and color of clothes readily separated people; peasants wore yellow, whereas lepers had to be dressed in yellowish brown *(kaki-iro)* (Amino 1993:13–36). Hairstyles and hats were important markers, such that people even wore hats *(eboshi)* while asleep; to cut hair without individual consent was a capital crime (Takahashi 1984:323–324). The visual representation of different status groups overlaid these markers through the use of different skin pigmentation; the pale figure of aristocrats exists in stark contrast to the dark-hued bodies of beggars (Sakurai 1981:35–37). Some putative ancestors of the Burakumin *(hinin)* were literally nonhuman (Amino 1978:146–147). How can they be considered Japanese when they were not even regarded as human beings?

Given territorial disunity, regional differentiation, cultural fragmentation, and status hierarchy, it is safe to conclude that popular national identity was not widespread before the Tokugawa period.

Tokugawa Japan (1603–1868)

During Tokugawa rule domestic pacification, the nationwide circulation of the local elite, the spread of interregional commerce, the efflorescence of urban culture, and the restriction of foreign contact contributed to national integration (Satō 1993:212–220). Contemporary Japanese are wont to identify with Tokugawa-era urbanites, at least as they are depicted in historical novels and television shows. The Tokugawa *bakufu* made some efforts to align ethnicity with the state (Howell 1994:74). Furthermore, a proto-nationalist ideology developed in the Tokugawa period (Ooms 1985:297). In particular, *Kokugaku* (nation studies, or nativism) writers searched for Japanese essences and articulated antiforeign sentiments (Harootunian 1988:437). Motoori Norinaga, for example, expressed sentiments of Japanese superiority (Mitani 1997:20–25). In addition, *Mitogaku* (Mito studies) scholars proposed the idea of a *kokutai* (national body) (Wakabayashi 1986:51–57; Koschmann 1987:64–77), which provided ideological inspiration for prewar ultranationalists (Yasumaru 1977:11–12; Noguchi 1993a:302). As Marius Jansen (1992:86) argues, "In the Tokugawa period the Japanese first became aware of themselves as a national entity."

The extent of nationalist ideology and identity was, however, severely curtailed in the Tokugawa period. The Tokugawa *bakufu* did not rely on nationalist ideology (Matsumoto 1975:42; Watanabe 1985:23–27). Furthermore, the Tokugawa state neither made a serious effort nor had the capacity to penetrate popular consciousness. Given the absence of mass schooling and mass media, most farmers—the vast majority of the population—did not identify themselves beyond their village or domain *(han)*. National linguistic unification was far from complete (see Appendix). Regional differences persisted. Inter-*han* marriages were, for example, rare (Yun 1987:84–85). Not surprisingly, Edo travelers found the people and customs of Sado and Tsugaru "foreign" (Kikuchi 1991:81–82). There was very little sense of the larger entity of Japan, or national consciousness, outside of the literate elite (Tsukamoto 1991:176–177).

Rather than the nation, the *han* was the privileged unit of peoplehood. The Tokugawa policy of divide and conquer accentuated *han* identity (Maruyama 1996:235–237). To the extent that nationalism existed, it was principally *han* nationalism. As the first Prime Minister Itō Hirobumi observed in the late nineteenth century, "Patriotism during the feudal period was usually confined to the domain [*han*]" (Craig 1968:100). As late as the mid-nineteenth century, the vast majority of reform-minded samurai had more of *han* than national consciousness. The young samurai from Satsuma and Chōshū maintained a strong sense of *han* consciousness, even as they called for a major political reform (Inuzuka 1994:104–109). "At the end of the Tokugawa period, [the anti-*bakufu*] samurai were Ōkubo of Satsuma or Kido of Chōshū. If we look for a samurai who was free from *han*, we can only regard . . . Sakamoto Ryōma and a few others. Even Sakamoto Ryōma only began to catch an image of a unified Japan after several escapes from *han,* exile, and harassment from *han,* after which he died" (Asukai 1985:107; cf. Jansen 1961:342).

Finally, rigid status distinctions stunted the development of an inclusive identity. Tokugawa society was not only status-based; there was considerable intrastatus inequality (Minegishi 1989:chap. 2). Ogyū Sorai's (1987:51–55) early eighteenth-century tract, *Seidan* (Political Talk), is but one articulation of the ruling group's extreme abhorrence of lower status people. The very rationalization behind status hierarchy is the profound gulf separating distinct categories of people. The basis for samurai rule was honor and heredity that differentiated them completely from farmers and other social inferiors. Status-based societies are not incompatible with proto-nationalist sentiments or xenophobic expressions, but the ruling groups, whether aristocrats or samurai, believed strongly in a status hierarchy that was exclusionary (Matsumoto 1975:5). *Kokugaku* ideologues may have challenged the prevailing Sinocentric worldview, but they did not advocate an inclusionary political identity.

The premodern efflorescence of Japanese identity is an exceedingly dubious historical proposition. In effect, the argument presupposes that if one were to administer an imaginary survey, eighth- or eighteenth-century residents of the Japanese archipelago would identify themselves as Japanese. Prior to the Meiji Restoration, identities based on region and status were paramount. To return to Gellner's definition of nationalism, power-holders were separated from the rest of society in premodern Japan. If Japanese nationalism were widespread in the Tokugawa period, then we cannot make sense of the urgency of Meiji leaders to instill nationalism in the larger population (Maruyama 1974:366–367). It is emblematic that the samurai who encountered Commodore Perry's crew were antagonistic, whereas farmers and townspeople were generally friendly (Inoue 1953:213; Craig 1968:101). Although samurai and rich farmers constituted the social basis of nationalism in the late nineteenth century (Mitani 1997:345–346), Japanese nationalism and national identity remained inchoate until the Meiji Restoration.

Modern State-Making

The Meiji state integrated local authorities under central rule and promoted national identity. The state abolished status distinctions and sought to transform townspeople and peasants divided by regional and status differences into loyal national subjects. The modern Japanese state greatly accelerated national integration by developing mass education and enhancing nationwide circuits of transportation and communication. In other words, the state transformed people in Japan into Japanese nationals. The extensive encounter with the West and a series of wars also promoted national consciousness. However, because the creation of Japanese national identity was coeval with the formation of the Japanese empire, Japanese national identity did not imply monoethnicity.

In attempting to integrate the nation, the Meiji state faced significant obstacles. *Han* identity remained potent among the educated elite, and the vast majority of the population had little inkling of the larger national polity. As Fukuzawa Yukichi (1981a:183) memorably put it, "there is a government in Japan, but not a nation." He noted that Japanese are individuals without a common tie: "Several tens of millions of humanity in Japan are closed inside tens of millions of boxes" (Fukuzawa 1981a:204). Hence, the task was to create Japanese nationals who were willing to sacrifice their lives for the "country's freedom and independence" (Fukuzawa 1980:60). The situation of Meiji Japan was similar to post-Risorgimento Italy; as Massimo d'Azeglio noted after Italian unification, "We have made Italy, now we have to make Italians" (Hobsbawm 1990:44). The very term *kokumin* (nationals) was popularized by Fukuzawa (Asukai 1984:7–8), and the idea of nationalism itself was a Western import (Matsumoto 1996:130–139). The Meiji state relied less on native discourses and more on Western concepts to foment nationalism (Yasumaru 1977:32).

If the West was a threat to the Meiji leaders, then the Meiji state in turn was a "foreign" threat to the majority of the populace. Popular resistance—exemplified by the political activism of Tanaka Shōzō (Yui 1984) or Minakata Kumagusu (Kano 1986:114–124)—challenged the centralizing thrust of the Meiji state. Farmers regarded government bureaucrats as "outsiders" and "strangers," and the rumor that they were bloodsuckers proliferated (Yasumaru 1974:273–282). From this perspective, the Meiji regime colonized not only Hokkaidō and Okinawa but much of the Japanese archipelago as well.

Perhaps the most immediate spur to national identity formation was a series of encounters with the indisputable others. The effort to topple the *bakufu* under the slogan *sonnō jōi* ("Respect the Emperor, Expel the Barbarians") captured the two movements of the Meiji Restoration: regime transition and national protection. Whatever else the Meiji Restoration was, we cannot ignore the beginning of a nationalist impulse that emerged against foreign threat (Pyle 1969:19–20). The Western threat—from the Russian encroachment in the late eighteenth century to the coming of Commodore Perry—generated manifold discourses on the Japanese nation and nationalist ideals (Maruyama 1995a:60; Matsumoto 1996:11–12). Although Motoori Norinaga may have discussed the idea of Japan at length, the explicit equation of the idea of Japan with people living in Japan began with nineteenth-century thinkers, such as Yoshida Shōin, born in 1830 (Matsumoto 1975:70–71). As the fabled historian Tokutomi Sohō (1981:46) noted in his biography of Yoshida, originally published in 1894, "The idea of nationals *(kokumin)* is a relative one. Only in coming into contact with foreign countries does that idea first develop."

The shock of the new—the modern West—entailed encounters with strange people, goods, and ideas, which accentuated the sense of Japanese identity that superseded differences among the Japanese. The abstract awareness of foreign countries and people became concrete appreciation of national differences as people in Japan encountered Westerners, whether in Japan or abroad. The significance of regional identities—being a Chōshū or Satsuma person—paled in comparison to more global identities— being a Japanese or a Westerner. Mid-nineteenth-century travelers to the West, whether to observe *(shisetsudan)* or to study *(ryūgakusei),* shed their *han* consciousness in favor of a new national identity (Matsuzawa 1993:52–55; Inuzuka 1994:106–109).

The Meiji state also promoted educational and cultural integration (Ishii 1986:327–330). The national registry *(koseki)* system sought to account for (and potentially control) every citizen (Ishii 1981:10–11). The state suppressed local religious beliefs and practices and tried to instill a new quasi-religious national identity (Yasumaru 1979:177–179). It instituted a national language *(kokugo)* and a centrally controlled school system. Influenced by the Prussian and other systems of education, Inoue Kowashi and other Meiji leaders sought to instill patriotism through schooling, exemplified in the Imperial Rescript on Education (Ōtsuki and Matsumura 1970). Another major agent of nationalist socialization was the military. Universal male conscription brought people from across the archipelago into the cauldron of discipline and national identity (Kamishima 1961:170–171).

Meiji state-building and military expansion promoted the emperor ideology *(tennōsei).* Blending elements of *Kokugaku* and Western ideas, the

Meiji state projected itself as the family-state *(kazoku kokka)* (Ishida 1954:6–17), basing a national unity on the family *(ie)* and the local community *(mura)* (Kinbara 1985:304–311). The nation-state was portrayed as an organic entity, encapsulated in the idea of the *kokutai* (national body or essence) (Tsurumi S. 1982:43–44). Loyalty and patriotism came to constitute the supreme political virtues (Haga 1984:72–73).

The development of the modern state was therefore coeval with the dissemination of national identity. By the 1880s a sense of the nation was manifest among urban intellectuals, exemplified in the ideology of Japanism *(Nihonshugi)* and codified in the 1889 Constitution and the 1890 Imperial Rescript on Education (Gluck 1985:21–23; Ishida 1989:16–169). Thereafter, a series of major wars—the Sino-Japanese War, the Russo-Japanese War, World War I, and World War II—stimulated xenophobic and racist rhetoric and patriotic jingoism (Nada 1992:132). As I noted in the previous chapter, the influx of Burakumin, Okinawans, and Koreans in the urban secondary labor market enhanced the distinction between Japanese and non-Japanese identities in the early twentieth century. Certainly by the 1920s popular nationalism penetrated urban areas (Miyachi 1973:248–253; Tazaki 1985:190–197). In this regard, Taishō Democracy was very much a phenomenon associated with urban-based national consciousness (Tsutsui 1984:43–48; Matsuo 1990:286).

In spite of considerable advances, however, the extent of national integration and national identity was limited as of 1945. The majority of Japanese people were farmers who lived in villages (Fukutake 1981:32–38). Rural-urban divides and regional differences remained prominent (Miyamoto 1984a:306, 1984b:187–196). In this context many farmers in the countryside remained farmers rather than Japanese, with tepid support for imperialist expansion and warfare (Kamishima 1961:39; Katō 1995:10–15). Even for educated urbanites, the allegiance to family and friends remained more powerful than the belief in the emperor or the *kokutai* (Hirota 1980:254; Nihon Senbotsu Gakusei Kinenkai 1982:14, 150). The emperor ideology and ultranationalism were not indelibly etched on Japanese consciousness (Yasumaru 1992:262–274), which should not be surprising when even the emperor was more interested in biology than Shintō (Ishida 1956:6–7).

More significantly, national identity—precisely at the moment of its widespread diffusion—was inflected by imperialism, which projected a multiethnic vision of the Japanese nation-state. The dominant conception of Japanese national identity in the early twentieth century was multiethnic, not monoethnic.

Nationalism and Imperialism

One may very well locate the belief in monoethnic Japan in the 1899 nationality law that granted Japanese citizenship principally to offspring of Japanese fathers or in the family-state ideology (Yun 1997:98–191; Weiner 1997:8). The early twentieth-century Japanese polity has often been described as fascist or ultranationalist (Eguchi 1993:364; cf. Gordon 1991:333–339). Mass mobilization from the 1930s and ultranationalist discourses in the 1940s glorified the cult of the emperor and the national essence *(kokutai)* (Maruyama 1976:221–224; Matsumoto 1996:130–139). At its extreme, everything of worth, including the Buddha and Jesus, was said to hail from Japan (Matsuyama 1993:289–305).

The ideology of "one nation, one people" was not, however, dominant in prewar Japan. The reason is simple: Japan was an imperial power. Whatever else empires may be, they are not monoethnic. The colonization of Taiwan and Korea may have promoted Japanese ethnonational chauvinism but the empire had to justify colonial rule beyond naked power. Hence, from the annexation of Taiwan in 1896 to 1945, the fundamental impulse of imperial Japan was to assert the multiethnic origins and constitution of Japan. The imperialist multiethnic ideology did not suppress all dissenting voices, but even some of the leading exponents of the monoethnic view, such as Inoue Tetsujirō, changed his mind by the time of the Korean annexation (Oguma 1995:113–115). The empire mobilized Japanese people *(kokumin)*, but the goal was the Greater East Asia Co-Prosperity Sphere, which included Koreans and Taiwanese as integral members (Ishida 1979:98–99). After the Russo-Japanese War, Japan was a Pacific state, and imperialist multiethnicity superseded monoethnic nationalism (Shinobu 1992:14–15). Some writers even went so far as to locate the reason for Japan's victory in the Russo-Japanese War in the beneficial effects of the ethnic hybridity of Japanese people (Oguma 1995:77–79). Imperial Japan was a melting pot that sought to assimilate "incomplete Japanese" ranging from the Ainu to the Taiwanese (Morris-Suzuki 1998b:175). The policy of assimiliation and the belief in superiority were compatible.

Consider the place of Korea in the Japanese imperial imagination. The prewar colonial ideology asserted the common origins of Korean and Japanese people *(Nissen dōsoron)*. The Japanese annexation of Korea was a form of "restoration," or a "natural" process (Oguma 1995:88–90). The educational bureaucrat Shiohara Tokisaburō noted in the 1930s, "The idea is to Japanize Koreans (Senjin). . . . In a word, because Koreans are Japanese Sinified, we can peel off the Sinification and make them into Japanese as they originally were" (Isoda 1993:119). During Japanese rule all Koreans, as well as Taiwanese, were Japanese citizens *(teikoku shinmin)*, with the guarantee of legal equalities (Gotō 1992:151–153). Koreans were *tennō no sekishi* (the emperor's baby) or *kōkoku shinmin* (imperial subjects) (Miyata 1994:152–153). Rather than referring to them as Koreans, the preferred term was *hantō no hito* (people from the peninsula). The very mention of the word colony never occurred in referring to Korea. Although a distinction was made between *naichi* (inland) and *gaichi* (outland), both were integral parts of Japan (Unno 1995:230).

Nationalist Koreans resented Japanese actions, and most Japanese people deemed Koreans to be inferior, but Japanese colonial rule sought to homogenize Korea and Japan, including the promotion of interethnic marriage between Koreans and Japanese (Suzuki Y. 1992:75–87). The 1911 government document on Korean education regarded as its mission "the cultivation of loyal nationals *(kokumin)*" (Ōe 1992a:25). The institution of the same curriculum in 1938 and the enforced use of Japanese names *(sōshi kaimei)* in 1940 are part and parcel of thoroughgoing Japanization efforts (Miyata 1994:161–163). If the nationalist ideology called for a family-state, then Koreans were siblings of Japanese people (Miyata 1994:166–167). In one articulation the ethnic hierarchy reflected the colonial birth order: Okinawans as the eldest, Taiwanese as the second, and Koreans as the third (Ishida T. 1998:70).

The dominance of the multiethnic worldview can also be gleaned in prewar writings. The hybrid origins of Japanese people were taken for granted. Speculations about the Jewish, Greek, and Hittite origins of Japanese people became popular in the 1910s and 1920s (Matsuyama 1993:289–305). Writing in 1912, Nitobe Inazō (1972b:89) noted, "Thus the farther we trace our lineage, the more entangled grow the threads which as warp and woof went to weave our nationality." The Japanese are "a race so diversified in its origin" (Nitobe 1972b:91). Similarly, Matsubara Hiroshi (1936:130) observed that Japanese people are a mixed race. Needless to say, there were competing discourses of Japaneseness, as well as conflicting theories of nation and ethnicity (Doak 1994:132–133, 1998:186). Nonetheless, the idea of the ethnoracial heterogeneity of the Japanese people was widely accepted in the early twentieth century. A 1918 geography text, for example, noted that Japan is multiethnic: "The majority of nationals *(kokumin)* are Yamato people *(minzoku)*. . . . In addition, there are Koreans . . . and Chinese. And there are Ainu in Hokkaidō and Ainu and other aborigines *(dojin)* in Karafuto" (Oguma 1995:161). Similarly, a 1942 publication by the Ministry of Education remarked, "Japanese ethnicity *(minzoku)* was not established as homogeneous" (Oguma 1995:1).

The multiethnic reality of the Japanese empire clarifies some of the puzzling aspects of Japanese nationalist thought. Kita Ikki, who is ritually described as an ultranationalist and even a fascist (Matsuzawa 1979:211), believed that Koreans were a "people most close" to Japanese, who were in turn of mixed-blood origins (Okamoto 1996:193). His espousal of Esperanto, in this regard, makes sense in the light of his colonial universalism (Okamoto 1996:218–224). The multiethnic ideal found its most idealistic articulation in Manchuria. The politically correct ideology of Manchukuo was multiethnic harmony *(minzoku kyōwa)* (Yamamuro 1993:9–13). Rather than regarding this as a deviation, it should be seen as a logical correlate of the dominant prewar Japanese mindset.

It is possible to locate a European-style racist, monoethnic discourse in prewar Japan. German philosophy introduced the ideology of blood and soil (Dower 1986:265–266), but Japanese discourses on ethnonational differences never highlighted the significance of blood, race, and monoethnicity in the same way that Nazi ideology did (Abe 1975:356; Brooker 1991:210–211). This should not be surprising in a culture that has traditionally downplayed the significance of blood ties (Nakane 1977:44–47; Miyamoto 1984a:44). Mori Ōgai's classic story, "Shibue Chūsai," delineates the communal nature of a premodern household, which was not based simply on blood relations (cf. Tanigawa 1985:214–217). Japan may have been a family-state, but Koreans and others could join it. Discussions of the national essence were not about monoethnicity. As Tosaka Jun's (1977:136–140) prewar critique of Japanese ideology reveals, the Japanese spirt evoked abstract platitudes, such as "unselfish love" and "harmony."

Rather than regarding prewar Japanese nationalism as a monoethnic ideology, it is important to highlight its multiethnic character. I am not denying that nationalism, chauvinism, xenophobia, and even racism were rampant in modern Japan. Like all colonizers, many Japanese assumed that they were superior to the colonized people. My assertion is that the dominant ethnonational worldview in the first half of the twentieth century did not assert Japanese monoethnicity but rather took the multiethnic constitution of Japan for granted. As I showed in the previous chapter, this is as it should be.

The Origins of Monoethnic Ideology

The spread of Japanese national identity was coeval with the making of multiethnic Japan. When Japan was an empire, the dominant ideology was multiethnic, not monoethnic. When and why, then, did the idea of monoethnic Japan arise?

The collapse of the empire radically reduced ethnic diversity in Japan. The sudden and complete loss of the empire, and the rapid departure of many colonials from the archipelago, occurred in a country that had become significantly integrated in terms of infrastructure as well as culture. This is the fundamental social context underlying the rise and dominance of monoethnic ideology. But this is far from adequate: there were still Koreans, Chinese, and other former Japanese imperial subjects, as well as Ainu, Burakumin, and Okinawans, in the Japanese archipelago. I argue that the discourse of Japaneseness emerged as the dominant response to the question of Japanese identity in the late 1960s. The new monoethnic ideology resonated well with the new nationalism born of prosperity.

The 1955 System, or the Emergence of Contemporary Japan

The 1955 system *(1955-nen taisei)* refers to the postwar Japanese political arrangement; in 1955 conservative parties united to form the Liberal Democratic Party, which ruled Japan uninterruptedly until 1993 (Ōtake 1995). The system can be seen not only in politics and economics but in society at large. By the mid-1950s, postwar Japanese society had crystallized its institutions and practices after the flux of the immediate postwar years. What most people identify as features of Japaneseness have their proximate origins in the immediate postwar decade (Amemiya 1997:chap. 4).

Needless to say, there were continuities between the prewar and postwar decades, but it would be foolhardy to deny the fundamental ruptures. Most important, the dominant institutions of imperial Japan either disappeared or were transformed beyond recognition. A constitutional monarchy transformed into a democracy as robust as that of any other advanced industrial society (Curtis 1988:249). The dominance of ultranationalism collapsed after 1945 (Maruyama 1964:161). The emperor was no longer the sovereign deity but the human symbol of the nation. The survival of a few fanatical believers in the emperor system should not belie its thoroughgoing secularization in the postwar period (Yasumaru 1992:288–292). A militarist nation was succeeded by a profoundly pacifist one. The large landlords and large capitalists who dominated the prewar Japanese economy virtually vanished (Tsuru 1993:18–22). What had been an agrarian society became indisputably urban (Amemiya 1997:14–16). Hierarchical domination based on age, gender, and status gave away to egalitarian social interactions. Indeed, egalitarianism became a hegemonic value in postwar Japan (Nimura 1994:68–70). People professed romantic love, began to change their underwear every day, and by the early 1960s endlessly watched television (Hidaka 1960:331–334; Kawauchi 1979:135–142; Ueno 1994:177–178). The historian Irokawa Daikichi (1990:82) goes so far as to argue that "the golden 1960s" marked a breaking point from the previous few centuries of popular culture.

The fundamental social transformations in the decade after the end of World War II provided the conditions for popular nationhood. The two major impediments to national consciousness, regional diversity and status hierarchy, dissipated substantially. The sense of belonging to the Japanese nation, rather than to a particular region, became paramount. Status hierarchy and income inequality declined significantly in the postwar period (Allinson 1997:12–18). The final years of total war mobilization had contributed to an egalitarian ethos (Amemiya 1997:14–16). Japan became a culturally integrated nation by the 1960s; the claim of cultural homogeneity became plausible to ordinary Japanese people.

The postwar transformation also dissolved traditional sources of solidarity. Farming households and village communities rapidly declined in numbers and symbolic significance (Kandatsu 1991:26–47). In prewar Japan the solidity of the family (ie) and the community (mura) was taken for granted. They were the fundamental agents of socialization and sustained the universe in which the majority of Japanese people lived (Fukutake 1981:39). The family-state ideology promoted the ideals of loyalty and filial piety, and family was regarded as the foundation of morality and society (Kawashima 1950:22–23). The postwar reforms dissolved the legal foundations of the patriarchal family (Fukushima 1967:38–40). The Western ideal of the nuclear family and my home-ism (mai hōmushugi) became the postwar norm (Minami et al. 1983:193–194; Yasuda 1987:312–313), characterized by low birth rates (from 3.7 in 1950 to 2.1 in 1970) (Naka-gawa 1993:267). While the mean household size was 4.9 people in 1955, it dropped to 3.6 by 1970 (Kurihara 1982:88). Whereas life continued to center on the home, domesticity became merely one element within a modern, complex environment. For example, as late as 1950, 95 percent of Japanese people were born at home; by 1960 this figure had declined to 50 percent, and by 1980 to .5 percent (Amemiya 1997:147).

The "tsunami of modernization" pulverized the stability of time (tradition) and place (*furusato* or *kokyō*—home or ancestral village) (Irokawa 1990:159). A rapid exodus undermined rural social solidarity (Smith 1978:chap. 8). Village solidarity, characterized by harmony, cooperation, and social control, eroded (Dore 1985:350–354), thereby shattering "that feeling of unconditional connectedness" that characterized Japan in the 1930s (Singer 1973:75). The widespread popularity of songs about home in the late 1950s is a harbinger of this nationwide deracination (Mita 1978:191–194). In response, the construction of ancestral villages or homelands (*furusato zukuri*) became a popular activity (Irokawa 1990:164–168). Jennifer Robertson's (1991) study of Kodaira, a city near metropolitan Tokyo, is telling. By 1985 only 1 percent of Kodaira residents regarded themselves as "natives," as opposed to "newcomers" (Robertson 1991:8). The deracinated urbanites generated an appetite for national nostalgia, including the domestic tourism industry, which is famously dependent on a nostalgia for lost local communities (Graburn 1995; cf. Ivy 1995:29–31). Nostalgia for *furusato* became a pervasive theme in postwar Japan (Kelly 1992:221–224).

If the traditional family and community eroded in the postwar period, so too did their spiritual overlay. Religion became a marginal social phenomenon. The Meiji state had sought to suppress local religious institutions and practices, such that "the religious history of modern Japan is the history of religious suppression" (Murakami 1978:33). State Shintō deified the emperor and promoted patriotic militarism (Murakami 1978:8–10), but it became nearly forgotten by the 1960s (Murakami 1970:i–ii; Hardacre 1989:142). According to Joseph Kitagawa (1966:331–332), "One of the basic problems in postwar Japan is the rootlessness of the Japanese people. . . . The tragedy of postwar Japan is that the people have lost this fundamental religious orientation." I am not sure whether it is a "problem," let alone a "tragedy," but there is certainly nothing like a recognizable national religion in contemporary Japan. Postwar Japan is characterized both by religious diversity and anomie (NHK Yoron Chōsabu 1991:92–97). Beginning in the 1950s, only about a third of surveyed Japanese have reported belief in a religion (Ozawa 1995:148), making Japan one of the least religious countries in the world (Nishihira 1982:60–67). Indeed, Yamaori Tetsuo (1996:2) characterizes the dominant Japanese belief as "nebulous atheism" *(bakuzentaru mushinkyō)* (cf. Yoshimoto 1984:3).

Instead of the family, community, and ultranationalism, the mass media became a major source of socialization and solidarity. When the folklorist Miyamoto Tsuneichi (1984a:27) visited Tsushima in the prewar period, no one had a radio; by the 1980s when I visited Tsushima, there was hardly a household without a television set. As Katō Shūichi (1964:236) argues: "Less than a lifetime ago there was no radio, television, or cinema; there were not even bestsellers or magazines of wide circulation. There were only newspapers which . . . fewer than 0.2 per cent of the people read. The mass media constitute one of the truly dramatic innovations in Japan today." It was not until the late 1950s that over 80 percent of Japanese households owned a radio; the same figure was reached for television ownership by the mid-1960s (Tanaka A. 1991:37). By then, Japan had become considerably more culturally homogeneous than it had been. Ironically, as I argued in Chapter 3, Japanese national popular culture turned out be multiethnic through and through.

The Nullity of Japaneseness

Ironically, once popular national identity had been achieved, there was no compelling answer to the question of what constitutes Japaneseness. After the catastrophic defeat in 1945 and the dizzying convulsions thereafter, the collapse of prewar ideals was complete (Hidaka 1960:260–264). As the critic Katō Shūichi (1959:51) observed, "We cannot see anywhere in Japan today what the Tōjō regime created. Japanese militarists only created graves and ruins, which was not the case in Italy or, for that matter, in Germany." More generally, postwar Japanese forgot, or tried to forget, the prewar years. However, some were not successful at distancing themselves from the recent past. Maruyama Masao (1982:114) famously called the immediate postwar Japanese intellectuals the "community of repentance" *(kaikon kyōdōtai)*. As a contrite war criminal memorably put it: "If I were to be born again, I would not want to be born as Japanese. . . . I would like to be a shell" (Ishida 1989:234).

Although the denial of Japanese war guilt undoubtedly has invidious motives, such as personal and collective guilt avoidance, all aspects of prewar Japan had in fact become delegitimated (Barshay 1998:284–286). The emperor had been a sovereign, patriarch, and even god for Japanese people (Fujita 1974:7–8), but he no longer represented for most Japanese people in the postwar period their deepest ideals or their cultural uniqueness. State Shintō gave way to religious eclecticism, the Imperial Rescript on Education was replaced by the democratic creed, and prewar imperialist history and geography were transformed into postwar progressive history and geography. Although some scholars insist on the continuing significance of the emperor system and the ideology of *kokutai* in postwar Japan, it is important to underscore the amnesia of prewar ideals and ideologies. For example, most contemporary Japanese would identify *kokutai* not with the prewar nationalist idea but as an acronym for the National Amateur Athletic Competition (Irokawa 1970:266).

Postwar Japan experienced not only six years of U.S. occupation but also an indiscriminate emulation of American life (Yasuda 1995). Whether in terms of material culture or social values, the United States dominated the immediate postwar decades in Japan (Sakuta 1972:395–397), such that Americanization came to be seen as inevitable (Hayashi 1973:107–108). As Bernard Rudofsky (1982:13) wrote in the 1960s, "Anybody who wants to study Americanization had better go to Japan these days." Kume Masao went so far as to suggest in 1950 that Japan should become part of the United States (Tsuda 1973:29–31). In the early 1950s, when sixth-graders were asked which nationality they would prefer to have been born as, 53 percent answered American, 22 percent Swiss, and only 16 percent Japanese (Ishida 1989:234). In an early 1960s national survey the person Japanese people most respected was Abraham Lincoln; Hirohito (Emperor Shōwa) was ranked fourteenth, tied with Madame Curie, behind Florence Nightingale (Mita 1965:69).

After the immediate tasks of postwar reconstruction and material improvement were achieved (Maruyama 1995b:104), reflective Japanese began once again to ponder Japanese identity. The question of Japanese identity became all the more pressing with the rapid economic growth of the 1960s and its symbolic apogee in the 1964 Tokyo Olympics (Kano 1995:187–188). Curious foreigners also queried incessantly about what it means to be Japanese (Yamamoto 1989:6; Rauch 1992:3). As I have suggested, the dominant discourses in the 1950s negated or nullified the idea of Japan and emphasized instead the shortcomings that had led to the fiasco of militarism and ultranationalism and prevented the achievements of universalistic (Western) ideals (Yoshino 1992:35–36; Ishida T. 1998:169). Hence, most answers in the 1960s were rather vague and banal. In one best-selling book published in 1962, *zenshū* (collected works) and gifts were said to exemplify Japanese wisdom (Hayashiya et al. 1973). In fact, the practice of publishing *Gesammelte Werke* (collected works) is a German import, and gifts are surely a cultural universal. Perhaps the most coherent answer in the early 1960s depicted Japan as an eclectic and syncretic culture, or a confluence of diverse influences and forces. Maruyama Masao (1961) suggested that Japanese thought has no essence or axis, such as Christianity in the West or Confucianism in China. In a similar vein, Katō Shūichi (1956) characterized Japanese culture as hybrid *(zasshu bunka).*

Most Japanese people in the 1960s, however, had no compelling response to the question of Japanese identity (Katō 1968:163, 1976:22). As Ezra Vogel (1971:87) found in the early 1960s, a typical middle-class suburbanite "has not had an accurate definition of what is distinctly Japanese, and he has, therefore, been less prepared for the sudden massive assault of Western culture." When the political scientist Ishida Takeshi (1973:170) asked college-age students "what is Japan?" in 1965, the most common answers included "The country I happened to be born in" or the murky "It probably won't go away." Their associations with the word "Japan" were equally nebulous: "the Japanese archipelago," "nothing," or "the mountain where I played as a child" (Ishida 1973:170). Having lost the dominant prewar worldview and having experienced rapid Americanization, most Japanese were confused as to what exactly constitutes Japaneseness. In a 1960 survey the thing that Japanese people wished most to preserve was "peace" (Yasumaru 1977:221). The newfound ideal of pacifism or the particular attachment to "the mountain where I played as a child" or Americanized material culture provided poor candidates for the nature and meaning of Japaneseness.

New Nationalism and Monoethnic Ideology

The contemporary discourse of Japaneseness that I described in Chapter 2 emerged to proffer a usable narrative of Japanese identity and uniqueness in the late 1960s. It described Japan as remarkable for its homogeneity, which arose from history (the Tokugawa state policy of seclusion, or *sakoku*) and geography (Japan is an island nation, or *shimaguni*).

The 1968 celebration of the Meiji Centennial provided the initial explicit articulation of this narrative. The novelist Ishihara Shintarō wrote in 1968, "There is no other country like Japan, people who are virtually monoethnic, who speak the same language which is like no other country's, and which has a unique culture" (Oguma 1995:358). More trenchantly, Mishima Yukio (1976:386) published in the same year his celebrated essay on "cultural defense": "Japan is a country rare in the world in that it is monoethnic and monolingual." He went on to underscore Japan's "cultural continuity" and the equivalence of "ethnicity *(minzoku)* and nation *(kuni),*" but his fundamental intention was to highlight that only the emperor could function as a "value in itself" *(wert an sich)* or as a "cultural concept" to define Japan (Mishima 1976:401). Sensibly, he was aware that Japanese monoethnicity was a postwar phenomenon (Mishima 1976:387).

Later articulations usually dropped the emperor and stressed monoethnicity as the differentiating predicate of Japaneseness. Ishida Takeshi (1973:172), for example, wrote, "Japan is defined by all people having the same color of hair and eyes, speaking the same language, and living in the same way." Once the idea of monoethnic Japan arose as an essential feature of Japaneseness, few questioned it, and many who should have known better reproduced it (Ishida 1970:70–75; Matsuo 1990:286). In this regard the discourse of Japaneseness, articulated as the *Nihonjinron* (theory of Japaneseness), entered a prolonged boom from 1970, the year of the Osaka Expo (Minami 1994:217–234). Kimura Takeo's early 1970s study (1973:38, 43) is prototypical in highlighting two special Japanese characteristics: first, it is an island nation *(shimaguni);* second, "it is a monoethnic country rare in the world." "Racial homogeneity," "island nation," and "same language" became truisms in many articulations of Japaneseness (e.g., Shimizu 1985:94). Western writers confidently and dutifully recycled and reported these truisms as essential features of Japanese society (Buckley 1990:82; Feiler 1991:135; Rauch 1992:82, 85).

As I have repeatedly emphasized, each of the major propositions of the discourse of Japaneseness, and especially the idea of monoethnicity, is misleading or mistaken. A common explanation for Japanese homogeneity is that Japan experienced nearly three centuries of seclusion *(sakoku)* during the Tokugawa period. Hence, the Japanese are insular and parochial: "History and geographic isolation have been combined with this racial unity to fuel a strong sense of national identity" (Buckley 1990:82). *Sakoku* implied the state monopoly of trade and foreign relations, not complete seclusion of society from foreign influences. All East Asian states featured state monopoly of trade, and the Tokugawa state had extensive contact with other sovereign states (Yamaguchi 1993:41–47). Tokugawa-era intellectuals had extensive knowledge of the world beyond the Japanese archipelago, and eagerly sought Chinese and, later, Western knowledge. The very idea of *sakoku* only became popular after the Meiji Restoration to mark off the premodern period from the modern period of enlightenment and civilization (Arano 1988:ii). Furthermore, being surrounded by ocean actually encouraged intercultural contact; water transportation is much more useful than land transportation in the rugged terrain that characterizes the Japanese archipelago (Hara 1978:20; Amino 1992:35–37). Certainly, Japan is not unique in being an island nation-state. Neither is Japan a monolingual society (see Appendix). Not only was the monoethnic thesis inaccurate; it was hardly a basis for uniqueness because many Japanese regard other nation-states as monoethnic as well.

Why, then, did the discourse of Japaneseness and, in particular, the idea of monoethnicity become so popular? I have already suggested some reasons: postwar Japan had become considerably more ethnically homogeneous after the loss of its colonies, including Okinawa; postwar Japan had achieved national integration and popular national consciousness; and there were few compelling alternative answers to the question of Japanese national identity. Equally significant, however, was the rise of a new nationalism born of newfound prosperity.

The two authors I cited as the pioneering interlocutors in the nascent discourse of Japaneseness—Ishihara and Mishima—were also the most vocal exponents of Japanese nationalism and conservatism in the 1960s. Indeed, Japanese right-wing thought began to recover in the 1960s from its thorough delegitimation. The first major postwar statement had been published in 1964 by Hayashi Fusao, who defended the Pacific War as an effort to liberate Asian nations from Western colonialism (cf. Watanabe S. 1995:351). Others soon followed, seeking to revive Japanese nationalism; some notable landmarks include the formation of the Japanese Culture Conference (Nihon Bunka Kaigi) in 1968 and the publication of the explicitly nationalist journal *Shokun* in 1969 (Yamada 1989:228). Indeed, the prewar elements in the ruling Liberal Democratic Party or the state bureaucracies made numerous attempts to revive prewar nationalism. For example, the Ministry of Education has insistently promoted the singing of the national anthem and the raising of the national flag in schools since the 1950s (Yoshino 1992:206). Most notably, Prime Minister Kishi Nobusuke's regime in the late 1950s sought to reestablish continuities with prewar Japan (Gotō, Uchida, and Ishikawa 1982:5).

Nonetheless, prewar nationalism, with its stress on the emperor system, imperialism, and militarism, had become thoroughly delegitimated after 1945. If prewar nationalism had survived or been revived in a more vigorous form, there would have been many more plausible candidates for Japanese uniqueness: most obviously, as Mishima emphasized, the emperor system or perhaps the samurai and their way *(bushidō)*. The collapse of the prewar ideals had, however, destroyed imperial and martial virtues as plausible sources of Japanese identity. Efforts to revive prewar nationalism—whether in the guise of Kishi's explicit political attempt or Mishima's utopian venture—were ultimately rebuffed by the Japanese people. At the time of the 1968 Meiji Centennial, "the intense criticism of historians, the cynicism of the left, and the general indifference of the public" punctured the effort to resuscitate nationalist pride (Large 1992:179).

The nationalist right has been loud but weak; the right-wing thinker Watase Shūkichi (1987) symptomatically narrates its history as one of continual oppression. Throughout the postwar period any mention of the Japanese spirit and other prewar nationalist sentiments inevitably evoked pejorative labels, such as "conservative, reactionary" *(hoshu handō)*, and were summarily dismissed (Yuasa 1995:176). Even seemingly innocent gestures of patriotism, such as saluting the flag and singing the national anthem, remained controversial in postwar Japan, associated as they were with the dreaded prewar past (Yasuoka 1991a:3–5). Patriotism, in other words, was equated with militarism in postwar Japan (Ishida 1989:234–235). No wonder, then, that it has been so weak; in a 1980s survey, whereas over 70 percent of Americans and South Koreans were willing to sacrifice individual interests for the national good, only 16 percent of Japanese were willing to do so (Nishihira 1987:98). As Nishihira Shigeki (1987:99) concludes: "Japanese people do not hold much pride in their country, patriotism is weak, and state consciousness is generally weak."

Paradoxically, then, the belief in monoethnicity arose in part because of the limitations of traditional prewar nationalism. It was a truncated expression that highlighted not what was intrinsic to Japan but what made Japan different from others. Rather than revanchist nationalism, what emerged in the 1960s was a new, or postwar, nationalism. New nationalism did not celebrate the emperor or *kokutai* but economic recovery and corporate capitalism. It was not anti-Western or anti-American but pro-Western and pro-American. Most crucially, it found support in the Japanese people's everyday conservatism or satisfaction with rapid economic growth. This undeniable affluence contradicted the prevailing denunciation or dismissal of everything Japanese, which had been dominant in the 1950s. Most Japanese people were not pining for prewar nationalism but for ideas that reflected the achievements of postwar economic growth. The writer Sakaiya Taichi's (1991:331) comment is hardly unique: "That Japan is 'special' *(tokushu)* is neither shameful nor criminal. We should not hesitate to claim Japanese particularity *(tokushusei)*." By 1988 over 95 percent of Japanese people were "glad to be born in Japan" (Yasumaru 1995:327). Nonetheless, neither the hollowness of affluence (Americanization is not a cogent predicate of Japaneseness) nor the revival of the prewar ideals provided a resonant reply to the question of Japanese identity.

The new nationalism and the idea of Japanese monoethnicity drew on and only made explicit the hegemonic postwar ethnonational worldview, which arose in conscious opposition to the imperialist and multiethnic worldview. Because the empire was equated with multiethnicity, the condemnation of the one had led to the condemnation of the other. Instead of the Greater East Asia Co-Prosperity Sphere, the idea of a small Japan—Japan as the Switzerland of Asia, as Douglas MacArthur put it—became the dominant ideal. Hence, prewar critics of imperialism, such as Ishibashi Tanzan (1984:101–121) who advocated a nonimperialist or "small" Japan *(shōkoku Nihon)* (Masuda 1990:7–10), silenced prewar enthusiasts. The historian Tsuda Sayukichi equated empire with multiethnicity, and counterposed to that the Japanese people and a monoethnic nation-state; the philosopher Watsuji Tetsurō—an ur-theorist of *Nihonjinron* (Yuasa 1995:12–13)—also championed a monoethnic and peaceful Japan in contradistinction to multiethnic and militarist Japan (Oguma 1995:340–345). More generally, ethnic nationalism emerged as an antiimperialist and antistatist ideology (Doak 1997:299–305).

Progressive intellectuals shared the new ethnonational worldview and the discourse of Japaneseness. Many communists and leftists were sympathetic to the plight of ex-colonials and minorities, but the dominant belief in the socialist revolution—or at least progressive and egalitarian ideals—turned their attention to other demands and problems. The fate of minorities was, in brief, to disappear qua minorities. In this view the Ainu and Burakumin were premodern remnants who were bound to disappear, and antiimperialist ideology mandated the repatriation of Koreans, Chinese, and other erstwhile colonials.

To be sure, monoethnicity was not so much a source of pride as one of shame, for it expressed the insularity of Japanese culture. Quite often, Japanese homogeneity was blamed for Japanese ethnocentrism. The anthropologist Nakane Chie (1967:53–54, 187–188) advanced the theory of Japan as a homogeneous society in part to chide Japanese people: "In the case of Japan, the reason that culture shock is severe is because Japanese society is monoethnically constituted. It is an island nation, and it does not interact with different cultures. . . . The opportunity to know the existence of systems other than our own is non-existent" (Nakane 1972:14). Scholars also avoided prewar topics, including ethnicity *(minzoku)* (Kuroda 1971:293–294). Motivated by Marxism or modernization theory, most postwar Japanese social scientists ignored particularistic problems, including ethnic minorities (Mihashi 1992:117; Fukuoka 1996:233–235). To the extent that ethnicity and nationalism were discussed seriously, the problem of ethnicity *(minzoku mondai)* focused on Japanese people threatened by imperialism (Tōyama 1968:106–159; Nagahara 1978:63–68), not on ethnic minorities.

Because universalistic theories, whether Marxism or modernization theory, did not explain Japanese peculiarities, progressive intellectuals were bereft of concepts and tools to understand the concrete experience of Japan. Hence, they uncritically accepted the predominant postwar ethnonational view of Japan. In this context folklore studies, especially the work of Yanagita Kunio, reinforced the belief in monoethnicity (Yasumaru 1995:293). The "new *Kokugaku*"—the project to define Japan's national essence—was another effort to resuscitate in print what has been lost in time and place (cf. Harootunian 1990). Yanagita elevated ordinary people such as farmers as the basis of true Japaneseness (cf. Fukuta 1992:52–53), which ignored inequality, discrimination, and heterogeneity (Akamatsu 1995:145).

Finally, the discourse of Japaneseness resonated well with postwar conservative rule. The ambivalence of colonialism—the desire for assimilation and the belief in Japanese superiority—manifested itself in differing attitudes toward minorities. On the one hand, the Ainu, Burakumin, and Okinawans became targets of continued Japanization. On the other hand, Koreans, Taiwanese, and other former Japanese imperial subjects were dismissed as non-Japanese. In so doing, the Japanese state disengaged from the colonies and their attendant problems, including repatriating displaced peoples and redressing wartime damages (Ishida T. 1998:169). In the bureaucratic and conservative mindset the habit of ultranationalism remained, albeit without the crucible of the emperor system and the empire.

Thus, the idea of monoethnic Japan arose as a contingent and serviceable answer to the question of Japanese identity in the late 1960s. When tradition had been so thoroughly pulverized, the search for identity defied all logic and evidence. Natsume Sōseki (1986:38) once lamented the fanatical and foolish Japanese who prided themselves on Mt. Fuji when faced with Western superiority. Even right-wingers could not be content with highlighting Fujiyama, geisha, haiku, ukiyoe, zen, and kabuki as sources of Japanese uniqueness in postwar Japan (Yamamoto 1989:i, 4). Monoethnicity became the nationalism of fools in postwar Japan.

Memories of Multiethnicity

Beyond the material and discursive context, generational change was significant in effacing the memory of Japanese multiethnicity and making the monoethnicity thesis plausible. Not only did Japanese people attempt to erase the prewar period, but the passage of time obliterated it. As early as the mid-1950s, the postwar generation *(sengo sedai)* became the dominant intellectual and cultural presence (Hidaka 1960:363–370). By the mid-1960s, the majority of Tokyo and Osaka residents were bereft of any memory of World War II (Takeuchi 1982:153). When I inquired in the mid-1980s about key references to the war years, such as battles and slogans (Mikuni 1985), many Japanese people expressed only the vaguest recollection, mostly from history books. Certainly, such allusions were not infused with meaning as they were for their parents' or grandparents' generation.

Furthermore, the centrality of Tokyo in the national imagination is important. To put it simply, Tokyo has come to stand for all of Japan (Isoda 1978:118–126). The Tokyo-centric media is especially crucial in sustaining the myth of monoethnicity. In other regions, whether Hokkaidō with the Ainu or Osaka with many Korean Japanese and Burakumin, the idea of monoethnic Japan is readily contradicted by the multiethnic reality. In a city where everyone attempts to pass as a native Tokyoite rather than country bumpkins, passing and assimilating as a homogeneous national subject have become normative (Nakajima 993:269). In this context it is not surprising that Tokyoites tend to efface regional and other forms of identities and accentuate their national *(kokumin)* identity (Takegawa 1990:266).

Finally, the inescapable presence of the United States should not be ignored. Many canards about Japanese difference or uniqueness arose from comparing Japan to the United States. To the Japanese the United States was not only an imperialist country but also a country with a serious racial discrimination problem (Oguma 1995:356). Japan, in contrast, was a small country, nonimperialistic, and therefore nonmultiethnic. One cannot ignore the role of U.S. racial ideology in the American reading of Japan, and vice versa. Unlike Europeans, who tend to be sensitive to ethnonational differences, Americans saw Japan through the black-white racial prism, in which ethnic differences among European Americans were compressed into the singular category of whiteness. From this perspective, Japan impressed most American observers as remarkably homogeneous. To put it crudely, they all looked alike. Donald Keene (1950:23) wrote of "the unusual physical homogeneity of the population of Japan." Delmer Brown (1955:7) remarked that Japan is "one of the most racially homogeneous people in the world." This is, of course, quite different from earlier European observers of Japan. From Elvin von Beltz to Bruno Taut, late nineteenth-century and early twentieth-century Europeans observed the remarkable diversity among Japanese facial types and physiognomy (Oguma 1995:22–23; cf. Kamishima 1973:14).

Nonetheless, the prewar imperialist, multiethnic ideology and reality have not been completely forgotten in the postwar period. As the political scientist Kamishima Jirō (1982:17–18) wrote, "In prewar Japan, everyone said that Yamato people are hybrid people *(zasshu minzoku)*, and mixed people *(kongō minzoku)*. . . . But, rather strangely, in the postwar period, beginning with progressive intellectuals, people began to say that Japan is monoethnic. There is no basis for this." Not everyone has forgotten Japan's prewar imperial multiethnicity or the recent nature of Japanese national integration.

The discursive dominance of monoethnic ideology cannot, after all, completely efface historical records or individual memories. It is quite remarkable how many life stories of Japanese people are colored by the experience of the Japanese empire and its ethnic mixing. Even in the seemingly isolated village of Suye Mura—the site of the classic ethnography of agrarian Japan—many villagers had been, or had family or friends, in Korea, Manchuria, and elsewhere (Smith and Wiswell 1982:134–136). In fact, Japanese colonial expansion has not been completely effaced from popular consciousness. As one older man told Hatada Kunio (1990:133), "Co-existence? That's impossible. As long as anyone born before the mid-1930s is around, that's definitely impossible. We are solidified by our prejudice against foreigners. Even if they are really good people, this problem is different. For us, 'co-existence' traces back to the Greater East Asia Co-Prosperity Sphere. To be one means only to dominate [foreigners]." An extreme right-wing nationalist, who was against the influx of foreign workers because that would lead to mixed-blood children *(konketsuji)*, was in fact conflicted because of his sentimental feeling *(naniwabushiteki kibun)* that Asia is a singular entity.

Just as historical documents from the prewar era bear the inevitable impress of imperialist, multiethnic Japan, memories of multiethnicity have not been expunged in many elder Japanese people. This was clear from my interviews. A small factory owner in his seventies ranted and raved about the "lowest" *(saitei)* Koreans and the weak and dirty Chinese. His racist utterances were infused with imperial nostalgia that extended to the ethnic inferiors. He spoke fondly, for example, of a Korean classmate who was very bright. As one man in his sixties who lived in Ueno, a poor central area of Tokyo, said, "Iranians are only the latest among foreigners who have come to Ueno. There were Koreans who came and stayed here, even before me. After the war, a lot of people came from the countryside *(inaka)*. Country bumpkins *(inakamono)* didn't speak the language *(kotoba)*, but they all assimilated." The grumpy man hinted at the subversive idea that the very establishment of Japanese national identity was far from complete even in his lifetime. Regional differences were acute enough so that easy communication was difficult, and people from the Japanese periphery were as different as Koreans or Iranians who had come to Ueno before and after them. These private voices, however, have been silenced by the rote repetition of monoethnic ideology.

The Anatomy of Silence

What allowed so many Japanese to believe that they have lived and continue to live in a monoethnic society is the silence of the actually existing minority groups. In the previous chapter I traced the development of the major ethnic groups in Japan. The Ainu, as we have seen, were not only few in number but their culture was devastated by a century of Japanization efforts. Okinawans, in the southern periphery, were occupied by the United States until 1972. The silence of these two groups is, therefore, not difficult to explain. Given their geographical distance and isolation, they were mere scratches on the minds of most Japanese people. But how about the two larger groups: the Korean Japanese and Burakumin? Why weren't they seen and heard?

First, both groups were socially isolated. In the postwar period many Burakumin and Korean Japanese remained residentially segregated. Furthermore, employment discrimination minimized the opportunities for Burakumin and Koreans to work alongside Japanese. Hence, most Japanese, especially in Tokyo, were unlikely to encounter large groups of Burakumin or Korean Japanese.

Second, the ideology of monoethnicity justified neglect by the government and the public. The government recognized no Burakumin neighborhoods in Tokyo, for example (Yagi 1984:175) despite their significant presence (cf. Honda 1990). The putative nonexistence of ethnic minorities legitimated passivity on the part of local and national government. The ideology of monoethnicity, in other words, released the Japanese government from addressing the demands of various minority groups. The Korean Japanese scholar Pak Kyŏng-sik (1992:81) has observed, "When we demand equality, we get 'monoethnic state-society.'" The dominant belief was that "passivity and silence" would eliminate Burakumin discrimination (Yagi 1984:250). Korean Japanese, in this regard, were expected to return imminently to their "home" in North or South Korea.

Third, assimilation, or Japanization, superseded ethnic mobilization. Given the fact of discrimination, individual Burakumin and Korean Japanese sought to assimilate into mainstream society. In the postwar period these two groups were not racialized—they were not physiologically or culturally distinct from the ethnic Japanese population. Most Burakumin, as I have noted, share the contemporary Japanese view that they are ethnically Japanese (Fujiwara 1993:298–299). One consequence of ethnic denial is the virtual ignorance about Burakumin, especially in the Tokyo area. The Japanese American sociologist I. Roger Yoshino found "few in the Tokyo area who had any knowledge of the Burakumin" (Yoshino and Murakoshi 1977:v). Indeed, more Japanese were aware of the black liberation movement in the United States than about the Burakumin liberation movement in their own country (Yoshino and Murakoshi 1977:2).

Most Korean Japanese, in contrast, did not regard themselves as in any way Japanese. The prevailing self-identification until the 1960s was as so-journers. To the extent that they participated in Japanese economic and social life, they found it easier to pass as Japanese. Even in the 1990s less than a tenth use their Korean names (Harajiri 1997:29). Their collective political energy was focused on homeland politics and on the division between Chongryun and Mindan, Korean Japanese organizations allied, respectively, to North and South Korea.

Passing as a widespread individual strategy closed the vicious circle of monoethnic ideology. Assimilation is possible only for selected individuals as long as discrimination is widespread. Because a collective challenge to monoethnic ideology and ethnic discrimination was not sought, the status quo was sustained. Both Burakumin and Koreans could become Japanese as individuals, but, in so doing, they could not, as collectives, become part of Japan.

By the 1980s, however, the situation of different ethnic groups had transformed sufficiently to usher in discourses and movements for the recognition of Japanese multiethnicity. The transformation of ethnic politics stemmed from changing social situations. Residential and employment segregation weakened. In particular, the labor shortages of the 1960s incorporated Burakumin within the mainstream Japanese labor market (Tsurushima 1984:108–109).

Precisely when assimilation advanced, ethnic identity was asserted. Although almost all Ainu, Burakumin, Chinese, Koreans, Okinawans, and other ethnic minorities in Japan are culturally indistinguishable from their Japanese counterparts, a powerful centrifugal force against assimilation emerged from the 1960s. For Korean Japanese, the first-generation's concern for homeland politics was superseded by the second- and third-generations' interest in Japanese politics (Chŏng 1984:38). As early as the late 1940s, perhaps a third of Koreans in Japan could not speak Korean fluently (Pak 1992:612). Among third- or fourth-generation Korean Japanese, fluency in the Korean language is extremely rare, and there is little memory of the homeland (Kim 1991:11; Ryang 1997:64–65). Younger Korean Japanese are culturally Japanese, albeit with some Korean identification (Fukuoka and Kim 1997:161).

Finally, various social movements and intellectual currents encouraged ethnic mobilization (Hanami 1995). Both the New Left and the new social movements in Japan took up the causes of various oppressed social groups. The global dissemination of human rights and antidiscrimination, both as ideas and as organized efforts, accelerated after the 1960s (Tsurushima 1984:110–111). Many Korean Japanese people I met were extremely curious about the fate of the Korean diaspora in the United States in general and the idea of being Korean American in particular. One such collective expression was the effort to construct a Koreatown in Kawasaki, which was in part inspired by the existence of a Koreatown in Los Angles.

The myth of monoethnic Japan is fundamentally a post–World War II construct. The recent vintage of monoethnic ideology does not prevent the imagined present from transforming the misty past in its image. Nationalist historiography and the nationalist imagination impose a vision of Japan that has been monoethnic from the beginning to the present. In the myth's contemporary articulation, as I suggested in Chapter 1, it is only the coming of Asian migrant workers in the late 1980s that posed the first serious threat of multiethnicity in Japanese history. The truth of the matter is that Japan has always been multiethnic.

6

Classify and Signify

"Ramos is Japanese," said Yamamoto, a college student. When I asked him how a shaggy-haired, dark-skinned professional soccer star from Brazil could possibly be Japanese, he retorted, "He acts like a Japanese person. He is a team player. He has guts *(konjō)*." He went on to say that Akebono, the Hawaiian sumō wrestler, is also Japanese because he seeks to be part of Japanese society. In contrast, Konishiki, another Hawaiian sumō wrestler, is not Japanese because he doesn't attempt to assimilate into Japanese society. Even as he sorted some foreign-born athletes into the category of Japanese people, Yamamoto insisted that Japan is a monoethnic society.

"I think it's a matter of race *(jinshu)*, what you can see *(mikake)*." For Suzuki, a housewife in her thirties, the salient distinction is whether someone can look, or pass as, Japanese. She insisted that other Asians look different, although she acknowledged that after living in Japan for a while, some Asians may begin to look Japanese. In this vein, she said that Korean Japanese are really Japanese. She was skeptical, however, whether Ainu people were in fact Japanese, precisely because of their somatic differences. In the end, she nonetheless articulated a powerful plea for a world free of prejudice and discrimination: "we are all human beings."

A successful *sararīman* in his forties, Nomura prided himself on his realistic view of Japanese society. Although he recognizes that there was discrimination in the past, he feels that it has vanished in contemporary Japan. The new foreign workers or Korean Japanese suffer to the extent that they refuse to assimilate into Japanese society. He could not see Iranians, Filipinos, or even the ethnic Japanese from Peru or Brazil leading the life of a *sararīman*—commuting from afar to work long hours and becoming part of a corporate team, which means being considerate and caring about colleagues. Neither could he envision Korean Japanese becoming Japanese. However, he emphasized that *kikoku shijo*, the children of Japanese parents working abroad, are "of course" Japanese because their parents are Japanese. He insisted that this is the case even if the child does not speak Japanese. For Nomura, Japan is an island country that is monoethnic. The island spirit *(shimaguni konjō)* is the basis, or the depth psychology *(shinsō shinri)*, of Japanese people.

These brief sketches demonstrate a considerable divergence in Japanese outlook on ethnic differences. Yamamoto, a fairly strident believer in Japanese superiority, denies the salience of physical differences. In contrast, Suzuki, who is deeply ashamed of Japanese aggression in World War II and is critical of contemporary Japanese society, highlights the importance of appearances. People are often inconsistent, if not contradictory. Nomura regards *kikoku shijo*, even when they are unable to speak Japanese, as Japanese, whereas he denies the Japaneseness of the ethnic Japanese from Latin America.

One idea no one seems to question is the validity of the very category of Japaneseness, the premise of the various discourses on Japanese identity, difference, and uniqueness. In Chapter 2, I discussed the contemporary discourse of Japaneseness as it was articulated against the new foreign workers. In Chapter 5, I sought to explain the origins of the monoethnic ideology. Here I will probe its conceptual foundations.

The Category of Japaneseness

The category of Japaneseness appears innocent and obvious. After all, there are Japanese people who are identified as Japanese by themselves as well as by others. Indeed, one of the characteristics of being Japanese is the ability to distinguish Japanese from non-Japanese people. It seems only natural, then, that people should generate generalizations about them. However, as we have seen from the three opening vignettes, the logic of classification that people employ can be different and contradictory. Although some use ascribed characteristics, such as physical appearance, others rely on achieved criteria, such as knowledge of language and culture. People even disagree on who should be regarded as Japanese. Rules of classification are rarely articulated explicitly and therefore tend to be a complex amalgam of commonsense intuitions and idiosyncratic ideas. Hence, as much as some people are confident in declaiming sources of

Japaneseness, many others are confused about what in fact makes people Japanese. What no one questions is the starting point. The category of Japaneseness, which is the foundation of the discourse of Japaneseness, is at once its subject and object. Rather than engaging in endless queries about the empirical adequacy of propositions about Japaneseness, it is important to interrogate it and to dethrone it from its transcendent perch.

Conflating Categories of Peoplehood

"What is the difference between citizenship and nationality?" This, perhaps the most common question that people I interviewed asked me, revealed the pervasive conflation of the state, nation, ethnicity, and race in contemporary Japan. My presence often provoked confusion and generated such conversation as:

"What is your citizenship?"
"American."
"What is your nationality, then?"
"American."
"But why do you speak Japanese so well?"
"I spent my childhood here."
"Were you born in Japan?"
"No, I was born in South Korea."
"Shouldn't your nationality be Korean, then?"

There is, in fact, no intrinsic distinction between citizenship and nationality. However, most Japanese regard *shiminken* (citizenship) as a relatively foreign concept, whereas *kokuseki* (nationality) appears to be an extension of *koseki* (household registry), and hence a native or natural concept. In this view nationality is an extension of the family; one belongs, organically as it were, to a nation as one does to a family. Whereas nationality is a matter of fate, citizenship, in contrast, strikes many Japanese people as superficial because people can choose and change it.

What underlies the confusion between citizenship and nationality is the blurred distinction between state membership and ethnonational identity. Because many people know that immigrants can become American citizens, citizenship strikes them as artificial, unlike the seeming solidity of nationality. Whereas state membership is considered mobile, ethnonational membership is not. In becoming a naturalized citizen, one becomes, in a manner of speaking, a non-national national. My interviewees wondered why a person of Korean descent *(Kankokujin)*, such as myself, can be an American citizen *(Amerika no shimin)*. Needless to say, naturalization *(kika)* is possible in Japan; I could in theory—however difficult it may be in practice—become a Japanese citizen. However, most Japanese are wont to bypass the plasticity of nationality, which they see as an almost natural—indeed, racial—category. One is born, reared, and dies a Japanese; in this worldview the category of nationality is immutable from cradle to grave.

At the same time, most Japanese people conflate the potentially discrete categories of nation, ethnicity, and race. The Japanese language distinguishes between nationals *(kokumin)* and ethnics *(minzoku)*, although *minzoku* is often used to refer to nationals as well. A Japanese person may be a member of *Nihon koku* (Japanese nation) or *Nihon* (or *Yamato*) *minzoku* (Japanese, or Yamato, ethnicity or people). It is, however, extremely rare to refer to *Nihon koku,* which is a vocabulary of politicians and bureaucrats, or *Nihon,* or *Yamato, minzoku,* which is used mainly by right-wing nationalists. When people speak of *Nihon koku* or *Nihon minzoku,* they sound stiff; idiomatic speech would use *Nihon* and *Nihonjin.* Similarly, *jinshu* (race) is rarely mentioned, except when people talk about racism or racial discrimination *(jinshu sabetsu).*

In ordinary conversation, nationality, ethnicity, and race are one and the same thing. Most Japanese refer to their fellow Japanese as *Nihonjin.* In fact, the most common way to refer to a group of people is to add the suffix *jin* (literally, people). In so doing, Japanese conflate categories of peoplehood. In the United States, for example, "white" and "black" are racial categories; "French" and "German" are national or citizenship categories; and "Italian American" and "Armenian American" are ethnic categories. In contrast, these distinctions are usually elided in Japanese: one can be a white person *(hakujin)* in the same way that one can be a German person *(Doitsujin).* In this line of reasoning, everyone belongs to a homologous category of peoplehood; everyone is some sort of *jin.*

The category of peoplehood is permanent and homogeneous. In the dominant way of thinking, nationals share descent; others are foreigners forever. Japanese are Japanese, and Koreans are Koreans, whether they were born or live in South Korea, Japan, or the United States. They remain, respectively, *Nihonjin* and *Kankokujin,* which are mutually exclusive. The anthropologist Dorinne Kondo (1990:11–14) found herself a "conceptual anomaly" in Japan as a Japanese American. Exceptions prove the rule that one can belong to only one ethnonational group. Some Japanese people regard Korean Japanese as fundamentally Japanese, thereby denying their difference as well as the possibility of a hybrid category.

Not surprisingly, the Japanese vocabulary for minority groups is impoverished. There is, to be sure, a common way to refer to ethnic minorities by using the suffix *kei* (related, via). Hence, Japanese Americans are *Nikkei Amerikajin* and Japanese Brazilians are *Nikkei Burajirujin*. In general, however, they are usually called *Nikkeijin*, denoting a distinct category of people—a sort of ex-Japanese. Almost no one refers to people of Korean descent who were born in Japan as *Kankokukei Nihonjin* ([South] Korean Japanese) or *Koriakei Nihonjin* (Korean Japanese). For older Japanese, they are *Chōsenjin* (*Chōsen* is the old Japanese term for Korea) or any number of racial epithets. For many others, they are *Zainichi Kankoku, Chōsenjin* (Resident South and North Koreans in Japan); the simpler *Zainichi Korian* (Resident Koreans in Japan) is popular among progressives in the 1990s. Similarly, Chinese Japanese are usually called *Chūgokujin* (Chinese) or *Kakyō* (Overseas Chinese). Occasionally, some Japanese use the term *Zainichi Chūgokujin* or *Taiwanjin* (Resident Chinese or Taiwanese in Japan). This nomenclature implies that even third-generation Korean Japanese and Taiwanese Japanese are foreigners (nationals), not ethnic minorities in Japan.

In contrast, Japanese do not use the suffix *jin* to refer to other ethnic minorities in Japan. An Ainu person is usually called Ainu. Occasionally, people refer to Ainu *minzoku* (Ainu ethnicity) but not to Ainu*jin*. An Okinawan is referred to as Okinawa *no hito* (a person of, or from, Okinawa) or, more formally, Okinawa *kenmin* (a person of Okinawa Prefecture). This is the same way in which people reckon regional differences, as when people speak of Kyūshū *danji* (Kyūshū man), Kumamoto *shusshin* (of Kumamoto Prefecture origin), Satsuma *no hito* (person from Satsuma, the Tokugawa-era name of present-day Kagoshima), or Kagoshima *kenmin*. A Burakumin is usually called Burakumin and, occasionally, *buraku no hito* (a person of, or from, the hamlet). The nomenclature for a person of mixed ancestry is *konketsuji* (a child of mixed blood) or *hāfu* (half). A politically correct alternative is *daburu* (double), which attempts to underscore the benefits of mixed ancestry (double, rather than half). As I noted above, ethnic Japanese who have emigrated abroad are usually called *Nikkeijin* regardless of whether they are still in Brazil or are living in Japan.

When I asked about what kind of people live in Japan, almost everyone answered by dividing people into Japanese *(Nihonjin)* and non-Japanese *(gaijin)*. People differed on the variety of outsiders; some spoke of Koreans, Chinese, whites, and Africans, whereas others mentioned Asians, Arabs, whites, and Africans, and yet others of Asians, Americans, Europeans, and blacks. Blacks *(kokujin)* are distinguished from Americans because *Amerikajin* are taken to be white. Although many people are aware that blacks in Japan are often African Americans, the dominant ethnoracial classification consigns them to a different category of peoplehood. The same confusion occurs at times for Jewish Americans, who are often referred to as *Yudayajin* (Jews). Some Japanese divide the world into three major races: white *(hakujin)*, black *(kokujin)*, and yellow *(ōshokujin)*, but they are often not very consistent in applying this racial scheme. Although they may be comfortable about dividing foreigners into these three races, they are reluctant to cast Japanese people into any of them.

Some people are sophisticated enough to realize the ethnic heterogeneity in the United States or the geographical complexity of the world—for example, that Africa is not a country but rather a continent, or that Arabs are a rather loose category of people in the Middle East. Quiz shows, documentaries, and travel supplement the school curriculum in making good geographers out of many Japanese people. Rote memorization and regurgitation serve people well when they are asked to point to Chicago or, for that matter, Cameroon on a map.

The cosmopolitan geographer turns out to be, however, a poor sociologist. The most erudite of geographers engages in ethnonational or ethnoracial conflation. Because other nation-states are presumed to be like Japan, the Japanese perceive other nations as ethnically homogeneous. This is, of course, paradoxical given that many Japanese regard Japanese ethnic homogeneity as one of their unique characteristics. However, if only by a habit of thought, the category "nation" presumes ethnic homogeneity. One person who had spent several months in Brussels and Amsterdam expressed her shock at the ethnic diversity in these cities. She had assumed that everyone would be white, and not the actual mix she found of people with ancestors from Africa, Asia, and elsewhere. In other words, most Japanese conflate race, ethnicity, and nation not only for Japan but for other countries as well. I should add, however, that this confusion is not unique to Japanese. Most Americans, as much as they live in a multiethnic society, are shocked to learn that a black person can be British—in the ordinary American ethnic worldview, black Briton is an oxymoron (Dawes 1996:21). Or, for that matter, many Americans still find it difficult to transcend the black-white racial prism, and assume that everyone else are recent immigrants or foreigners. The anticipated answer to the question, "where are you from?," posed to an Asian American is a country in Asia, not some state in the United States.

In summary, Japanese tend to conflate distinct categories of peoplehood into a singular one *(jin)*. The dominant mode of ethnoracial or ethnonational classification posits homogeneous categories of peoplehood.

Japanese versus Others

The discourse of Japaneseness counterposes Japanese against not only the new foreign workers, as we saw in Chapter 2, but all other non-Japanese groups as well. As many long-term foreign residents in Japan bemoan, it is difficult for them to shed their outsider status. A German businessman, who had lived in Japan for over two decades, said, "I have been in many places where my sense of being German was intensified; Japan is the only place where I merely feel that I am not Japanese" (cf. Buruma 1989:227–228). To be sure, the *unheimlich* is a common lament of exiles and expatriates around the world. There is no doubt, however, that the distinction between inside *(uchi)* and outside *(soto)* finds great resonance in everyday Japanese life and language (Nakano 1983:329–331). It is, however, a cultural universal, which may be articulated differently, as, for example, between natives and strangers. As Georg Simmel (1950:402) put it: "The stranger, like the poor . . . is an element of the group itself"; the stranger, the outsider, is everywhere.

The contrast between inside and outside is transposed to that between Japanese and others, thereby strengthening the boundary of Japaneseness. The fundamental belief that there is something distinct about being Japanese—that there is a significant barrier or boundary between Japanese and non-Japanese people—makes possibile the diverse and proliferating discourses on being Japanese, or the discourse of Japaneseness. The belief in Japanese difference or uniqueness is frequently shared by foreign observers. Nearly all non-Japanese writers highlight differences between the Japanese and others (Moeran 1989:182). As Lafcadio Hearn (1972:180) warned his readers, however, the assertion of difference points both ways: "One should be able to study those old drawings in order to comprehend just how we appeared to the Japanese of that era; how ugly, how grotesque, how ridiculous." After years of living in Japan, Hearn (1904:9–10) cautioned against overhasty generalizations. His humility, however, remains very much an exception.

Consider one of the first Western characterizations of the Japanese by the Jesuit missionary Luis Frois (1532–1597), who spent thirty-five years in Japan. According to the historian Donald Lach (1965:684), Frois demonstrated an "understanding and appreciation of the arts and achievement of Japan and [studied] sympathetically all levels of Japanese society and various branches of its culture." In his 1585 treatise Frois makes a series of cultural contrasts between European ("our") culture and Japanese culture. He notes, for example, that although Europeans spit, Japanese do not (Frois 1991:29). The contemporary Japanese annotator is puzzled by this assertion because he notes that Japanese are well known to spit in public (Frois 1991:29). My observation is, rather, that most middle-class Japanese, or Americans for that matter, do not often expectorate in public. Frois (1991:56) also writes that men cook in Japan, whereas women do so in Europe. His observations extend to the ways in which Japanese cut melons (sideways, as opposed to Europeans, who cut them top down) (Frois 1991:95).

It is possible to read Frois's account not as a window into the past but as yet another lamentable instance of Orientalism. As Edward Said (1978:1) memorably noted, "The Orient was almost a European invention, and had been since antiquity a place of romance, exotic beings, haunting memories and landscapes, remarkable experiences." Although Said's observation was principally about European writings on the Middle East, his generalization applies remarkably well to Western writings on Japan. Certainly, they often tell us more about the writers themselves and their milieu than about Japan. However, it would surely be a mistake to castigate Frois and other early European travelers to Japan. Said's (1978:3) argument that "Orientalism [is] a Western style for dominating, restructuring, and having authority over the Orient" risks being hoisted on its own petard—that is, doing unto Orientalists what they purportedly did to the Orient.

Be that as it may, what interests me here is the ravage that historical transformations wreak on cultural generalizations. Confident characterizations come to seem absurd in a matter of decades, if not years. More significantly, because Frois presumes the Japanese to be so different from Europeans, he can only note differences and thereby fortify the very categorical distinction with which he begins. Although people may change beyond recognition, the categories remain robust. Hence, rather than considering each proposition critically, we need to question Frois's very use of the category of Japanese culture. As I noted in the previous chapter, it is very difficult to talk of Japan as an integral entity before the Meiji Restoration. The category of Japaneseness is an external attribution. Few people living in Japan in the sixteenth century had a national consciousness, divided as they were by region and status. In other words, the nation (Japan) is the wrong unit of analysis.

Because Frois wrote four centuries ago, it would be easy to dismiss his cultural generalizations. Contemporary ones may seem more plausible, but the faulty logic of cultural distinction remains suspiciously similar.

Nihonjinron and the Discourse of Japaneseness

An explicit articulation of the discourse of Japaneseness is the *Nihonjinron:* an extensive body of writings on theories of Japaneseness. The objective is to identify the defining and different qualities of Japanese people. Although these writings are taken as yet another unique characteristic of Japan, all major nation-states can point to numerous writings on their national identity. Whether as a state ideology to promote national integration or as a form of civil religion, there are interminable and inconclusive discussions on what it means to be a member of a particular nation-state and how that nation-state differs from others. Nationalist historiography traces a nation-state's birth and growth, whereas nationalist social sciences establish the nature and characteristics of a nation and its inhabitants. Books on *The Germans* (Elias 1996) or *The French* (Zeldin 1982) are perennially popular and inform popular discussions on Germany and Germans, or France and the French.

Thus, the *Nihonjinron* are merely a Japanese variant of the universal discourse of modern nation-states. The earliest European narratives of national characteristics, like many *Nihonjinron* writings, collected and classified simple epithets (van Delft 1993:87–104). Speculations on Japaneseness, beside the early proto-national writings of *Kokugaku* and *Mitogaku* writers in the Tokugawa period, initially took off in the late 1880s, with the publication of the journal *Nihonjin* in 1888 and the newspaper *Nihon* in 1889 (Tominaga 1990:209–210). They were products at once of nation-building and of reaction to the West (Pyle 1969:53–55).

Many contemporary Japanese people eagerly purchase and peruse *Nihonjinron* books and readily discuss them at offices and bars. According to Nomura Sōgō Kenkyūsho's 1979 bibliography, about 700 books on *Nihonjinron* appeared between 1946 and 1978, and many more have appeared since then (Aoki 1990:24). Critics charge that they promote a conservative ideology by encouraging cultural or chauvinistic nationalism (Dale 1986; Befu 1990). Brian Moeran (1989:183–184) suggests that the *Nihonjinron* are "a means whereby [Japan] can practise on the West precisely the kind of orientalism from which it has had to suffer, and to some extent still suffers, at the hands of Westerners." In other words, the Japanese discourse on Japaneseness is a form of Occidentalism, or rendering the West as the other (Aoki 1990:149–150), as it is also a form of auto-Orientalism. For others, however, these writings are a matter of serious scholarship. At one conference a major theorist of *Nihonjinron* spoke scathingly of ideological critics, claiming that they do to *Nihonjinron* writings what they claim *Nihonjinron* writers do to the Japanese. *Nihonjinron* writings, whatever their intellectual merit, are plainly good business as many books on what it means to be Japanese become best-sellers in Japan.

The diversity of perspectives is in part a reflection of the changing historical context. If the early *Nihonjinron* writings expressed the prevailing sense of Japanese inferiority vis-à-vis the West, more recent writings claimed a sense of equality and even superiority. *Nihonjinron* writings became especially popular after the rapid economic growth of the 1960s, when they also became much more positive about Japanese people and culture (Aoki 1990:82). It is not surprising that Ezra Vogel's (1979) paean to the Japanese miracle, with its propitious title of *Japan as Number One*, should have become one of the all-time best-selling nonfiction books in Japan (Aoki 1990:123).

Beyond their social origins and functions, what unifies all *Nihonjinron* writings are their fundamental assumption and central conclusion that Japanese people are different and even unique. The sine qua non of the *Nihonjinron* is the salience of the category of Japaneseness; the only taboos are to say that Japanese are just like other people or to question the category itself. The most common narrative pattern is to stress one or another feature of Japanese national character or collective psychology, such as curiosity (Tsurumi 1972), collectivism (Hamaguchi and Kumon 1982), or self-uncertainty (Minami 1983).

The *Nihonjinron* discourse shows symptomatic shortcomings. Like

Frois's pronouncements, they are replete with errors and become quickly outdated. Indeed, one of the family failings of the *Nihonjinron* is the temptation to seek *aeterna veritas*, not truths that are contingent and in flux. For example, Michael Lewis (1992:18) writes that "the pattern of Japan's domestic, social, and economic arrangements . . . hadn't changed in 200 years," when it has changed rather dramatically. The author of *The Kimono Mind*, originally published in 1965, found Japanese to be "unpunctual" (Rudofsky 1982:108), when contemporary Japanese are exceedingly punctual. As soon as one egregious effort is derided or ignored, equally implausible generalizations appear.

Beyond ignoring historical changes, *Nihonjinron* writers typically lack comparative perspective. In 1993 I was shocked by a distinguished Japanese sociologist's assertion that only Japanese criminals cover their face because Japan has a unique culture of shame. When I pointed out that South Korean criminals act in a similar fashion, he replied that, somehow, they must be different. Japanese characteristics are in fact frequently shared by East Asian and other cultures. *Amae* (dependence) is an idea made popular by the Japanese psychoanalyst Doi Takeo (1993) in a book originally published in 1971. Although this characteristic is widely believed by Japanese to be unique to Japan, Lee O-Young (1983:12–14), among others, asserts the existence of the same phenomenon in South Korea. Others argue that the Japanese are notorious for apologizing constantly. Paul Barker (1996:36) notes in this regard, "The English air is alive with the sound of 'Sorry!' London is the only capital city where the person you bump into apologizes." Politeness is, I hope, unique neither to the Japanese or the English.

Let me elaborate on the symptomatic failings of the *Nihonjinron* by considering several characteristics deemed representative of Japaneseness: loyalty, militarism, and harmony. The indelible images of the samurai and kamikaze pilots lead some people to envision Japanese as maniacally loyal and martial in nature. *Chūshingura*, translated by Donald Keene as *The Tale of 47 Ronin*, is often taken as a paradigmatic account of the Japanese spirit (Okonogi 1978:233–234). The story about forty-seven samurai who vanquish the man who dishonored their master is taken as heroic because it exemplifies the virtues of loyalty and self-sacrifice (Tsurumi and Yasuda 1983:111–115). What the celebration of *Chūshingura* misses is that it can be read as a Bakhtinian carnival (Maruya 1984) or that its parody, *Tōkaidō Yotsuya Kaidan* (Fantastic Tales of Tōkaidō Yotsuya) (Tsuruya 1956), has often been just as popular. The wartime mobilization of the 1930s and 1940s resurrected various tales of loyalty and sacrifice, inscribing them as quintessential Japanese attributes. Nitobe Inazō (1972c:282–295), writing in 1936, highlighted many samurai virtues as Japanese national character-istics, including patriotism, unity, loyalty, self-abnegation, the sense of duty, sense of honor, and so on. When I mentioned this passage to Japa-nese people in their twenties and thirties, most of them found the senti-ment outdated. Similarly, General Nogi's suicide in 1912—when he atoned for a military defeat during the Russo-Japanese War at the time of the Meiji emperor's death (Lifton, Katō, and Reich 1979:58–66)—struck youn-ger Japanese as bizarre and foreign.

Beside loyalty, samurai and kamikaze pilots evoke the image of Japa-nese people as militaristic. However, the historian Mary Elizabeth Berry (1994:xv) writes, "Before the modern era, war was unusual in Japan." The centuries of domestic peace during the Tokugawa period rendered martial arts nonviolent; violence was regarded as uncivilized (Kōno 1991:376–379). Farmers resisted military conscription during the Meiji era (Ōe S. 1981:64–76). In the postwar period pacifism became something of a hege-monic ideology. The anthropologist Mary Ellen Goodman (1957:996) found in the mid-1950s, merely a decade after the end of World War II, that "Japanese children . . . totally ignore all roles related to the military or to the national defense." Article 9 of the Japanese Constitution reads "the Japanese people forever renounce war as a sovereign right of the nation. . . . Land, sea, and airforces, as well as other war potential, will never be main-tained. The right of belligerency of the state will not be recognized." Al-though significant rearmament has occurred (Ōtake 1988:174–181), it would be difficult to characterize contemporary Japanese society as milita-ristic. A peace activist confidently told me that few Japanese would will-ingly risk their lives for the sake of the country. Both the domestic peace movement and the intellectual effort to acknowledge war guilt have been significant elements of postwar Japanese life (Ōnuma 1985).

Another received wisdom about Japanese culture is the stress on har-mony (wa). Whether in business management or everyday interactions, many write confidently of the Japanese emphasis on cooperation and com-promise. Although there are examples of harmony throughout Japanese history, there are also counterexamples. In early sixteenth-century Kyoto "we find monks battering abbots after religious debates, townspeople pummeling tax collectors with furniture, shogunal deputies torching the shrines of uncooperative priests, rivals for office assassinating their brothers" (Berry 1994:104). The psychiatrist Nakai Hisao (1992:80–81) recalls the ubiquity of street fighting in prewar Japan and speculates on the military influence in fomenting public displays of naked power. The immediate postwar years were notable for the ferocity and frequency of labor-management conflict (Moore 1983).

Some may find the assertion of militaristic Japanese contradicting that of harmonious Japanese, but *Nihonjinron* writers revel in ostensible or real contradictions. Yamazaki Masakazu (1990:83–84), for example, finds two distinct traditions in Japanese history: the family-based society *(ie shakai)* of samurai and farmers and the individualistic society of merchants. More commonly, however, an inescapable shibboleth about Japan is the distinction between *honne* (inner thought) and *tatemae* (outer expression), which reflects the quintessential Japanese mindset (Doi 1985:25–42). No civilization is, however, without some form of distinction between what Erving Goffman (1959:106–112) called the front and back regions. Certainly, Jean-Jacques Rousseau's (1960:34–47) lament about Molière's *Le misanthrope* suggests that Japanese people are far from unique in distinguishing thought and speech from act.

Furthermore, logical inconsistency may be taken as yet another defining characteristic of Japan (Smith 1983:110–112). There is in fact a venerable tradition of highlighting logical inconsistency in describing Japanese people and culture. As Ruth Benedict (1946:2–3) emphasized in *The Chrysanthemum and the Sword,* "The Japanese are, to the highest degree, both aggressive and unaggressive, both militaristic and aesthetic, both insolent and polite, rigid and adaptable, submissive and resentful of being pushed around, loyal and treacherous, brave and timid, conservative and hospitable to new ways." Given the phenomenal popularity of Benedict's book in postwar Japan, it is no wonder that most Japanese were confused as to what exactly constitutes Japaneseness. According to Bernard Rudofsky (1982:17), Japanese "are at once geniuses and copycats, aesthetes and vulgarians, their politeness is as exquisite as their rudeness, their wisdom often indistinguishable from stupidity." Similarly, the journalist Pico Iyer (1991:329) confesses, "For my own part, I began to realize that every statement I made about Japan applied just as surely in the opposite direction." Jonathan Rauch (1992:5–6) writes, "Japan is big and powerful and unstoppable. . . . But it is also small and vulnerable and hesitant and delicate. . . . These are two prevalent pictures, and they aren't consistent. Yet both seem truthful." Hence, Kishida Shū (1982:12) may very well be right in pronouncing that the "Japanese people are schizophrenic."

Why are these facile generalizations proffered? Beyond individual lapses in observation and judgment, there are several factors that contribute to the proliferation of cultural contrasts. Wielding ignorance with swagger, without shame, remains a permissible journalistic and scholarly activity. In a very narrow sense, many Western writers on Japan simply do not know much about Japanese language, history, or culture. Charles Cleaver (1976:vii) confesses at the beginning of his book comparing Japanese and American culture, "I read and write no Japanese, and my conversation with Japanese people is perfectly satisfactory to me only if they are under the age of five." Jonathan Rauch (1992:11) remarks, "I understood almost nothing except what came to me through English speakers or what was directed to me in simple, patient Japanese." John Elder's (1993:5) "journey [was] founded upon enthusiasm rather than professional expertise" (cf. Downer 1989:8). Having taken two years of Japanese, he spends a year in Kyoto to write on Bashō and classical Japanese culture. Would someone who had taken two years of Italian and spent a year in Siena dare to write a book on Dante and classical Italian culture?

To be sure, there is a classical sociological truism about outsiders, or the stranger, being able to find out important facts and to identify significant insights about another culture (Simmel 1950:406). Outsiders ignorant of language, history, and culture make acute observations from time to time. However, English-language speakers are not representative of Japanese people at large; the way many Japanese interact with white foreigners is not necessarily the way Japanese interact with others in general. In neglecting these concerns, many writers deluge readers with ethnocentric presumptions, cultural solecisms, and fanciful speculations. Consider the following entry from *Conversations in Japan*, a result of David Riesman and Evelyn Thompson Riesman's (1976:6, 31) two-month visit to Japan in the mid-1960s: "In the streets, most people we see are in Western suits. . . . I am beginning to see more variety and beauty in Japanese faces." Such an insight can only emerge against the stereotype of Japanese people articulated by Roland Barthes (1982:95–96): "a skinny creature, wearing glasses, of no specific age, in correct and lusterless clothes, a minor employee of a gigantic country."

Several years before Barthes's visit to Japan, Katō Shūichi (1986:289) found that Parisian intellectuals' knowledge of Japan comprised "*Rasho-*

mon, Kurosawa." The mother of Katō's journalist friend wondered whether there were fish and eggs in Japan. More fantastically but poetically, Pico Iyer (1991:4–5) discovered "a Wordsworthian moment" in Narita, the site of the major international airport near Tokyo. "There were many features of Japan that might have reminded me of England: the small villages set amidst rich green hills . . . the self-enclosure of an island apart from the world . . . a sense of political aloofness . . . even the sense of immovable hierarchy." Banalities and speculations abound because individuals and their thoughts remain inaccessible behind the linguistic barrier. In the absence of contacts and conversations, preconceptions shape perceptions. Given the proliferation and ready availability of *Nihonjinron* writings, foreign observers often unwittingly reproduce them.

Superficial observations lead, not surprisingly, to cursory conclusions. As Jonathan Rauch (1992:11) recognized in his state of ignorance, "Everywhere I saw surfaces, but nothing beneath. Inevitably, then, the first reaction is aesthetic." This is an extremely apt description of Barthes's *Empire of Signs* (1982), which the French critic wrote after a short visit to Japan. Although I assumed Barthes was joking, many others regard it as a valid source of information on Japan: "Roland Barthes's *Empire of Signs* . . . provides interesting insights into Japanese behavior" (Feiler 1991:312). Hence, book after book on Japan takes on the uncanny litany of repeated, common conclusions.

The problem is also one of systematic distortion of perspectives. As in the case of Frois, only differences, and not commonalities, are worthy of note. Because of the significance of the United States in postwar Japan, Japanese characteristics are noted only when they diverge from those of the United States. Such a mindset searches only for what is different or exotic, whether in the arts, popular culture, or everyday life. For example, when an American film critic sought venerable Japanese influences on Kitano Takeshi's films, the Japanese critic Hasumi Shigehiko proposed instead Jean-Luc Godard and Jerry Lewis (Camhi 1998:16). At times, observations may merely reveal the author's ignorance of his own culture. Bruce Feiler (1991:21) found evidence for rank and hierarchy consciousness among Japanese because "even the titles for the two secretaries showed rank." The ranking of secretaries is a fairly common feature of bureaucracies in most industrial societies.

Imagine, moreover, observers of Japan from other cultures; a Muslim traveler may seize on monogamy or a Hindu writer may stress materialism as different and defining characteristics of Japanese culture (Befu 1990:92–

93). The conclusion that Japan is a monogamous society, or that it is industrialized and materialist, would be of no interest to Americans, who are seeking differences, not similarities. That Japanese drink coffee and Coke or that they spend an inordinate amount of time watching television is not interesting or exotic to those engaging in tea ceremony or kabuki appreciation. In 1942 Sakaguchi Ango (1987:244–246) mocked the disjuncture between the ideal of Japaneseness—for example, Buddhist temples in Kyoto cherished by foreigners such as Bruno Taut—and the reality of contemporary Japanese life. Taut's search for "pure Japanese culture rooted in the distinctive tradition of Japan led him to Shinto and to the emperor system" (Nishikawa 1996:253). The discursive universe from Frois to Taut to contemporary *Nihonjinron* writers constitutes a mythological universe of fixed epithets and tropes.

Furthermore, historical transformations or internal variations are systematically ignored. Particular experiences generate heroic conclusions. In the immediate postwar years Japan is presented as a land of poverty and of an inferiority complex; in the bubble-economy years of the late 1980s, it is a land of wealth and has a superiority complex. Neither Tokyo nor Kyoto offers the essence of Japan, just as neither New York nor San Francisco presents the quintessential United States.

What I have said about Western writers on Japan is not significantly different from what Said argued about European writers on the Middle East. Ethnocentrism, lamentably but predictably, characterizes most writings on foreign culture. At worst, writers see merely a uniformity that verges on nullity. Peregrine Hodson (1992:64) writes: "This is Japan. It's the same everywhere. A sameness. Nothing, nothing, nothing." Japan is, however, not unique in generating the discourse of "no there there." James Bryce (1891:ii, 695) observed in his influential treatise *The American Commonwealth* that the besetting American weakness is uniformity: "it is hard to imagine how new points of repulsion and contrast are to arise, new diversities of sentiment and doctrine to be developed." It may very well be that "in America's vast emptiness . . . there are truths to sustain any fiction" (Conrad 1980:5), but in writings about America there are constant traits and themes. *Amerikajinron* is, in other words, just as flourishing a genre as *Nihonjinron*, being a wild mixture of insight and ignorance, with its canonical texts, such as Alexis de Tocqueville's *Democracy in America*, generating discourses both in the United States and abroad, such as in France (Echeverria 1957:282; Mathy 1993:251).

Why do Japanese people read foreigners' accounts of Japan and Japanese? More curiously, why do Japanese writers repeat the same observations and conclusions? In spite of the manifest limitations of *Nihonjinron* writings, many of the books are eagerly read by Japanese seeking knowledge of themselves because of the authority of the West and of curiosity about what outsiders think. As Ronald Dore (1978:248) concludes, "Few peoples in the world are as nationally self-conscious as the Japanese, as preoccupied with what it means to be a Japanese and what being a Japanese means for one's place is in the world." Although Japanese people tend to care deeply about what other people think of Japan (Aoki 1990:114), this trait can be found in many societies. The Turkish novelist Orhan Pamuk (1997:34) writes of "an oversensitivity, on our part, to opinions about Turkey expressed by foreigners and, above all, Westerners. I do not know if the same phenomenon occurs anywhere else" (cf. Yoshino 1992:40–43). A character in Robertson Davies's *The Lyre of Orpheus* (1992:844) says, "Do you like Canada? That's a silly question, of course, but you must forgive me; we always ask visitors if they like Canada as soon as they step off the plane." According to James Bowman (1992:27), "Americans have always been, more than the people of most nations, solicitous of the opinions of foreigners about their country." James Bryce (1891:i, 1) wrote over a century ago: "'What do you think of our institutions?' is the question addressed to the European traveller in the United States by every chance acquaintance." Few modern societies are indifferent to outsiders; few tourists can escape the query "how do you find our country?" As visitors grow in number, however, the frequency of the question declines.

Occasionally, Japanese people referred to one or another *Nihonjinron* book to substantiate their claim about some aspect of Japanese history or culture. Japanese people are reflexive, and Western academic discourse about Japan has had an impact on Japanese views of themselves. This, too, is not unique to the Japanese. "Apocryphal stories abound in professional folklore about the American Indian informant who, in response to the ethnographer's question, consults the work of Alfred Kroeber, or the African villager in the same situation who reaches for his copy of Meyer Fortes" (Marcus and Fischer 1986:36). Not surprisingly, Ruth Benedict's (1946) *The Chrysanthemum and the Sword* appeared to be something of a sentimental favorite, although people who referred to it clearly had not read the book carefully. They were content to rehash the proposition about Japan being a culture of shame.

The vast majority of writings on Japan underplay historical transformations, regional variations, social inequality, and, of course, ethnic diversity in Japanese society. Eurocentrism, Orientalism, and *Nihonjinron* are homologous discourses (Williams 1996; Lie 1997). The assumption of Japanese difference is, in effect, combined with the presumption of national cultural uniformity, which highlights intercultural variations at the expense of intracultural differences. Hence, the logical destination of most discussions of Japanese people is to emphasize Japanese uniqueness (Hendry 1987:3; Sugimoto 1997:2–5). Japan emerges as a valid unit of generalization, which is unchanging, homogeneous, and distinct. These characteristics reflect a particular style of thought: typological thinking.

The Pitfalls of Typological Thinking

A fundamental problem with the kind of generalizations about Japanese people, culture, and identity that I have reviewed is not only their empirical inadequacy but their conceptual shortcomings. In typological thinking a dogmatically asserted category defines a class of objects. Categorical assertions of difference ignore historical transformations and internal heterogeneity (Mayr 1991:27–31). Homogeneity and constancy characterize typological categories, which imply essential identities. The category of Japaneseness constitutes an expressive totality, in which each Japanese person becomes a bearer of the category and its attributes. In speaking of the category, one speaks of Japanese people *tout court*. Any Japanese represents the essential Japaneseness and is as good as any other in making sense of the category. Thus, the constitution of Japanese society is like a fractal; no matter where you cut it, one finds the homologous face of Japaneseness, like *Kintarō ame* or Brighton Rock. Japanese people are, as it were, ineffably Japanese; one Japanese is like any other in their shared Japaneseness. Indeed, there is really no need to examine anyone because the category already presumes its essential attributes.

Typological thinking is immune to empirical refutation. Changes and differences are negated by definition (cf. Althusser 1977:203). If someone or some characteristics change or do not seem to exemplify the essences, then there is one of two possibilities: either the transforming or heterogeneous elements express a yet deeper uniformity, or they are inessential or epiphenomenal. Alternatively, the presumption of an essence leads to its identification. Encountering a Japanese person, the typological mindset seeks to identify elements of Japaneseness, just as much as one might look for aesthetic greatness in reading a Shakespeare play or a Rembrandt self-portrait (Gombrich 1979:87). The plausibility of assertions depends not so much on logical consistency and empirical adequacy but rather on the sense of aesthetic appropriateness. Therefore, the typological formulation is frequently lapidary, however much worse it may be for the facts of the matter. In other words, the essentialized characterizations may be aesthetically pleasing—just as a Brancusi sculpture of a bird may be beautiful—but they are inadequate to achieve descriptive accuracy, whether of 125 million Japanese people or of concrete birds in flight.

Furthermore, predicates of typological categories are fundamentally indeterminate. A typological category can swallow all heterogeneous or changing elements. Diversity and change are rendered as different expressions of the same patterns. The only restriction is that the category and its attributes should be different from that of other categories. Consider in this regard that the category of the nation-state is formally isomorphic (e.g., all nations claim history, symbols, and so on), but its substance is heteromorphic (i.e., all nations perforce have different history and symbols). The dialectic of distinctions is a play of synchrony, not diachrony. Sacred symbols and characteristics change, but they must continue to differentiate one nation from another.

The discourse of Japaneseness is a palimpsest on which many contradictory things can be noted. The distinguishing quality of Japanese can be rice, the flag, or Mt. Fuji. Needless to say, many cultures eat rice, all nation-states have a flag of their own, many of which in turn look suspiciously similar, and several mountains resemble Mt. Fuji. If rice doesn't really distinguish Japanese from other peoples, then Mt. Fuji does. If Mt. Fuji seems a rather hollow source of distinction for Japanese people, then perhaps they are remarkable for their loyalty and militarism. The point is that something can always be adduced to prove the categorical distinction of Japanese from others. The idea of Japaneseness (or Frenchness or Filipino Americanness) is an empty and floating signifier; there is nothing essential except essentialization and distinction.

Beneath and Beyond the Discourse of Japaneseness

Consider the multitude of individuals who are Japanese by the conventional ethnonational classifications: rural or urban, rich or poor, schooled in the emperor ideology or democratic ideology. Given the inevitable heterogeneity, any assertion of Japanese identity is bound to be problematic; in fact, it often teeters close to being racist characterization.

The claim of Japanese essence—the existence of Japaneseness—is exceedingly dubious to anyone who knows anything about contemporary Japan, characterized as it is by rapid change and considerable diversity. Most Japanese people I know well are certainly not clones of one or another archetype. Karl Taro Greenfeld's (1994) romp through urban Tokyo introduces us to a Korean Japanese drug dealer and an English hostess, as well as pornographers and gangsters. Although Greenfeld's cast of characters may strike many American readers as deviant and delinquent, the presumption of conformity and homogeneity hardly does justice to the actually existing practices of urban Japanese youths. Consider what I saw: elementary school pupils reading manga that depict not merely nudity but sexual intercourse; teenage girls who sell their underwear with their signed photos in *burusera* shops (there were even vending machines); college, and even some high school, students who date and even prostitute themselves in *aijin banku* (lovers' banks); students and OLs (office ladies) in the most minimal of clothing gyrating madly on stage at Juliana and other discos. And I am merely a garden-variety academic who by and large dutifully commuted between my apartment and my office. In contrast, the symbol of 1970s deviance, motorcycle gangs, seems downright tame (Sato 1991). A study of 1960s deviance in a poor area of Tokyo reads like a study in conformity: "Many Japanese are still part of a 'heritage of endurance,' still part of a 'Japanese' culture that organizes its people both individually and collectively toward the realization of ends that are often collectively perceived" (Wagatsuma and De Vos 1984:447).

It would be easy to retort that just as motorcycle gang members became ordinary adults (Sato 1991:176–177), oversexed girls may become the most demure of housewives. Alternatively, the latest transformations may in fact exemplify broadly Japanese patterns (White 1993:160–166). Although there is more than a grain of truth in both views, the proverbial procrustean bed should not be stretched beyond recognition. Does it really make sense to tame every transgression of traditional patterns as expressing, ineffably but deeply, elements of Japaneseness? It is the same mindset that frames every foreign element in Japanese life—whether Jesus or jazz, baseball or Buddhism, Chinese characters or Chinese food—as ultimately conforming to certain deep Japanese patterns. Indeed, the very incorporation of foreign elements becomes yet another—and unique—expression of Japanese people and culture, as if other cultural traditions were not syncretic.

Contemporary Japanese people are neither particularly uniform nor inevitably exemplify some stereotypes of Japaneseness. Rather, individualism and deviance are well cultivated. Manga as a genre is particularly rife with diversity; we can read about cannibalism and rape in Ōtomo Katsuhiro (1986) or the importance of privacy and human rights in Mōri Jinpachi and Uoto Osamu (1990). Academics, by and large staid people, say wild things in Japan; Komuro Naoki (1993:213) seriously proposed annexing the United States to Japan, whereas Tada Michitarō (1988:28) claimed that "I quit brushing my teeth when I was about 30 because I was told that my mouth smelled." He felt that people complaining about his halitosis was the beginning of fascism. In a collection of essays on fifty years of the postwar period, Iida Momo argues that Japan should perish, Watanabe Kazuomi believes Japan to be a totalitarian society, and Hagiwara Yōko thinks that all the Japanese have become idiots (Yasuhara 1995).

The diversity of sentiments that flourish beneath the discursive space of Japaneseness is nothing new. One need only consider the reactions to the end of World War II. If we believed the discourse of Japaneseness, the emperor's announcement of surrender *(gyokuon hōsō)* on August 15, 1945, might have led to fanatical outbursts by loyal, martial, and patriotic Japanese. In fact, the reactions were manifold (Irokawa 1978:162–176; Isoda 1983b:18–33). To begin with, many people had difficulty deciphering what the emperor was saying (Ishida 1968:146–147). Far from expressing dejection and despair, the critic Hayashi Tatsuo (1973:107) remembered reading Alphonse Daudet on that fateful day. Many Ainu, Koreans, and leftists—all Japanese citizens at the time—celebrated the day (Ogawa 1997:377–379). Okiura Kazumitsu (1990:32) recalled that people around him mainly worried about their family members.

Even for believers and partial-believers in the emperor and the war, the turnaround was very quick. The novelist Yasuoka Shōtarō (1991a:17–18) listened to the broadcast, heard a baby cry, and got on an empty train: "I probably lost my patriotism the moment when I heard the baby cry." The publisher Ogawa Kikumatsu "could not prevent tears from falling [when he heard the broadcast], but he planned for the publication of a Japanese-English conversation text on the same day," which went on to sell 3.6 million copies (Akazawa 1994:176). The rapid conversion of Ogawa was symptomatic; Tsuda Michio (1973:23) beat up a friend who exchanged the Japanese flag for chocolate bars from GIs but went on to make the same trade a week later. As I emphasized in the previous chapter, the penetration of national identity, and especially of the ultranationalistic creed of the emperor and militarism, remained incomplete even in 1945, especially in rural areas. As a 49-year-old farmer noted in 1943: "I feel no gratitude for having been born in Japan. Being born in Japan is regrettable, I think, and I loathe the emperor" (Dower 1993:143). In fact, a great deal of popular antipathy to wartime militarism existed, including antagonism toward the emperor (Araki 1986:154–170). So much for the 100 million Japanese—30 million of whom were colonized people—united in the sacred war effort.

The Poverty of Holism

Typological thinking exemplifies a style of thought common in the social sciences. Recall once again Émile Durkheim's (1984:chaps. 2–3) celebrated contrast between mechanical and organic solidarity. Complex societies, according to Durkheim, are unified by differences making for organic solidarity. In a society of mechanical solidarity, as the Latin root of identity— *idem* (sameness)—suggests, any assertion of identity presupposes elements of sameness or similarity among disparate individuals. One is a French person or a Filipino American because of some shared characteristics with fellow French people or Filipino Americans. Yet a French person in the 1990s may be of Alsatian or Algerian descent, Catholic or Jewish, French speaking or Breton speaking, republican or racist, and so on. Similarly, a Filipino American may have a father of Chinese or African American descent, a knowledge of one of the Filipino languages, such as Tagalog or Ilocano, or none of them, may have been born in the Philippines or Saudi Arabia, and so on. This does not mention the multitude of possible personality types, lifestyle choices, educational attainments, or political orientations.

To conceive of society as one of mechanical solidarity has nonetheless been a privileged mode of social theorizing. Baron de Montesquieu (1949:293), one of the precursors of modern sociology, wrote, "Mankind are influenced by various causes: by the climate, by the religion, by the laws, by the maxims of government, by precedents, morals, and customs; whence is formed a general spirit of nations. In proportion as, in every country, any one of these causes acts with more force, the others in the same degree are weakened. Nature and the climate rule almost alone over the savages; customs govern the Chinese; the laws tyrannize in Japan." Few today would accuse Japan of being tyrannized by law (Upham 1998). Each variable, in fact, is significantly diverse in Japan: there are distinct climate zones in Japan (Fujimoto 1988:14–19), and there is considerable religious diversity (Murakami 1978:78–107).

Modern complex societies are not holistic in the sense implied by mechanical solidarity, that of being an organism or expressing inner essences (Phillips 1976:122–123). Among the Japanese there are overall similarities, sometimes similarities of detail, but certainly no essences. Contemporary Japanese society is a complex amalgam of transnational institutions and social networks, constituted by various organizations and regions. Although useful generalizations may be made about Japanese society as a whole, they should not be regarded as expressing the underlying unity and uniformity of Japanese people. Any serious study would inevitably uncover a messy reality—complexity, diversity, and change.

To assume the singularity of Japanese people, or essential features of Japaneseness, misses the fundamental fact that there is no Japanese people as such. In this regard, Ludwig Wittgenstein (1968:32) suggested that, rather than looking for essence, we should look for family resemblance. He used the example of games: "What is common to them all?—Don't say: 'There *must* be something common, or they would not be called "games."' For if you look at them you will not see something that is common to *all*, but similarities, relationships, and a whole series of them and that. . . . We see a complicated network of similarities overlapping and criss-crossing: sometimes overall similarities, sometimes similarities of detail" (Wittgenstein 1968:31–32).

The discourse of Japaneseness, like all nationalist discourses, is ultimately a form of mythology. Mythology is static, rehashing a repertoire of utterances (Lévi-Strauss 1979:40). The category of Japaneseness posits naturalized essences, which are inimical to serious empirical examination. As R. H. Tawney once quipped, you can peel an onion layer by layer, but you can't skin a tiger stripe by stripe. Arguing with Japaneseness is like that; just as Tawney believed that one cannot transform capitalism piecemeal, typological thinking resists empirical examination. It is not possible to argue an empirical point fact by fact or criteria of Japaneseness criterion by criterion. Because the category of thought is dogmatically asserted, there is no way to use empirical propositions to question or to engage in logical disputation. Assertions of Japaneseness are quasi-religious utterances. That propositions prove to be mutually contradictory, or do not reflect reality, does not disrupt the category. Although mythology may promote social solidarity, it does not promote accurate knowledge. As Georges Canguilhem (1988:32–33) argued, "The essence of false science is that it never encounters falsehood, never renounced anything, and never has to change its language. . . . The assertions of a false science can never be falsified. Hence false science has no history."

Some Consequences of the Prison House of Japaneseness

One consequence of the discourse of Japaneseness is that it circumscribes the culturally accepted boundaries of Japanese utterance and behavior. Strong norms about what it means to be Japanese translate into strong sanctions to squelch deviance. There are in fact many ways in which Japanese lives are prescribed and circumscribed. Michel Foucault (1977:227–228), in one of the memorable passages in *Discipline and Punish,* discusses the rise of a disciplinary society in which norms are not prescribed from above but rather instituted from below. Certainly, a vision of disciplinary society in which everyone is a warden—a heady mixture of Kafka and Foucault—is a commonly expressed sentiment about contemporary Japanese society (cf. Kurihara 1982).

It is precisely because of the persistence of strong norms that many Japanese are wont to remark that "I am not really Japanese." What they mean, of course, is not that they doubt their citizenship status or ethnonational membership, but that they find it difficult to conform to societal norms. The quality of being Japanese is not so much descriptive as prescriptive. If the *Nihonjinron* writings offer something of a civil religion for Japanese people, then that creed—how to be Japanese—is just as difficult for Japanese to follow as the Ten Commandments are for Christians. A Briton describes his Japanese girlfriend: "She didn't want to behave in a Japanese way. Why did she have to change the way she was to suit Japanese people? What was this Japanese way of doing things? She wasn't going to be turned into a Japanese girl. And what was so special about Japanese girls anyway?" (Hodson 1992:107–108). A housewife in her forties told me that, as easy as it may seem to be Japanese, it is in fact very tiring to be so. Some foreigners complain about how difficult it is to relax in Japan because of the oppressive character of Japanese manners (Sha 1988:96–98). Norms of interpersonal interaction demand surface conformity; deviants are stigmatized as somehow un-Japanese, evoking the wartime epithet *hikokumin* (non-national) that stifled dissent (Kawamura 1993:18–19), or its postwar variants, such as *Nihonjin banare* (deviating from Japanese) or *bata kusai* (smelling like butter, a shorthand for foreign).

The category of Japaneseness has considerable social significance. As in other nation-states, citizenship provides various privileges, ranging from suffrage, to welfare benefits, to employment opportunities. But being Japanese—fitting the image of what it means to be Japanese—is one of the fundamental ways in which society is organized. I have already mentioned several instances when clearly non-Japanese people, such as the sumō wrestler Akebono or the soccer star Ramos, were regarded as Japanese because of their putatively Japanese behavior and thought patterns. The sociologist Takeuchi Yō (1995:232–234) argues that employment and mobility advantages are given to people who exemplify what I have been calling Japaneseness. Cultural capital for Japanese, in other words, is to embody and enact Japaneseness.

The Classificatory Impulse and the Hermeneutic Urge

The impulse to classify is universal. Beyond evolutionary and utilitarian reasons, the very operations of our cognition depend on classification. The biologist John Moore (1993:181–182) writes, "classification is the most powerful method we possess for packaging information. It is so much a part of our lives that we forget how basic it is." Some categories are rooted in nature; others are relatively independent of it. Although the distinction between nature and society is an easy one to deconstruct, classification systems of color or of plants and animals exhibit commonality across cultures (Berlin and Kay 1969; Hardin and Maffi 1997). The same cannot be said, however, for classification of human beings. Although physiological and other biological features are often invoked to distinguish one group of people from another, the fundamental basis of classification is social, not biological. Biologically, the basal taxonomic unit of humanity is the species Homo sapiens.

Social life dictates the imposition of classification and categorization. Mature members of one tribe have no trouble identifying their own members from those of other tribes. Modern nation-states seek to forge a sense of nationhood that supersedes competing identities. In either case, the categories of peoplehood are given, not generated by individuals. Everyone relies on socially disseminated categories to identify and divide people. Although individuals, especially children, may devise idiosyncratic systems of classification—thin versus fat people, or people with or without spectacles—they must align their inchoate schemes with socially accepted systems of classification. In the case of Japanese people, the ready-made categories of peoplehood are taught in schools and saturate the mass media.

That society imposes classificatory schemes does not mean that there is only one system or that people do not struggle over these schemes. Even in the natural world, matters of classification come to the fore from time to time. Consider the relatively trivial case of the planet Pluto. "Pluto's minuteness and its membership in a swarm of like objects mean that it should be classified as a 'minor planet,' as asteroids and comets are. Others are outraged by the idea, insisting that regardless of how its identity has changed, demoting Plato would dishonor astronomical history and confuse the public" (Freedman 1998:22).

Social classification, which is born of convenience, often becomes reified. Although there may be no solid bedrock—no principle to justify the classificatory scheme—many people nonetheless think and live according to the reified schemes. Hindsight frequently reveals the arbitrary nature of social classification. For example, the Quiller-Couch edition of *The Oxford Book of Victorian Verse,* published in 1913, contains recognizably Victorian poets such as John Greenleaf Whittier and Lord Tennyson. By 1987, when the Ricks edition of *The New Oxford Book of Victorian Verse* appeared, we could ask, whither Whittier? What is even more remarkable is that the redoubtable Quiller-Couch had included James Joyce and Ezra Pound in the 1913 volume. Joyce and Pound as Victorians? In fact, Carol T. Christ (1984) makes a very persuasive case for the continuities between what we call Victorian and modernist poetry.

Needless to say, we cannot do away with classificatory schemes and categories. In their absence individuals place a seemingly deviant case in one of the available categories. In this regard, scholars have attributed many works to Daniel Defoe under the assumption that it is better to attribute an anonymous work to a specific author (Furbank and Owens 1988:30–31). In a similar fashion Pisanello's paintings have been attributed to Piero della Francesca, Albrecht Dürer, and Leonardo da Vinci (Fenton 1996). In the contemporary United States there are murky debates on the racial classification of mixed-race people. Until recently the one-drop rule had defined whether a person of mixed descent should be classified as white or black (Davis 1991). As absurd as the classificatory scheme may seem in retrospect, to which side of the ethnoracial divide one belonged had tremendous impact on the life chances of individuals. Ethnoracial classification has often implied a difference between freedom and slavery, life and death.

The classificatory impulse combines well with the hermeneutic urge. As cultural beings, human beings impose meanings on the chaotic world. When I have divided a classroom of students into two groups, and asked the groups to generate generalizations about one another, they almost always do so based on arbitrary divisions. Should it be surprising then that received categories should be the object of endless imputations, and permutations, of meaning? One of the principal reasons that the category of Japaneseness seems so natural and obvious is that people have invested it with profound meaning, articulated in long-standing discourses. Given the subject of Japanese, we are awash with predicates of Japaneseness.

Reflective individuals query the meaning of self and identity. Everyone is a sociologist; hence, everyone has an implicit system of social classification, replete and redolent with meaning. Most individual reflections, however, tend to be fleeting and superficial. In Anton Chekhov's 1887 story, "The Kiss," a woman mistakenly and mysteriously kisses the protagonist. Anxiously attempting to convey the wondrous experience to his comrades, Ryabovitch "began describing very minutely the incident of the kiss, and a moment later relapsed into silence. In the course of that moment he had told everything, and it surprised him dreadfully to find how short a time it took him to tell it. He had imagined that he could have been telling the story of the kiss till next morning" (Chekhov 1984:199). It takes a masterly writer, such as Chekhov, to transmogrify the moment into meaning; lesser mortals can at best hope to reproduce the received rhetoric and available trope.

Most Japanese people, like Chekhov's Ryabovitch, responded curtly and vaguely when I asked them explicitly about what makes Japanese Japanese. Many people were silent, others repeated banalities, some quoted authorities, and others offered their considered reflections. What distinguished them from their 1960s counterparts—many of whom were puzzled about the nature of Japaneseness, as we saw in the previous chapter—was the proliferation of ready-made predicates of Japaneseness, supplied by decades of *Nihonjinron* writings.

Contemporary Japanese people draw on a large and proliferating discourse on what it means to be Japanese, thereby bringing closure to the cycle of the classificatory impulse and the hermeneutic urge. Each response in turn reproduces the category of Japaneseness. The sociologist Merry White (1993:215) observes that "[b]eing Japanese is a significant factor in [Japanese children's] identity and they feel that Japan and the Japanese are in some ways different or unique." Confronted by a strange foreigner, or asked to answer questions about Japanese characteristics, students cannot but generate discourses of difference and uniqueness. Indeed, the trope of "we Japanese" becomes the dominant mode of responding to curious foreigners. "Always, it was 'ware, ware Nihonjin desu,'—'we Japanese'—an identification, I was to learn, that had less to do with the name of a nation state than with an idea, a self-defining concept two thousand years old" (Shapiro 1989:12). Of course, few native Japanese speakers will say "ware, ware Nihonjin desu." While the elite college students in the 1960s were stumped by the question of what it meant to be Japanese, by the 1990s almost all Japanese knew—thanks to the discourse of Japaneseness—a thing or two about the meaning of Japaneseness.

The category of Japaneseness generates endless discussions of essentialized characteristics. For the reasons I adduced in the previous chapter, mono-ethnicity became a key predicate of Japaneseness by the late 1960s. As Friedrich Nietzsche (1982:9) observed: "All things that live long are gradually so saturated with reason that their origin in unreason thereby becomes improbable." Although the idea of monoethnic Japan may be relatively new, it had become almost as sacrosanct in the early 1990s as the divinity of the emperor was sixty years ago. This is not necessarily a ground for despair, however. As rapidly as the secularization of the emperor ideology occurred, we may also see the imminent demise of the idea of monoethnicity.

Conclusion

Perhaps the largest collective project in Japanese sociology is the decennial survey on Stratification and Social Mobility (SSM). In the 1980s Japanese sociologists began to consider seriously the gender dimension of inequality and mobility. When I asked them in 1985 about analyzing ethnicity, the uniform answer was that the category of ethnicity, whether for counting or for analysis, was not necessary because there were so few minorities in Japan. The inevitable consequence of ignoring ethnicity is that the SSM surveys record no ethnic minority in Japan. The count of zero becomes a scientific fact that justifies the presumption of ethnic homogeneity—yet another instance of a self-fulfilling prophecy.

Power produces knowledge—sometimes. As a scholar I am constantly reminded of the equation between academe and irrelevance; few seem to read academic work, and even fewer seem to appreciate it. However, social research has been repeatedly called on to serve the needs of governments and other interests, whether it be anthropology in the service of colonialism (Stauder 1986) or genetics in the service of eugenics (Kevles 1985). The social sciences in the contemporary world play a minor but discernible role in shaping public opinion, the commonsense consensus that has such a significant impact on politics. When Japanese sociologists write and speak with all their authority about monoethnic Japan, they contribute in a small but potentially significant way to the continuing nonrecognition and exclusion of non-Japanese ethnics in contemporary Japanese society. Knowledge is power—sometimes.

The Politics of Recognition and Inclusion

Japan has always been multiethnic. Ethnic diversity began neither with the coming of the new foreign workers in the 1980s, nor with the influx of colonial subjects in the early twentieth century, nor even with the arrival of *toraijin* from the Korean peninsula over a millennium ago. Japanese history and multiethnic Japan are coeval; one cannot speak of Japan without speaking of ethnic diversity. Nonetheless, many Japanese continue to believe that they live in a monoethnic society. For them, Ainu, Okinawans, Burakumin, Koreans, Chinese, and others are about to disappear, are really Japanese, or are foreigners. Non-Japanese Japanese are not granted their place in Japanese society, either in the present or in the past, and they face disadvantages and discrimination in seeking jobs or spouses. Because they don't exist, they can't rectify their place in Japanese society.

The prevailing individualistic solution has been to attempt to pass as ordinary Japanese. Living in the ethnic closet, however, non-Japanese Japanese suffer from psychological anguish. Their sufferings go beyond routine slights; their life stories are often heartbreaking. It was not unusual to hear in interviews that I was the first person outside family members to be told about an interviewee's ethnic background. It is difficult enough to face, or constantly expect to face, discrimination in employment or ordinary social interactions; it is wrenching to suffer the further ordeal of hiding, as it were, an elemental self-identity. For what is personal identity but a sense of whence one came and who one is? Anyone who cannot tell others of their name or ethnonational descent cannot hope to lead a life of dignity and respect.

Against the prevalent belief that Japan is a monoethnic society, non-Japanese Japanese engage in a politics of recognition. To achieve a decent and dignified life, they must first eradicate ethnic discrimination and seek full-scale inclusion in Japanese life. Here the single most important institutional impediment against the advancement of non-Japanese Japanese remains the state bureaucracies, which continue to be exclusionary against cultural Japanese without state citizenship. By ignoring systematic disadvantages of the Ainu, Burakumin, or Okinawans, they also encourage efforts by ethnic activists to remedy their collective situation.

The struggles for recognition and inclusion necessarily incorporate other pressing concerns in Japanese life. The movements for Ainu or Okinawan cultural autonomy promote the environmental protection of Hokkaidō and Okinawa (Hanazaki 1993). Just as the new social movements of the 1960s and 1970s inspired Ainu, Burakumin, Korean, and other activists, their continuing struggles cannot but touch other efforts to ameliorate the neglected and impoverished sectors of Japanese life (Kano 1985; Honda 1993b). In this regard, there are powerful voices heard not only among the non-Japanese Japanese but also among ethnic Japanese people. There are numerous scholarly efforts to rectify the recent dominance of the monoethnic worldview. Indeed, I have drawn heavily on the academic excavation of Japanese multiethnicity.

The idea of multiethnicity is not an unalloyed good in itself, however. As we saw in Chapter 5, prewar imperialists promoted an ideology of multiethnicity to justify colonialism. In the 1990s some conservative Japanese nationalists began to promote the idea of Japanese ethnic hybridity and multiethnicity, presenting a kinder and gentler version of prewar pan-Asian identity (Oguma 1995:396–399; cf. Hein and Hammond 1995:16–17). Ishihara Shintarō (1995:158)—one of the pioneering ideologues of Japanese monoethnicity in the late 1960s—was spouting Japanese multiethnicity in order to legitimate pan-Asian ideals by the mid-1990s: "We are an Asian people, ethnically and culturally. Japan is not a unique, homogeneous country."

Are Japanese Racists?

In struggling for recognition and inclusion, some have come to regard Japanese society as hopelessly and irremediably racist. Japanese critics frequently concur and cite Japanese racism as a recalcitrant and reprehensible feature of contemporary Japanese society (e.g., Koyama 1981:6). Indeed, it is something of an American stereotype that Japanese people are irrevocably racist and xenophobic (Fallows 1994:104). The grand historian Paul Kennedy (1993:143) detects "a deep streak of racism, which is particularly manifested in Japanese views of Koreans, Chinese, American blacks, and many other ethnic groups abroad, as well as the *burakumin* ('outcasts') at home." For the philosopher Allan Bloom (1990:22), Japanese people "seem to be racists. They consider themselves superior; they firmly resist immigration; they exclude even Koreans who have lived for generations among them." In Michael Crichton's (1992) novel, *Rising Sun*, Conner, whom the protagonist thought "had been Japanese himself," says that Japanese people are "the most racist people on the planet. . . . I got tired of the exclusion. . . . I got tired of being a nigger."

The American accusation of Japanese racism seems misplaced, however. White Europeans and Americans are, in general, treated extremely well as honored guests, and their complaints reveal the extent to which they are pampered. For example, a young American man was happy to learn that I was of Korean descent. He explained that when he went to Seoul, the first thing that happened to him was that he got into a screaming match with a cabdriver. The experience sounded horrible to me, but he countered: "After living in Tokyo for a year, where everyone, all the time, is so nice and friendly, I was going bonkers. It was such a relief to meet a rude person. Shouting at him, I felt alive." The British expatriate Peregrine Hodson (1992:211), in contrast, writes, "I remember I'm a *gaijin* and it hurts like poverty or injustice. It's the pain of being other." The only concrete experience of painful injustice in his book is a rude bank clerk; otherwise, his life in Japan seems to revolve around meeting beautiful women and engaging in interesting conversations. Similarly, the journalist Pico Iyer's (1991) account of his year in Kyoto, *The Lady and the Monk,* is more about the former topic than the latter. C. W. Nichol (1993:17) expounds at length about encountering an obnoxious drunk—the only time in thirty years that he encountered something like racism in Japan.

Nonetheless, white *gaijin* frequently complain bitterly. Ivan Hall (1998) accuses Japanese intellectual life of "academic apartheid" (cf. Buruma 1989:227–228). In contrast, I found remarkable indulgence accorded to white academics and intellectuals; the analogy with second-rate foreign baseball players feted in Japan is appropriate (cf. Yamaguchi 1978:66–71). I know of no non-American academic at a U.S. university who cannot carry an ordinary conversation in English, whereas there are *hakujin* academics teaching at Japanese universities who have trouble ordering from a set menu. It is, of course, easier to condemn Japanese as xenophobic than to learn Japanese. In any case, Westerners have been more likely to inflict derogatory comments on Japanese people.

Japanese people are more likely to hurl racist epithets at African Americans and Africans. Kokubo Masao, a regional politician, said, "We know in our heads that discrimination is bad, but our feelings are different. . . . When you shake hands with someone who is completely black, you feel your hands getting black" (*International Herald Tribune,* March 19, 1993). Prime Minister Nakasone Yasuhiro made international headlines in the mid-1980s by making racist remarks against American ethnic minorites: "There are quite a few blacks, Puerto Ricans, and Mexicans in America, and their [intelligence] is on average still extremely low" (Nakasone 1986:152). The implication of Nakasone's statement was elaborated in 1990 by the Minister of Justice Kajiyama Seiroku, who invoked Gresham's law to state, "In the United States, blacks *(kuro)* came in and pushed out whites *(shiro)*" (Terazawa 1990:65). The decline of the United States resulted in this ethnic allegory of multiethnicity; the ascent of Japan was, in contrast, due to monoethnicity. However, it is far from clear that negative Japanese stereotypes about African Americans and Africans are transhistorical truths. The Iwakura Mission in the mid-nineteenth century reported: "There is no relationship between skin color and intelligence" (Tokumei Zenken Taishi 1977:218). A 1950s study of Japanese novels showed that "Negroes are always described favorably" (Adachi 1959:59). Some contemporary Japanese people hold negative stereotypes about African Americans (Wagatsuma and Yoneyama 1967:88–91; Russell 1991:86– 108; Honda 1993b:99–104), but they learned them proximately and principally from Americans and the American media.

Certainly, xenophobic sentiments and exclusionary discourses have existed at least since the Tokugawa effort to extirpate Christianity (Norman 1957:338–339). The colonial period was rife with statements of Japanese superiority and Asian inferiority, which penetrated even the countryside (Smith and Wiswell 1982:21; Shibuya 1986:4–5). This is not surprising given that virtually all the colonized people worked in subordinate positions (Hidaka 1980:32–33). Negative stereotypes that derive from colonial rule afflict contemporary Japanese perceptions of Koreans and other Asians (Kang 1993:122–128).

Nonetheless, we should not assume an unbroken continuity of the prewar colonial discourse in contemporary Japan. At a rowdy bar in the now-seedy Golden Street *(Gōrudengai)* in Shinjuku, a clearly inebriated man ranted and raved about "Chankoro." My Japanese friend was, however, ignorant of this racial epithet for Chinese. On another occasion a female teacher used the phrase "*baka de mo Chon de mo*" (even fools and Koreans) to express her disgust at some slow students. The phrase is used to denote that even fools and Koreans can do a simple task: hence the term *bakachon kamera* for a foolproof camera. When I asked her if she was conscious of the racial epithet *Chon* for Koreans, she became embarrassed, and said that she had used it unconsciously. As these examples suggest, the survival of racist epithets and phrases should not necessarily be taken to mean that the prewar ethnoracial worldview remains robust. Simply to castigate contemporary Japanese people as racist obscures more than it illuminates about the nature of the contemporary Japanese ethnonational worldview.

Consider a major incident that occurred in 1993. After complaints from some citizens, the authorities banned the large weekly gathering of Iranians in Yoyogi Park. An Iranian youth concluded that "Japanese are fascists and racists." Certainly, the decision exemplified the authoritarian streak in Japanese life. The complaints, according to the authorities, focused on the "threatening" crowd. Several Japanese people told me that they were scared of Iranians gathering in a crowd, although the fear remained unspecified and the worst offense I heard was that Iranian men try to pick up Japanese women. Because foreigners and bad behavior are both rare, the combination—foreigners behaving badly—stands out. There was a widespread suspicion among the Japanese about the criminal behavior of the new foreign workers even though the evidence was at best ambiguous (Komai 1993:187–191; Sekiguchi 1993:78). They were reproducing the reified category and the racist rhetoric associated with it. One young woman who suggested that foreign workers were "scary" or a recent college graduate who said that they were "strange" both admitted that they had never talked to, or for that matter come close to, any foreign worker.

I would argue that most Japanese people are, at worst, passive racists. It is very difficult to locate irrefutable evidence of Japanese racism; rather, I mainly heard statements that indict other Japanese. For example, when a friend was considering marriage with a Burakumin man, her parents and friends repeatedly told her that her life, and especially that of her future children, would be ruined. In this line of reasoning, individuals are not racists but, rather, the society at large. Passive racism expresses the structure of irresponsibility illuminated by the political theorist Maruyama Masao (1964:106–128). He argued that Japanese soldiers and officers denied their responsibility for World War II and blamed their superiors. The ladder of irresponsibility eventually reached the top, namely, the emperor, and all below him were, in effect, absolved of their responsibility. In other words, blaming others left everyone blameless. A paradigmatic instance of passive racism is residential discrimination. When I looked for an apartment for a South Korean scholar near the University of Tokyo, eight brokers simply refused to consider renting to foreigners. All of them blamed either landlords or neighbors for disliking foreigners. In castigating someone else, the structure of irresponsibility assured the perpetuation of residential segregation.

Many situations that can be construed as instances of Japanese racism are in fact much more ambiguous. Consider again residential discrimination, which stems from a concatenation of concerns. Although a single negative experience with a Japanese renter does not lead to a ban on renting to Japanese, one bad experience with a non-Japanese person often leads to a decision never to rent to foreigners (Komai 1993:172–173). Many foreign workers, due to the prohibitively high cost of housing and the difficulty of locating suitable lodging, overcrowd their apartments and thereby contribute to their undesirability as tenants (Ishiyama 1989:15). In addition, ignorance of local norms leads newcomers to behave in ways that make them unwelcome (Okuda and Tajima 1991:165–166), and the complicated system of rental, including the provision of guarantors (*hoshōnin*), makes it difficult for newcomers to find housing. The most commonly expressed complaints about the new foreign workers by neighbors—their inability to park their bicycles properly or to place their garbage—were often matters that a few minutes of conversation might very well have solved (Okuda and Tajima 1991:148).

Misunderstandings are rife among people who do not share a common language (Tokyo Toritsu Rōdō Kenkyūsho 1994:312–313). One day I was speaking with a young European American man in Shibuya when a politician began, as is customary in Japan, to make a soporific speech that nonetheless blared painfully and loudly. The annoyed American shouted at the rotund speaker to "shut up," sprinkling his request with colorful epithets. The speaker smiled, pointed at the man, and thanked the unknown *gaijin* profusely for the enthusiastic support.

Finally, many problematic aspects of Japanese life affect both foreigners and Japanese. Some foreigners felt that they were under constant surveillance. Rey Ventura (1992:171) thought that he had "lived in hiding," but he found out that the police merely "pretended not to see us. When public opinion demanded, they made a token raid." Police surveillance of foreigners is something of a historical constant in modern Japan (Honda 1992:58). However, police surveillance often extends to ordinary Japanese as well, and surveillance goes well beyond the police. Many Japanese urban neighborhoods remain realms of face-to-face interactions and of strong communal social control (Bestor 1989:205–213). In this context any newcomers or strangers are greeted with a degree of suspicion, whether or not they are foreigners. In this regard, urban life in Japan is challenging even for most Japanese. In the crowded Tokyo metropolitan area, a great deal of local knowledge is necessary to maneuver around town; navigating the labyrinthine train and subway system requires considerable local knowledge and survival skills. Anyone moving at less than peak efficiency is bound to suffer, even those with linguistic fluency. Japanese from out of town, the elderly, and those with physical disabilities all find urban life difficult.

My intention is not to exculpate Japanese rudeness or racism. Rather, my point is that Japanese racism is far from being an essential Japanese characteristic. In the extensive debate on the foreign workers, there was no well-organized xenophobic movement or widespread public expressions of racism. In Europe, in contrast, immigration politics unleashed a variety of right-wing nationalist movements (Freeman 1979:280–294). It is, of course, possible that such a movement will arise in Japan. Scattered evidence of far-right, even neo-Nazi, sentiments existed (*Asahi Shinbun,* April 7, 1993). However, government publications were remarkably tempered and often expressed concerns for the welfare and human rights of the foreign workers (e.g., Keizai Kikakuchō Sōgō Keikakukyoku 1989:86–95; Ministry of Labour 1992:173–176; Ministry of Foreign Affairs 1992:183–185). Most publications on the problem of foreign workers were careful to point out human rights abuses even when they were less than supportive of open immigration (e.g., Ōmura 1990).

My interviews with government officials and ordinary citizens yielded very little in the way of statements that could be construed as racist—and this was no different when my Japanese colleagues interviewed them. Some local political authorities, such as the Kanagawa Prefecture, have set up agencies to disseminate information to and assist foreign residents (Kanagawa Zainichi Gaikokujin Mondai Kenkyūkai 1992; cf. Tezuka, Miyajima, Tou, and Itō 1992). In one booklet subtitled, "I Would Like to Meet You More," there are articles that explain why foreign workers are in Kanagawa, information on medical services, schools, and Japanese-language courses, and guides in English, Korean, Chinese, Thai, Tagalog, Spanish, and Portuguese (Kanagawa Zainichi Gaikokujin Mondai Kenkyūkai 1993).

Some progressive unions, such as Zentōitsu, have actively organized the migrant workers in construction and other industries (Gaikokujin Rōdōsha Kenri Hakusho Henshū Iinkai 1995). I found a very informative and useful book for employers who wished to hire foreign workers (Gaikokujin Kōyō Mondai Kenkyūkai 1990), as well as a guidebook that apprised Asian workers of their rights in eighteen languages (Osaka Bengoshikai 1992). Support groups, such as HELP and Kalabaw no Kai, assist foreigners in a variety of ways, ranging from legal counsel to language training (Ajiajin Rōdōsha Mondai Kondankai 1988:456–460; Stevens 1997:86–88). Several books provided guidance on, and even encouraged, international marriage (Kokusai Kekkon o Kangaerukai 1987; Moriki 1991). Many people I interviewed spoke up on behalf of the new immigrant workers. One elite office worker decried the unfair treatment of foreign workers; invoking the philosopher Immanuel Kant, he fulminated that people should be treated as ends rather than as means. An attorney who did pro bono work for the Asian migrant workers insisted that his only regret was that he could not spend more time helping them, and I had no reason to doubt his sincerity.

Given that there are Japanese racists and racist discourses in Japanese society, the temptation to heighten the social evil is understandable, but it obfuscates more than it illuminates. If Japanese people are, somehow, transhistorically and systematically racist, then there is really no solution. Racists are, after all, not born. History, particularly bad history, is not destiny. At the least, we should not expunge a significant body of anticolonial or counterracist writings, ranging from Matsuura Takeshiro and Yanagi Muneyoshi on the Ainu (Hanazaki 1988:305–321; Yanagi 1981:530) to Nakae Chōmin and Sakai Toshihiko on the Burakumin (Neary 1989:39–40). Neither should we ignore the existence of antiracist discourses and movements in contemporary Japanese society.

In spite of the seeming omnipotence of the state in modern Japanese history, change has been constant. To take one example, the emperor system was largely meaningless before the Meiji Restoration and has become profoundly secularized in the postwar period. There have been at least two unheralded efforts to create an independent country in Japan: the 1869 independence movement in Hokkaidō led by Enomoto Takeaki (singing *La Marseillaise* no less) and the 1945 founding of the Yaeyama Republic (Yaeyama *kyōwakoku*) in the Okinawa archipelago (Shinobu 1992:352–357). The fundamental transformation of Japanese society since 1945 leaves open the possibility that we may also see a far-reaching change in ethnic relations. Already by the early 1980s, interethnic marriage rates for ethnic Chinese and Koreans in Japan were over two-thirds (Ichikawa 1987:271; Yazawa 1985:36). We should not ignore the most recent advances: the 1996 Law for the Measures for Promotion of Human Rights Protection (principally for Burakumin), and the 1997 Act on the Promotion of Ainu Culture and the Dissemination and Education of Knowledge Concerning Ainu Traditions.

Nationalism and Its Discontents

Japanese monoethnic ideology is hardly unique and is in fact simply a more virulent form of nationalism, which is a powerful and ubiquitous ideology of modernity. Nationalism is an ideological and institutional project that seeks to achieve cultural and linguistic unification of diverse peoples into a singular nationality within clearly defined political boundaries. But it encounters the recalcitrant reality of multiethnic populations within any sizable bounded territory. All large nation-states have been willy-nilly multiethnic.

The case of contemporary Japanese ethnic ideology is a subset of nationalist ideology, and is hardly unique in contemporary world history. I have already touched on the cases of Britain and France. In spite of the right-wing nationalist discourse that posits only British in Britain or French in France, there are numerous people of different and mixed descent who can nonetheless claim their place in Britain or France. There are other societies where minorities hanker for recognition; consider the Palestinians in Israel.

In the mid-1990s about a million Palestinians in Israel constituted nearly a fifth of that country's population (Khalidi 1997:207). The establishment of the Israeli state in 1948 and the ensuing nationalist policies had generated refugees and effaced non-Jewish Israelis (Sternhell 1998:43–47). For three decades Palestinians were nearly nonexistent. "Dulles said in the 1950s that the Palestinians would disappear, and Golda Meir spoke in 1969 as if they had disappeared, going so far as to declare that they had never existed in the first place" (Khalidi 1997:209). Edward Said (1979:5) wrote in the late 1970s, "The fact of the matter is that today Palestine does not exist, except as a memory or, more importantly, as an idea, a political and human experience, and an act of sustained political will." The Palestinian past has been erased by tendentious scholarship, which has led to "the deliberate fragmentation of a fundamentally unified region" of what was once Roman Arabia (Bowersock 1988:186).

Palestinians therefore engaged in a politics of recognition. "My specific task was . . . to make the case for Palestinian presence, to say that there *was* a Palestinian people" (Said 1994:xvi). Palestinian and Arab political movements, symbolized by the *intifada,* have redressed the neglect of Palestinian existence (Landau 1993:169–173). By the 1990s few would altogether deny the existence of Palestinians, even in Israel. Although multiethnic Israel may sound as strange as multiethnic Japan, the idea lags behind the reality in both countries. By raising the question of Palestine, my intention is to underscore that monoethnic ideology is not unique to Japan. And the recognition by Israel does not, as Edward Said (1994:xlvi) reminds us, "necessarily answer Palestinian needs." Palestinian identity is, after all, not singular; in ethnonational terms, many identify as Arabs, which is far from a singular or settled identity (Rodinson 1981:12).

Just as the claim of Palestinians may raise the ire of some Zionists, my case for multiethnic Japan may annoy some Japanese people. When I have given talks on this topic at Japanese universities, one of the most common responses was to seize on my Korean ancestry and to question whether the case of contemporary South Korea would be all that different from the supposed accusation I was making against Japan. Needless to say, this book, as well as my talk, was on Japan, not South Korea. And the case of monoethnic nationalism in South Korea does not vitiate my argument about Japan; it only points out that Japan is not unique. In this regard, the anthropologist Edward Evans-Pritchard (1962:129) was right to stress that "[o]nly by understanding other cultures and societies does one see one's own in perspective, and come to understand it better against a background of the totality of human experience and endeavor."

The tenacious hold of monoethnic ideology is not confined to Japan, South Korea, and Israel. There are numerous other cases, such as the denied existence of an estimated 25 million Kurds in Turkey, Iraq, and other countries (Randal 1997:14–16). And, more disturbingly, there continue to be efforts to create a monoethnic society by means of mass killing, whether in Sri Lanka (Tambiah 1986), Rwanda (Destexhe 1995), or Bosnia (Sells 1996). Even in the United States—a multiethnic country par excellence—versions of monoethnic ideology have prevailed from time to time. The frontier thesis presumed the nonexistence, or the impending disappearance, of American Indians. The United States once regarded itself as a white republic, so much so that there were efforts to exclude even European immigrants. William Appleman Williams (1955:379) noted, "One of the central themes of American historiography is that there is no American Empire." In part because of the efforts by Williams and others, no serious history of the United States in the late 1990s would ignore the American empire or American multiethnicity.

The Necessity of Concrete Politics

One may very well wonder whether it would not be more prudent to ignore ethnic diversity altogether. Would it not be more sensible, as postwar modernization theorists and Marxists did, to assume that particularistic identities will wither away in favor of more universalistic ones? Shouldn't we take Article 14 of the Japanese Constitution for granted: "All of the people are equal under the law and there shall be no discrimination in political, economic or social relations because of race, creed, sex, social status or family origin"? Don't we risk reifying the ethnic categories, thereby fomenting interethnic conflict and suppressing intraethnic differences? Shouldn't we attempt to free ourselves from the alienated categories of peoplehood, such as ethnicity or nation? Although I am profoundly sympathetic to universalistic ideals and cosmopolitan concerns, I am afraid that abstract universals cannot emerge without concrete struggles for recognition and inclusion.

The pursuit of abstract universals carries the danger of empty formalism, thereby reproducing the discourse of monoethnicity and the phenomena of passive racism and passing. When Japanese students were asked whether they would marry Burakumin, most claimed that they would (Kanegae 1991:161). Very few, however, were willing to do so after they were shown a video on Burakumin discrimination (cf. Fukuoka 1985:146–149). The converse of passive racism is the prevalence of passing. Many Korean Japanese who have become Japanese citizens nonetheless continue to hide the fact of naturalization and live in fear of exposure of their Korean ancestry (Fukuoka and Tsujiyama 1990:103). Although police officers are taught to ignore ascriptive characteristics, such as nationality and Burakumin status (Bayley 1976:85–86), several Korean Japanese told me that they are frequently harassed by the police.

In the meantime, well-meaning Japanese, steeped as they may be in the ideology of universal human rights and democracy, reiterate the ideology of monoethnic Japan. Consider in this regard the shortcomings of the Japanese social sciences. In nearly 700 pages, contributors to a volume on contemporary Japanese society had nothing to say about minorities in Japan (Watanabe 1996). The critical overview of Japanese society by the progressive sociologist Mita Munesuke (1996) similarly bypasses ethnic questions. When Western postmodern and postcolonial scholars revived the issues of nation and ethnicity in the 1980s, some Japanese scholars followed the fashion. Their writings are replete with *katakana* (a script used for foreign words)—*nēshon* and *esunishitī*, not *kokka* and *minzoku*—but devoid of actually existing Japanese minorities (e.g., Ōsawa 1996). Non-Japanese Japanese are not mentioned even when a book argues for the multiethnic nature of contemporary Japanese society (Yamauchi et al. 1991:10).

Abstract universals must be achieved through concrete particulars. As alienated and particularistic as ethnic categories may be, we cannot wish them away. Rather, we need to struggle through concrete concerns of prejudice, discrimination, and denial in order to address them in the hopes of overcoming them.

Beyond Boundaries

In his incomparable essay on the origins of inequality, Jean-Jacques Rousseau (1992:43) wrote, "The first person who, having fenced off a plot of ground, took it into his head to say *this is mine* and found people simple enough to believe him, was the true founder of civil society. What crimes, wars, murders, what miseries and horrors would the human Race have been spared by someone who, uprooting the stakes or filling in the ditch, had shouted to his fellows: Beware of listening to this impostor; you are lost if you forget that the fruits belong to all and the Earth to no one!" Rousseau was, of course, writing about the rise of property and of inequality. In a similar spirit, we should beware of people who draw social boundaries and declare people on one side of the line to be typologically distinct from those on the other. As ubiquitous as the socially imposed lines are, there have inevitably been crossings and interactions, impurity and hybridity. Yet the insistence on the line, to create purity and homogeneity, underlies many discourses of racial, ethnic, and national distinction. The ethnonational or ethnoracial divides are often manipulated, and the ethnonational or ethnoracial others are blamed for one or another social ill, when they may have nothing to do with them.

Once upon a time, Europeans fought one another over religion, and different varieties of the same religion at that. Now, horizontal divides in the world are rarely those of religions; they are predominantly those of race, ethnicity, and nation (peoplehood). Perhaps one day we will look back on our long period of racial struggles, ethnic fratricides, and national divisions with amazement, as some do on centuries of religious wars. Just as religious wars have receded in many parts of the world, perhaps ethnonational conflicts may wane in the not-so-distant future. Efforts to underscore their intractability—to damn the contemporary era as the age of ethnic conflict—seem ultimately counterproductive. As immobile and permanent as ethnic divides may seem at any given place and time, they are neither natural nor necessary. To root the monoethnic ideology in Japan in national character or something deeper is not only contrary to historical fact; it does little to inform efforts to challenge it.

At least in Japan the politics of ethnic recognition have made considerable advances: there are serious efforts to include all permanent non-Japanese residents in full civic life. I would like to believe that the time is not so far off when this book will have become obsolete; when readers will wonder why the author belabors the obvious; and ponder how it was possible that so many people believed that Japan was a monoethnic society.

Appendix:
Multilingual Japan

"Since the natural inclination to language is universal to man, and since all men must carry the key to the understanding of all languages in their minds, it follows automatically that the form of all languages must be fundamentally identical and must always achieve a common objective" (Humboldt 1972:193). Wilhelm von Humboldt and Noam Chomsky (1972:71) are just two of the many linguists who underscore language as a cultural universal. The human universal of language competence does not, of course, deny the particularities of each language, which offer a powerful basis of social distinction. Because language is inextricably intertwined with social life, Raymond Williams's (1973:215) suggestion that "the most deeply known human community is language itself" is shared by many philosophers—"And to imagine a language means to imagine a form of life" (Wittgenstein 1968:8). If two people do not share a common language, then it is difficult to presume any sense of solidarity and, therefore, identity between them.

Nihonjinron writers have often identified the Japanese language as the basis of Japanese uniqueness. Roy Miller (1982:32) calls it the "major sustaining myth of Japanese society." Like most *Nihonjinron* arguments, however, much of the evidence for the uniqueness of the Japanese language turns out to be absurd, banal, fanciful, wrong, or mystical. In *Atama no yosugiru Nihonjin* (Japanese Who Are Too Bright), one of Takemitsu Makoto's (1990:77) proofs for Japanese intellectual superiority is that ordinary Japanese use 140,000 words, whereas their English or French counterparts only use 10,000 words. Slightly more plausibly, a school teacher told me that "there are things that cannot be expressed in any other language:

think of miso and *nattō*" (fermented beans). Although many languages outside of Japan lack the word for miso and *nattō,* the absence can be easily rectified. Consider in this regard that about a seventh of the words used in ordinary Japanese conversation are foreign words (Honna 1995:45). Furthermore, without Western imports such as society *(shakai)*, love *(ren'ai)*, or freedom *(jiyū)*, even elementary conversations in Japanese would be difficult (Yanabu 1982).

The poet and language maven Ōno Susumu (1966:11–14) observes that the Yamato (proto-Japanese) language had no word for nature *(shizen)*, which indicates that Japanese did not clearly distinguish between nature and humanity, and therefore Japanese, unlike Westerners, live in harmony with nature. Although such a proposition may convince impressionistic foreigners and Japanese (Morley 1985:78–79), Japan's recent history of industrial pollution would cast serious doubt on it (Tsuru 1993:129–138). A white-collar worker (or *sararīman*) who was an aficionado of the *Nihonjinron* told me that Japanese is the only language to use different syllabaries. In fact, as Walter J. Ong (1982:88) notes, "Many writing systems are in fact hybrid systems, mixing two or more principles." Several people I talked with pointed to the subtleties of the Japanese language that they felt could not possibly be captured in translation. All translations are problematic, just as all languages are undoubtedly capable of subtleties. However, these claims, along with those that argue that elements of Japanese syntax, morphology, and phonetics are different from all the other languages, neither prove Japanese uniqueness—for all languages are distinct in some way—nor prevent non-Japanese from acquiring the language.

The equivalence of Japanese language and Japanese people is not a transhistorical truth. In general, as Edward Sapir (1921:215) pointed out, there is no strict correlation among language, culture, nation, or race. In spite of repeated efforts to seek a mystical connection between a particular language and culture, all such efforts have failed (Sapir 1921:219). In any case, the origin of the Japanese language is mixed, not pure (Nakamoto 1985:51–52; Murayama 1995:2).

Most significantly, the linguistic unification of the Japanese archipelago occurred only recently. The development of a common language requires national integration, whether by a centralizing state or a colonial power (Fabian 1991:8–10). In the case of France, "The Third Republic found a France in which French was a foreign language for half the citizens" (Weber 1976:70). As late as the mid-nineteenth century no more than 3 percent of people living in present-day Italy understood Italian (Steinberg 1987:198). In the absence of nationwide circuits of people and media most people rely on regional tongues. The literate elite in Japan shared a common language twelve centuries ago, but that was written Chinese. In the main Japanese islands the first common tongue developed among samurai in the early seventeenth century (Komatsu 1985:69–70; Mizuhara 1994:24–26). Naoki Sakai (1991:335–336) argues that Japanese language and culture were invented in the eighteenth century. Although mutually intelligible communication was increasingly common during the Tokugawa period, regional differentiation, as well as status difference, prevented popular linguistic unification (Maeda 1978:27–29; Hida 1992:187–188). In the early Meiji period people from Tōhoku and Kyūshū could not communicate with each other (Isoda 1983a:41). Even in the postwar period the novelist Yasuoka Shōtarō (1991b:18) found the Tōhoku dialect to be "a truly foreign language."

Standard Japanese *(hyōjungo)* arose from the samurai language of Edo (later Tokyo) (Isoda 1978:24–27; Tanaka 1983:90–92). The rise of urbanization and rural-urban transportation, the expansion of the state bureaucracy, including the military, the centralized system of schooling, and the development of mass communication, such as radio, are some of the factors that ensured that Japanese from across the archipelago are able to communicate fluently with each other. Schools in particular instilled a common tongue, punishing pupils for speaking in dialects by marking them with *hōgen fuda* (dialect sign) (Tanaka 1978:56–60). In the prewar period linguistic difference played an important role in the social distinction between Okinawans and Japanese. A common test of Korean ethnicity was to have people pronounce syllables most difficult for native Korean speakers to enunciate (e.g., *zu*).

The road to linguistic unification was far from smooth or swift. It is not out of whim that the Minister of Education Mori Arinori seriously entertained the proposal to institute English as the national language *(kokugo)* in the late nineteenth century. Even the relatively invariant written Japanese underwent significant modifications in the past century. Most important, contemporary written Japanese is the consequence of the *genbun itchi* movement (the effort to align the written with the spoken) in the 1880s (Suga 1995:8) and *gendai kanazukai* (the articulation of different syllabaries), which was promulgated in 1946 (Tsukishima 1986:2–3). The instability of the modern Japanese language provides a wonderful source of literary inventions. Dazai Osamu's (1989) famous story, "Dasu Gemeine," originally published in 1935, offers a potpourri of literary references: Radiguet, Valéry, Cocteau, Gide, and Mann. Hence, the title is often taken to be a German word, but it is in fact a phrase in Tōhoku dialect, which means "therefore, no good" *(dasuke maine)*. Even in the 1990s people accustomed to standard spoken Japanese find it difficult to understand regional dialects (Amino 1991:15–17). As Masayoshi Shibatani (1990:185) writes, "Japan is extremely rich in dialectal variations. Different dialects are often mutually unintelligible." Given that only in 1944 did the majority of Japanese households own a radio (Oku 1993:274–275), some scholars suggest that the linguistic unification of Japan occurred in the postwar period (Tanaka 1996:24–27).

Finally, there are various linguistic communities and language schools, including Ainu, Korean, Chinese, and English, for long-term residents of Japan (Maher 1995). Japan is, in other words, a multilingual society.

References

Abe Hakujun. 1975. *Nihon fashizumu kenkyū josetsu.* Tokyo: Miraisha.

Abella, Manolo I. 1995. "Asian Migrant and Contract Workers in the Middle East." In Robin Cohen, ed., *The Cambridge Survey of World Migration,* pp. 418–423. Cambridge: Cambridge University Press.

Abelmann, Nancy, and John Lie. 1995. *Blue Dreams: Korean Americans and the Los Angeles Riots.* Cambridge, Mass.: Harvard University Press.

Adachi, Kenichi. 1959. "The Image of America in Contemporary Japanese Fiction." In Hidetoshi Kato, ed., *Japanese Popular Culture: Studies in Mass Communication and Cultural Change,* pp. 47–59. Rutland, Vt.: Charles E. Tuttle.

Ainu Association of Hokkaido. [1984/1985] 1993. "A Proposal for Legislation Concerning the Ainu People," trans. John Lie and Hideaki Uemura. In n.a., *Nibutani Forum '93: shiryōshū,* pp. 92–95. Biratori, Japan: Nibutani Forum '93 Jimukyoku.

Ainu Minzoku Hakubutsukan, ed. 1993. *Ainu bunka no kiso chishiki.* Tokyo: Sōfūkan.

Ajiajin Rōdōsha Mondai Kondankai, ed. 1988. *Ajiajin dekasegi techō.* Tokyo: Akashi Shoten.

Akamatsu Keisuke. 1995. *Sabetsu no minzokugaku.* Tokyo: Akashi Shoten.

Akazawa Shirō. 1994. "Sengo shisō to bunka." In Masanori Nakamura, ed., *Kindai Nihon no kiseki.* Vol. 6: *Senryō to sengo kaikaku,* pp. 174–195. Tokyo: Yoshikawa Kōbunkan.

Akisada Yoshikazu. 1993. *Kindai to buraku sangyō.* Osaka: Buraku Kaihō Kenkyūsho.

Akutagawa Ryūnosuke. [1927] 1978. "Aru aho no isshō." In Ryūnosuke Akutagawa, *Akutagawa Ryūnosuke zenshū,* vol. 9, pp. 309–338. Tokyo: Iwanami Shoten.

Allen, Matthew. 1994. *Undermining the Japanese Miracle: Work and Conflict in a Coalmining Community.* Cambridge: Cambridge University Press.

Allinson, Gary D. 1997. *Japan's Postwar History.* Ithaca, N.Y.: Cornell University Press.

Althusser, Louis. [1965/1969] 1977. *For Marx,* trans. Ben Brewster. London: NLB.

Amano Ikuo. 1983. *Shiken no shakaishi: kindai Nihon no shiken, kyōiku, shakai.* Tokyo: Tokyo Daigaku Shuppankai.

Amemiya Shōichi. 1997. *Senji sengo taiseiron.* Tokyo: Iwanami Shoten.

Amino Yoshihiko. 1978. *Muen, kugai, raku: Nihon chūsei no jiyū to heiwa.* Tokyo: Heibonsha.

———. 1990. *Nihonron no shiza: rettō no shakai to kokka.* Tokyo: Shōgakukan.

———. 1991. *Nihon no rekishi o yominaosu.* Tokyo: Chikuma Shobō.

———. 1992. *Umi to rettō no chūsei.* Tokyo: Nihon Editā Sukūru Shuppanbu.

———. [1986] 1993. *Igyō no ōken.* Tokyo: Heibonsha.

———. 1996. "Emperor, Rice, and Commoners," trans. Gavan McCormack. In Donald Denoon, Mark Hudson, Gavan McCormack, and Tessa Morris-Suzuki, eds., *Multicultural Japan: Palaeolithic to Postmodern,* pp. 235–244. Cambridge: Cambridge University Press.

Anderson, Benedict O'G. [1983] 1990. *Imagined Communities,* expanded ed. London: Verso.

Aniya Masaaki. 1977. "Imin to dekasegi: sono haikei." In Okinawa Rekishi Kenkyūkai, ed., *Kindai Okinawa no rekishi to minshū,* pp. 143–165. Tokyo: Shigensha.

Aoki Hideo. 1989. *Yoseba rōdōsha no sei to shi.* Tokyo: Akashi Shoten.

———. 1992. "Nihon no āban-esunishiti: toshi kasō no chōsa kara." *Shakaigaku hyōron* 42: 346–359.

Aoki Tamotsu. 1990. *"Nihon bunkaron" no hen'yō: sengo Nihon no bunka to aidentiti.* Tokyo: Chūō Kōronsha.

Arakawa Shōji. 1995. "Kokumin seishin sōdōin to taiseiyokusan undō." In Masaomi Yui, ed., *Kindai Nihon no kiseki.* Vol. 5: *Taiheiyō sensō,* pp. 139–166. Tokyo: Yoshikawa Kōbunkan.

Araki Moriaki. 1986. "Tennō to 'tennōsei.'" In Rekishigaku Kenkyūkai, ed., *Tennō to tennōsei o kangaeru,* pp. 149–178. Tokyo: Aoki Shoten.

Arano Yasunori. 1988. *Kinsei Nihon to Higashi Ajia.* Tokyo: Tokyo Daigaku Shuppankai.

———. 1994. "Kinsei no taigaikan." In Naohiro Asao, Yoshihiko Amino, Susumu Ishii, Masanao Kano, Shōhachi Hayakawa, and Yasuo Yasumaru, eds., *Iwanami kōza Nihon tsūshi.* Vol. 13: *Kinsei 3,* pp. 211–249. Tokyo: Iwanami Shoten.

Araragi Shinzō. 1994. *"Manshū imin" no rekishi shakaigaku.* Tokyo: Gyōrosha.

Arasaki Moriteru. 1995. "Okinawa ni totte sengo to wa nanika." In Masanori Nakamura, Akira Amakawa, Kŏn-ch'a Yun, and Takeshi Igarashi, eds., *Sengo Nihon senryō to sengo kaikaku.* Vol. 5: *Kako no seisan,* pp. 197–232. Tokyo: Iwanami Shoten.

Arita Yoshifu. 1994. *Utaya Miyako Harumi.* Tokyo: Kōdansha.

Arnold, Matthew. [1869] 1993. "Preface to *Culture and Anarchy.*" In Matthew Arnold, *Culture and Anarchy and Other Writings*, ed. Stefan Collini, pp. 188–211. Cambridge: Cambridge University Press.

Asada Kyōji. 1993. "Manshū nōgyō imin to nōgyō, tochi mondai." In Shinobu Ōe, Kyōji Asada, Taichirō Mitani, Ken'ichi Gotō, Hideo Kobayashi, Sōji Takasaki, Masahiro Wakabayashi, and Minato Kawamura, eds., *Iwanami kōza kindai Nihon to Shokuminchi*. Vol.3: *Shokuminchika to sangyōka*, pp. 77–102. Tokyo: Iwanami Shoten.

————. 1994. "Higashi Ajia no 'teikoku' Nihon." In Kyōji Asada, ed., *Kindai Nihon no kiseki*. Vol. 10: *"Teikoku" Nihon to Ajia*, pp. 1–33. Tokyo: Yoshikawa Kōbunkan.

Asahi Shinbun Ainu Minzoku Shuzaihan. 1993. *Kotan ni ikiru*. Tokyo: Iwanami Shoten.

Asahi Shinbun Shakaibu, ed. 1989. *Chikakute chikai Ajia*. Tokyo: Gakuyō Shobō.

Asahi Shinbunsha, ed. 1990. *Kokusai sinpojiumu: kodai Nihon no kokusaika*. Tokyo: Asahi Shinbunsha.

Asukai Masamichi. 1984. "'Kokumin' no sōshutsu—kokumin bunka no keisei, josetsu." In Masamichi Asukai, ed., *Kokumin bunka no keisei*, pp. 3–66. Tokyo: Chikuma Shobō.

————. 1985. *Bunmei kaika*. Tokyo: Iwanami Shoten.

Bade, Klaus J. 1992. "Einheimische Ausländer: 'Gastarbeiter,' Dauergäste, Enwanderer." In Klaus J. Bade, ed., *Deutsche im Ausland—Fremde in Deutschland: Migration in Geschichte und Gegenwart*, pp. 393–401. München: Beck.

Banno Junji. [1989] 1993. *Taikei Nihon no rekishi*. Vol. 13: *Kindai Nihon no shuppatsu*. Tokyo: Shōgakukan.

Barker, Paul. 1996. "England, Whose England?" *Times Literary Supplement*, July 12, p. 36.

Barshay, Andrew E. 1998. "Postwar Social and Political Thought, 1945–1990." In Bob Tadashi Wakabayashi, ed., *Modern Japanese Thought*, pp. 273–355. Cambridge: Cambridge University Press.

Barthes, Roland. [1970] 1982. *Empire of Signs*, trans. Richard Howard. New York: Hill & Wang.

Barzun, Jacques. 1954. *God's Country and Mine: A Declaration of Love Spiced with a Few Harsh Words*. Boston: Little, Brown.

Bayley, David H. 1976. *Force of Order: Police Behavior in Japan and the United States*. Berkeley: University of California Press.

Befu, Harumi. [1987] 1990. *Ideorogī to shite no Nihon bunkaron*, expanded ed. Tokyo: Shisō no Kagakusha.

Benedict, Ruth F. 1946. *The Chrysanthemum and the Sword*. Boston: Houghton Mifflin.

Berlin, Brent, and Paul Kay. 1969. *Basic Color Terms: Their Universality and Evolution*. Berkeley: University of California Press.

Bernstein, Gail Lee. 1983. *Haruko's World: A Japanese Farm Woman and Her Community*. Stanford, Calif.: Stanford University Press.

Berry, Mary Elizabeth. 1994. *The Culture of Civil War in Kyoto*. Berkeley: University of California Press.

Bestor, Theodore C. 1989. *Neighborhood Tokyo*. Stanford, Calif.: Stanford University Press.

Bitō Masahide. 1993. *Nihon bunkaron*. Tokyo: Hōsō Daigaku Kyōiku Shinkōkai.

Bloch, Marc. 1954. "Les aliments de l'ancienne France." In Jean-Jacques Hémardinquer, ed., *Pour une histoire de l'alimentation*, pp. 231–235. Paris: Armand Colin.

Bloom, Allan. [1988] 1990. "Western Civ." In Allan Bloom, *Giants and Dwarfs: Essays, 1960–1990*. New York: Simon & Schuster.

Bogdanor, Vernon. 1997. "Sceptred Isle—or Isles?" *Times Literary Supplement*, Sept. 26, pp. 4–6.

Bourdieu, Pierre. [1979] 1984. *Distinction: A Social Critique of the Judgment of Taste*, trans. Richard Nice. Cambridge, Mass.: Harvard University Press.

Bowersock, G. W. 1988. "Palestine: Ancient History and Modern Politics." In Edward Said and Christopher Hitchens, eds., *Blaming the Victims: Spurious Scholarship and the Palestinian Question*, pp. 181–191. London: Verso.

Bowman, James. 1992. "Through Alien Eyes." *Times Literary Supplement*, June 12, p. 27.

Brinton, Crane. 1948. *From Many, One: The Process of Political Integration, The Problem of World Government*. Cambridge, Mass.: Harvard University Press.

Brinton, Mary C. 1993. *Women and the Economic Miracle*. Berkeley: University of California Press.

Brooker, Paul. 1991. *The Faces of Fraternalism: Nazi Germany, Fascist Italy, and Imperial Japan*. Oxford: Clarendon Press.

Brown, Delmer M. 1955. *Nationalism in Japan: An Introductory Historical Analysis*. Berkeley: University of California Press.

———. 1993. "Introduction." In Delmer M. Brown, ed., *The Cambridge History of Japan*. Vol. 1: *Ancient Japan*, pp. 1–47. Cambridge: Cambridge University Press.

Bruck, Connie. 1997. "The Big Hitter." *New Yorker*, Dec. 8, pp. 82–93.

Bryce, James. 1891. *The American Commonwealth*, 2d ed., 2 vols. London: Macmillan.

Buckley, Roger. [1985] 1990. *Japan Today*, 2d ed. Cambridge: Cambridge University Press.

Bungei Shunjūsha, ed. 1992. *Dai ankēto ni yoru shōnen shōjo manga besuto 100*. Tokyo: Bungei Shunjū.

Buruma, Ian. 1989. *God's Dust: A Modern Asian Journey*. New York: Farrar Straus Giroux.

Caillois, Roger. [1958/1961] 1979. *Man, Play and Games,* trans. Meyer Barash. New York: Schocken.

Calhoun, Craig. 1997. *Nationalism.* Minneapolis: University of Minnesota Press.

Camhi, Leslie. 1998. "The Serious Side of Japan's Favorite Nuisance." *New York Times,* Mar. 15, sec. 2, pp. 13,16.

Canguilhem, Georges. [1977] 1988. *Ideology and Rationality in the History of the Life Sciences,* trans. Arthur Goldhammer. Cambridge, Mass.: MIT Press.

Castles, Stephen, and Godula Kosack. [1973] 1985. *Immigrant Workers and Class Structure in Western Europe,* 2d ed. Oxford: Oxford University Press.

Chekhov, Anton. [1895] 1967. *The Island: A Journey to Sakhalin,* trans. Luba Terpak and Michael Terpak. New York: Washington Square Press.

———. [1887/1917] 1984. "The Kiss." In Anton Chekhov, *The Tales of Chekhov.* Vol. 4: *The Party and Other Stories,* pp. 173–205. New York: Ecco Press.

Chi Tong-Wook. 1997. *Zainichi o yamenasai.* Tokyo: Za Masada.

Chikappu Mieko. 1991. *Kaze no megumi: Ainu minzoku no bunka to jinken.* Tokyo: Ochanomizu Shobō.

Ching, Leo. 1996. "Imaginings in the Empires of the Sun: Japanese Mass Culture in Asia." In John Whittier Treat, ed., *Contemporary Japan and Popular Culture,* pp. 169–194. Honolulu: University of Hawaii Press.

Ch'oe Chŏng-nim, ed. [1982/1985] 1987. *Kankoku zaibatsu no sōsuitachi.* Tokyo: Kōbunsha.

Chomsky, Noam. [1968] 1972. *Language and Mind,* expanded ed. New York: Harcourt Brace Jovanovich.

Chŏng In-hwa. [1985] 1989. *Itsuno hi ka kaikyō o koete: Kankoku puroyakyū ni kaketa otokotachi.* Tokyo: Bungei Shunjū.

Chŏng Kyŏng-mo. 1984. "Dō ikiru bekika." *Sharehimu,* Aug., pp. 35–136.

Chŏng Tae-sŏng. 1992. *Shokubunka no naka no Nihon to Chōsen.* Tokyo: Kōdansha.

Christ, Carol T. 1984. *Victorian and Modern Poetics.* Chicago: University of Chicago Press.

Christy, Alan S. 1993. "The Making of Imperial Subjects in Okinawa." *Positions* 1: 607–639.

Cleaver, Charles Grinnell. 1976. *Japanese and Americans: Cultural Parallels and Paradoxes.* Minneapolis: University of Minnesota Press.

Cole, Robert E. 1979. *Work, Mobility, and Participation: A Comparative Study of American and Japanese Industry.* Berkeley: University of California Press.

Colley, Linda. 1992. *Britons: Forging the Nation 1707–1837.* New Haven, Conn.: Yale University Press.

Conrad, Peter. 1980. *Imagining America.* New York: Oxford University Press.

Conze, Werner, and Jürgen Kocka. 1985. "Einleitung." In Werner Conze and Jürgen Kocka, eds., *Bildungsbürgertum im 19. Jahrhundert.* Vol. 1:

Bildungssystem und Professionalisierung in internationalen Vergleichen, pp. 9–26. Stuttgart: Klett-Cotta.

Cornell, John B. 1967. "Individual Mobility and Group Membership: The Case of the Burakumin." In R. P. Dore, ed., *Aspects of Social Change in Modern Japan,* pp. 337–372. Princeton, N.J.: Princeton University Press.

Craig, Albert M. 1968. "Fukuzawa Yukichi: The Philosophical Foundations of Meiji Nationalism." In Robert E. Ward, ed., *Political Development in Modern Japan,* pp. 99–148. Princeton, N.J.: Princeton University Press.

Creighton, Millie R. 1995. "The Non-Vanishing Ainu: A Damming Development Project, Internationalization and Japan's Indigenous Other." *American Asian Review* 13: 69–96.

Crichton, Michael. 1992. *Rising Sun.* New York: Knopf.

Curtis, Gerald L. 1988. *The Japanese Way of Politics.* New York: Columbia University Press.

Cuyler, P. L. [1979] 1985. *Sumo: From Rite to Sport,* rev. ed. New York: Weatherhill.

Dale, Peter N. 1986. *The Myth of Japanese Uniqueness.* New York: St. Martin's.

Davies, Robertson. [1988] 1992. *The Lyre of Orpheus.* In Robertson Davies, *The Cornish Trilogy,* pp. 739–1136. Harmondsworth, U.K.: Penguin.

Davis, F. James. 1991. *Who Is Black? One Nation's Definition.* University Park: Pennsylvania State University.

Dawes, Kwame. 1996. "Diary." *London Review of Books,* Feb. 8, p. 21.

Dazai Osamu. [1935] 1989. "Dasu gemaine." In Osamu Dazai, *Dazai Osamu zenshū,* vol. 1, pp. 301–332. Tokyo: Chikuma Shobō.

DeChicchis, Joseph. 1995. "The Current State of the Ainu Language." In John C. Maher and Kyoko Yashiro, eds., *Multilingual Japan,* pp. 103–124. Clevedon, U.K.: Multilingual Matters.

Denoon, Donald, Mark Hudson, Gavan McCormack, and Tessa Morris-Suzuki, eds. 1996. *Multicultural Japan: Palaeolithic to Postmodern.* Cambridge: Cambridge University Press.

Destexhe, Alain. [1994] 1995. *Rwanda and Genocide in the Twentieth Century,* trans. Alison Marschner. New York: New York University Press.

Doak, Kevin M. 1994. *Dreams of Difference: The Japan Romantic School and the Rise of Modernity.* Berkeley: University of California Press.

———. 1997. "What Is a Nation and Who Belongs? National Narratives and the Ethnic Imagination in Twentieth-Century Japan." *American Historical Review* 102: 283–309.

———. 1998. "Culture, Ethnicity, and the State in Early Twentieth-Century Japan." In Sharon A. Minichiello, ed., *Japan's Competing Modernities: Issues in Culture and Democracy, 1900–1930,* pp. 181–205. Honolulu: University of Hawai'i Press.

Doi Takeo. 1985. *Omote to ura*. Tokyo: Kōbundō.

———. [1971] 1993. *"Amae" no kōzō*, annotated ed. Tokyo: Kōbundō.

Dore, R. P. 1958. *City Life in Japan: A Study of a Tokyo Ward*. Berkeley: University of California Press.

———. 1964. "Latin America and Japan Compared." In John J. Johnson, ed., *Continuity and Change in Latin America*, pp. 227–249. Stanford, Calif.: Stanford University Press.

———[Ronald P. Dore]. 1978. *Shinohata: A Portrait of a Japanese Village*. New York: Pantheon.

———. [1959] 1985. *Land Reform in Japan*. New York: Schocken.

Dower, John W. 1986. *War without Mercy: Race and Power in the Pacific War*. New York: Pantheon.

———. 1993. *Japan in War and Peace: Selected Essays*. New York: New Press.

Downer, Lesley. 1989. *On the Narrow Road: Journey into a Lost Japan*. New York: Summit.

———. 1994. *The Brothers: The Hidden World of Japan's Richest Family*. New York: Random House.

Durkheim, Émile. [1893] 1984. *The Division of Labor in Society*, trans. W. D. Halls. New York: Free Press.

Duus, Peter. 1995. *The Abacus and the Sword: The Japanese Penetration of Korea, 1895–1910*. Berkeley: University of California Press.

Eberhard, Wolfram. 1982. *China's Minorities: Yesterday and Today*. Belmont, Calif: Wadsworth.

Ebina Kenzō. 1983. *Hokkaidō takushoku kaihatsu keizairon*. Tokyo: Shinhyōron.

Echeverria, Durand. 1957. *Mirage in the West: A History of the French Image of American Society to 1815*. Princeton, N.J.: Princeton University Press.

Eguchi Keiichi. [1989] 1993. *Taikei Nihon no rekishi*. Vol. 14: *Futatsu no taisen*. Tokyo: Shōgakukan.

Ehara Takekazu. 1984. *Gendai kōtō kyōiku no kōzō*. Tokyo: Tokyo Daigaku Shuppankai.

Elder, John. 1993. *Following the Brush: An American Encounter with Classical Japanese Culture*. Boston: Beacon Press.

Elias, Norbert. [1989] 1996. *The Germans*, ed. Michael Schröter, trans. Eric Dunning and Stephen Mennell. New York: Columbia University Press.

Engels, Frederick. [1844] 1975. "The Condition of the Working-Class in England: From Personal Observations and Authentic Sources," trans. Florence Kelley-Wischnewetzing. In Karl Marx and Frederick Engels, *Collected Works*, vol. 4, 295–583. New York: International Publishers.

Evans-Pritchard, E. E. 1962. *Social Anthropology and Other Essays*. New York: Free Press.

Fabian, Johannes. [1986] 1991. *Language and Colonial Power: The Appropriation of Swahili in the Former Belgian Congo 1880–1938.* Berkeley: University of California Press.

Fallows, James. 1994. *Looking at the Sun: The Rise of the New East Asian Economic and Political System.* New York: Pantheon.

Feifer, George. 1993. "Okinawa: After the Volcano." *The Atlantic Monthly,* Sept., pp. 22–27.

Feiler, Bruce S. 1991. *Learning to Bow: An American Teacher in a Japanese School.* New York: Ticknor & Fields.

Fenton, James. 1996. "The Best of Both Worlds." *New York Review of Books,* Aug. 8, pp. 21–24.

Field, Norma. 1991. *In the Realm of a Dying Emperor: A Portrait of Japan at Century's End.* New York: Pantheon.

Ford, Caroline. 1993. *Creating the Nation in Provincial France: Religion and Political Identity in Brittany.* Princeton, N.J.: Princeton University Press.

Foucault, Michel. [1975] 1977. *Discipline and Punish: The Birth of the Prison,* trans. Alan Sheridan. New York: Pantheon.

Fowler, Edward. 1996. *San'ya Blues: Laboring Life in Contemporary Tokyo.* Ithaca, N.Y.: Cornell University Press.

Freedman, David. 1998. "When Is a Planet Not a Planet?" *The Atlantic Monthly,* Feb., pp. 22–33.

Freeman, Gary P. 1979. *Immigrant Labor and Racial Conflict in Industrial Societies: The French and British Experience.* Princeton, N.J.: Princeton University Press.

Frois, Luis. [1585/1965] 1991. *Yōroppa bunka to Nihon bunka,* trans. and annot. Akio Okada. Tokyo: Iwanami Shoten.

Frow, John. 1995. *Cultural Studies and Cultural Value.* Oxford: Clarendon Press.

Fujimoto Hideo. [1982] 1994. *Chiri Mashiho no shōgai.* Tokyo: Sōfūkan.

Fujimoto Tsuyoshi. 1988. *Mō futatsu no Nihon bunka.* Tokyo: Tokyo Daigaku Shuppankai.

Fujimura Michio. 1973. *Nisshin sensō: Higashi Ajia kindai no tenkanten.* Tokyo: Iwanami Shoten.

Fujino Yutaka. 1994. "Hisabetsu buraku." In Naohiro Asao, Yoshihiko Amino, Susumu Ishii, Masanao Kano, Shōhachi Hayakawa, and Yasuo Yasumaru, eds., *Iwanami kōza Nihon tsūshi.* Vol. 18: *Kindai 3,* pp. 133–167. Tokyo: Iwanami Shoten.

Fujisaki Yasuo. 1991. *Dekasegi Nikkei gaikokujin rōdōsha.* Tokyo: Akashi Shoten.

Fujita Shōzō. [1966] 1974. *Tennōsei kokka no shihai genri,* 2d ed. Tokyo: Miraisha.

Fujitake Akira. 1985. "Katei no bunka hen'yō." In Shōichi Nakamura and Osamu Nakano, eds., *Taishū no bunka: nichijō seikatsu no shinjō o saguru,* pp. 141–161. Tokyo: Yūhikaku.

Fujitani, T. 1996. *Splendid Monarchy: Power and Pageantry in Modern Japan.* Berkeley: University of California Press.

Fujiwara Akira. 1987. "Tennō to Okinawasen." In Akira Fujiwara, ed., *Okinawasen to tennōsei,* pp. 9–45. Tokyo: Rippū Shobō.

Fujiwara Hiroshi. 1993. *Chōshō tennōsei to buraku gensō.* Tokyo: San'ichi Shobō.

Fukuoka Yasunori. 1985. *Gendai shakai no sabetsu ishiki.* Tokyo: Akashi Shoten.

———. 1993. *Zainichi Kankoku, Chōsenjin: wakai sedai no aidentiti.* Tokyo: Chūō Kōronsha.

———. 1996. "Sabetsu kenkyū no genjō to kadai." In Shun Inoue, Chizuko Ueno, Masachi Ōsawa, and Shun'ya Yoshimi, eds., *Iwanami kōza gendai shakaigaku.* Vol. 15: *Sabetsu to kyōsei no shakaigaku,* 233–248. Tokyo: Iwanami Shoten.

Fukuoka Yasunori and Myung-Soo [Myŏng-su] Kim. 1997. *Zainichi Kankokujin seinen no seikatsu to ishiki.* Tokyo: Tokyo Daigaku Shuppankai.

Fukuoka Yasunori and Yukiko Tsujiyama. 1990. "'Kika' e no ishi o jōsei suru mono." *Kaihō shakaigaku* 4: 103–131.

Fukuoka Yasunori, Hiroaki Yoshii, Atsushi Sakurai, Shūsaku Ejima, Haruhiko Kanegae, and Michihiko Noguchi, eds. 1987. *Hisabetsu no bunka, hansabetsu no ikizama.* Tokyo: Akashi Shoten.

Fukushima Masao. 1967. *Nihon shihonshugi to "ie" seido.* Tokyo: Tokyo Daigaku Shuppankai.

Fukuta Ajio. 1992. *Yanagita Kunio no minzokugaku.* Tokyo: Yoshikawa Kōbunkan.

Fukutake Tadashi. 1981. *Nihon shakai no kōzō.* Tokyo: Tokyo Daigaku Shuppankai.

Fukuzawa Yukichi. [1876] 1980. "Gakumon no susume." In Yukichi Fukuzawa, *Fukuzawa Yukichi senshū,* vol. 3, pp. 53–176. Tokyo: Iwanami Shoten.

———. [1875] 1981a. "Bunmeiron no gairyaku." In Yukichi Fukuzawa, *Fukuzawa Yukichi senshū,* vol. 4, pp. 5–254. Tokyo: Iwanami Shoten.

———. [1881] 1981b. "Datsuaron." In Yukichi Fukuzawa, *Fukuzawa Yukichi senshū,* vol. 7, pp. 221–224. Tokyo: Iwanami Shoten.

Furbank, P. N., and W. R. Owens. 1988. *The Canonisation of Daniel Defoe.* New Haven, Conn.: Yale University Press.

Furuta Takahiko. 1989. *Bōdāresu sosaieti jidai wa "Shōwa-Genroku" kara "Heisei-Kyōhō" e.* Tokyo: PHP Kenkyūsho.

Gabe Masao. 1979. *Meiji kokka to Okinawa.* Tokyo: San'ichi Shobō.

———. 1992. "Nihon no kindaika to Okinawa." In Shinobu Ōe, Kyōji Asada, Taichirō Mitani, Ken'ichi Gotō, Hideo Kobayashi, Sōji Takasaki, Masahiro Wakabayashi, and Minato Kawamura, eds., *Iwanami kōza kindai Nihon to shokuminchi.* Vol. 1: *Shokuminchi teikoku Nihon,* pp. 101–119. Tokyo: Iwanami Shoten.

Gabe Masao and Megumu Kawabata. 1994. "Kaitaku seisaku to 'Ryūkyū shobun.'" In Akira Tanaka, ed., *Kindai Nihon no kiseki. Vol. 1: Meiji ishin,* pp. 220–243. Tokyo: Yoshikawa Kōbunkan.

Gabler, Neal. 1988. *An Empire of Their Own: How the Jews Invented Hollywood.* New York: Crown.

Gaikokujin Kōyō Mondai Kenkyūkai. [1989] 1990. *Toraburu o okosanai tame no gaikokujin kōyō no jitsumu,* rev. ed. Tokyo: Shōji Nōmu Kenkyūkai.

Gaikokujin Rōdōsha Kenri Hakusho Henshū Iinkai. 1995. *Gaikokujin rōdōsha kenri hakusho: hataraku nakama, gaikokujin rōdōsha.* Tokyo: Gaikokujin Rōdōsha Kenri Hakusho Henshū Iinkai.

Gallie, W. B. 1964. *Philosophy and the Historical Understanding.* London: Chatto & Windus.

Gellner, Ernest. 1983. *Nations and Nationalism.* Oxford: Blackwell.

Gilroy, Paul. [1987] 1991. *"There Ain't No Black in the Union Jack": The Cultural Politics of Race and Nation.* Chicago: University of Chicago Press.

Gluck, Carol. 1985. *Japan's Modern Myths: Ideology in the Late Meiji Period.* Princeton, N.J.: Princeton University Press.

Goffman, Erving. 1959. *The Presentation of Self in Everyday Life.* Garden City, N.Y.: Anchor.

Gombrich, E. H. [1965] 1979. "The Logic of Vanity Fair: Alternatives to the Study of Historicism in the Study of Fashions, Style and Taste." In E. H. Gombrich, *Ideals and Idols: Essays on Values in History and in Art,* pp. 60–92. London: Phaidon.

Goodman, David G., and Masanori Miyazawa. 1995. *Jews in the Japanese Mind: The History and Uses of a Cultural Stereotype.* New York: Free Press.

Goodman, Mary Ellen. 1957. "Values, Attitudes, and Social Concepts of Japanese and American Children." *American Anthropologist* 59: 979–999.

Goodman, Roger. 1990. *Japan's "International Youth": The Emergence of a New Class of Schoolchildren.* Oxford: Clarendon Press.

Gordon, Andrew. 1991. *Labor and Imperial Democracy in Prewar Japan.* Berkeley: University of California Press.

———. 1998. "The Invention of Japanese-Style Labor Management." In Stephen Vlastos, ed., *Mirror of Modernity: Invented Traditions of Modern Japan,* pp. 19–36. Berkeley: University of California Press.

Gotō Jun'ichi. 1990. *Gaikokujin rōdō no keizaigaku: kokusai bōekiron kara no apurōchi.* Tokyo: Tōyō Keizai Shinpōsha.

Gotō Ken'ichi. 1992. "Taiwan to Nan'yō: 'Nanshin' mondai to no kanren de." In Shinobu Ōe, Kyōji Asada, Taichirō Mitani, Ken'ichi Gotō, Hideo Kobayashi, Sōji Takasaki, Masahiro Wakabayashi, and Minato Kawamura, eds., *Iwanami kōza kindai Nihon to shokuminchi.* Vol. 2: *Teikoku tōji no kōzō,* pp. 147–175. Tokyo: Iwanami Shoten.

Gotō Motoo, Kenzō Uchida, and Masumi Ishikawa. 1982. *Sengo hoshuseiji no kiseki: Yoshida naikaku kara Suzuki naikaku made.* Tokyo: Iwanami Shoten.

Gotō Yasushi. 1985. "'Chū ishiki' no mujun: kaikyū to kaisō." In Rekishigaku Kenkyūkai and Nihonshi Kenkyūkai, eds., *Kōza Nihon rekishi.* Vol. 13: *Rekishi ni okeru genzai,* pp. 139–164. Tokyo: Tokyo Daigaku Shuppankai.

Graburn, Nelson H. H. 1995. "The Past in the Present in Japan: Nostalgia and

Neo-Traditionalism in Contemporary Japanese Domestic Tourism." In Richard Butler and Douglas Pearce, eds., *Change in Tourism: People, Places, and Processes*, pp. 47–70. London: Routledge.

Greenbie, Barrie B. 1988. *Space and Spirit in Modern Japan*. New Haven, Conn.: Yale University Press.

Greenfeld, Karl Taro. 1994. *Speed Tribes: Days and Nights with Japan's Next Generation*. New York: HarperCollins.

Grillo, R. D. 1985. *Ideologies and Institutions in Urban France: The Representation of Immigrants*. Cambridge: Cambridge University Press.

Guttmann, Allen. 1978. *From Ritual to Record: The Nature of Modern Sports*. New York: Columbia University Press.

Hachiya Takashi. 1992. "Gaikokujin rōdōsha mondai: ukeire to seifu, keizaikai no tachiba." *Kikan rōdōhō* 164: 42–57.

Haga Shōji. 1984. "Meiji zenki ni okeru aikoku shisō no keisei." In Masamichi Asukai, ed., *Kokumin bunka no keisei*, pp. 69–119. Tokyo: Chikuma Shobō.

Hall, Ivan P. 1998. *Cartels of the Mind: Japan's Intellectual Closed Shop*. New York: Norton.

Halperin, David M. 1995. *Saint=Foucault: Towards a Gay Hagiography*. New York: Columbia University Press.

Hamaguchi Eshun and Shunpei Kumon, eds. 1982. *Nihonteki shūdanshugi: sono shinka o tou*. Tokyo: Yūhikaku.

Hamashima Akira. 1985. "Daikigyō taiseika no rōdōsha ishiki." In Hiroshi Hazama and Takayoshi Kitagawa, eds., *Keiei to rōdō no shakaigaku*, pp. 95–128. Tokyo: Tokyo Daigaku Shuppankai.

Hanami Makiko. 1995. "Minority Dynamics in Japan: Towards a Society of Sharing." In John C. Maher and Gaynor Macdonald, eds., *Diversity in Japanese Culture and Language*, pp. 121–146. London: Kegan Paul International.

Hanazaki Kōhei. 1988. *Shizuka na daichi: Matsuura Takeshirō to Ainu minzoku*. Tokyo: Iwanami Shoten.

———. 1993. *Aidentiti to kyōsei no tetsugaku*. Tokyo: Chikuma Shobō.

Haneda Arata. 1987. "Joron Nihon no dekasegi." In Sakae Watanabe and Arata Haneda, eds., *Dekasegi no sōgōteki kenkyū*, pp. 1–5. Tokyo: Tokyo Daigaku Shuppankai.

Hanihara Kazurō. 1996. *Nihonjin no tanjō: jinrui harukana tabi*. Tokyo: Yoshikawa Kōbunkan.

Hanley, Susan B. 1997. *Everyday Things in Premodern Japan: The Hidden Legacy of Material Culture*. Berkeley: University of California Press.

Hara Katsurō. [1917] 1978. *Tōyama jidai ni okeru ichi shinshi no seikatsu*. Tokyo: Kōdansha.

Harada Nobuo. 1993. *Rekishi no naka no kome to niku: shokumotsu to tennō, sabetsu*. Tokyo: Heibonsha.

Harajiri Hideki. 1997. *Nihon teijū Korian no nichijō to seikatsu: bunkajinruigakuteki apurōchi.* Tokyo: Akashi Shoten.

Hardacre, Helen. 1989. *Shintō and the State, 1868–1988.* Princeton, N.J.: Princeton University Press.

Hardin, C. L., and Luisa Maffi, eds. 1997. *Color Categories in Thought and Language.* Cambridge: Cambridge University Press.

Hargreaves, Alec G. 1995. *Immigration, "Race" and Ethnicity in Contemporary France.* London: Routledge.

Harootunian, H. D. 1988. *Things Seen and Unseen: Discourse and Ideology in Tokugawa Nativism.* Chicago: University of Chicago Press.

———. 1990. "Disciplining Native Knowledge and Producing Place: Yanagita Kunio, Origuchi Shinobu, and Takata Yasuma." In J. Thomas Rimer, ed., *Culture and Identity: Japanese Intellectuals during the Interwar Years,* pp. 99–127. Princeton, N.J.: Princeton University Press.

Hasegawa Akira. 1993. *Sumō no tanjō.* Tokyo: Shinchōsha.

Hashizume Daizaburō. 1989. *Bōken to shite no shakaikagaku.* Tokyo: Mainichi Shinbunsha.

Hatada Kunio. 1990. "Maruchi-nashonaru sutorīto: Ōkubo-dori ni 'taminzoku kokka Nihon' no asu ga aru!" *Bessatsu Takarajima* 106: 130–137.

Hattori Yukio. [1970] 1993. *Edo kabuki,* rev. ed. Tokyo: Iwanami Shoten.

Havens, Thomas R. H. 1987. *Fire across the Sea: The Vietnam War and Japan, 1965–1975.* Princeton, N.J.: Princeton University Press.

Hayashi Fusao. 1964. *Daitōa sensō kōteiron.* Tokyo: Banchō Shobō.

Hayashi Tatsuo. 1973. *Kyōsanshugiteki ningen.* Tokyo: Chūō Kōronsha.

Hayashiya Tatsusaburō. 1953. *Chūsei bunka no kichō.* Tokyo: Tokyo Daigaku Shuppankai.

Hayashiya Tatsusaburō, Tadao Umesao, Michitarō Tada, and Hidetoshi Katō. [1962] 1973. *Nihonjin no chie.* Tokyo: Chūō Kōronsha.

Hearn, Lafcadio. 1904. *Japan: An Attempt at Interpretation.* New York: Macmillan.

———. [1896] 1972. *Kokoro: Hints and Echoes of Japanese Inner Life.* Rutland, Vt.: Charles E. Tuttle.

Hebdige, Dick. 1979. *Subculture: The Meaning of Style.* London: Methuen.

———. 1988. *Hiding in the Light: On Images and Things.* London: Routledge.

Hein, Laura, and Ellen H. Hammond. 1995. "Homing in on Asia: Identity in Contemporary Japan." *Bulletin of Concerned Asian Scholars* 27(3): 3–17.

Hendry, Joy. 1987. *Understanding Japanese Society.* London: Croom Helm.

Hida Yoshifumi. 1992. *Tōkyōgo seiritsushi no kenkyū.* Tokyo: Tōkyōdō.

Hidaka Rokurō. 1960. *Gendai ideorogī.* Tokyo: Keisō Shobō.

———. 1980. *Sengo shisō o kangaeru.* Tokyo: Iwanami Shoten.

Hinago Akira. 1986. "Japayukisan no keizaigaku." *Bessatsu Takarajima* 54: 130–157.

Hippō Yasuyuki. 1992. *Nihon kensetsu rōdōron: rekishi, genjitsu to gaikokujin rōdōsha.* Tokyo: Ochanomizu Shobō.

Hiraishi Naoaki. 1994. "Kindai Nihon no 'Ajiashugi.'" In Yūzō Mizoguchi, Takeshi Hamashita, Naoaki Hiraishi, and Hiroshi Miyajima, eds., *Ajia kara kangaeru*. Vol. 5: *Kindaika zō*, pp. 265–291. Tokyo: Tokyo Daigaku Shuppankai.

Hirano Kunio. 1993. *Kikajin to kodai kokka*. Tokyo: Yoshikawa Kōbunkan.

Hiraoka Masaaki. 1993. *Yokohamateki: geinō toshi sōseiron*. Tokyo: Seidosha.

Hirota Hisako. 1979. *Gendai joshi rōdō no kenkyū*. Tokyo: Rōdō Kyōiku Sentā.

Hirota Masaki. 1980. *Bunmei kaika to minshū ishiki*. Tokyo: Aoki Shoten.

Hirota Teruyuki. 1997. *Rikugun shokō no kyōiku shakaishi: risshin shusse to tennōsei*. Yokohama: Seshoku Shobō.

Hirowatari Seigo. 1992. "Gaikokujin ukeire no hōteki ronri." In Toshio Iyotani and Takamichi Kajita, eds., *Gaikokujin rōdōsharon: genjō kara riron e*, pp. 63–97. Tokyo: Kōbundō.

Hobsbawm, E. J. 1990. *Nations and Nationalism since 1780: Programme, Myth, Reality*. Cambridge: Cambridge University Press.

Hodson, Peregrine. 1992. *A Circle Round the Sun: A Foreigner in Japan*. London: Heinemann.

Hokama Shuzen. 1986. *Okinawa no rekishi to bunka*. Tokyo: Chūō Kōronsha.

Hokusei Katsushika and Naoki Urasawa. 1993. *Master Keaton [Masutā Kīton]*, vol.14. Tokyo: Shōgakukan.

Hollifield, James F. 1992. *Immigrants, Markets, and States: The Political Economy of Postwar Europe*. Cambridge, Mass.: Harvard University Press.

Honda Hideo. 1982. *Sonzai shinai kodomotachi: Okinawa no mukokusekiji mondai*. Tokyo: Chōbunsha.

Honda Junryō. 1992. "Konnichi no gaikokujin rōdōsha mondai." *Rōdō undō* 326: 54–63.

Honda Katsuichi. 1993a. *Ainu minzoku*. Tokyo: Asahi Shinbunsha.

———. 1993b. *The Impoverished Spirit in Contemporary Japan: Selected Essays of Honda Katsuichi*, ed. John Lie, trans. Eri Fujieda, Masayuki Hamazaki, and John Lie. New York: Monthly Review Press.

Honda Yasuharu. 1987. *"Sengo": Misora Hibari to sono jidai*. Tokyo: Kōdansha.

Honda Yutaka. 1990. *Burakushi kara mita Tokyo*. Tokyo: Aki Shobō.

Honig, Emily. 1992. *Creating Chinese Ethnicity: Subei People in Shanghai, 1850–1980*. New Haven, Conn.: Yale University Press.

Honna, Nobuyuki. 1995. "English in Japanese Society: Language within Language." In John C. Maher and Kyoko Yashiro, eds., *Multilingual Japan*, pp. 45–62. Clevedon, U.K.: Multilingual Matters.

Horiba Kiyoko. 1990. *Inaguya Nanabachi: Okinawa joseishi o saguru*. Tokyo: Domesu Shuppan.

Horiuchi Kōichi. [1986] 1993. *Matsuromanu hitobito Ainu*, expanded ed. Tokyo: Shinsensha.

Howell, David L. 1994. "Ainu Ethnicity and the Boundaries of the Early Modern Japanese State." *Past and Present* 142: 69–93.

————. 1995. *Capitalism from Within: Economy, Society, and the State in a Japanese Fishery.* Berkeley: University of California Press.

————. 1996. "Ethnicity and Culture in Contemporary Japan." *Journal of Contemporary History* 31: 171–190.

Hoyano Hatsuko. 1993. "Yakinikuten fukyō o kui hōdai." *Aera,* Dec. 20, pp. 37–38.

Humboldt, Wilhelm von. [1836/1971] 1972. *Linguistic Variability and Intellectual Development,* trans. George C. Buck and Frithjof A. Raven. Philadelphia: University of Pennsylvania Press.

Hunter, Janet E., ed. 1984. *Concise Dictionary of Modern Japanese History.* Berkeley: University of California Press.

Hwang Min-gi. 1992. "Rikidōzan densetsu." *Oruta* 1: 49–57.

Ichikawa Nobuchika. 1987. *Kakyō shakai keizairon josetsu.* Fukuoka, Japan: Kyūshū Daigaku Shuppankai.

Ienaga Saburō. [1959] 1982. *Nihon bunkashi,* 2d ed. Tokyo: Iwanami Shoten.

Ijūin Shizuka. 1989. *Anoko no kānēshon.* Tokyo: Bungei Shunjū.

Ike Satoko. 1995. "Jirei 1: Burajiru de no Okinawakei e no sabetsu." In Masako Watanabe, ed., *Kyōdō kenkyū dekasegi Nikkei Burajirujin, ge: shiryōhen,* pp. 199–204. Tokyo: Akashi Shoten.

Ikei Masaru. 1991. *Yakyū to Nihonjin.* Tokyo: Maruzen.

Ikemiyagushiku Shūi. 1996. *Hankotsu no jānarisuto.* Naha, Japan: Niraisha.

Inagami Takeshi, Yasuo Kuwahara, and Kokumin Kin'yū Kōko Sōgō Kenkyūsho. 1992. *Gaikokujin rōdōsha o senryakuka suru chūshō kigyō.* Tokyo: Chūshō Kigyō Risāchi Sentā.

Ino Kenji. 1993. *Yakuza to Nihonjin.* Tokyo: Gendai Shokan.

Inomata Tsunao. [1934] 1982. *Kyūbō no nōson.* Tokyo: Iwanami Shoten.

Inoue Kiyoshi. 1953. *Tennōsei.* Tokyo: Tokyo Daigaku Shuppankai.

Inoue Tadashi. 1989. "Gendai no gaishoku to gurume." In Takeshi Moriya, ed., *Gendai Nihon bunka ni okeru dentō to hen'yō.* Vol. 6: *Nihonjin to asobi,* pp. 133–149. Tokyo: Domesu Shuppan.

Inui Takashi. 1971. *Sengoshi: Nihonjin no ishiki.* Tokyo: Rironsha.

Inuzuka Takaaki. 1994. "Bakufu kengaishisetsudan to ryūgakusei." "Kaitaku seisaku to 'Ryūkyū shobun.'" In Akira Tanaka, ed., *Kindai Nihon no kiseki.* Vol. 1: *Meiji ishin,* pp. 89–113. Tokyo: Yoshikawa Kōbunkan.

Ireland, Patrick. 1994. *The Policy Challenge of Ethnic Diversity: Immigrant Politics in France and Switzerland.* Cambridge, Mass.: Harvard University Press.

Iriye, Akira. 1989. "Japan's Drive to Great-Power Status." In Marius B. Jansen, ed., *The Cambridge History of Japan.* Vol. 5: *The Nineteenth Century,* pp. 721–782. Cambridge: Cambridge University Press.

Irokawa Daikichi. 1970. *Meiji no bunka.* Tokyo: Iwanami Shoten.

————. [1975] 1978. *Aru Shōwashi: jibunshi no kokoromi.* Tokyo: Chūō Kōronsha.

————. 1990. *Shōwashi sesōhen.* Tokyo: Shogakukan.

Ishi, Angelo. 1995. "Nikkei Burajirujin o torimaku uwasa to jiken." In Masako Watanabe, ed., *Kyōdō kenkyū dekasegi Nikkei Burajirujin, jo: ronbunhen,* pp. 289–308. Tokyo: Akashi Shoten.

Ishibashi Tanzan. 1984. *Ishibashi Tanzan hyōronshū,* ed. Takayoshi Matsuo. Tokyo: Iwanami Shoten.

Ishida, Hiroshi. 1993. *Social Mobility in Contemporary Japan.* Stanford, Calif.: Stanford University Press.

————. 1998. "Educational Credentials and Labour-Market Entry Outcomes in Japan." In Yossi Shavit and Walter Müller, eds., *From School to Work: A Comparative Study of Educational Qualifications and Occupational Destinations,* pp. 287–309. Oxford: Clarendon Press.

Ishida Takeshi. 1954. *Meiji seiji shisōshi kenkyū.* Tokyo: Miraisha.

————. 1956. *Kindai Nihon seiji kōzō no kenkyū.* Tokyo: Miraisha.

————. 1968. *Nihon kindaishi taikei.* Vol. 8: *Hakyoku to heiwa.* Tokyo: Tokyo Daigaku Shuppankai.

————. 1970. *Nihon no seiji bunka: dōchō to kyōsō.* Tokyo: Tokyo Daigaku Shuppankai.

————. 1973. *Heiwa to henkaku no ronri.* Tokyo: Renga Shobō.

————. 1979. "'Fashizumuki' Nihon ni okeru 'kokumin undō' no soshiki to ideorogī." In Tokyo Daigaku Shakaikagaku Kenkyūsho, ed., *Fashizumuki no kokka to shakai.* Vol. 6: *Undō to teikō jo,* pp. 57–112. Tokyo: Tokyo Daigaku Shuppankai.

————. 1983. *Kindai Nihon no seiji bunka to gengo shōchō.* Tokyo: Tokyo Daigaku Shuppankai.

————. 1984. *Nihon no shakaikagaku.* Tokyo: Tokyo Daigaku Shuppankai.

————. 1989. *Nihon no seiji to kotoba.* Vol. 2: *"Heiwa" to "kokka."* Tokyo: Tokyo Daigaku Shuppankai.

————. 1995. *Shakaikagaku saikō: haisen kara hanseiki no dōjidaishi.* Tokyo: Tokyo Daigaku Shuppankai.

————. 1998. "'Dōka' seisaku to tsukurareta kannen to shite no 'Nihon,'" 2 parts. *Shisō* 892: 47–75, 893: 141–174.

Ishige Naomichi. 1989. "Pachinko—asobi no naka no shigoto." In Takeshi Moriya, ed., *Gendai Nihon bunka ni okeru dentō to hen'yō.* Vol. 6: *Nihonjin to asobi,* pp. 173–196. Tokyo: Domesu Shuppan.

Ishihara Masaie. 1992. "Okinawasen no shosō to sono haikei." In Ryūkyū Shinpōsha, ed., *Shin Ryūkyūshi: kindai, gendai hen,* pp. 249–283. Naha, Japan: Ryūkyū Shinpōsha.

Ishihara Michihiro, ed. [3rd century/1951] 1985. *Gishi wajinden ta sanpen,* new ed., trans. Michihiro Ishihara. Tokyo: Iwanami Shoten.

Ishihara Shintarō. 1995. "Co-Prosperity in the 21st Century." In Mahathir bin

Mohamad and Shintarō Ishihara, *The Voice of Asia: Two Leaders Discuss the Coming Century,* trans. Frank Baldwin, pp. 133–159. Tokyo: Kodansha International.

Ishii Ryōsuke. 1981. *Ie to koseki no rekishi.* Tokyo: Sōbunsha.

Ishii Shirō. 1986. *Nihon kokuseishi kenkyū.* Vol. II: *Nihonjin no kokka seikatsu.* Tokyo: Tokyo Daigaku Shuppankai.

Ishiko Junzō. 1975. *Sengo mangashi nōto.* Tokyo: Kinokuniya Shoten.

Ishio Yoshihisa. 1986. *Buraku kigenron: sono rironteki shomondai.* Tokyo: San'ichi Shobō.

Ishiyama Eiichirō. 1989. *Firipin dekasegi rōdōsha: yume o oi Nihon ni ikite.* Tokyo: Shashiku Shobō.

Ishizuka Hiromichi. 1993. "Fukoku kyōhei to korera: seikimatsu no 'teito' Tokyo." In Ryūji Sasaki and Akira Yamada, eds., *Shinshiten Nihon no rekishi.* Vol. 6: *Kindaihen,* pp. 132–137. Tokyo: Shinjinbutsu Ōraisha.

Isoda Kazuo. 1993. "Kōminka kyōiku to shokuminchi no kokushi kyōkasho." In Shinobu Ōe, Kyōji Asada, Taichirō Mitani, Ken'ichi Gotō, Hideo Kobayashi, Sōji Takasaki, Masahiro Wakabayashi, and Minato Kawamura, eds., *Iwanami kōza kindai Nihon to shokuminchi.* Vol. 4: *Tōgō to shihai no ronri,* pp. 113–135. Tokyo: Iwanami Shoten.

Isoda Kōichi. 1978. *Shisō to shite no Tokyo: kindai bungakushiron nōto.* Tokyo: Kokubunsha.

———. 1983a. *Rokumeikan no keifu: kindai Nihon bungeishi shi.* Tokyo: Bungei Shunjū.

———. 1983b. *Sengoshi no kūkan.* Tokyo: Shinchōsha.

Itō Ruri. 1992. "'Japayukisan' genshō saikō—80-nendai Nihon e no Ajia josei ryū'nyū." In Toshio Iyotani and Takamichi Kajita, eds., *Gaikokujin rōdōsharon: genjō kara riron e,* pp. 293–332. Tokyo: Kōbundō.

Ivy, Marilyn. 1995. *Discourses of the Vanishing: Modernity, Phantasm, Japan.* Chicago: University of Chicago Press.

Iwamoto Noriaki. 1985. "Nihon keizai no kaikaku to fukkō." In Rekishigaku Kenkyūkai and Nihonshi Kenkyūkai, eds., *Kōza Nihon rekishi.* Vol. 11: *Gendai 1,* pp. 77–106. Tokyo: Tokyo Daigaku Shuppankai.

Iwamura Toshio. 1972. *Zainichi Chōsenjin to Nihon rōdōsha kaikyū.* Tokyo: Azekura Shobō.

Iwanaga Kenkichirō. 1985. *Sengo Nihon no seitō to gaikō.* Tokyo: Tokyo Daigaku Shuppankai.

Iwao, Sumiko. 1993. *The Japanese Woman: Traditional Image and Changing Reality.* New York: Free Press.

Iwata Masami. 1995. *Sengo shakaifukushi no tenkai to daitoshi saiteihen.* Kyoto: Mineruva Shobō.

Iwauchi Ryōichi, Atsushi Kadowaki, Etsuo Abe, Yasuhiko Jinnouchi, and Shunta Mori. 1992. *Kaigai Nikkei kigyō to jinteki shigen.* Tokyo: Dōbunkan.

Iyer, Pico. 1988. *Video Night in Kathmandu*. New York: Random House.

———. 1991. *The Lady and the Monk: Four Seasons in Kyoto*. New York: Knopf.

Jansen, Marius B. 1961. *Sakamoto Ryōma and the Meiji Restoration*. Princeton, N.J.: Princeton University Press.

———. 1980. *Japan and Its World: Two Centuries of Change*. Princeton, N.J.: Princeton University Press.

———. 1992. *China in the Tokugawa World*. Cambridge, Mass.: Harvard University Press.

Japan Immigration Association. 1992. *Basic Plan for Immigration Control*. Tokyo: Japan Immigration Association.

Johnson, Douglas. 1993. "The Making of the French Nation." In Mikuláš Teich and Roy Porter, eds., *The National Question in Europe in Historical Context*, pp. 35–62. Cambridge: Cambridge University Press.

Kagotani Jirō. 1994. *Kindai Nihon ni okeru kyōiku to kokka no shisō*. Kyoto: Aunsha.

Kaiho Mineo. 1989. "Wajinchi kenryoku no keisei." In Eiichi Katō, Manji Kitajima, and Katsumi Fukaya, eds., *Bakuhansei kokka to iiki, ikoku*, pp. 47–87. Tokyo: Azekura Shobō.

Kaiho Yōko. 1992. *Kindai hoppōshi: Ainu minzoku to josei to*. Tokyo: San'ichi Shobō.

Kajiwara Ikki and Noboru Kawasaki. 1966–1971. "Kyojin no hoshi." *Shōnen magajin*.

Kamada Motokazu. 1988. "Nihon kodai no 'kuni.'" In Naohiro Asao, Yoshihiko Amino, Keiji Yamaguchi, and Takashi Yoshida, eds., *Nihon no shakaishi*. Vol. 6: *Shakaiteki shoshūdan*, pp. 17–35. Tokyo: Iwanami Shoten.

Kamata Satoshi. 1984. *Dokyumento rōdōsha! 1967–1984*. Tokyo: Chikuma Shobō.

Kamei Shunsuke. 1994. "Nihon no kindai to hon'yaku." In Shunsuke Kamei, ed., *Kindai Nihon no hon'yaku bunka*, pp. 7–50. Tokyo: Chūō Kōronsha.

Kamiesu Tomokatsu. 1996. *Tennōsei ka no Okinawa*. Tokyo: San'ichi Shobō.

Kamijō Horiyuki. 1994. "Kyōiku sōzō to minshū bunka." In Samon Kinbara, ed., *Kindai Nihon no kiseki*. Vol. 4: *Taishō Demokurashī*, pp. 126–148. Tokyo: Yoshikawa Kōbunkan.

Kamishima Jirō. 1961. *Kindai Nihon no seishin kōzō*. Tokyo: Iwanami Shoten.

———. 1973. "Nihon no kindaika." In Jirō Kamishima, ed., *Nihon kindaika no tokushitsu*, 7–38. Tokyo: Ajia Keizai Kenkyūsho.

———. 1982. *Jiba no seijigaku*. Tokyo: Iwanami Shoten.

Kamiya Atsuyuki. 1989. "Tai-Mei seisaku to Ryūkyū shihai." In Eiichi Katō, Manji Kitajima, and Katsumi Fukaya, eds., *Bakuhansei kokka to iiki, ioku*, pp. 247–289. Tokyo: Azekura Shobō.

Kamiya Nobuyuki. 1990. *Bakuhansei kokka no Ryūkyū shihai*. Tokyo: Azekura Shobō.

Kanagawa Zainichi Gaikokujin Mondai Kenkyūkai. 1992. *Tabunka, taminzoku shakai no shinkō to gaikokujin ukeire no genjō*. Yokohama: Kanagawa Zainichi Gaikokujin Mondai Kenkyūkai.

———. 1993. *Zaijū gaikokujin, tomo ni kurasu Kanagawa: motto anata ni deaitai*. Yokohama: Kanagawa Zainichi Gaikokujin Mondai Kenkyūkai.

Kandatsu Haruki. 1991. *Sengo sonraku keikan no henbō*. Tokyo: Ochanomizu Shobō.

Kanegae Haruhiko. 1991. "Gendai daigakusei no buraku sabetsu ishiki no ichisokumen." *Kaihō shakaigaku* 5: 144–162.

Kaneko Masaru. 1985. "'Kōdo seichō' to kokumin seikatsu." In Rekishigaku Kenkyūkai and Nihonshi Kenkyūkai, eds., *Kōza Nihon rekishi*. Vol. 12: *Gendai 2*, pp. 45–86. Tokyo: Tokyo Daigaku Shuppankai.

Kang Chae-on and Tong-hun Kim. 1989. *Zainichi Kankoku, Chōsenjin—rekishi to tenbō*. Tokyo: Rōdōkeizaisha.

Kang Sang-jung. 1993. "Shakaikagakusha no shokuminchi ninshiki: shokuminseisakugaku to orientarizumu." In Yasushi Yamanouchi et al., eds., *Iwanami kōza shakaikagaku no hōhō*. Vol. 3: *Nihon shakaikagaku no shisō*, pp. 101–130. Tokyo: Iwanami Shoten.

Kang Tŏk-sang. 1975. *Kantō daishinsai*. Tokyo: Chūō Kōronsha.

Kano Masanao. 1985. "Gendai ningenron." In Rekishigaku Kenkyūkai and Nihonshi Kenkyūkai, eds., *Kōza Nihon rekishi*. Vol. 13: *Rekishi ni okeru genzai*, pp. 213–234. Tokyo: Tokyo Daigaku Shuppankai.

———. [1972] 1986. *Nihon kindaika no shisō*. Tokyo: Kōdansha.

———. 1987. *Sengo Okinawa no shisōzō*. Tokyo: Asahi Shinbunsha.

———. 1993. *Okinawa no en: Iha Fuyuu*. Tokyo: Iwanami Shoten.

———. 1995. "Nihon bunkaron to rekishi ishiki." In Naohiro Asao, Yoshihiko Amino, Susumu Ishii, Masanao Kano, Shōhachi Hayakawa, and Yasuo Yasumaru, eds., *Iwanami kōza Nihon tsūshi, bekkan 1*, pp. 187–213. Tokyo: Iwanami Shoten.

Kantō Bengoshikai Rengōkai, ed. 1989. *Gaikokujin rōdōsha to keizai shakai no shinro*. Tokyo: Akashi Shoten.

———. 1990. *Gaikokujin rōdōsha no shūrō to jinken*. Tokyo: Akashi Shoten.

Kaplan, Justin, and Anne Bernays. 1997. *The Language of Names*. New York: Simon & Schuster.

Karatani Kōjin. [1990] 1995. *Shūen o megutte*. Tokyo: Kōdansha.

Kariya Tetsu and Akira Hanasaki. 1985. *Oishinbo*, vol. 3. Tokyo: Shōgakukan.

Kasamatsu Hiroshi. 1984. *Hō to kotoba no chūseishi*. Tokyo: Heibonsha.

Kasuya Ken'ichi. 1992. "Chōsen sōtokufu no bunka seiji." In Shinobu Ōe, Kyōji Asada, Taichirō Mitani, Ken'ichi Gotō, Hideo Kobayashi, Sōji Takasaki, Masahiro Wakabayashi, and Minato Kawamura, eds., *Iwanami kōza kindai Nihon to shokuminchi*. Vol. 2: *Teikoku tōji no kōzō*, pp. 121–146. Tokyo: Iwanami Shoten.

Kata Kōji. 1979. *Kamishibai Shōwashi*. Tokyo: Ōbunsha.

———. [1975] 1985. *Uta no Shōwashi*. Tokyo: Jiji Tsūshinsha.

Katō Hidetoshi. 1977. *Meiji Taishō shokuseikatsu sesōshi*. Tokyo: Shibata Shoten.

———. [1954] 1980. "Hābādo e." In Hidetoshi Katō, *Katō Hidetoshi chosakushū*, vol. 8 *(geppō)*, pp. 1–8. Tokyo: Chūō Kōronsha.

———. [1969] 1981. "Chikyū to ningen." In Hidetoshi Katō, *Katō Hidetoshi chosakushū*, vol. 5, pp. 7–28. Tokyo: Chūō Kōronsha.

Katō Shūichi. 1956. *Zasshu bunka—Nihon no chiisana kibō*. Tokyo: Kōdansha.

———. 1959. *Gendai Yōroppa no seishin*. Tokyo: Iwanami Shoten.

———. 1964. "The Mass Media: A. Japan." In Robert E. Ward and Dankwart A. Rustow, eds., *Political Modernization in Japan and Turkey*, pp. 236–254. Princeton, N.J.: Princeton University Press.

———. 1968. *Hitsuji no uta: waga kaisō*, 2 vols. Tokyo: Iwanami Shoten.

———. 1971. *Bungaku to wa nanika*. Tokyo: Kadokawa Shoten.

———. 1976. *Nihonjin to wa nanika*. Tokyo: Kōdansha.

———. 1986. "Sengo sekai to Nihon." In Rokurō Hidaka, ed., *Sengo Nihon o kangaeru*, pp. 285–301. Tokyo: Chikuma Shobō.

———. 1995. "Sōron 'kako no kokufuku' oboegaki." In Masanori Nakamura, Akira Amakawa, Kŏn-ch'a Yun, and Takeshi Igarashi, eds., *Sengo Nihon senryō to sengo kaikaku*. Vol. 5: *Kako no seisan*, pp. 1–18. Tokyo: Iwanami Shoten.

Katō Tetsurō. 1992. *Shakai to kokka*. Tokyo: Iwanami Shoten.

Katsumata Shizuo. 1994. "15–16 seiki no Nihon." In Naohiro Asao, Yoshihiko Amino, Susumu Ishii, Masanao Kano, Shōhachi Hayakawa, and Yasuo Yasumaru, eds., *Iwanami kōza Nihon tsūshi*. Vol. 1: *Chūsei 4*, pp. 1–57. Tokyo: Iwanami Shoten.

Kawamura Minato. 1994a. *Umi o watatta Nihongo*. Tokyo: Seidosha.

———. 1994b. *Nan'yo, Karufuto no Nihon bungaku*. Tokyo: Chikuma Shobō.

———. 1995. *Sengo bungaku o tou: sono taiken to rinen*. Tokyo: Iwanami Shoten.

Kawamura Nozomu. [1982] 1993. *Nihon bunkaron no shūhen*. Tokyo: Ningen no Kagakusha.

Kawashima Takeyoshi. [1948] 1950. *Nihon shakai no kazokuteki kōsei*. Tokyo: Nihon Hyōronsha.

Kawauchi Masahiro. 1979. "Bakuhatsu suru rejā." In Hiroyoshi Ishikawa, ed., *Yoka no sengoshi*, pp. 115–208. Tokyo: Tokyo Shoseki.

Kayano Shigeru. 1994. *Our Land Was a Forest: An Ainu Memoir*, trans. Kyoko Selden and Lili Selden. Boulder, Colo.: Westview Press.

Kayatori Mitsugu. 1980. *Sengo manga shisōshi*. Tokyo: Miraisha.

Kazama Hideto. 1994. "Shokuminchi jinushisei to nōgyō." In Kyōji Asada, ed., *Kindai Nihon no kiseki*. Vol. 10: *"Teikoku" Nihon to Ajia*, pp. 108–130. Tokyo: Yoshikawa Kōbunkan.

Keene, Donald. 1950. *Living Japan*. Garden City, N.Y.: Doubleday.

————. 1984. *Dawn to the West—Japanese Literature in the Modern Era: Fiction.* New York: Holt, Rinehart and Winston.

Keizai Dōyūkai. 1989. *Gaikokujin to no kyōsei o mezashite.* Tokyo: Keizai Dōyūkai.

Keizai Kikakuchō Kokumin Seikatsukyoku, ed. 1987. *Kokusaika to kokumin ishiki.* Tokyo: Ōkurashō Insatsukyoku.

Keizai Kikakuchō Sōgō Keikakukyoku. 1989. *Gaikokujin rōdōsha to keizai shakai no shinro.* Tokyo: Ōkurashō Insatsukyoku.

Kelly, William W. [1990] 1992. "Regional Japan: The Price of Prosperity and the Benefits of Dependency." In Carol Gluck and Stephen R. Graubard, eds., *Showa: The Japan of Hirohito,* pp. 208–227. New York: Norton.

Kennedy, Paul. 1993. *Preparing for the Twenty-First Century.* New York: Random House.

Kerr, George H. 1958. *Okinawa: The History of an Island People.* Rutland, Vt.: Charles E. Tuttle.

Kevles, Daniel J. 1985. *In the Name of Eugenics: Genetics and the Uses of Human Heredity.* New York: Knopf.

Khalidi, Rashid. 1997. *Palestinian Identity: The Construction of Modern National Consciousness.* New York: Columbia University Press.

Kikuchi Isao. 1984. *Bakuhan taisei to Ezochi.* Tokyo: Yūzankaku.

————. 1989. "Kinsei kōki no bakuhan kenryoku to Ainu." In Eiichi Katō, Manji Kitajima, and Katsumi Fukaya, eds., *Bakuhansei kokka to iiki, ikoku,* pp. 89–139. Tokyo: Azekura Shobō.

————. 1991. *Hoppōshi no naka no kinsei Nihon.* Tokyo: Azekura Shobō.

————. 1995. "Kaibō to hoppō mondai." In Naohiro Asao, Yoshihiko Amino, Susumu Ishii, Masanao Kano, Shōhachi Hayakawa, and Yasuo Yasumaru, eds., *Iwanami kōza Nihon tsūshi.* Vol. 14: *Kinsei 4,* pp. 221–252. Tokyo: Iwanami Shoten.

Kikuchi Kyōko. 1992. "Gaikokujin rōdōsha okuridashikoku no shakaiteki mekanizumu—Firipin no baai." In Toshio Iyotani and Takamichi Kajita, eds., *Gaikokujin rōdōsharon: genjō kara riron e,* pp. 169–201. Tokyo: Kōbundō.

Kikuyama Masaaki. 1992. "Okinawa tōgō kikō no sōsetsu." In Ryūkyū Shinpōsha, ed., *Shin Ryūkyūshi: kindai, gendai hen,* pp. 63–88. Naha, Japan: Ryūkyū Shinpōsha.

Kim Ch'an-jŏng. 1985. *Ipōjin wa Kimigayomaru ni notte: Chōsenjin Ikaino no keiseishi.* Tokyo: Iwanami Shoten.

Kim Kyu-sŭng. 1987. *Nihon no shokuminchi hōsei no kenkyū.* Tokyo: Shakai Hyōronsha.

Kim Mun-sŏn. 1991. *Horōden: Shōwashi no naka no Zainichi.* Tokyo: Sairyūsha.

Kim Yŏng-sin. 1994. "Hangug'in iyŏ uridŭl ingan ŭro taehaedao." *Sin Tong'a,* July, pp. 492–507.

Kim Yŏng-un. 1983. *Kankokujin to Nihonjin.* Tokyo: Saimaru Shuppankai.

Kimura Kenji. 1989. *Zaichō Nihonjin no shakaishi.* Tokyo: Miraisha.

Kimura Takeo. 1973. *Nihon nashonarizumu shiron.* Tokyo: Waseda Daigaku Shuppanbu.

Kinbara Samon. 1985. "Ie to mura to kokka no ideorogī." In Rekishigaku Kenkyūkai and Nihonshi Kenkyūkai, eds., *Kōza Nihon rekishi.* Vol. 8: *Kindai 2,* pp. 277–313. Tokyo: Tokyo Daigaku Shuppankai.

Kinmonth, Earl H. 1981. *The Self-Made Man in Meiji Japanese Thought: From Samurai to Salary Man.* Berkeley: University of California Press.

Kiridōshi Risaku. 1993. *Kaijū tsukai to shōnen: Urutoraman no sakka tachi.* Tokyo: Takarajimasha.

Kishida Shū. [1977] 1982. *Monogusa seishinbunseki.* Tokyo: Chūō Kōronsha.

Kitade Seigorō. [1980] 1991. "Taihō, sono sugao." In Akira Yoshimura, ed., *Nihon no meizuihitsu bekkan.* Vol. 2: *Sumō,* pp. 149–159. Tokyo: Sakuhinsha.

Kitagawa, Joseph M. 1966. *Religion in Japanese History.* New York: Columbia University Press.

Kitamura Hideo. 1983. "Terebi to Nihon bunka." In Hideo Kitamura and Osamu Nakano, eds., *Nihon no terebi bunka,* pp. 233–268. Tokyo: Yūhikaku.

Kitō Kiyoaki. 1975. "Nihon minzoku no keisei to kokusaiteki keiki." In Hidesaburō Hara, Sumio Minegishi, Junnosuke Sasaki, and Masanori Nakamura, eds., *Taikei Nihon kokkashi.* Vol. 1: *Kodai,* pp. 67–119. Tokyo: Tokyo Daigaku Shuppankai.

Kiyasu Yukio. 1979. *Taiwantō kōnichi nisshi.* Tokyo: Hara Shobō.

Kō Sekai. 1972. *Nihon tōjika no Taiwan.* Tokyo: Tokyo Daigaku Shuppankai.

Ko Sŏn-mi. 1995. "'Shin-Kankokujin'" no teijūka." In Hiroshi Komai, ed., *Kōza gaikokujin teijū mondai.* Vol. 2: *Teijūku suru gaikokujin,* pp. 227–254. Tokyo: Akashi Shoten.

Kobayashi Kengo. 1992. "Yoseba no gaikokujin rōdōsha." In Ajiajin Rōdōsha Mondai Kondankai, ed., *Okasareru jinken gaikokujin rōdōsha,* pp. 73–85. Tokyo: Daisan Shokan.

Kobayashi Ken'ichi. 1977. *Rōdō keizai no kōzō henkaku.* Tokyo: Ochanomizu Shobō.

Kobayashi Nobuhiko. 1997. *Gendai "shigo" nōto.* Tokyo: Iwanami Shoten.

Kobayashi Shigeru. 1979. *Buraku "kaihōrei" no kenkyū.* Osaka: Buraku Kaihō Shuppansha.

———. 1985. *Buraku sabetsu no rekishiteki kenkyū.* Tokyo: Akashi Shoten.

Kobayashi Yoshinori. 1993. *Gōmanizumu sengen,* vol. 1. Tokyo: Fusōsha.

Koike Kazuo. 1981. *Nihon no jukuren: sugureta jinzai keisei sisutemu.* Tokyo: Yūhikaku.

Koizumi Fumio. 1977. *Nihon no oto: sekai no naka no Nihon ongaku.* Tokyo: Seidosha.

———. 1984. *Kayōkyoku no kōzō.* Tokyo: Tōkisha.

————. 1985. *Minzoku ongaku no sekai*, ed. Gen'ichi Tsuge. Tokyo: Nihon Hōsō Shuppan Kyōkai.

Koizumi Shinzō. 1966. *Fukuzawa Yukichi*. Tokyo: Iwanami Shoten.

Kojima Tomiko. 1982. *Nihon ongaku no kosō*. Tokyo: Shunjūsha.

Kokusai Kekkon o Kangaerukai, ed. 1987. *Kokusai kekkon handobukku*. Tokyo: Akashi Shoten.

Kokusai Kyōryoku Jitsugyōdan. [1992] 1994. "Heisei 4-nendo Nikkeijin honpō shūrōsha jittai chōsa hōkokusho." In Hiroshi Komai, ed., *Gaikokujin rōdōsha mondai shiryō shūsei*, vol. 1, pp. 115–179. Tokyo: Akashi Shoten.

Komai Hiroshi. 1993. *Gaikokujin rōdōsha teijū e no michi*. Tokyo: Akashi Shoten.

Komatsu Hisao. 1985. *Edojidai no kokugo Edogo*. Tokyo: Tōkyōdō.

Komuro Naoki. 1993. *Kokumin no tame no keizai genron*. Vol. 2: *Amerika heigō hen*. Tokyo: Kōbunsha.

Konaka Yōtarō. 1993. "Terebi bangumi kara mita Nihon shakai." In Katsumasa Harada and Ryūji Sasaki, eds., *Shinshiten Nihon no rekishi*. Vol. 7: *Gendaihen*, pp. 218–223. Tokyo: Shinjinbutsu Ōraisha.

Kondo, Dorinne K. 1990. *Crafting Selves: Power, Gender, and Discourses of Identity in a Japanese Workplace*. Chicago: University of Chicago Press.

Kondō Masami. 1992. "Taiwan sōtokufu no 'riban' taisei to Musha jiken." In Shinobu Ōe, Kyōji Asada, Taichirō Mitani, Ken'ichi Gotō, Hideo Kobayashi, Sōji Takasaki, Masahiro Wakabayashi, and Minato Kawamura, eds., *Iwanami kōza kindai Nihon to shokuminchi*. Vol. 2: *Teikoku tōji no kōzō*, pp. 35–60. Tokyo: Iwanami Shoten.

Kōno Yoshinori. 1991. *Tsurugi no seishinshi*. Tokyo: Shin'yōsha.

Kosaka, Kenji. 1994. "Perceptions of Class and Status." In Kenji Kosaka, ed., *Social Stratification in Contemporary Japan*, pp. 93–117. London: Kegan Paul International.

Koschmann, J. Victor. 1987. *The Mito Ideology: Discourse, Reform, and Insurrection in Late Tokugawa Japan, 1790–1864*. Berkeley: University of California Press.

Kotani Hiroyuki. 1992. "Kindai Nihon no jiko ninshiki to Ajiakan." In Yasunori Arano, Masatoshi Ishii, and Shōsuke Murai, eds., *Ajia no naka no Nihonshi*. Vol. 1: *Ajia to Nihon*, pp. 59–79. Tokyo: Tokyo Daigaku Shuppankai.

Koyama Hirotake. 1981. "Sōron." In Shinsensha Henshūbu, ed., *Gendai Nihon no henken to sabetsu*, pp. 5–21. Tokyo: Shinsensha.

Kubo Kiriko. 1987. *Imadoki no kodomo*, vol. 1. Tokyo: Shōgakukan.

Kuhaulua, Jesse (Daigoro Takamiyama), with John Wheeler. 1973. *Takamiyama: The World of Sumo*. Tokyo: Kodansha International.

Kumagai, Fumie. 1996. *Unmasking Japan Today: The Impact of Traditional Values on Modern Japanese Society*. Wesport, Conn: Praeger.

Kumakura Isao. 1988. "Nihon no shokuji bunka ni okeru gairai no shoku." In Isao Kumakura and Naomichi Ishige, eds., *Shoku no bunka fōramu: gairai no shoku no bunka*, pp. 13–29. Tokyo: Domesu Shuppan.

Kumazaka Kenji. 1985. "'Wakamonotachi no kamigami.'" *Asahi jānaru,* May 31, pp. 108–113.

Kumazawa Makoto. 1981. *Nihon no rōdōshazō.* Tokyo: Chikuma Shobō.

———. 1983. *Minshushugi wa kōjō no monzen de tachisukumu.* Tokyo: Tabata Shoten.

Kumito Fujiko. 1990. "Josei rōdōsha no byōtō yōkyū no hatten." In Joseishi Sōgō Kenkyūkai, ed., *Nihon josei seikatsushi,* vol. 5, pp. 69–100. Tokyo: Tokyo Daigaku Shuppankai.

Kunitomo Ryūichi. 1992. *Dokomade susumu Nihon no naka no kokusaika chizu.* Tokyo: Nihon Jitsugyō Shuppansha.

Kurasawa Aiko. 1992. "Tōnan Ajia no minshū dōin." In Shinobu Ōe, Kyōji Asada, Taichirō Mitani, Ken'ichi Gotō, Hideo Kobayashi, Sōji Takasaki, Masahiro Wakabayashi, and Minato Kawamura, eds., *Iwanami kōza kindai Nihon to shokuminchi.* Vol. 2: *Teikoku tōji no kōzō,* pp. 243–266. Tokyo: Iwanami Shoten.

Kure Tomofusa. 1986. *Gendai manga no zentaizō: taibō shiteita mono, koeta mono.* Tokyo: Jōhō Sentā Shuppankyoku.

———. 1993a. *Chi no shūkaku.* Tokyo: Media Fakutorī.

———. 1993b. *Saru no seigi.* Tokyo: Futabasha.

———. 1993c. "Konjō no shūhen ni tsuite kataro!" *Border* 1: 84–85.

Kurihara Akira. 1982. *Kanri shakai to minshū risei: nichijō ishiki no seijishakaigaku.* Tokyo: Shin'yōsha.

Kurihara Akira, ed. 1996. *Kōza sabetsu no shakaigaku.* Vol. 1: *Sabetsu no shakai riron.* Tokyo: Kōbundō.

Kuroda Toshio. 1971. "Minzoku bunkaron." In Rekishigaku Kenkyūkai and Nihonshi Kenkyūkai, eds., *Kōza Nihonshi.* Vol. 9: *Nihonshigaku ronsō,* pp. 283–312. Tokyo: Tokyo Daigaku Shuppankai.

———. 1987. "Chūsei no mibun ishiki to shakaikan." In Naohiro Asao, Yoshihiko Amino, Keiji Yamaguchi, and Takeshi Yoshida, eds., *Nihon no shakaishi.* Vol. 7: *Shakaikan to sekaizō,* pp. 51–86. Tokyo: Iwanami Shoten.

Kuwabara Masato. 1993. *Senzenki Hokkaidō no shiteki kenkyū.* Sapporo: Hokkaidō Daigaku Tosho Kankōkai.

Kuwahara Yasuo. 1991. *Kokkyo o koeru rōdōsha.* Tokyo: Iwanami Shoten.

Lach, Donald F. 1965. *Asia in the Making of Europe,* vol. 1. Chicago: University of Chicago Press.

Landau, Jacob M. 1993. *The Arab Minority in Israel, 1967–1991: Political Aspects.* Oxford: Clarendon Press.

Large, Stephen S. 1992. *Emperor Hirohito and Shōwa Japan: A Political Biography.* London: Routledge.

Leavis, Q. D. [1932] 1979. *Fiction and the Reading Public.* Harmondsworth, U.K.: Penguin.

Lebra, Joyce. [1976] 1978. "Conclusion." In Joyce Lebra, Joy Paulson, and Elizabeth Powers, eds., *Women in Changing Japan*, pp. 297–304. Stanford, Calif.: Stanford University Press.

Lebra, Takie Sugiyama. 1993. *Above the Clouds: Status Culture of the Modern Japanese Nobility*. Berkeley: University of California Press.

Lee O-Young [Yi O-yŏng]. 1983. *"Chijimi" shikō no Nihonjin*. Tokyo: Gakuseisha.

Lévi-Strauss, Claude. [1978] 1979. *Myth and Meaning*. New York: Schocken.

Lewis, Michael. [1991] 1992. *Pacific Rift*. New York: Norton.

Lewis, W. Arthur. 1985. *Racial Conflict and Economic Development*. Cambridge, Mass.: Harvard University Press.

Lie, John. 1987. "The Discriminated Fingers: The Korean Minority in Japan." *Monthly Review* 38(8): 17–23.

————. 1995. "The Transformation of Sexual Work in 20th-Century Korea." *Gender & Society* 9: 310–327.

————. 1997. "Sociology of Contemporary Japan." *Current Sociology* 44: 1–101.

————. 1998. *Han Unbound: The Political Economy of South Korea*. Stanford, Calif.: Stanford University Press.

Lifton, Robert Jay, Shūichi Katō, and Michael R. Reich. 1979. *Six Lives, Six Deaths: Portraits from Modern Japan*. New Haven, Conn.: Yale University Press.

Machimura Takashi. 1993. "Ekkyō suru media to Nihon shakai." *Hitotsubashi ronsō* 110: 255–273.

Maeda Ai. 1978. *Genkei no Meiji*. Tokyo: Asahi Shinbunsha.

Maehira Fusaaki. 1994. "19-seiki no Higashi Ajia kokusai kankei to Ryūkyū mondai." In Yūzō Mizoguchi, Takeshi Hamashita, Naoaki Hiraishi, and Hiroshi Miyajima, eds., *Ajia kara kangaeru*. Vol. 3: *Shūen kara no rekishi*, pp. 243–271. Tokyo: Tokyo Daigaku Shuppankai.

Maher, John C. 1995. "The *Kakyo*: Chinese in Japan." In John C. Maher and Kyoko Yashiro, eds., *Multilingual Japan*, pp. 125–138. Clevedon, U.K.: Multilingual Matters.

Maher, John C., and Gaynor Macdonald, eds. 1995. *Diversity in Japanese Culture and Language*. London: Kegan Paul International.

Mainichi Shinbun Gaishinbu. 1990. *Daisan no kaikoku: sekai o "tadayou tami."* Tokyo: Asahi Sonorama.

Mainichi Shinbun Tokyo Honsha Shakaibu, ed. [1989] 1990. *Jipangu: Nihon o mezasu gaikokujin rōdōsha*, rev. ed. Tokyo: Mainichi Shinbunsha.

Makino Hirotaka. 1992. "Shikake to shite no Amerika no keizai seisaku." In Ryūkyū Shinpōsha, ed., *Shin Ryūkyūshi: kindai, gendai hen*, pp. 315–357. Naha, Japan: Ryūkyū Shinpōsha.

Mamada Takao. 1990. "Kaisō kizoku ishiki." In Junsuke Hara, ed., *Gendai Nihon no kaisō kōzō*. Vol. 2: *Kaisō ishiki no dōtai*, pp. 23–45. Tokyo: Tokyo Daigaku Shuppankai.

Manabe Shunji. 1990. *Kokusaika no ishiki kakumei: shinjidai e no pasupōto*. Kyoto: Hōritsu Bunkasha.

Marcus, George E., and Michael M. J. Fischer. 1986. *Anthropology as Cultural Critique: An Experimental Movement in the Human Sciences.* Chicago: University of Chicago Press.

Marks, Jonathan. 1995. *Human Biodiversity: Genes, Race, and History.* New York: Aldine de Gruyter.

Maruya Saiichi. 1984. *Chūshingura to wa nanika.* Tokyo: Kōdansha.

Maruyama Masao. 1961. *Nihon no shisō.* Tokyo: Iwanami Shoten.

———. [1957] 1964. *Gendai seiji no shisō to kōdō,* expanded ed. Tokyo: Miraisha.

———. [1952] 1974. *Studies in the Intellectual History of Tokugawa Japan,* trans. Mikiso Hane. Tokyo: University of Tokyo Press.

———. [1946] 1976. "Meiji kokka no shisō." In Masao Maruyama, *Senchū to sengo no aida: 1936–1957,* pp. 202–250. Tokyo: Misuzu Shobō.

———. 1982. "Kindai Nihon no chishikijin." In Masao Maruyama, *Kōei no ichi kara: "Gendai seiji no shisō to kōdō" tsuiho,* pp. 71–133. Tokyo: Miraisha.

———. [1951] 1995a. "Nihon ni okeru nashonarizumu." In Masao Maruyama, *Maruyama Masao shū,* vol. 5, pp. 57–78. Tokyo: Iwanami Shoten.

———. [1951] 1995b. "Sengo Nihon no nashonarizumu no ippanteki kōsatsu." In Masao Maruyama, *Maruyama Masao shū,* vol. 5, pp. 89–122. Tokyo: Iwanami Shoten.

———. [1944] 1996. "Kokuminshugi no 'zenkiteki' keisei." In Masao Maruyama, *Maruyama Masao shū,* vol. 2, 225–269. Tokyo: Iwanami Shoten.

Mason, David. 1995. *Race and Ethnicity in Modern Britain.* Oxford: Oxford University Press.

Masuda Hiroshi. 1990. *Ishibashi Tanzan kenkyū: "shō Nihonshugisha" no kokusai ninshiki.* Tokyo: Tōyō Keizai Shinpōsha.

Masuda Kō. [1918] 1974. *New Japanese-English Dictionary,* 4th ed. Tokyo: Kenkyūsha.

Matayoshi Morikiyo. 1992. "Taiwan shokuminchi to Okinawa no kakawari." In Shinobu Ōe, Kyōji Asada, Taichirō Mitani, Ken'ichi Gotō, Hideo Kobayashi, Sōji Takasaki, Masahiro Wakabayashi, and Minato Kawamura, eds., *Iwanami kōza kindai Nihon to shokuminchi,* vol. 2 *(geppō),* pp. 3–5. Tokyo: Iwanami Shoten.

Mathy, Jean-Philippe. 1993. *Extrême-Occident: French Intellectuals and America.* Chicago: University of Chicago Press.

Matsubara Hiroshi. 1936. *Minzokuron.* Tokyo: Mikasa Shobō.

Matsubara Nobuko. 1983. "Joshi pātotaimu rōdōsha no zōka to rōdō jōken." In Hisako Takahashi, ed., *Kawariyuku fujin rōdō: jakunen tanki mikongata kara chūkōnen kikongata e,* pp. 100–123. Tokyo: Yūhikaku.

Matsubara Ryūichirō. 1994. *Kakutōgi to shite no dōjidai ronsō.* Tokyo: Keisō Shobō.

Matsuda Yoshitaka. 1981. *Sengo Okinawa shakai keizaishi kenkyū.* Tokyo: Tokyo Daigaku Shuppankai.

Matsumori, Akiko. 1995. "Ryūkyūan: Past, Present and Future." In John C. Maher and Kyoko Yashiro, eds., *Multilingual Japan*, pp. 19–44. Clevedon, U.K.: Multilingual Matters.

Matsumoto Sannosuke. 1975. *Nihon seiji shisōshi gairon*. Tokyo: Keisō Shobō.

————. 1996. *Meiji shisōshi*. Tokyo: Shin'yōsha.

Matsuo Takayoshi. 1990. *Taishō demokurashī no gunzō*. Tokyo: Iwanami Shoten.

Matsuyama Iwao. 1993. *Uwasa no enkinhō*. Tokyo: Seidosha.

Matsuyama Yukio. 1985. *Kokusai taiwa no jidai*. Tokyo: Asahi Shinbunsha.

Matsuzaka Hideaki and Tsuneko Matsuzaka. 1993. *Musume—Matsuzaka Keiko e no "yuigon."* Tokyo: Kōbunsha.

Matsuzawa Hiroaki. 1993. *Kindai Nihon no keisei to Seiō keiken*. Tokyo: Iwanami Shoten.

Matsuzawa Tetsunari. 1979. *Ajiashugi to fashizumu: tennō teikokuron hihan*. Tokyo: Renga Shobō Shinsha.

Mayr, Ernst. 1991. *One Long Argument: Charles Darwin and the Genesis of Modern Evolutionary Thought*. Cambridge, Mass.: Harvard University Press.

McCormack, Gavan. 1996. *The Emptiness of Japanese Affluence*. Armonk, N.Y.: M. E. Sharpe.

McGregor, Richard. 1996. *Japan Swings: Politics, Culture, and Sex in the New Japan*. St. Leonards, Australia: Allen & Unwin.

McNeill, William H. 1986. *Polyethnicity and National Unity in World History*. Toronto: University of Toronto Press.

————. 1989. *Arnold J. Toynbee: A Life*. New York: Oxford University Press.

————. 1990. *Population and Politics since 1750*. Charlottesville: University Press of Virginia.

Mennell, Stephen. 1985. *All Manners of Food: Eating and Taste in England and France from the Middle Ages to the Present*. Oxford: Blackwell.

Mihashi Osamu. 1992. "Sabetsu no teigi o megutte jo." In Sabetsu o Kangaeru Kenkyūkai, ed., *Nenpō sabetsu mondai kenkyū*, vol. I, pp. 107–122. Tokyo: Akashi Shoten.

Miki Takeshi. 1988. *Okineshia bunkaron: seishin no kyōwakoku o mezashite*. Osaka: Kaifūsha.

————. 1992. "Sōmō no minshūshi: Iriomote tankō." In Ryūkyū Shinpōsha, ed., *Shin Ryūkyūshi: kindai, gendai hen*, pp. 215–248. Naha, Japan: Ryūkyū Shinpōsha.

Mikuni Ichirō. 1985. *Senchū yōgoshū*. Tokyo: Iwanami Shoten.

Miller, Roy Andrew. 1982. *Japan's Modern Myth: The Language and Beyond*. New York: Weatherhill.

Mills, C. Wright. 1959. *The Sociological Imagination*. London: Oxford University Press.

Minami Hiroshi. 1983. *Nihonteki jiga*. Tokyo: Iwanami Shoten.

———. 1994. *Nihonjinron: Meiji kara kyō made.* Tokyo: Iwanami Shoten.

Minami Hiroshi and Shakai Shinri Kenkyūsho, eds. 1983. *Nihonjin no seikatsu bunka jiten.* Tokyo: Keisō Shobō.

Minegishi Kentarō. 1989. *Kinsei mibunron.* Tokyo: Azekura Shobō.

Ministry of Foreign Affairs. 1992. "Issues Associated with Foreign Labour in Japan." In Association for Promotion of International Cooperation, ed., *Japan and International Migration: Challenges and Opportunities,* pp. 177–185. Tokyo: Association for Promotion of International Cooperation.

Ministry of Labour. 1992. "Foreign Workers and Labour Market in Japan." In Association for Promotion of International Cooperation, ed., *Japan and International Migration: Challenges and Opportunities,* pp. 161–176. Tokyo: Association for Promotion of International Cooperation.

Minoshima Hirotaka. 1993. "Yomikata oshiete." *Aera,* Aug. 3, pp. 44–45.

Mishima Yukio. [1968] 1976. "Bunka bōeiron." In Yukio Mishima, *Mishima Yukio zenshū,* vol. 33, pp. 366–401. Tokyo: Shinchōsha.

———. [1970] 1996. "Gekiga ni okeru wakamonoron." In Shinbō Minami, ed., *Nihon no meizuihitsu.* Vol. 62: *Manga,* pp. 108–111. Tokyo: Sakuhinsha.

Misumi Kazuko. 1990. "Kaikyū kizoku ishiki." In Junsuke Hara, ed., *Gendai Nihon no kaisō kōzō.* Vol. 2: *Kaisō ishiki no dōtai,* pp. 71–95. Tokyo: Tokyo Daigaku Shuppankai.

Mita Munesuke. 1965. *Gendai Nihon no seishin kōzo.* Tokyo: Kōbundō.

———. [1968] 1978. *Kindai Nihon no shinjō no rekishi: ryūkōka no shakai shinrishi.* Tokyo: Kōdansha.

———. 1996. *Gendai shakai no riron: jōhōka, shōhika shakai no genzai to mirai.* Tokyo: Iwanami Shoten.

Mitani Hiroshi. 1997. *Meiji ishin to nashonarizumu.* Tokyo: Yamakawa Shuppansha.

Mitchell, Richard H. 1967. *The Korean Minority in Japan.* Berkeley: University of California Press.

———. 1983. *Censorship in Imperial Japan.* Princeton, N.J.: Princeton University Press.

Miyachi Masato. 1973. *Nichirosengo seijishi no kenkyū.* Tokyo: Tokyo Daigaku Shuppankai.

Miyadai Masaji, Hideki Ishihara, and Akiko Ōtsuka. 1993. *Sabukaruchā shinwa kaitai.* Tokyo: Paruko Shuppan.

Miyajima Takashi. 1989. *Gaikokujin rōdōsha mukaeire no ronri: senshin shakai no jirenma no nakade.* Tokyo: Akashi Shoten.

Miyamoto Tokuzō. 1985. *Rikishi hyōhaku: sumō no arukeorojī.* Tokyo: Ozawa Shoten.

Miyamoto Tsuneichi. [1960] 1984a. *Wasurerareta Nihonjin.* Tokyo: Iwanami Shoten.

————. [1943] 1984b. *Kakyō no oshie*. Tokyo: Iwanami Shoten.

Miyata Setsuko. 1985. *Chōsen minshū to 'kōminka' seisaku*. Tokyo: Miraisha.

————. 1994. "Tennōsei kyōiku to kōminka seisaku." In Kyōji Asada, ed., *Kindai Nihon no kiseki*. Vol. 10: *"Teikoku" Nihon to Ajia*, pp. 152–172. Tokyo: Yoshikawa Kōbunkan.

Mizuhara Akito. 1994. *Edogo, Tōkyōgo, hyōjungo*. Tokyo: Kōdansha.

Moeran, Brian. 1989. *Language and Popular Culture in Japan*. Manchester: Manchester University Press.

Montesquieu, Baron de. [1748] 1949. *The Spirit of the Laws*, trans. Thomas Nugent. New York: Hafner Press.

Moore, Joe. 1983. *Japanese Workers and the Struggle for Power, 1945–1947*. Madison: University of Wisconsin Press.

Moore, John A. 1993. *Science as a Way of Knowing: The Foundations of Modern Biology*. Cambridge, Mass.: Harvard University Press.

Mori Akihide. 1981. *Enka no kaikyō*. Tokyo: Shōnensha.

Mori, Hiromi. 1997. *Immigration Policy and Foreign Workers in Japan*. New York: St. Martin's Press.

Mōri Jinpachi and Osamu Uoto. 1990. *Kasai no hito*, vol. 3. Tokyo: Shōgakukan.

Morieda Takashi. 1988. "Nihonka shita Chōsen hantō no shoku." In Isao Kumakura and Naomichi Ishige, eds., *Shoku no bunka fōramu: gairai no shoku no bunka*, pp. 176–186. Tokyo: Domesu Shuppan.

————. 1989. *Karē raisu to Nihonjin*. Tokyo: Kōdansha.

Moriki Kazuo. 1991. *Irasutoban kokusai kekkon gaidobukku*. Tokyo: Akashi Shoten.

Morita Kirirō, ed. 1987. *Kokusai rōdōryoku idō*. Tokyo: Tokyo Daigaku Shuppankai.

Morita Komi. 1993. "Gendai no shozō: tachigyōji 28-dai Kimura Shōnosuke." *Aera*, July 20, pp. 53–57.

Morita Yoshinori. 1995. *Chūsei senmin to zatsu geinō no kenkyū*. Tokyo: Yūzankaku.

Morley, John David. 1985. *Pictures from the Water Trade: An Englishman in Japan*. London: André Deutsch.

Morris-Suzuki, Tessa. 1998a. *Re-inventing Japan: Time, Space, Nation*. Armonk, N.Y.: M. E. Sharpe.

————. 1998b. "Becoming Japanese: Imperial Expansion and Identity Crises in the Early Twentieth Century." In Sharon A. Minichiello, ed., *Japan's Competing Modernities: Issues in Culture and Democracy, 1900–1930*, pp. 157–180. Honolulu: University of Hawai'i Press.

Motoyama Yoshihiko. 1991. *Yutakana kuni, mazushii kuni*. Tokyo: Iwanami Shoten.

Mouer, Ross, and Yoshio Sugimoto. 1989. "A Multi-dimensional View of Stratification: A Framework for Comparative Analysis." In Yoshio Sugimoto and

Ross E. Mouer, eds., *Constructs for Understanding Japan,* pp. 157–201. London: Kegan Paul International.

Mukai Kiyoshi. 1992. "'Sotetsu jigoku.'" In Ryūkyū Shinpōsha, ed., *Shin Ryūkyūshi: kindai, gendai hen,* pp. 191–213. Naha, Japan: Ryūkyū Shinpōsha.

Mun Kyŏng-su. 1995. "Zainichi Chōsenjin ni totte no 'sengo.'" In Masanori Nakamura, Akira Amakawa, Kŏn-ch'a Yun, and Takeshi Igarashi, eds., *Sengo Nihon senryō to sengo kaikaku.* Vol. 5: *Kako no seisan,* pp. 159–196. Tokyo: Iwanami Shoten.

Murai Osamu. [1992] 1995. *Nantō ideorogī no hassei: Yanagita Kunio to shokuminchishugi,* rev. ed. Tokyo: Ōta Shuppan.

Murai Shōsuke. 1987. "Chūsei ni okeru Higashi Ajia shochiiki to no kōtsū." In Naohiro Asao et al., eds., *Nihon no shakaishi.* Vol. 1: *Rettō naigai no kōtsū to kokka,* pp. 97–138. Tokyo: Iwanami Shoten.

———. 1993. *Chūsei Wajinden.* Tokyo: Iwanami Shoten.

Murai Yoshinori. 1988. *Ebi to Nihonjin.* Tokyo: Iwanami Shoten.

Murakami Haruki and Mizumaru Anzai. 1986. *Murakami Asahidō no gyakushū.* Tokyo: Asahi Shinbunsha.

Murakami Shigeyoshi. 1970. *Kokka shintō.* Tokyo: Iwanami Shoten.

———. 1978. *Gendai shūkyō to seiji.* Tokyo: Tokyo Daigaku Shuppankai.

Murakami Yasusuke. 1984. *Shin chūkan taishū no jidai—sengo Nihon no kaibōgaku.* Tokyo: Chūō Kōronsha.

Murayama Shichirō. 1995. *Nihongo no hikaku kenkyū.* Tokyo: San'ichi Shobō.

Murphy-Shigematsu, Stephen. 1994. "Okinawa no Nichibei Hāfu ni taisuru sutereotaipu." In Okinawa Shinrigakkai, ed., *Okinawa no hito to kokoro,* pp. 53–57. Fukuoka, Japan: Kyūshū Daigaku Shuppankai.

Nada Inada. 1992. *Minzoku to iu na no shūkyō—hito o matomeru genri, haijo suru genri.* Tokyo: Iwanami Shoten.

Nagahara Keiji. 1978. *Rekishigaku josetsu.* Tokyo: Tokyo Daigaku Shuppankai.

———. 1990. "The Medieval Peasant," trans. Suzanne Gay. In Kozo Yamamura, ed., *The Cambridge History of Japan.* Vol. 3: *Medieval Japan,* pp. 301–343. Cambridge: Cambridge University Press.

Nagai Katsuichi. [1987] 1996. "Sōkangō to 'Kamuiden.'" In Shinbō Minami, ed., *Nihon no meizuihitsu.* Vol. 62: *Manga,* pp. 52–59. Tokyo: Sakuhinsha.

Nagai Michio. 1988. *Sekai kara Nihon e, Nihon kara sekai e.* Tokyo: Kōdansha.

Nagano Takeshi. 1994. *Zainichi Chūgokujin: rekishi to aidentiti.* Tokyo: Akashi Shoten.

Nagata Yōichi. 1994. *Bēsubōru no shakaishi: Jimmī Horio to Nichibei yakyū.* Tokyo: Tōhō Shuppan.

Nagel, Joane. 1996. *American Indian Ethnic Renewal: Red Power and the Resurgence of Identity and Culture.* New York: Oxford University Press.

Naitō Konan [1925] 1976. *Nihon bunkashi kenkyū,* 2 vols. Tokyo: Kōdansha.

Nakagami Kenji. [1975] 1978. "Misaki." In Kenji Nakagami, *Misaki*, pp. 171–266. Tokyo: Bungei Shunjū.

———. [1977] 1980. *Karekinada.* Tokyo: Kawade Shobō Shinsha.

———. 1983. *Chi no hate shijō no toki.* Tokyo: Shinchōsha.

———. 1987. *Ten no uta: shōsetsu Miyako Harumi.* Tokyo: Mainichi Shinbunsha.

———. 1993. *Izoku.* Tokyo: Kōdansha.

Nakagawa Hiroshi. 1995. *Shoku no sengoshi.* Tokyo: Akashi Shoten.

Nakagawa Kiyoko. [1975] 1983. "Ishiki chōsa ni mita sabetsu ishiki no kōzō." In Eiichi Isomura, ed., *Dōwa gyōseiron,* vol. 1, pp. 345–386. Tokyo: Akashi Shoten.

Nakagawa Kiyoshi. 1993. "Toshi nichijō seikatsu no naka no sengo: minshū ni totte no jinkō ninshin chūzetsu." In Ryūichi Narita, ed., *Kindai Nihon no kiseki.* Vol. 9: *Toshi to minshū,* pp. 263–288. Tokyo: Yoshikawa Kōbunkan.

Nakai Hisao. 1992. *Kioku no shozō.* Tokyo: Misuzu Shobō.

Nakajima Misaki. 1983. *Chikyū jidai no kōsōryoku.* Tokyo: Daiyamondosha.

Nakajima Ramo. 1993. *Bijinesu-nansensu jiten.* Tokyo: Kōdansha.

Nakamoto Masachie. 1985. *Nihongo no keifu.* Tokyo: Seidosha.

Nakamura Akira. 1982. *Kōjō ni ikiru hitobito: uchigawa kara egakareta rōdōsha no jitsuzō.* Tokyo: Gakuyō Shobō.

Nakamura Hajime. 1960. *Hikaku shisōron.* Tokyo: Iwanami Shoten.

Nakamura Kōsuke. 1987. *Seiō no oto, Nihon no mimi: kindai Nihon bungaku to Seiō ongaku.* Tokyo: Shunjūsha.

Nakamura Shin'ichirō. [1963] 1983. *Sengo bungaku no kaisō,* expanded ed. Tokyo: Chikuma Shobō.

Nakane Chie. 1967. *Tate shakai no ningen kankei: tan'itsu shakai no riron.* Tokyo: Kōdansha.

———. 1970. *Japanese Society.* Berkeley: University of California Press.

———. 1972. *Tekiō no jōken: Nihonteki renzoku no shikō.* Tokyo: Kōdansha.

———. 1977. *Kazoku o chūshin to shita ningen kankei.* Tokyo: Kōdansha.

———. 1978. *Tate shakai no rikigaku.* Tokyo: Kōdansha.

Nakano Osamu. 1995. "Taishū bunkaron." In Naohiro Asao, Yoshihiko Amino, Susumu Ishii, Masanao Kano, Shōhachi Hayakawa, and Yasuo Yasumaru, eds., *Iwanami kōza Nihon tsūshi.* Vol. 20: *Gendai 1,* pp. 265–309. Tokyo: Iwanami Shoten.

Nakano Shūichirō, 1993. "Indoshina nanmin." In Shūichirō Nakano and Kōjirō Imazu, eds., *Esunishiti no shakaigaku: Nihon shakai no minzokuteki kōsei,* pp. 66–84. Kyoto: Sekai Shisōsha.

Nakano Shūichirō and Kōjirō Imazu, eds. 1993. *Esunishiti no shakaigaku: Nihon shakai no minzokuteki kōsei.* Kyoto: Sekai Shisōsha.

Nakano Takashi. 1983. "Uchi to soto." In Tōru Sagara, Masahide Bitō, and Ken

Akiyama, eds., *Kōza Nihon shisō.* Vol. 3: *Chitsujo,* pp. 329–364. Tokyo: Tokyo Daigaku Shuppankai.

Nakasone Yasuhiro. 1986. "Zensairoku Nakasone shushō 'chiteki suijun' kōen." *Chūō Kōron,* Nov., pp. 146–162.

Namikawa Kenji. 1992. *Kinsei Nihon to hoppō shakai.* Tokyo: Sanseidō.

Naoi Michiko. 1979. "Kaisō ishiki to kaikyū ishiki." In Ken'ichi Tominaga, ed., *Nihon no kaisō kōzō,* pp. 365–388. Tokyo: Tokyo Daigaku Shuppankai.

Natsume Sōseki. [1912] 1986. "Gendai Nihon no kaika." In Sōseki Natsume, *Sōseki bunmeironshū,* ed. Yukio Miyoshi, pp. 7–38. Tokyo: Iwanami Shoten.

Neary, Ian. 1989. *Political Protest and Social Control in Pre-War Japan: The Origins of Buraku Liberation.* Atlantic Highlands, N.J.: Humanities Press International.

———. 1997. "Burakumin in Contemporary Japan." In Michael Weiner, ed., *Japan's Minorities: The Illusion of Homogeneity,* pp. 50–78. London: Routledge.

NHK Hōsō Yoron Chōsabu, ed. 1983. *Nihonjin no shokuseikatsu.* Tokyo: Nihon Hōsō Shuppan Kyōkai.

NHK Yoron Chōsabu, ed. 1991. *Gendai Nihonjin no ishiki kōzō,* 3rd ed. Tokyo: Nihon Hōsō Shuppan Kyōkai.

Nichol, C. W. 1993. "Waga tomo Nihonjin e," trans. Yōko Mori. In Tetsuya Tsukishi, ed., *Nihon nikki: gaikokujin ga mita Nihon,* pp. 7–19. Tokyo: Fukutake Shoten.

Nietzsche, Friedrich. [1881] 1982. *Daybreak: Thoughts on the Prejudices of Morality,* trans. R. J. Hollingdale. Cambridge: Cambridge University Press.

Nihon Keizai Shinbunsha, ed. 1982. *Nihon to wa nanika: shin kaikokuron.* Tokyo: Nihon Keizai Shinbunsha.

Nihon Senbotsu Gakusei Kinenkai, ed. [1949] 1982. *Kike wadatsumi no koe: Nihon senbotsu gakusei no shuki.* Tokyo: Iwanami Shoten.

Niigata Nippō Hōdōbu. 1985. *Mura wa kataru.* Tokyo: Iwanami Shoten.

Nimura Kazuo. 1992. "The Trade Union Response to Migrant Workers." In Glenn D. Hook and Michael A. Weiner, eds., *The Internationalization of Japan,* pp. 246–266. London: Routledge.

———. 1994. "Sengo shakai no kiten ni okeru rōdō kumiai undō." In Junji Banno et al., eds., *Sirīzu Nihon kingendaishi kōzō to henkaku.* Vol. 4: *Sengo kaikaku to gendai shakai no keisei,* pp. 37–78. Tokyo: Iwanami Shoten.

Ninouya Tetsuichi. 1993. *Nihon chūsei no mibun to shakai.* Tokyo: Hanuka Shobō.

———. 1994. "Hinin, kawaramono, sanjo." In Naohiro Asao, Yoshihiko Amino, Susumu Ishii, Masanao Kano, Shōhachi Hayakawa, and Yasuo Yasumaru, eds., *Iwanami kōza Nihon tsūshi.* Vol. 8: *Chūsei 2,* pp. 215–254. Tokyo: Iwanami Shoten.

Nishihira Shigeki. 1982. "Shūkyō." In Tōkei Sūri Kenkyūsho and Kokuminsei Chōsa Iinkai, eds., *Dai-4 Nihonjin no kokuminsei,* pp. 53–70. Tokyo: Idemitsu Shoten.

————. 1987. *Yoron chōsa ni okeru dōjidaishi*. Tokyo: Burēn Shuppan.

Nishijima Sadao. 1994. *Yamataikoku to Wakoku: kodai Nihon to Higashi Ajia*. Tokyo: Yoshikawa Kōbunkan.

Nishikawa Nagao. 1996. "Two Interpretations of Japanese Culture," trans. Mikiko Murata and Gavan McCormack. In Donald Denoon, Mark Hudson, Gavan McCormack, and Tessa Morris-Suzuki, eds., *Multicultural Japan: Palaeolithic to Postmodern*, pp. 245–264. Cambridge: Cambridge University Press.

Nishinarita Yutaka. 1997. *Zainichi Chōsenjin no "sekai" to "teikoku" kokka*. Tokyo: Tokyo Daigaku Shuppankai.

Nishio Kanji. 1988. *Senryakuteki "sakoku"ron*. Tokyo: Kōbunkan.

————. 1989a. *"Rōdō sakoku" no susume: gaikokujin rōdōsha ga Nihon o horobosu*. Tokyo: Kōbunkan.

————. 1989b. "'Rōdō kaikoku' wa dō kentōshitemo fukanō da." *Chūō Kōron*, Sept., pp. 312–330.

Nishizawa Akihito. 1995. *Inpeisareta gaibu: toshi kasō no esunogurafi*. Tokyo: Sairyūsha.

Nitobe Inazō. [1909] 1972a. "Thoughts and Essays." In Inazo Nitobe, *The Works of Inazo Nitobe*, vol. 1, pp. 155–463. Tokyo: University of Tokyo Press.

————. [1912] 1972b. "The Japanese Nation." Inazo Nitobe, *The Works of Inazo Nitobe*, vol. 2, pp. 3–302. Tokyo: University of Tokyo Press.

————. [1936] 1972c. "Lectures on Japan." In Inazo Nitobe, *The Works of Inazo Nitobe*, vol. 4, pp. 3–367. Tokyo: University of Tokyo Press.

————. [1933] 1984. *Seiō no jijō to shisō*. Tokyo: Kōdansha.

Nitta Ichirō. 1994. *Sumō no rekishi*. Tokyo: Yamakawa Shuppan.

Noguchi Takehiko. 1993a. *Edo shisōshi no chikei*. Tokyo: Perikansha.

————. 1993b. *Nihon shisōshi nyūmon*. Tokyo: Chikuma Shobō.

Noma Hiroshi. [1947–1971] 1966–1971. *Seinen no wa*, 5 vols. Tokyo: Kawade Shobō Shinsha.

Noma Hiroshi and Kazuteru Okiura. 1983. *Ajia no sei to sen: hisabetsumin no rekishi to bunka*. Kyoto: Jinbun Shoin.

————. 1986. *Nihon no sei to sen: kinsei hen*. Kyoto: Jinbun Shoin.

Nomura Susumu. 1996. *Korian sekai no tabi*. Tokyo: Kōdansha.

Norman, E. H. [1945] 1957. "Feudal Background of Japanese Politics." In E. H. Norman, *Origins of the Modern Japanese State: Selected Writings of E. H. Norman*, ed. John W. Dower, pp. 317–464. New York: Pantheon.

Nyūkan Kyōkai. 1993. *Zairyū gaikokujin tōkei*. Tokyo: Nyūkan Kyōkai.

Nyūkan Tōkei Kenkyūkai, ed. 1990. *Waga kuni o meguru kokusai jinryū no henbō*. Tokyo: Ōkurashō Insatsukyoku.

O Kyu-sang. 1992. *Zainichi Chōsenjin kigyō katsudō keiseishi*. Tokyo: Yūzankaku.

O'Brien, David J., and Stephen S. Fugita. 1991. *The Japanese American Experience*. Bloomington: Indiana University Press.

Ochiai Eishū. 1974. *Ajiajin rōdōryoku yu'nyū*. Tokyo: Gendai Hyōronsha.

Ōe Kenzaburō. [1973] 1981. "Hakaisha Urutoraman." In Kenzaburō Ōe, *Ōe Kenzaburō dōjidaironshū.* Vol. 9: *Kotoba to jōkyō,* pp. 155–168. Tokyo: Iwanami Shoten.

Ōe Shinobu. 1981. *Chōheisei.* Tokyo: Iwanami Shoten.

————. 1992a. "Higashi Ajia shin-kyū teikoku no kōkan." In Shinobu Ōe, Kyōji Asada, Taichirō Mitani, Ken'ichi Gotō, Hideo Kobayashi, Sōji Takasaki, Masahiro Wakabayashi, and Minato Kawamura, eds., *Iwanami kōza kindai Nihon to shokuminchi.* Vol. 1: *Shokuminchi teikoku Nihon,* pp. 3–31. Tokyo: Iwanami Shoten.

————. 1992b. "Shokuminchi sensō to sōtokufu no seiritsu." In Shinobu Ōe, Kyōji Asada, Taichirō Mitani, Ken'ichi Gotō, Hideo Kobayashi, Sōji Takasaki, Masahiro Wakabayashi, and Minato Kawamura, eds., *Iwanami kōza kindai Nihon to shokuminchi.* Vol. 2: *Teikoku tōji no kōzō,* pp. 3–33. Tokyo: Iwanami Shoten.

Ogata Sadako. 1992. "Interdependence and Internationalization." In Glenn D. Hook and Michael A. Weiner, eds., *The Internationalization of Japan,* pp. 63–71. London: Routledge.

Ogawa Masahito. 1997. *Kindai Ainu kyōiku seidoshi kenkyū.* Sapporo: Hokkaidō Daigaku Tosho Kankōkai.

Ogawa Masahito and Shin'ichi Yamada, eds. 1998. *Ainu minzoku: kindai no kiroku.* Tokyo: Sōfūkan.

Oguma Eiji. 1995. *Tan'itsu minzoku shinwa no kigen: "Nihonjin" no jigazō no keifu.* Tokyo: Shin'yōsha.

————. 1998. *"Nihonjin" no kyōkai: Okinawa, Ainu, Taiwan, Chōsen shokuminchi shihai kara fukki undō made.* Tokyo: Shin'yōsha.

Ogyū Sorai. [c. 1725] 1987. *Seidan,* annot. Tatsuya Tsuji. Tokyo: Iwanami Shoten.

Oh, Sadaharu, and David Falkner. 1984. *Sadaharu Oh: A Zen Way of Baseball.* New York: Times Books.

Ōhashi Ryūken. 1971. *Nihon no kaikyū kōsei.* Tokyo: Iwanami Shoten.

Ohnuki-Tierney, Emiko. 1993. *Rice as Self: Japanese Identities through Time.* Princeton, N.J.: Princeton University Press.

Oinuma Yoshihiro. 1994. *Sumō shakai no kenkyū.* Tokyo: Fumidō.

Okabe Kazuaki. 1991. *Taminzoku shakai no tōrai.* Tokyo: Ochanomizu Shobō.

Okakura Kakuzō. [1904] 1928. *The Awakening of Japan.* New York: Japan Society.

Okamoto Kōji. 1996. *Kita Ikki—tenkanki no shisō kōzō.* Kyoto: Mineruva Shobō.

Okamoto Tarō. 1972. *Okinawa bunkaron—wasurerareta Nihon.* Tokyo: Chūō Kōronsha.

Okano Ben. 1988. *Enka genryū kō.* Tokyo: Gakugei Shorin.

Okazaki Takashi. 1993. "Japan and the Continent." In Delmer M. Brown, ed., *The Cambridge History of Japan.* Vol. 1: *Ancient Japan,* pp. 268–316. Cambridge: Cambridge University Press.

Ōkida Mamoru. 1996. *Okinawa no kokoro no genten.* Tokyo: Tokyo Shoseki.

Okiura Kazumitsu. 1990. *Tennō no kuni, senmin no kuni—ryōkyoku no tabū.* Tokyo: Kōbundō.

Ōkōchi Kazuo. [1949] 1980. *Shakai seisaku (sōron),* expanded ed. Tokyo: Yūhikaku.

Okonogi Keigo. 1978. *Moratoriamu ningen no jidai.* Tokyo: Chūō Kōronsha.

Oku Sumako. 1993. "Rajio no fukkyū wa Nihon no shakai o dō kaetaka." In Ryūji Sasaki and Akira Yamada, eds., *Shinshiten Nihon no rekishi.* Vol. 6: *Kindaihen,* pp. 274–279. Tokyo: Shinjinbutsu Ōraisha.

Okuda Michihiro and Junko Tajima, eds. 1991. *Ikebukuro no Ajiakei gaikokujin.* Tokyo: Mekon.

————. 1993. *Shinjuku no Ajiakei gaikokujin.* Tokyo: Mekon.

Ōmae Ken'ichi. 1989. *Shin kokufuron.* Tokyo: Kōdansha.

Ōmameuda Minoru. 1993. *Kindai Nihon no shokuryō seisaku.* Kyoto: Mineruva Shobō.

Ōmori Maki. 1990. *Gendai Nihon no josei rōdō.* Tokyo: Nihon Hyōronsha.

Ōmura Yasuki. 1990. "Gaikokujin rōdōsha no jinken hoshō to kenpō." *Hōgaku seminā* 42: 120–127.

Ong, Walter J. 1982. *Orality and Literacy: The Technologizing of the Word.* London: Methuen.

Ōno Susumu. 1966. *Nihongo no nenrin.* Tokyo: Shinchōsha.

Ōnuma Yasuaki. 1985. *Tokyo saiban kara sengo sekinin no shisō e.* Tokyo: Yūshindō.

————. 1986. *Tan'itsu minzoku shakai no shinwa o koete: Zainichi Kankoku, Chōsenjin to shutsu'nyūkoku kanri taisei.* Tokyo: Tōshindō.

————. 1988a. *Wakoku to Kyokutō no aida: rekishi to bunmei no naka no "kokusaika."* Tokyo: Chūō Kōronsha.

————. 1988b. "'Gaikokujin rōdōsha' dō'nyū rongi ni kakerumono." *Chūō kōron,* May, pp. 148–162.

Ōoka Shōhei and Yutaka Haniya. 1984. *Futatsu no dōjidaishi.* Tokyo: Iwanami Shoten.

Ooms, Herman. 1985. *Tokugawa Ideology: Early Constructs, 1570–1680.* Princeton, N.J.: Princeton University Press.

————. 1996. *Tokugawa Village Practice: Class, Status, Power, Law.* Berkeley: University of California Press.

Orwell, George. [1937] 1958. *The Road to Wigan Pier.* New York: Harcourt Brace Jovanovich.

Osaka Bengoshikai, ed. 1992. *18 gengo no gaikokujin jinken handobukku.* Tokyo: Akashi Shoten.

Ōsawa Mari. 1993. *Kigyō chūshin shakai o koete.* Tokyo: Jiji Tsūshinsha.

Ōsawa Masachi. 1996. "Nēshon to esunishiti." In Shun Inoue, Chizuko Ueno,

Masachi Ōsawa, Munesuke Mita, and Shun'ya Yoshimi, eds., *Iwanami kōza gendai shakaigaku*. Vol. 24: *Minzoku, kokka, esunishiti*, pp. 27–66. Tokyo: Iwanami Shoten.

Ōshiro Masayasu. 1985. *Konketsuji: Okinawa kara no kokuhatsu, kokuseki no nai seishun*. Tokyo: Kokusai Jōhōsha.

Ōshiro Tatsuhiro. 1993. "Arata na michi no mokusa o." *Shin Okinawa bungaku* 95: 19–24.

Ōta Masahide. 1972. *Kindai Okinawa no seiji kōzō*. Tokyo: Keisō Shobō.

———. 1976. *Okinawa no minshū ishiki*. Tokyo: Shinsensha.

Ōtake Hideo. 1988. *Saigunbi to nashonarizumu: hoshu, riberaru, shakaiminshushugisha no bōeikan*. Tokyo: Chūō Kōronsha.

———. 1994. *Jiyūshugiteki kaikaku no jidai—1980-nendai zenki no Nihon seiji*. Tokyo: Chūō Kōronsha.

———. 1995. "55-nen taisei no keisei." In Masanori Nakamura, Akira Amakawa, Kŏn-ch'a Yun, and Takeshi Igarashi, eds., *Sengo Nihon senryō to sengo kaikaku*. Vol. 6: *Sengo kaikaku to sono isan*, pp. 23–57. Tokyo: Iwanami Shoten.

Ōtomo Katsuhiro. 1986. *Shōto-pīsu: Ōtomo Katsuhiro kessakushū*, vol. 3. Tokyo: Futabasha.

Ōtsuki Takeshi and Ken'ichi Matsumura. 1970. *Aikokushin kyōiku no shiteki kyūmei*. Tokyo: Aoki Shoten.

Ōyama Chōjō. 1997. *Okinawa dokuritsu sengen: Yamato wa kaerubeki "sokoku" de wa nakatta*. Tokyo: Gendai Shorin.

Ozaki Hotsuki. 1971. *Kyū shokuminchi bungaku no kenkyū*. Tokyo: Keisō Shobō.

Ozawa Hiroshi. 1995. "Shūkyō ishiki no genzai." In Naohiro Asao, Yoshihiko Amino, Susumu Ishii, Masanao Kano, Shōhachi Hayakawa, and Yasuo Yasumaru, eds., *Iwanami Nihon tsūshi*. Vol. 21: *Gendai 2*, pp. 145–183. Tokyo: Iwanami Shoten.

Pak Kyŏng-sik. 1992. *Zainichi Chōsenjin, kyōsei renkō, minzoku mondai*. Tokyo: San'ichi Shobō.

———. 1995. "Chōsenjin kyōsei renkō." In Naohiro Asao, Yoshihiko Amino, Susumu Ishii, Masanao Kano, Shōhachi Hayakawa, and Yasuo Yasumaru, eds., *Iwanami kōza Nihon tsūshi*. Vol. 19: *Kindai 4*, pp. 363–379. Tokyo: Iwanami Shoten.

Pamuk, Orhan. 1997. "On the Periphery." *Times Literary Supplement*, Aug. 8, p. 34.

Passin, Herbert. [1965] 1982. *Society and Education in Japan*. Tokyo: Kodansha International.

Pearson, Richard. 1996. "The Place of Okinawa in Japanese Historical Identity." In Donald Denoon, Mark Hudson, Gavan McCormack, and Tessa Morris-Suzuki, eds., *Multicultural Japan: Palaeolithic to Postmodern*, pp. 95–116. Cambridge: Cambridge University Press.

Peattie, Mark R. 1988. *Nan'yō: The Rise and Fall of the Japanese in Micronesia, 1885–1945.* Honolulu: University of Hawaii Press.

———. 1992. "Nihon shokuminchi shihai ka no Mikuroneshia," trans. Masao Gabe. In Shinobu Ōe, Kyōji Asada, Taichirō Mitani, Ken'ichi Gotō, Hideo Kobayashi, Sōji Takasaki, Masahiro Wakabayashi, and Minato Kawamura, eds., *Iwanami kōza kindai Nihon to shokuminchi.* Vol. 1: *Shokuminchi teikoku Nihon,* pp. 189–215. Tokyo: Iwanami Shoten.

Petkanas, Christopher. 1993. "It's Not Easy Behaving Well in France, Critics Say." *International Herald Tribune,* Aug. 31, pp. 1ff.

Phillips, D. C. 1976. *Holistic Thought in Social Science.* Stanford, Calif.: Stanford University Press.

Piore, Michael J. 1979. *Birds of Passage: Migrant Labor and Industrial Societies.* Cambridge: Cambridge University Press.

Plath, David W. 1964. *The After Hours: Modern Japan and the Search for Enjoyment.* Berkeley: University of California Press.

———. [1990] 1992. "My-Car-isma: Motorizing the Showa Self." In Carol Gluck and Stephen R. Graubard, eds., *Showa: The Japan of Hirohito,* pp. 229–244. New York: Norton.

Plessner, Helmuth. 1959. *Die Verspätete Nation: Über die politische Verführbarkeit bürgerlichen Geistes,* 2d ed. Stuttgart: W. Kohlhammer.

Potts, Lydia. [1988] 1990. *The World Labour Market: A History of Migration,* trans. Terry Bond. London: Zed.

Pyle, Kenneth B. 1969. *The New Generation in Meiji Japan: Problems of Cultural Identity, 1885–1895.* Stanford, Calif.: Stanford University Press.

Quiller-Couch, Arthur, ed. 1913. *The Oxford Book of Victorian Verse.* Oxford: Clarendon Press.

Randal, Jonathan C. 1997. *After Such Knowledge, What Forgiveness? My Encounters with Kurdistan.* New York: Farrar, Straus and Giroux.

Rauch, Jonathan. 1992. *The Outnation: A Search for the Soul of Japan.* Boston: Harvard Business School Press.

Rei Rokusuke. 1969. *Heinintachi no geinōshi.* Tokyo: Banchō Shobō.

Reischauer, Edwin O. 1988. *The Japanese Today: Change and Continuity.* Cambridge, Mass.: Harvard University Press.

Renan, Ernest. [1882] 1990. "What Is a Nation?," trans. Martin Thom. In Homi K. Bhabha, ed., *Nation and Narration,* pp. 8–22. London: Routledge.

Rex, John, and Sally Tomlinson. 1979. *Colonial Immigrants in a British City: A Class Analysis.* London: Routledge and Kegan Paul.

Ricks, Christopher, ed. 1987. *The New Oxford Book of Victorian Verse.* Oxford: Oxford University Press.

Riesman, David, and Evelyn Thompson Riesman. [1967] 1976. *Conversations in Japan: Modernization, Politics, and Culture.* Chicago: University of Chicago Press.

Rimer, J. Thomas. [1990] 1992. "High Culture in the Showa Period." In Carol Gluck and Stephen R. Graubard, eds., *Showa: The Japan of Hirohito*, pp. 265–278. New York: Norton.

Robertson, Jennifer. 1991. *Native and Newcomer: Making and Remaking a Japanese Society*. Berkeley: University of California Press.

Rodinson, Maxime. [1979] 1981. *The Arabs*, trans. Arthur Goldhammer. Chicago: University of Chicago Press.

Rohlen, Thomas P. 1983. *Japan's High Schools*. Berkeley: University of California Press.

Rosenberger, Nancy. 1992. "Images of the West: Home Style in Japanese Magazines." In Joseph J. Tobin, ed., *Re-Made in Japan: Everyday Life and Consumer Taste in a Changing Society*, pp. 106–125. New Haven, Conn.: Yale University Press.

Rousseau, Jean-Jacques. [1758] 1960. *Politics and the Arts: Letter to M. D'Alembert on the Theatre*, trans. Allan Bloom. Glencoe, Ill.: Free Press.

———. [1755] 1992. "Discourse on the Origin and Foundations of Inequality among Men." In Jean-Jacques Rousseau, *Collected Writings of Rousseau*. Vol. 3: *Discourse on the Origins of Inequality (Second Discourse), Polemics, and Political Economy*, ed. Roger D. Masters and Christopher Kelly, trans. Judith R. Bush, Roger D. Masters, Christopher Kelly, and Terence Marshall, pp. 1–95. Hanover, N.H.: University Press of New England.

Rudofsky, Bernard. [1965] 1982. *The Kimono Mind: An Informal Guide to Japan and the Japanese*. New York: Van Nostrand Reinhold.

Russell, Conrad. 1993. "John Bull's Other Nations." *Times Literary Supplement*, Mar. 12, pp. 3–4.

Russell, John G. 1991. *Nihonjin no kokujinkan: mondai wa "Chibikuro Sanbo" dake de wa nai*. Tokyo: Shinhyōron.

Ryang, Sonia. 1997. *North Koreans in Japan: Language, Ideology, and Identity*. Boulder, Colo.: Westview Press.

Said, Edward W. 1978. *Orientalism*. New York: Random House.

———. 1979. *The Question of Palestine*. New York: Times Books.

———. 1994. *The Politics of Dispossession: The Struggle for Palestinian Self-Determination, 1969–1994*. New York: Pantheon.

Saiki, Maggie Kinser. 1994. "Japan's Answer to Beavis and Butthead." *Wall Street Journal*, Feb. 11, p. A13.

Saimon Fumi. 1990–1991. *Tokyo rabu sutōrī*, 4 vols. Tokyo: Shōgakukan.

Saitō Takao. 1995. *Yūyake o miteita otoko: hyōden Kajiwara Ikki*. Tokyo: Shinchōsha.

Sakabe Megumi. 1990. *Fuzai no uta—Kuki Shūzō no sekai*. Tokyo: TBS Buritanika.

Sakaguchi Ango. [1942] 1987. "Nihon bunka shikan." In Ango Sakaguchi, Seiichi Funabashi, Jun Takami, and Fumiko Enchi, *Shōwa bungaku zenshū*, vol. 12, pp. 224–238. Tokyo: Shōgakukan.

Sakai, Naoki. 1991. *Voices of the Past: The State of Language in Eighteenth-Century Japanese Discourse.* Ithaca, N.Y.: Cornell University Press.

Sakaiya Taichi. 1991. *Nihon to wa nanika.* Tokyo: Kōdansha.

Sakurai Yoshirō. 1981. *Chūsei Nihon bunka no keisei: shinwa to rekishi jojutsu.* Tokyo: Tokyo Daigaku Shuppankai.

Sakuta Keiichi. 1972. *Kachi no shakaigaku.* Tokyo: Iwanami Shoten.

Sapir, Edward. 1921. *Language: An Introduction to the Study of Speech.* New York: Harcourt Brace & World.

Sasaki Ken. 1990. "Ajia no rōdōryoku idō to Nihon shihonshugi no kiki." *Mado* 4: 44–57.

Sasaki Takeshi. 1986. *Hoshuka to seijiteki imi kūkan.* Tokyo: Iwanami Shoten.

Sasaki, Yuzuru, and George De Vos. 1966. "A Traditional Urban Outcaste Community." In George De Vos and Hiroshi Wagatsuma, eds., *Japan's Invisible Race: Caste in Culture and Personality,* pp. 129–136. Berkeley: University of California Press.

Sassen, Saskia. 1988. *The Mobility of Labor and Capital: A Study in International Investment and Labor Flow.* Cambridge: Cambridge University Press.

Sato Ikuya. 1991. *Kamikaze Biker: Parody and Anomy in Affluent Japan.* Chicago: University of Chicago Press.

Satō Kenji. 1992. *Gojira to Yamato to bokura no minshushugi.* Tokyo: Bungei Shunjū.

Satō Seizaburō. 1992. *"Shi no chōyaku" o koete: Seiō no shōgeki to Nihon.* Tokyo: Toshi Shuppan.

Satō Shōichirō. 1985. "Sengo no Okinawa." In Rekishigaku Kenkyūkai and Nihonshi Kenkyūkai, eds., *Kōza Nihon rekishi.* Vol. 12: *Gendai 2,* pp. 239–283. Tokyo: Tokyo Daigaku Shuppankai.

Satō Susumu. 1992. "Gaikokujin rōdōsha to shakaihoshōhō no shomondai." In Susumu Satō, ed., *Gaikokujin rōdōsha no fukushi to jinken.* Kyoto: Horitsu Bunkasha.

Satō Toshiki. 1993. *Kindai, soshiki, shihonshugi: Nihon to Seiō ni okeru kindai no chihei.* Kyoto: Mineruva Shobō.

Sawa Takamitsu. 1991. *Korekara no keizaigaku.* Tokyo: Iwanami Shoten.

———. 1992. *Songen naki taikoku.* Tokyo: Kōdansha.

Sawada Yōtarō. 1995. *Yamato kokka wa torai ōchō.* Tokyo: Shinsensha.

Schiller, Friedrich. [1795/1954]. 1965. *On the Aesthetic Education of Man,* trans. Reginald Snell. New York: Frederick Ungar.

Schodt, Frederik L. 1996. *Dreamland Japan: Writings on Modern Manga.* Berkeley, Calif.: Stone Bridge Press.

Seki Hideshi. 1983. "Imin to chiiki shakai no seiritsu." In Hideshi Seki, ed., *Hokkaidō no kenkyū.* Vol. 5: *Kin-gendai hen I.* Osaka: Seibundō.

Sekiguchi Chie. 1993. "Gaikokujin hōdō no hanzai." *Inpakushon* 79: 77–79.

Sekikawa Natsuo. [1984] 1988. *Kaikyō o koeta hōmuran.* Tokyo: Asahi Shinbunsha.

———. 1993. *Suna no yō ni nemuru: mukashi "sengo" to iu jidai ga atta.* Tokyo: Shinchōsha.

———. [1991] 1996. *Chiteki taishū shokun, kore mo manga da.* Tokyo: Bungei Shunjū.

Sellek, Yoko, and Michael A. Weiner. 1992. "Migrant Workers: The Japanese Case in International Perspective." In Glenn D. Hook and Michael A. Weiner, eds., *The Internationalization of Japan,* pp. 205–228. London: Routledge.

Sells, Michael A. 1996. *The Bridge Betrayed: Religion and Genocide in Bosnia.* Berkeley: University of California Press.

Senda Akihiko. 1995. *Nihon no gendai engeki.* Tokyo: Iwanami Shoten.

Sengoku Hideyo. 1993. "Nakagami Kenji to Faulkner." In Mitsuo Sekii, ed., *Nakagami Kenji,* pp. 58–62. Tokyo: Shibundō.

Sha Shinhatsu. 1988. *Darenimo kakenakatta Nihonjin.* Tokyo: Keisō Shobō.

Shapiro, Michael. 1989. *Japan: In the Land of the Brokenhearted.* New York: Henry Holt.

Shi Gang. 1993. *Shokuminchi shihai to Nihongo.* Tokyo: Sangensha.

Shibata Minao. 1984. *Gusutafu Mārā.* Tokyo: Iwanami Shoten.

Shibatani, Masayoshi. 1990. *The Languages of Japan.* Cambridge: Cambridge University Press.

Shibuya Shigemitsu. 1991. *Taishō sōsa no keifu.* Tokyo: Keisō Shobō.

Shibuya Teisuke. 1986. *Nōmin aishi kara 60-nen.* Tokyo: Iwanami Shoten.

Shiga Naoya. [1946] 1955. "Kokugo mondai." In Naoya Shiga, *Shiga Naoya zenshū,* vol. 9, pp. 125–128. Tokyo: Iwanami Shoten.

Shiga Nobuo. 1990. *Shōwa terebi hōsōshi,* vol. 1. Tokyo: Hayakawa Shobō.

Shimada Haruo. 1991. *Nihon keizai: mujun to saisei.* Tokyo: Chikuma Shobō.

———. [1993] 1994. *Japan's "Guest Workers": Issues and Public Policies,* trans. Roger Northridge. Tokyo: University of Tokyo Press.

Shimada Kinji. 1970. "Nihon kindaibungaku no hitotsu no mikata." In Shirō Masuda, ed., *Seiō to Nihon: hikaku bunmeishiteki kōsatsu,* pp. 121–164. Tokyo: Chūō Kōronsha.

Shimahara Nobuo. [1984] 1991. "Social Mobility and Education: Burakumin in Japan." In Margaret A. Gibson and John U. Ogbu, eds., *Minority Status and Schooling: A Comparative Study of Immigrant and Involuntary Minorities,* pp. 327–353. New York: Garland.

Shimazaki Tōson. [1906] 1957. *Hakai.* Tokyo: Iwanami Shoten.

Shimizu Ikutarō. [1980] 1985. *Sengo o utagau.* Tokyo: Kōdansha.

Shinano Mainichi Shinbunsha, ed. 1992. *Tobira o akete: ruporutāju gaikokujin rōdōsha no seikatsu to jinken.* Tokyo: Akashi Shoten.

Shindō Ken. 1977. *"Shisetsu" sengo kayōkyoku.* Tokyo: San'ichi Shobō.

————. 1985. *Taishū geinōron nōto*. Akita, Japan: Mumyōsha Shuppan.

Shindō Toyoo. 1985. *Nihon minshū no rekishi chiikihen*. Vol. 9: *Akai botayama no hi—Chikuhō, Miike no hitobito*. Tokyo: Sanseidō.

Shinobu Seizaburō. 1992. *Seidan no rekishigaku*. Tokyo: Keisō Shobō.

Shinsensha Henshūbu, ed. 1981. *Gendai Nihon no henken to sabetsu*. Tokyo: Shinsensha.

Shin'ya Gyō. [1972] 1977. *Ainu minzoku teikōshi: Ainu kyōwakoku e no taidō*, expanded ed. Tokyo: San'ichi Shobō.

Shioda Sakiko. 1985. "Kōdo seichōki no gijutsu kakushin to joshi rōdō no henka." In Masanori Nakamura, ed., *Gijutsu kakushin to joshi rōdō*, pp. 171–201. Tokyo: Tokyo Daigaku Shuppankai.

Shiozawa Miyoko. 1986. *Ajia no minshū vs. Nihon no kigyō*. Tokyo: Iwanami Shoten.

Shirato Sanpei. [1959–1962] 1976. *Ninja bugeichō*, 17 vols. Tokyo: Shōgakukan.

————. [1965–1971] 1979. *Kamuiden*, 15 vols. Tokyo: Shōgakukan.

Shōji Kōkichi. 1982. "Gendai Nihon no kaikyū to shakai ishiki." *Shakaigaku hyōron* 33: 20–40.

Shōwa no ōzumō 60-nen. 1986. Tokyo: Nihon Supōtsu Shuppansha.

Shūkan Daiyamondo Bessatsu. 1993. *Nippon nandemo 10-ketsu*. Tokyo: Daiyamondosha.

Siddle, Richard. 1996. *Race, Resistance and the Ainu of Japan*. London: Routledge.

————. 1997. "Ainu: Japan's Indigenous People." In Michael Weiner, ed., *Japan's Minorities: The Illusion of Homogeneity*, pp. 17–49. London: Routledge.

Silberman, Bernard S. 1964. *Ministers of Modernization: Elite Mobility in the Meiji Restoration, 1868–1973*. Tucson: University of Arizona Press.

Silverman, Maxim. 1992. *Deconstructing the Nation: Immigration, Racism and Citizenship in Modern France*. London: Routledge.

Simmel, Georg. 1950. *The Sociology of Georg Simmel*, trans. and ed. Kurt H. Wolff. New York: Free Press.

Singer, Kurt. 1973. *Mirror, Sword and Jewel: A Study of Japanese Characteristics*. New York: George Braziller.

Sjöberg, Katarina. 1993. *The Return of the Ainu: Cultural Mobilization and the Practice of Ethnicity in Japan*. Chur, Switzerland: Harwood Academic.

Skeldon, Ronald. 1992. "International Migration within and from the East and Southeast Asia Region: A Review Essay." *Asian and Pacific Migration Journal* 1: 19–63.

Smith, Donald. 1996. "The 1932 Asō Coal Strike: Korean-Japanese Solidarity and Conflict." *Korean Studies* 20: 93–122.

Smith, Herman W. 1995. *The Myth of Japanese Homogeneity: Social-Ecological Diversity in Education and Socialization*. Commack, N.Y.: Nova Science.

Smith, Robert J. 1978. *Kurusu: The Price of Progress in a Japanese Village, 1951–1975*. Stanford, Calif.: Stanford University Press.

————. 1983. *Japanese Society: Tradition, Self and the Social Order*. Cambridge: Cambridge University Press.

Smith, Robert J., and Ella Lury Wiswell. 1982. *The Women of Suye Mura*. Chicago: University of Chicago Press.

Smits, Gregory. 1999. *Visions of Ryukyu: Identity and Ideology in Early-Modern Thought and Politics*. Honolulu: University of Hawai'i Press.

Sofue Takao. 1993. *Shusshinken de wakaru hitogara no hon: Nihonjin no jōshiki*. Tokyo: Dōbun Shoin.

Sōmuchō Seishōnen Taisakuhonbu, ed. 1996. *Seishōnen hakusho*. Tokyo: Ōkurashō Insatsukyoku.

Sonoda Shigeto. 1993. "Fuīrudo to shite no Ajia." In Yūzō Mizoguchi, Takeshi Hamashita, Naoaki Hiraishi, and Hiroshi Miyajima, eds., *Ajia kara kangaeru*. Vol. 1: *Kōsaku suru Ajia*, pp. 13–32. Tokyo: Tokyo Daigaku Shuppankai.

Sōrifu. 1988. *Gaikokujin no nyūkoku to zairyū ni kansuru yoron chōsa*. Tokyo: Sōrifu.

————. 1990. *Gaikokujin rōdōsha mondai ni kansuru yoron chōsa*. Tokyo: Sōrifu.

————. 1992. "Gaikokujin rōdōsha ni kansuru yoron chōsa." *Rōdō hōritsu junpō* 1263: 73–81.

Stauder, Jack. 1986. "The 'Relevance' of Anthropology to Colonialism and Imperialism." In Les Levidow, ed., *Radical Science Essays*, pp. 38–61. London: Free Association Books.

Steinberg, Jonathan. 1987. "The Historian and the *Questione della Lingua*." In Peter Burke and Roy Porter, eds., *The Social History of Language*, pp. 198–209. Cambridge: Cambridge University Press.

Sternhell, Zeev. [1996] 1998. *The Founding Myths of Israel: Nationalism, Socialism, and the Making of the Jewish State*, trans. David Maisel. Princeton, N.J.: Princeton University Press.

Steven, Rob. 1983. *Classes in Contemporary Japan*. Cambridge: Cambridge University Press.

————. 1990. *Japan's New Imperialism*. Armonk, N.Y.: M. E. Sharpe.

Stevens, Carolyn S. 1997. *On the Margins of Japanese Society: Volunteers and the Welfare of the Urban Underclass*. London: Routledge.

Strom, Stephanie. 1999. "2nd American in Top Rank as Diversity Hits Sumo." *New York Times*, May 27, p. A9.

Stronach, Bruce. 1989. "Japanese Television." In Richard Gid Powers and Hidetoshi Kato, eds., *Handbook of Japanese Popular Culture*, pp. 127–165. Westport, Conn.: Greenwood.

Suga Hidemi. 1995. *Nihon kindai bungaku no "tanjō": genbun itchi undō to nashonarizumu*. Tokyo: Ōta Shuppan.

Sugawara Kōsuke. 1979. *Nihon no kakyō*. Tokyo: Asahi Shinbunsha.

Sugimoto Yoshio. 1997. *An Introduction to Japanese Society*. Cambridge: Cambridge University Press.

Sugita Genpaku. [1815] 1959. *Rangaku kotohajime,* annot. Tomio Ogata. Tokyo: Iwanami Shoten.

Suigyū Kurabu, ed. 1990. *Mono tanjō: ima no seikatsu.* Tokyo: Shōbunsha.

Suzuki Jōji. 1992. *Nihonjin dekasegi imin.* Tokyo: Heibonsha.

Suzuki Kunio. [1988] 1990. *Shin uyoku: minzokuha no rekishi to genzai,* expanded ed. Tokyo: Sairyūsha.

Suzuki Sayoko. [1985] 1991. *Tachihara Masaaki: fūshiden.* Tokyo: Chūō Kōronsha.

Suzuki Takao. 1990. *Nihongo to gaikokugo.* Tokyo: Iwanami Shoten.

Suzuki Yūko. 1992. *Jūgun ianfu, naisen kekkon.* Tokyo: Miraisha.

———. 1993. "Karayukisan, 'jūgun ianfu,' senryōgun 'ianfu.'" In Shinobu Ōe, Kyōji Asada, Taichirō Mitani, Ken'ichi Gotō, Hideo Kobayashi, Sōji Takasaki, Masahiro Wakabayashi, and Minato Kawamura, eds., *Iwanami kōza kindai Nihon to shokuminchi.* Vol. 5: *Bōchō suru teikoku no jinryū,* pp. 223–250. Tokyo: Iwanami Shoten.

Tada Michitarō. 1974. *Asobi to Nihonjin.* Tokyo: Chikuma Shobō.

———. [1979] 1988. *Amanojaku Nihon fūzokugaku.* Tokyo: PHP Kenkyūsho.

Tada Tetsunosuke. 1972. *Tabemono Nihonshi: Man'yō no aji kara rāmen made.* Tokyo: Shinjinbutsu Ōraisha.

Taeuber, Irene B. 1958. *The Population of Japan.* Princeton, N.J.: Princeton University Press.

Taira, Koji. 1997. "Troubled National Identity: The Ryukyuans/Okinawans." In Michael Weiner, ed., *Japan's Minorities: The Illusion of Homogeneity,* pp. 140–177. London: Routledge.

Takagi Hiroshi. 1994. "Ainu minzoku e no dōka seisaku no seiritsu." In Rekishigaku Kenkyūkai, ed., *Kokumin kokka o tou,* pp. 166–183. Tokyo: Aoki Shoten.

Takahashi Masaaki. 1984. "Chūsei no mibunsei." In Rekishigaku Kenkyūkai and Nihonshi Kenkyūkai, eds., *Kōza Nihon rekishi.* Vol. 3: *Chūsei 1,* pp. 293–334. Tokyo: Tokyo Daigaku Shuppankai.

Takara Kurakichi. 1987. "Ryūkyū, Okinawa no rekishi to Nihon shakai." In Naohiro Asao, Yoshihiko Amino, Keiji Yamaguchi, and Takeshi Yoshida, eds., *Nihon no shakaishi.* Vol. 1: *Rettō naigai no kōtsū to kokka,* pp. 353–384. Tokyo: Iwanami Shoten.

———. 1992a. "Kindai, gendai e no sasoi." In Ryūkyū Shinpōsha, ed., *Shin Ryūkyūshi: kindai, gendai hen,* pp. 9–22. Naha, Japan: Ryūkyū Shinpōsha.

———. 1992b. "Daitōjima no shiten." In Ryūkyū Shinpōsha, ed., *Shin Ryūkyūshi: kindai, gendai hen,* pp. 377–384. Naha, Japan: Ryūkyū Shinpōsha.

———. 1993. *Ryūkyū ōkoku.* Tokyo: Iwanami Shoten.

Takarajima, ed. 1992. *Bokura no jidai dai'nenpyō.* Tokyo: JICC.

Takasaki Sōji. 1993. *"Han nichi kanjō": Kankoku-Chōsenjin to Nihonjin.* Tokyo: Kōdansha.

Takayama Toshio. 1992. "Gaikokujin o shimedasu iryō, fukushi." In Ajiajin Rōdōsha Mondai Kondankai, ed., *Okasareru jinken gaikokujin rōdōsha,* pp. 127–145. Tokyo: Daisan Shokan.

Takeda Seiji. 1983. *"Zainichi" to iu konkyo.* Tokyo: Kokubunsha.

Takeda Taijun. [1958] 1972. "Mori to mizuumi no matsuri." In Taijun Takeda, *Takeda Tainjun zenshū,* vol. 7, pp. 3–392. Tokyo: Chikuma Shobō.

Takegawa Shōgo. 1990. "Jūmin ishiki, kokumin ishiki, kaikyū ishiki, jinrui ishiki." In Toshiaki Furuki, ed., *Sekai shakai no imēji to genjitsu,* pp. 237–268. Tokyo: Tokyo Daigaku Shuppankai.

Takemitsu Makoto. 1990. *Atama ga yosugiru Nihonjin.* Tokyo: Dōbun Shoin.

Takeuchi Osamu. 1995. *Sengo manga 50-nen shi.* Tokyo: Chikuma Shobō.

Takeuchi Shizuko. 1982. *1960-nendai.* Tokyo: Tabata Shoten.

Takeuchi Yō. 1995. *Nihon no meritokurashī: kōzō to shinsei.* Tokyo: Tokyo Daigaku Shuppankai.

Takeyama Michio. [1950] 1985. "Techō." In Michio Takeyama, *Shōwa no seishinshi,* pp. 169–341. Tokyo: Kōdansha.

Tambiah, S. J. 1986. *Sri Lanka: Ethnic Fratricide and the Dismantling of Democracy.* Chicago: University of Chicago Press.

Tamiya Takeshi. 1991. *Wakamono wa buraku mondai o dō miteiru no ka.* Osaka: Buraku Kaihō Kenkyūsho.

Tamura Sadao. 1992. "Naikoku shokuminchi to shite no Hokkaidō." In Shinobu Ōe, Kyōji Asada, Taichirō Mitani, Ken'ichi Gotō, Hideo Kobayashi, Sōji Takasaki, Masahiro Wakabayashi, and Minato Kawamura, eds., *Iwanami kōza kindai Nihon to shokuminchi.* Vol. 1: *Shokuminchi teikoku Nihon,* pp. 87–99. Tokyo: Iwanami Shoten.

Tanaka Akio. 1983. *Tōkyōgo—sono seiritsu no tenkai.* Tokyo: Meiji Shoin.

———. 1991. *Hyōjungo: kotoba no shōkei.* Tokyo: Scibundō.

———. 1996. "Tōkyogo to hyōjungo." In Kokugakuin Daigaku Nihon Bunka Kenkyūsho, ed., *Tōkyōgo no yukue: Edogo kara Tōkyōgo, Tōkyōgo kara sutandādo Nihongo e,* pp. 21–76. Tokyo: Tōkyōdō Shuppan.

Tanaka Akira. 1984. *"Datsua" no Meiji ishin: Iwakura shisetsudan o ou tabi kara.* Tokyo: Nihon Hōsō Kyōkai.

Tanaka Hiroshi. 1991. *Zainichi gaikokujin: hō no kabe, kokoro no mizo.* Tokyo: Iwanami Shoten.

Tanaka Katsuhiko. 1978. *Gengo kara mita minzoku to kokka.* Tokyo: Iwanami Shoten.

———. 1989. *Kokkago o koete: kokusaika no naka no Nihongo.* Tokyo: Chikuma Shobō.

Tanaka Osamu. 1986. *Nihon shihonshugi to Hokkaidō.* Sapporo: Hokkaidō Daigaku Tosho Kankōkai.

Tanaka Seiichi. 1988. "Nihonka shita Chūgoku no shoku to ryōri." In Isao

Kumakura and Naomichi Ishige, eds., *Shoku no bunka fōramu: gairai no shoku no bunka*, pp. 165–175. Tokyo: Domesu Shuppan.

Tanaka, Stefan. 1993. *Japan's Orient: Rendering Pasts into History*. Berkeley: University of California Press.

Tanaka Takeo. 1997. *Higashi Ajia tsūkōken to kokusai ninshiki*. Tokyo: Yoshikawa Kōbunkan.

Tanigawa Ken'ichi. [1975] 1985. *Onna no fūdoki*. Tokyo: Kōdansha.

Tanizawa Eiichi. 1991. *Taikoku Nihon no "shōtai."* Tokyo: Kōdansha.

Tansman, Alan M. 1996. "Mournful Tears and *Sake:* The Postwar Myth of Misora Hibari." In John Whittier Treat, ed., *Contemporary Japan and Popular Culture*, pp. 103–133. Honolulu: University of Hawaii Press.

Tazaki Nobuyoshi. 1985. "Toshi bunka to kokumin ishiki." In Rekishigaku Kenkyūkai and Nihonshi Kenkyūkai, eds., *Kōza Nihon rekishi*. Vol. 10: *Kindai 4*, pp. 167–198. Tokyo: Tokyo Daigaku Shuppankai.

Terada Torahiko. [1921] 1947. "Maruzen to Mitsukoshi." In Torahiko Terada, *Terada Torahiko zuihitsushū*, vol. 1, pp. 119–138. Tokyo: Iwanami Shoten.

Terazawa Masako. 1990. "Nihon shakai no heisasei to bunka." In Gyōzaisei Sōgō Kenkyūsho, ed., *Gaikokujin rōdōsha no jinken*, pp. 63–68. Tokyo: Ōtsuki Shoten.

Tezuka Kazuaki. 1989. *Gaikokujin rōdōsha*. Tokyo: Nihon Keizai Shinbunsha.

Tezuka Kazuaki, Hiroshi Komai, Gorō Ono, and Takaaki Ogata, eds. 1992. *Gaikokujin rōdōsha no shūrō jittai*. Tokyo: Akashi Shoten.

Tezuka Kazuaki, Takashi Miyajima, Tsuaen Tou, and Sukesada Itō, eds. 1992. *Gaikokujin rōdōsha to jichitai*. Tokyo: Akashi Shoten.

Thompson, John B. 1990. *Ideology and Modern Culture*. Stanford, Calif.: Stanford University Press.

Thornton, Emily. 1995. "French Links." *Far Eastern Economic Review*, Mar. 23, p. 70.

Toby, Ronald P. 1984. *The State and Diplomacy in Early Modern Japan: Asia in the Development of the Tokugawa Bakufu*. Princeton, N.J.: Princeton University Press.

Tokumei Zenken Taishi. 1977. *Bei-Ō kairan jikki*, vol. 1, ed. Kunitake Kume, annot. Akira Tanaka. Tokyo: Iwanami Shoten.

Tokutomi Sohō. [1894] 1981. *Yoshida Shōin*. Tokyo: Iwanami Shoten.

Tokyo Toritsu Rōdō Kenkyūsho. [1991] 1994. "Tōkyōto ni okeru gaikokujin rōdōsha no shūrō jittai." In Hiroshi Komai, ed., *Gaikokujin rōdōsha mondai shiryō shūsei*, vol. 2, pp. 275–585. Tokyo: Akashi Shoten.

Tominaga Ken'ichi. 1990. *Nihon no kindaika to shakai hendō*. Tokyo: Kōdansha.

Tomiyama Ichirō. 1990. *Kindai Nihon shakai to "Okinawajin."* Tokyo: Nihon Keizai Hyōronsha.

———. 1992. "Okinawa sabetsu to puroretariaka." In Ryūkyū Shinpōsha, ed.,

Shin Ryūkyūshi: kindai, gendai hen, pp. 169–189. Naha, Japan: Ryūkyū Shinpōsha.

———. 1995. "Colonialism and the Sciences of the Tropical Zone: The Academic Analysis of Difference in 'the Island Peoples.'" *Positions* 3: 367–391.

Torii Yumiko. 1993. "Kinsei Nihon no Ajia ninshiki." In Yūzō Mizoguchi, Takeshi Hamashita, Naoaki Hiraishi, and Hiroshi Miyajima, eds., *Ajia kara kangaeru.* Vol. 1: *Kōsaku suru Ajia*, pp. 219–252. Tokyo: Tokyo Daigaku Shuppankai.

Tosaka Jun. [1935] 1977. *Nihon ideorogīron.* Tokyo: Iwanami Shoten.

Totsuka Hideo. 1976. "Korean Immigration in Pre-war Japan." *Annals of the Institute of Social Science* 17: 89–110.

———. 1977. "Nihon teikokushugi no hōkai to 'i'nyū Chōsenjin rōdōsha.'" In Mikio Sumiya, ed., *Nihon rōshi kankeishi*, pp. 189–261. Tokyo: Tokyo Daigaku Shuppankai.

Totten, George O., and Hiroshi Wagatsuma. 1966. "Emancipation: Growth and Transformation of a Political Movement." In George De Vos and Hiroshi Wagatsuma, eds., *Japan's Invisible Race: Caste in Culture and Personality,* pp. 33–67. Berkeley: University of California Press.

Tou Namsen. 1992. "Nihon ni okeru 'gaikokujin rōdōsha' rongi no shomondai." In Hiroshi Momose and Mitsuo Ogura, eds., *Gendai kokka to imin rōdōsha,* pp. 11–37. Tokyo: Yūshindō.

Tōyama Shigeki. 1968. *Sengo no rekishigaku to rekishi ishiki.* Tokyo: Iwanami Shoten.

Toynbee, Arnold. [1948] 1976. "Civilization on Trial." In Arnold Toynbee, *Civilization on Trial and the World and the West*, pp. 9–229. New York: North American Library.

Toyota Aritsune. 1985. *Nihonjin to Kankokujin kokoga ōchigai.* Tokyo: Nesuko.

Tsuboi Hirofumi. 1979. *Imo to Nihonjin.* Tokyo: Miraisha.

Tsuda Michio. 1973. *Zōho Nihon nashonarizumuron.* Tokyo: Fukumura Shuppan.

Tsuge Yoshiharu. [1977] 1983. *Tsuge Yoshiharu tabi nikki.* Tokyo: Ōbunsha.

Tsuka Kōhei. 1990. *Musume ni kataru sokoku.* Tokyo: Kōbunsha.

Tsukada Takashi. 1992. "Ajia ni okeru ryō to sen." In Yasunori Arano, Masatoshi Ishii, and Shōsuke Murai, eds., *Ajia no naka no Nihonshi.* Vol. 1: *Ajia to Nihon,* pp. 297–316. Tokyo: Tokyo Daigaku Shuppankai.

Tsukamoto Manabu. 1991. *Tokai to inaka.* Tokyo: Heibonsha.

Tsukishima Hiroshi. 1986. *Rekishiteki kanazukai: sono seiritsu to tokuchō.* Tokyo: Chūō Kōronsha.

Tsuru Shigeto. 1993. *Japan's Capitalism: Creative Defeat and Beyond.* Cambridge: Cambridge University Press.

Tsurumi Kazuko. 1972. *Kōkishin to Nihonjin: tajūkōzō shakai no riron.* Tokyo: Kōdansha.

Tsurumi Shunsuke. 1982. *Senjiki Nihon no seishinshi: 1931–1945-nen.* Tokyo: Iwanami Shoten.

———. 1984. *Sengo Nihon no taishū bunkashi: 1945–1980-nen.* Tokyo: Iwanami Shoten.

———. 1989. *Shisō no otoshiana.* Tokyo: Iwanami Shoten.

Tsurumi Shunsuke and Takeshi Yasuda. 1983. *Chūshingura to Yotsuya kaidan: Nihonjin no komyu nikēshon.* Tokyo: Asahi Shinbunsha.

Tsurumi Yoshiyuki. 1982. *Ajia wa naze mazushii no ka.* Tokyo: Asahi Shinbunsha.

Tsurushima, Setsure. 1984. "Human Rights Issues and the Status of the Burakumin and Koreans in Japan." In George De Vos, ed., *Institutions for Change in Japanese Society,* pp. 83–113. Berkeley: Institute of East Asian Studies, University of California.

Tsuruta Kei. 1992. "Kinsei Nihon no yottsu no 'kuchi.'" In Yasunori Arano, Masatoshi Ishii, and Shōsuke Murai, eds., *Ajia no naka no Nihonshi.* Vol. 2: *Gaikō to sensō,* pp. 297–316. Tokyo: Tokyo Daigaku Shuppankai.

Tsuruya Nanboku. [1826] 1956. *Tōkaidō Yotsuya kaidan.* Tokyo: Iwanami Shoten.

Tsushima Tomoaki. 1992. "'Marebito Urutoraman' saikō." *Shin Okinawa bungaku* 93: 172–182.

Tsutsui Kiyoko and Hiroko Yamaoka. 1991. *Kokusaika jidai no joshi kōyō.* Tokyo: Chūō Keizaisha.

Tsutsui Kiyotada. 1984. *Shōwaki Nihon no kōzō: sono rekishishakaigakuteki kōsatsu.* Tokyo: Yūhikaku.

———. 1995. *Nihongata "kyōyō" no unmei: rekishishakaigakuteki kōsatsu.* Tokyo: Iwanami Shoten.

Turner, Victor. 1967. *The Forest of Symbols: Aspects of Ndembu Ritual.* Ithaca, N.Y.: Cornell University Press.

Uchida Ruriko. 1993. "Ajia no naka no Nihon ongaku." In Yasunori Arano, Masatoshi Ishii, and Shōsuke Murai, eds., *Ajia no naka no Nihonshi.* Vol. 6: *Bunka to gijutsu,* pp. 297–320. Tokyo: Tokyo Daigaku Shuppankai.

Ueda Atsushi. 1987. "Ryūkō to wa nanika." Michitarō Tada, ed., *Ryūkō no fūzokugaku,* pp. 42–66. Kyoto: Sekai Shisōsha.

Uemura Hideaki. 1987. "'Shosū minzoku' to wa nanika: Nihon seifu ni kesareta Ainu minzoku." *Sekai,* July, pp. 238–247.

———. 1990. *Kita no umi no kōekishatachi: Ainu minzoku no shakaikeizaishi.* Tokyo: Dōbunkan.

———. 1992a. *Senjū minzoku: "Koronbusu" to tatakau hitobito no rekishi to genzai.* Tokyo: Kaihō Shuppansha.

———. 1992b. *Sekai to Nihon no senjū minzoku.* Tokyo: Iwanami Shoten.

Ueno Chizuko. 1989. "Taishū shakai no shinwa to genjitsu." In Hirochika Nakamaki, ed., *Gendai Nihon bunka ni okeru dentō to hen'yō: gendai Nihon no "shinwa,"* pp. 48–69. Tokyo: Domesu Shuppan.

————. 1994. *Kindai kazoku no seiritsu to shūen.* Tokyo: Iwanami Shoten.

Ueno Kōshi. 1995. *Sengo saikō.* Tokyo: Asahi Shinbunsha.

————. [1989] 1996. "'Kyojin no hoshi' no chichi naru mono to gijutsushugi." In Shinbō Minami, ed., *Nihon no meizuihitsu.* Vol. 62: *Manga,* pp. 151–165. Tokyo: Sakuhinsha.

Ueno Terumasa. 1985. "Nashonarizumu to shinhoshushugi." In Rekishigaku Kenkyūkai and Nihonshi Kenkyūkai, eds., *Kōza Nihon rekishi.* Vol. 12: *Gendai 2,* pp. 87–130. Tokyo: Tokyo Daigaku Shuppankai.

Uesugi Satoshi. 1990. *Tennōsei to buraku sabetsu.* Tokyo: San'ichi Shobō.

Umemura Mataji. 1964. *Sengo Nihon no rōdōryoku: sokutei to hendō.* Tokyo: Iwanami Shoten.

Umesao Tadao. 1986. *Nihon to wa nanika: kindai Nihon bunmei no keisei to hatten.* Tokyo: Nihon Hōsō Shuppan Kyōkai.

Umetani Shun'ichirō. 1993. "Fuhō shūrō gaikokujin no jittai." In Tadashi Hanami and Yasuo Kuwahara, eds., *Anata no rinjin: gaikokujin rōdōsha,* pp. 76–104. Tokyo: Tōyō Keizai Shinpōsha.

Unno Fukuju. 1993. "Chōsen no rōmu dōin." In Shinobu Ōe, Kyōji Asada, Taichirō Mitani, Ken'ichi Gotō, Hideo Kobayashi, Sōji Takasaki, Masahiro Wakabayashi, and Minato Kawamura, eds., *Iwanami kōza kindai Nihon to shokuminchi.* Vol. 5: *Bōchō suru teikoku no jinryū,* pp. 103–130. Tokyo: Iwanami Shoten.

————. 1995. *Kankoku heigō.* Tokyo: Iwanami Shoten.

Unno Fukuju and Takaki Watanabe. 1975. "Meiji kokka to chihō jichi." In Hidesaburō Hara, Sumio Minegishi, Junnosuke Sasaki, and Masanori Nakamura, eds., *Taikei Nihon kokkashi.* Vol. 4: *Kindai I,* pp. 195–279. Tokyo: Tokyo Daigaku Shuppankai.

Upham, Frank K. 1987. *Law and Social Change in Postwar Japan.* Cambridge, Mass.: Harvard University Press.

————. 1998. "Weak Legal Consciousness as Invented Tradition." In Stephen Vlastos, ed., *Mirror of Modernity: Invented Traditions of Modern Japan,* pp. 48–64. Berkeley: University of California Press.

Ushijima Hidehiko. [1978] 1995. *Rikidōzan: ōzumō, puroresu, ura shakai,* rev. ed. Tokyo: Daisan Shokan.

Uzawa Hirofumi. 1974. *Jidōsha no shakaiteki hiyō.* Tokyo: Iwanami Shoten.

Valente, Waldemar. 1978. *O Japonês no nordeste agrário.* Recife, Brazil: Instituo Joaquim Nabuco de Pesquisas.

van Delft, Louis. 1993. *Littérature et anthropologie: nature humaine et caractère à l'âge classique.* Paris: Presses Universitaires de France.

Vasishth, Andrew. 1997. "A Model Minority: The Chinese Community in Japan." In Michael Weiner, ed., *Japan's Minorities: The Illusion of Homogeneity,* pp. 108–139. London: Routledge.

Veblen, Thorstein. [1899] 1953. *The Theory of the Leisure Class: An Economic Study of Institutions.* New York: Mentor.

Ventura, Rey. 1992. *Underground in Japan,* ed. James Fenton. London: Jonathan Cape.

Vogel, Ezra F. [1963] 1971. *Japan's New Middle Class: The Salary Man and His Family in a Tokyo Suburb,* 2d ed. Berkeley: University of California Press.

————. 1979. *Japan as Number One: Lessons for America.* Cambridge, Mass.: Harvard University Press.

Wada Haruki. 1990. *Hoppō ryōdo mondai o kangaeru.* Tokyo: Iwanami Shoten.

Wagatsuma, Hiroshi. 1966. "Postwar Political Militance." In George De Vos and Hiroshi Wagatsuma, eds., *Japan's Invisible Race: Caste in Culture and Personality,* pp. 68–87. Berkeley: University of California Press.

Wagatsuma, Hiroshi, and George De Vos. 1966. "The Ecology of Special Buraku." In George De Vos and Hiroshi Wagatsuma, eds., *Japan's Invisible Race: Caste in Culture and Personality,* pp. 113–128. Berkeley: University of California Press.

————. 1984. *Heritage of Endurance: Family Patterns and Delinquency Formation in Urban Japan.* Berkeley: University of California Press.

Wagatsuma Hiroshi and Toshinao Yoneyama. 1967. *Henken no kōzō: Nihonjin no jinshukan.* Tokyo: Nihon Hōsō Shuppan Kyōkai.

Wagner, Edward W. 1951. *The Korean Minority in Japan, 1904–1950.* Vancouver, Canada: Publication Centre, University of British Columbia.

Wakabayashi, Bob Tadashi. 1986. *Anti-Foreignism and Western Learning in Early-Modern Japan: The New Theses of 1825.* Cambridge, Mass.: Council on East Asian Studies, Harvard University.

Wakabayashi Masahiro. 1983. *Taiwan kōnichi undōshi kenkyū.* Tokyo: Kenbun Shuppan.

Waki Keihei and Takeo Ashizu. 1984. *Furutovengurā.* Tokyo: Iwanami Shoten.

Wakita Osamu. 1985. "Sabetsu no kakudai." In Buraku Mondai Kenkyūsho, ed., *Buraku no rekishi to kaihō undō: zen-kindai hen,* pp. 229–294. Osaka: Buraku Mondai Kenkyūsho Shuppanbu.

Walton, John K. 1992. *Fish and Chips and the British Working Class, 1870–1940.* Leicester, U.K.: Leicester University Press.

Watanabe Hiroshi. 1985. *Kinsei Nihon shakai to Sogaku.* Tokyo: Tokyo Daigaku Shuppankai.

Watanabe Kyōji. 1978. *Kita Ikki.* Tokyo: Asahi Shinbunsha.

Watanabe Makoto. 1964. *Nihon shokuseikatsushi.* Tokyo: Yoshikawa Kōbunkan.

Watanabe Masako. 1995. "Shutsu'nyūkoku kanrihō kaisei to Burajirujin shutsu'nyūkoku no suii." In Masako Watanabe, ed., *Kyōdō kenkyū dekasegi Nikkei Burajirujin, jo: ronbunhen,* pp. 19–37. Tokyo: Akashi Shoten.

Watanabe Naomi. 1994. *Nihonteki kindai bungaku to "sabetsu."* Tokyo: Ōta Shuppan.

Watanabe Osamu, ed. 1996. *Gendai Nihon shakairon*. Tokyo: Rōdō Junpōsha.

Watanabe Sakae and Arata Haneda, eds. 1977. *Dekasegi rōdō to nōson no seikatsu*. Tokyo: Tokyo Daigaku Shuppankai.

Watanabe Shōichi. 1995. *Kakute Shōwashi wa yomigaeru: jinshu sabetsu no sekai o tadakitsubushita Nihon*. Tokyo: Nihon Kuresutosha.

Watanabe Yoshio. 1990. *Minzoku chishikiron no kadai—Okinawa no chishiki jinruigaku*. Tokyo: Gaifūsha.

Watanabe Zenjirō. 1988. *Kyodai toshi Edo ga washoku o tsukutta*. Tokyo: Nōsan Gyōsan Bunka Kyōkai.

Watase Shūkichi. 1987. *Minzoku no saisei*, vol. 1. Wakayama, Japan: Kaiten.

Weber, Eugen. 1976. *Peasants into Frenchmen: The Modernization of Rural France, 1870–1914*. Stanford, Calif.: Stanford University Press.

Weiner, Michael. 1989. *The Origins of the Korean Community in Japan, 1910–1923*. Atlantic Highlands, N.J.: Humanities Press International.

———. 1994. *Race and Migration in Imperial Japan*. London: Routledge.

———. 1997. "The Invention of Identity: 'Self' and 'Other' in Pre-war Japan." In Michael Weiner, ed., *Japan's Minorities: The Illusion of Homogeneity*, pp. 1–16. London: Routledge.

White, Merry. 1988. *The Japanese Overseas: Can They Go Home Again?* New York: Free Press.

———. 1993. *The Material Child: Coming of Age in Japan and America*. New York: Free Press.

Whiting, Robert. 1977. *The Chrysanthemum and the Bat: Baseball Samurai Style*. New York: Dodd, Mead.

———. 1986. *Gaijin rikishi monogatari*, trans. Midori Matsui. Tokyo: Chikuma Shobō.

———. 1989. *You Gotta Have Wa*. New York: Macmillan.

Wigen, Kären. 1995. *The Making of a Japanese Periphery, 1750–1920*. Berkeley: University of California Press.

Williams, David. 1996. *Japan and the Enemies of Open Political Science*. London: Routledge.

Williams, Raymond. [1958] 1963. *Culture and Society, 1780–1950*. Harmondsworth, U.K.: Penguin.

———. 1973. *The Country and the City*. New York: Oxford University Press.

———. [1974] 1975. *Television: Technology and Cultural Form*. New York: Schocken.

———. 1977. *Marxism and Literature*. Oxford: Oxford University Press.

Williams, William Appleman. 1955. "The Frontier Thesis and American Foreign Policy." *Pacific Historical Review* 24: 379–395.

Willis, Paul E. 1978. *Profane Culture*. London: Routledge & Kegan Paul.

Wittgenstein, Ludwig. [1953] 1968. *Philosophical Investigations*, 3rd ed., trans. G. E. M. Anscombe. New York: Macmillan.

Wurth, Julie. 1998. "1st Palauan to Earn Doctorate among UI Graduates." *News-Gazette*, Aug. 18, pp. A1ff.

Yagi Kōsuke. 1984. "Buraku sabetsu no genjitsu to mondaiten." In Eiichi Isomura, Yasuko Ichibangase, and Tomohiko Harada, eds., *Kōza sabetsu to jinken*. Vol. 1: *Buraku I*, pp. 163–269. Tokyo: Yūzankaku.

Yamada Kō. 1989. *Sengo shisōshi*. Tokyo: Aoki Shoten.

Yamada Shōji. 1994. "Minzokuteki sabetsu to besshi." In Kyōji Asada, ed., *Kindai Nihon no kiseki*. Vol. 10: *"Teikoku" Nihon to Ajia*, pp. 173–192. Tokyo: Yoshikawa Kōbunkan.

Yamada Shūji. 1994. "Shokuminchi." In Naohiro Asao, Yoshihiko Amino, Susumu Ishii, Masanao Kano, Shōhachi Hayakawa, and Yasuo Yasumaru, eds., *Iwanami kōza Nihon tsūshi*. Vol. 18: *Kindai 3*, pp. 65–95. Tokyo: Iwanami Shoten.

Yamada Teruko. 1992. *Urutoraman shōten: M78-seiun wa Okinawa no kanata*. Tokyo: Asahi Shinbunsha.

Yamaguchi Keiji. 1993. *Sakoku to kaikoku*. Tokyo: Iwanami Shoten.

Yamaguchi Kikuo. 1983. *Sengo ni miru shoku no bunkashi*. Tokyo: Sanrei Shobō.

Yamaguchi Masao. 1978. *Chie no enkinhō*. Tokyo: Iwanami Shoten.

Yamakawa Tsutomu. 1989. *Seiji to Ainu minzoku*. Tokyo: Miraisha.

———. 1996. *Meijiki Ainu minzoku seisakuron*. Tokyo: Miraisha.

Yamamoto Akira. 1986. *Sengo fūzokushi*. Osaka: Osaka Shoseki.

Yamamoto Keizō. 1979. *Kokuseki*. Tokyo: Sanseidō.

Yamamoto Shichihei. 1989. *Nihonjin to wa nanika*, 2 vols. Tokyo: PHP Kenkyūsho.

Yamamoto Shigeru. 1993. *Ipōjin no kobushi*. Tokyo: Bēsubōru Magajinsha.

Yamamoto Tetsumi. 1995. *Hokori: ningen Harimoto Isao*. Tokyo: Kōdansha.

Yamamuro Shin'ichi. 1993. *Kimera: Manshūkoku no shozō*. Tokyo: Chūō Kōronsha.

Yamanaka Ichirō. 1989. *Heisei yakuza*. Tokyo: Chūō Āto Shuppansha.

Yamanaka, Keiko. 1993. "New Immigration Policy and Unskilled Foreign Workers in Japan." *Pacific Affairs* 66: 72–90.

Yamaori Tetsuo. 1996. *Kindai Nihonjin no shūkyō ishiki*. Tokyo: Iwanami Shoten.

Yamauchi Masayuki and Minzoku Mondai Kenkyūkai, eds., 1991. *Nyūmon sekai no minzoku mondai*. Tokyo: Nihon Keizai Shinbunsha.

Yamawaki Keizō. 1994. *Kindai Nihon to gaikokujin rōdōsha: 1890-nendai kōhan to 1920-nendai zenhan ni okeru Chūgokujin, Chōsenjin rōdōsha mondai*. Tokyo: Akashi Shoten.

Yamazaki Kesaya. [1924] 1982. "Jishin, kenpei, kaji, junsa." In Kesaya Yamazaki, *Jishin, kenpei, kaji, junsa*, ed. Eizaburō Morinaga, pp. 217–278. Tokyo: Iwanami Shoten.

Yamazaki Masakazu. 1990. *Nihon bunka to kojinshugi*. Tokyo: Chūō Kōronsha.

Yanabu Akira. 1982. *Hon'yakugo seiritsu jijō*. Tokyo: Iwanami Shoten.

Yanagi Muneyoshi. 1981. "Ainu ni okuru sho." In Muneyoshi Yanagi, *Yanagi Muneyoshi zenshū*, vol. 15, pp. 528–537. Tokyo: Chikuma Shobō.

———. [1920] 1984. "Chōsen no tomo ni okuru sho." In Muneyoshi Yanagi, *Mingei 40-nen*, pp. 19–45. Tokyo: Iwanami Shoten.

———. [1948] 1985. *Teshigoto no Nihon*. Tokyo: Iwanami Shoten.

Yanagita Kunio. [1930] 1976. *Meiji Taishōshi sesōhen*, 2 vols. Tokyo: Kōdansha.

———. [1952] 1978. *Kaijō no michi*. Tokyo: Iwanami Shoten.

Yanaihara Tadao. [1929] 1988. *Teikokushugi ka no Taiwan*. Tokyo: Iwanami Shoten.

Yano Tōru. 1988. *Nihon no kokusaika o kangaeru*. Tokyo: Nikkan Kōgyō Shinbunsha.

Yasuda Takeshi. 1985. *Shōwa seishun dokusho hishi*. Tokyo: Iwanami Shoten.

Yasuda Tsuneo. 1987. *Kurashi no shakai shisō: sono hikari to kage*. Tokyo: Keisō Shobō.

———. 1995. "Amerikanizēshon no hikari to kage." In Masanori Nakamura, Akira Amakawa, Kŏn-ch'a Yun, and Takeshi Igarashi, eds., *Sengo Nihon senryō to sengo kaikaku*. Vol. 3: *Sengo shisō to shakai ishiki*, pp. 251–285. Tokyo: Iwanami Shoten.

Yasuhara Ken. 1993. "Amerika no okama ni narisagatta Nihonjin." *Tosho shinbun*, Sept.4, p. 3.

Yasuhara Ken, ed. 1995. *Sengo 50-nen to watashi*. Tokyo: Metarōgu.

Yasumaru Yoshio. 1974. *Nihon no kindaika to minshū shisō*. Tokyo: Aoki Shoten.

———. 1977. *Nihon nashonarizumu no zen'ya*. Tokyo: Asahi Shinbunsha.

———. 1979. *Kamigami no Meiji ishin*. Tokyo: Iwanami Shoten.

———. 1992. *Kindai tennōzō no keisei*. Tokyo: Iwanami Shoten.

———. 1995. "Gendai no shisō jōkyō." In Naohiro Asao, Yoshihiko Amino, Susumu Ishii, Masanao Kano, Shōhachi Hayakawa, and Yasuo Yasumaru, eds., *Iwanami kōza Nihon*. Vol. 21: *Gendai 2*, pp. 291–336. Tokyo: Iwanami Shoten.

Yasumoto Biten. 1991. *Nihonjin to Nihongo no kigen*. Tokyo: Mainichi Shinbunsha.

Yasuoka Shōtarō. 1983. *Shōsetsuka no shōsetsukaron*. Tokyo: Fukutake Shoten.

———. [1964] 1991a. "'Aikokushin' ni tsuite." In Shōtarō Yasuoka, *Yasuoka Shōtarō zuihitsushū*, vol. 5, pp. 3–18. Tokyo: Iwanami Shoten.

———. [1980–1988]. 1991b. "Boku no Shōwashi." In Shōtarō Yasuoka, *Yasuoka Shōtarō zuihitsushū*, vol. 7, pp. 3–242. Tokyo: Iwanami Shoten.

Yazawa Kōsuke. 1985. "Taminzoku shakai to shite no Nihon." In Rekishigaku Kenkyūkai and Nihonshi Kenkyūkai, eds., *Kōza Nihon rekishi*. Vol. 13: *Rekishi ni okeru genzai*, pp. 25–47. Tokyo: Tokyo Daigaku Shuppankai.

Yokoyama Gennosuke. [1899] 1949. *Nihon no kasō shakai*. Tokyo: Iwanami Shoten.

Yoneda Yūsuke. 1984. "Kizoku bunka no tenkai." In Rekishigaku Kenkyūkai and

Nihonshi Kenkyūkai, eds., *Nihon rekishi*. Vol. 2: *Kodai 2*, pp. 211–246. Tokyo: Tokyo Daigaku Shuppankai.

Yoneyama Toshinao. 1989. *Shōbonchi uchū to Nihon bunka*. Tokyo: Iwanami Shoten.

Yorimitsu Masatoshi. 1993. "Nihon shakai to gaikokujin rōdōsha." In Tadashi Hanami and Yasuo Kuwahara, eds., *Anata no rinjin: gaikokujin rōdōsha*, pp. 2–35. Tokyo: Tōyō Keizai Shinpōsha.

Yoshida Sensha. 1990. *Utsurun desu*, vol. 1. Tokyo: Shōgakukan.

Yoshihiro Kōsuke. 1993. *Manga no gendaishi*. Tokyo: Maruzen.

Yoshimi Shunsuke. 1987. *Toshi no doramatourugī: Tokyo, Sakariba no shakaishi*. Tokyo: Kōbundō.

Yoshimi Yoshiaki. 1995. "Okinawa, haisen zengo." In Naohiro Asao, Yoshihiko Amino, Susumu Ishii, Masanao Kano, Shōhachi Hayakawa, and Yasuo Yasumaru, eds., *Iwanami kōza Nihon tsūshi*. Vol. 19: *Kindai 4*, pp. 135–168. Tokyo: Iwanami Shoten.

Yoshimoto Takaaki. [1976] 1984. *Saigo no Shinran*, new ed. Tokyo: Shunjūsha.

Yoshimura Sakuo. 1981. *Nihon henkyōron josetsu: Okinawa no tōji to minshū*. Tokyo: Ochanomizu Shobō.

Yoshimura Tsutomu. 1986. *Buraku sabetsu to rōdō mondai*. Tokyo: Akashi Shoten.

Yoshino, I. Roger, and Sueo Murakoshi. 1977. *The Invisible Visible Minority: Japan's Burakumin*. Osaka: Buraku Kaiho Kenkyusho.

Yoshino, Kosaku. 1992. *Cultural Nationalism in Contemporary Japan: A Sociological Enquiry*. London: Routledge.

Yoshiwara Kōichirō. 1973. *Okinawa minshū undō no dentō*. Tokyo: Fukumura Shuppan.

Yoshizawa Osamu. 1993. "AWAY ni umarete." *BART*, Sept. 13, pp. 16–17.

Young, Louise. 1998. *Japan's Total Empire: Manchuria and the Culture of Wartime Imperialism*. Berkeley: University of California Press.

Yuasa Yasuo. [1981] 1995. *Watsuji Tetsurō: kindai Nihon tetsugaku no unmei*. Tokyo: Chikuma Shobō.

Yui Masaomi. 1984. *Tanaka Shōzō*. Tokyo: Iwanami Shoten.

Yun Keun-cha [Kŏn-ch'a]. 1987. *Ishitsu to no kyōzon: sengo Nihon no kyōiku, shisō, minzokuron*. Tokyo: Iwanami Shoten.

———. 1994. *Minzoku gensō no satetsu: Nihonjin no jikozō*. Tokyo: Iwanami Shoten.

———. 1997. *Nihon kokuminron: kindai Nihon no aidentiti*. Tokyo: Chikuma Shobō.

Zakō Jun. 1983. *Itsumo kayōkyoku ga atta*. Tokyo: Shinchōsha.

Zeldin, Theodore. 1982. *The French*. New York: Pantheon.

Index